CHINA FACTOR
in
India-Vietnam Relations
(1991–2019)

CHINA FACTOR
in
India-Vietnam Relations
(1991–2019)

Tilottama Mukherjee

KNOWLEDGE WORLD
KW Publishers Pvt Ltd
New Delhi

ISBN 978-81-952858-9-1 Hardback
ISBN 978-81-952858-6-0 ebook

Published in India by Kalpana Shukla

KNOWLEDGE WORLD
KW Publishers Pvt Ltd
4676/21, First Floor, Ansari Road
Daryaganj, New Delhi 110002
Phone: +91 11 43528107
Marketing: kw@kwpub.in
Editorial: production@kwpub.in
Website: www.kwpub.in

Printed and Bound in India

I dedicate it to my parents, husband and Ghonti

for their unconditional love and unwavering support

Contents

List of Tables

Acknowledgements

Right at the outset, I would like to express my sincere gratitude to Dr. Tridib Chakraborti for supervising my research for all these years, the fruition of which is this book. His knowledge, guidance, advice and motivation have helped me immensely for writing this book. I also thank his entire family, especially Late Ms. Pragati Chakraborty, his elder sister, whose encouragement even when she was battling cancer, shall be etched in my memories forever. Special thanks to Dr. Paramita Bhattacharya for her tremendous support. I would like to thank Dr. Om Prakash Mishra, Head, Department of International Relations, Jadavpur University for his encouragement.

I also extend my thanks to Dr. Gundre Jaychandra Reddy, Director and Chairman, Board of Studies, Centre for Southeast Asian and Pacific Studies, Sri Venkateswara University, Tirupati, Dr. Le Hang Nga and her team at Institute for Indian and South West Asian Studies, Vietnam Academy of Social Sciences (VASS), Hanoi, Mr. Geetesh Sharma, President, Indo-Vietnam Solidarity Committee, Kolkata for continuously supporting, advising and motivating me to contribute significantly through my research.

I am grateful to faculty and staff at Institute for Indian and South West Asian Studies, VASS, Hanoi; Department of World History, Hanoi National University of Education; Institute of Southeast Asian Studies, VASS; Indian Council for Cultural Relations, Kolkata; Indo-Vietnam Solidarity Committee, Kolkata; UGC Centre for Southeast Asian and Pacific Studies, Sri Venkateswara University, Tirupati; Netaji Institute for Asian Studies, Kolkata; Maulana Abul Kalam Azad Institute for Asian Studies, Kolkata; National Library, Kolkata; Central Library, Departmental Library (of Department of International Relations) and Tarak Nath Das Research Centre, Jadavpur University,

Kolkata; Department of East Asian Studies, University of Delhi; Indian Council of World Affairs (ICWA), New Delhi; Institute for Defence Studies and Analyses (IDSA), New Delhi. I could never have conducted the research for this book without being greatly enriched by these institutes. Thank you very much.

I am indebted to my maternal uncle, Prof. Priyabrata Chakraborty, my maternal aunt, Mrs. Maitreyi Banerjee, and all my relatives for their love and prayers.

List of Abbreviations

ADB	Asian Development Bank
ADMM	ASEAN Defence Ministers Meeting
AIADMK	All India Anna Dravida Munnetra Kazhagam
AIDZ	Air Defence Identification Zone
AINTT	ASEAN- India Network of Think Tanks
AITIG	ASEAN-India Trade in Goods
AITTA	ASEAN-India Transit Transport Agreement
AMM	ASEAN Ministerial Meeting
APEC	Asia Pacific Economic Cooperation
ARC-ICT	Advanced Resource Centre-Information and Communication Technology
ARF	ASEAN Regional Forum
ASEAN	Association of South East Asian Nations
ASEAN PMC	Association of South East Asian Nations Post Ministerial Conference
ASEM	Asia Europe Meeting
ASEM	Asia Europe Meeting
ASSOCHAM	Associated Chambers of Commerce and Industry of India
BARC	Bhabha Atomic Research Centre
BIMSTEC and	Bay of Bengal Initiative for Multi-Sectoral Technical Economic Co-operation
BIPPA	Bilateral Investment Promotion and Protection Agreement
BISTEC Economic	Bangladesh, India, Sri Lanka and Thailand Cooperation
BJP	Bharatiya Janata Party
BOT	Build-Operate-Transfer

BRICS	Brazil Russia India China South Africa
BT	Build-Transfer
BTA	Bilateral Trade Agreement
BTA	Bilateral Trade Agreement
BTO	Build-Transfer-Operate
CAPEXIL	Chemical and Allied Product Export Promotion Council
CBM	Confidence Building Measure
CIS	Centre for Indian Studies
CLMV	Cambodia Laos Myanmar Vietnam
CMEA	Council for Mutual Economic Assistance
CPC	Communist Party of China
CPV	Communist Party of Vietnam
DOC	Declaration on the Conduct of Parties in the South China Sea
DRDO	Defence Research Development Organization
DRV	Democratic Republic of Vietnam
EAS	East Asia Summit
EDC	Entrepreneurship Development Centre
EEP	Educational Exchange Programme
EEZ	Exclusive Economic Zone
EU	European Council
EWGHMA	Expert Working Group for Humanitarian Mine Action
FDI	Foreign Direct Investment
FICCI	Federation of Indian Chambers of Commerce
FTA	Free Trade Agreement
FTP	Free Trade Partner
GCSS	General Cultural Scholarship Scheme
GDP	Gross Domestic Product
GERUCO	General Rubber Corporation
HAL	Hindustan Aeronautics Limited
HPC	High Performance Computing
IAEA	International Atomic Energy Agency

IAEC	Indian Atomic Energy Commission
IAI	Initiative for ASEAN Integration
IBSA	India Brazil South Africa
ICAR	Indian Council for Agricultural Research
ICCR	Indian Council for Cultural Relations
ICCS	International Commission of Control and Supervision
IFC	International Finance Corporation
IGHTCL	Indira Gandhi High Tech Crime Lab
IMF	International Monetary Fund
INC	Indian National Congress
IORA	Indian Ocean Rim Association
ISRO	Indian Space Research Organization
ITEC	Indian Technical and Economic Cooperation
IVCCI	Indo-Vietnam Chamber of Commerce and Industries
JeM	Jaish-e-Mohammed
JMSU	Joint Marine Seismic Undertaking
JWG	Joint Working Group
LAC	Line of Actual Control
LOC	Line of Credit
LOC	Line of Control
LPG	Liberalization Privatization Globalization
MFN	Most Favoured Nation
MGC	Mekong Ganga Cooperation
MoU	Memorandum/Memoranda of Understanding
MTCR	Missile Technology Control Regime
NDA	National Democratic Alliance
NEP	New Economic Policy
NEP	New Economic Policy
NLF	National Liberation Front
NPC	National People's Congress
NSG	Nuclear Suppliers Group
ODA	Official Development Assistance
ODA	Official Development Assistance
ONGC	Oil and Natural Gas Corporation

OVL	ONGC Videsh Limited
PEC	Public Equipment Corporation
PIDC	Petroleum Investment of Development Company
PIDC	Petroleum Investment and Development Company
PKOs	Peace Keeping Operations
PLA	People's Liberation Army
PLAN	People's Liberation Army Navy
PNTR	Permanent Normal Trade Relation
PoK	Pakistan occupied Kashmir
PRC	People's Republic of China
QIPs	Quick Impact Projects
QSD	Quadrilateral Security Dialogue
RCEP	Regional Comprehensive Economic Partnership
RV	Republic of Vietnam
SAARC	South Asian Association for Regional Cooperation
SAGAR	Security and Growth for All in the Region
SCO	Shanghai Cooperation Organization
SCS	South China Sea
SEATO	South East Treaty Organization
SED	Strategic Economic Dialogue
TAC	Treaty of Amity and Cooperation
TRAI	Telecom Regulatory Authority of India
UNCLCS	United Nations Commission on the Limits of Continental Shelf
UNCLOS	United Nations Convention on the Law of the Sea
UNCTAD	United Nations Conference on Trade and Development
UNESCAP for	United Nations Economic and Social Commission Asia and the Pacific
USA/US	United States of America/United States
VAAS	Vietnam Academy of Agricultural Sciences
VAEC	Vietnam Atomic Energy Commission
VCCI	Vietnam Chamber of Commerce and Industries
VICELT	Vietnam-English Language Training Centre

VIEDC	Vietnam-India Entrepreneurship Development Centre
VIEDC	Vietnam India Entrepreneurship Development Centre
VNTA	Vietnam Telecommunications Authority
VSC	Vietnam Steel Corporation
WTO	World Trade Organization

ONE

India's Relations with Vietnam in the Cold War Years and the China Factor

In the annals of world history, India's relations with Vietnam have deep historical and cultural roots tracing back more than 2000 years. This is evident from the Indian influence in Vietnamese folklore, religion, philosophy, art and architecture and such temples as the Champa Temple in the present day Ho Chi Minh City, formerly Saigon and in Danang in recent times.[1] With the passage of time, both countries have developed strong diplomatic ties spanning nearly five decades. Geographically speaking, Vietnam, being a strategically located country bordering China, Laos, Cambodia, the Gulf of Thailand, the Gulf of Tonkin, the South China Sea and the Pacific Ocean, has always enjoyed importance in global politics surpassing its significance in terms of its size, population, economic clout or its achievements in any other realm of foreign policy. The purpose of this chapter is to analyse the trajectory of India's overall relations with Vietnam during the Cold War period and how this was conditioned by the imperatives of the then superpower politics, marked by the ideological face-off between the two sides. This chapter purports to explain how non-aligned India's policies were shaped vis-à-vis Communist Vietnam's against the backdrop of Cold War politics and the 'China factor' in their bilateral ties. For better explanation, this chapter has been divided into various sub-headings, such as, the foundation of India-Vietnam relation; India-Vietnam relations under Mrs. Indira Gandhi, and India's role in Vietnam's national reconstruction.

Laying the Strong Foundation of Indo-Vietnam Relations: The Time-Tested Friendship Ties

Historically, Vietnam had to face thousand years of Chinese colonial rule (from 111 BC–940 AD), followed by the French colonial rule which began from 1887. During this time, both India and Vietnam had started their struggles against their respective colonial powers. At that crucial juncture, when India herself was fighting to gain independence from the oppressive British colonial rule, in as early as 1927, Pandit Jawaharlal Nehru, while formulating the first foreign policy statement of the Indian National Congress (INC) party, staunchly supported the anti-imperialist struggles in the rest of the Third World countries, including Vietnam. He also extended India's unwavering solidarity with such efforts in the foreign policy statement by declaring that India condemned the imperialist rule and would not participate on behalf of the British Army to resist such anti-imperialist wars in any Third World country. This principled foreign policy stance of Indian leaders at a time when the country was reeling under the British rule, not only guided India's mindset till independence, but almost immediately made India a champion of the cause of Asian solidarity.

During the course of the Second World War, Vietnam underwent tumultuous changes in its political structure when its coloniser, France was defeated by Germany under the leadership of the Nazi leader, Adolf Hitler. From then onwards the administration of Vietnam, Laos and Cambodia, that is the countries of Indo-China, which were so far under the French colonial rule, now came to be administered by the Vichy French government, which in reality was nothing but a puppet of the Nazi Germany. In 1941, the Vichy French government allowed Japan, an ally of the Nazi's in the 'Axis Powers' grouping, to extend its control over not only Vietnam, but over the entire Southeast Asian region. By March 1945, Japan not only summarily overthrew the Vichy French government, but also took direct control of Vietnam. However, shortly afterwards, in August 1945, Japan was defeated by the 'Allied Powers' and the Vietnamese nationalists, under the leadership of enigmatic Ho Chi Minh, proclaimed independence. However, their joy was short-lived as France, now a part of the 'Allied Powers' did not waste time in re-colonising Vietnam. This led to the outbreak of the First Indo-China War in 1946, culminating in the rout of France in the Battle of Dien Bien Phu in 1954. As for India, even while the First Indo-China War was in full swing, Pandit Nehru, as the head of the then constituted Provisional government of India which was preparing for its independence to be obtained shortly afterwards, hosted the Asian Relations Conference in March-April 1947 in New Delhi. During this time, India, despite having immense respect for the nationalism of Vietnam, did not actively lend support to either Ho Chi Minh's regime or Bao Dai's regime as the then leadership felt that it would not be prudent to interfere in Vietnam's internal affairs till it becomes clear as to which government would prevail.

As a result of the emerging impasse in the Indo-China region, the Geneva Conference was convened which culminated in the Geneva Accords of July 1954 that decided to divide the country into two halves along the 17 Parallel separating the military forces of the Viet Minh (national independence coalition, under the leadership of the Indo-Chinese Communist Party and Ho Chi Minh, which had fought valiantly against Japan and France) in the North and the military forces of the French in the South. North Vietnam came to be known as the Democratic Republic of Vietnam (DRV), which was led by the Communist Party of Vietnam (CPV) and Ho Chi Minh and South Vietnam came to be known as the Republic of Vietnam (RV), under the nominal leadership of the Vietnamese emperor Bao Dai. The Geneva Accords further stipulated that nationwide elections were to be held in 1956.

Hence, it becomes amply clear that right from the beginning of the Cold War, Vietnam found itself situated amidst the quandary of the Great Power politics, as a theatre where the Cold War paraphernalia was being increasingly played out. India, after achieving her own independence, started to condemn more vociferously the imperialist oppression in other parts of the world. That is why only five days after Ho Chi Minh took control over Hanoi after defeating France at Dien

Bien Phu in May 1954, Nehru paid a visit to Vietnam to express solidarity with Vietnam and met the charismatic Ho Chi Minh and was highly impressed by him. Nehru fondly wrote, "Dr. Ho Chi Minh impressed me as an unusually frank, straight-forward and likeable person…He struck me as a man of peace and goodwill…it was evident that Viet Minh was well-organized and disciplined."[2]

Most importantly, India was then functioning as the Chairman of the International Commission of Control and Supervision in Vietnam (ICCS), in-charge of the affairs of the Indo-China states, mandated by the Geneva Accords and also, according to the Accords, India was given the supervisory role for conducting nationwide elections in 1956. The ICCS was constituted in 1954 by the Geneva Conference and India was nominated its Chairman with a mediating role with Poland and Canada as two other members. Thus India's Chairmanship provided India with an opportunity to exhibit its leadership ability in crucial global affairs.[3]

It is interesting to note here that during this time, Vietnam's struggle was not only being actively supported by India, but also by the Mao Tse Tung-led People's Republic of China (PRC). The Communists had captured power in 1949 and India was the first country to recognize the Communist government in China in 1949. The PRC not only provided moral support to Ho Chi Minh and the Viet Minh at this crucial juncture, owing to ideological affinities, but also offered material support, military assistance and safe sanctuary to the Viet Minh forces. However, the United States of America (USA/US) was becoming increasingly paranoid of communist expansion in the Cold War years and therefore, particularly after Communist North Korea's invasion of South Korea and ally France's defeat at the hands of Communist Viet Minh, the US got actively embroiled in the affairs of Vietnam as its loss would have meant the realisation of their dreaded 'domino theory' and the loss of America's control over the entire Southeast Asian region. That is why, the US-backed Ngo Dinh Diem became the newly installed Premier of South Vietnam in 1954 and, interestingly enough, he flouted the stipulations of the Geneva Accords which had called for nationwide elections to be conducted in 1956. The Diem government backed by the US was strongly against the idea of such elections. In October 1955, he declared himself the President of the Republic of Vietnam, and conducted a referendum only in the territories of South Vietnam, thereby checking the possibility of any further Communist expansion. India, as the Chairman of the ICCS, criticised such activities whereas the US grew extremely critical of India's role as the Chairman of the ICCS. The Chairmanship of the ICCS further paved the way for India to develop extremely friendly ties with not only Vietnam, but also with China and the Soviet Union, further antagonising the US. Despite the fact that India established Consular relations with Vietnam in 1956, Diem paid a visit to India in November 1957 to win support for his regime in South Vietnam. The Foreign Minister of North Vietnam Pham Van Dong had visited India in April 1995 and extended whole-hearted support to India to fulfil her duties and obligations as the Chairman of the ICCS. That visit concluded very significantly with a joint declaration on cooperation, implementation of the Geneva Agreement and a call for free elections for subsequent unification of the two Vietnams.[4] President Ho Chi Minh paid a visit to India in February 1958 to further bolster their bilateral ties and to enhance the solidarity among the countries in Asia and Africa for the purpose of defending world peace. India made known her fondness for Ho Chi Minh when Mrs. Rameshwari Nehru, Chairman of the "President Ho Chi Minh Reception Committee" remarked, "you are loved and respected by us, the citizens of India as much as by your own people."[5] On this visit, Ho Chi Minh, during his speech at the banquet given by the President of India Rajendra Prasad, thanked 'the International Commission with India as its chairman for the efforts in the supervision and control of the implementation of the Geneva Agreements in Vietnam'.[6] Therefore, India's Chairmanship of the ICCS catapulted her to a position of eminence and allowed her to play a leadership role in the affairs of the region.

However, by the end of the 1950s, India's relations with China started to become bitter, which had a spillover effect in India's ties with Vietnam as well. India's hitherto excellent understanding with China started to lose its warmth particularly when, at the outset of 1959, the Tibetan uprising took place against PRC's effective control and imposition of socialist reforms over Tibet. The Dalai Lama had to flee Tibet along with his followers and he reached India through Assam. China was infuriated when India granted asylum to the Dalai Lama and his retinue (on the condition that no political activities could be undertaken from the Indian soil), which irrevocably threw their ties to the nadir. This was followed by the 1962 border clash between India and China when China invaded India owing to its border claims. Parallel to India's deterioration of ties with China, her ties with Vietnam started to deteriorate to some extent owing to China and North Vietnam's strengthening of mutual camaraderie as a result of common ideological affinities. Thus, with Vietnam being generously helped by the Soviet Union and China to counter the US in its soil in the Cold War milieu, Hanoi was in no position to criticise the Chinese incursions on the Indian soil in 1962. India retorted by making known its displeasure against Hanoi through the ICCS Report of June 1962, where it was reported for the first time, "Armed and unarmed personnel, arms, ammunitions and other supplies…sent from the zone in the North to the zone in the South".[7] Thus, it was a remarkable departure from India's previous position as the Chairman of the ICCS when she had repeatedly been unresponsive of South Vietnam's and US's allegations of revolutionary activities in South Vietnam carried out by the guerrillas and communist forces of the North. The stark change of position by India at this juncture was entirely due to the 'China factor'. The shocking defeat of India, at the hands of the People's Liberation Army (PLA) took place in 1962 and Prime Minister Jawaharlal Nehru passed away in 1964. He was succeeded by Lal Bahadur Shastri, who continued with the principled tenets of India's foreign policy, namely, adherence to the Panchasheel, following the non-aligned path and to play a neutral and constructive role as the Chairman of the ICCS. During the 1965 Indo-Pak border clash, China was in support of Pakistan and had provided the latter with the necessary logistical help,[8] probably this was the reason why Hanoi could never come forth with any criticism of China or Pakistan for getting involved in a border clash with India in 1965. With the US involved in its bloody war with Vietnam, the Soviet Union utilised the opportunity to broker peace between India and Pakistan at Tashkent, where the Tashkent Declaration was signed in 1966. India on her part, though continued to remain principally opposed to US's involvement in Vietnam, became less vociferous than before on the issue, because, owing to the bad shape of India's economic health in the mid and late 1960s, India increasingly fell into the lap of the US for importing food grains, a process which had started from Nehru's hugely successful visit to the US in 1956 and in 1959. When President Eisenhower touched down for visiting India, India was already obtaining economic aid from the US to the tune of $822 million and was covered under the PL 480 food programme. On one hand, at this time, while the official mouthpiece of the Communist Party of Vietnam, *Nhan Dan*, was reporting that the Kashmir issue was wrongly complicated and meddled with by the imperialist Western bloc to further their "warmongering plans in Asia" and that "the stand of the Indian Government is inappropriate, and at variance with the principle of respect for the national right of self-determination by the Kashmir people. In the conflict, India has expanded hostilities from Kashmir to Pakistan and at the same time sent troops to thrust deep in many other areas on Pakistan's territory. India has also shown its unwillingness to peacefully settle the Kashmir issue, but wants to expand further the conflict."[9] Slowly it began to be observed that China, Pakistan and North Vietnam were forming a triad in the Asian continent. Therefore, the period between Jawaharlal Nehru and Shastri eras saw ups and downs in India's relations with Vietnam (both North and South) and was solely determined by the Cold War politics.

Intensification of Indo-Vietnam Conviviality: The Pre-eminent Role of Mrs. Indira Gandhi as the Champion of the Vietnam Cause

With the fall of the Diem regime in South Vietnam in 1963, the instability caused by failed successions in South Vietnam led to intensification of subversive activities by the National Liberation Front (NLF) of North Vietnam in the territory of South Vietnam. Simultaneous to these occurrences, India too witnessed the untimely demise of Prime Minister Lal Bahadur Shastri in 1966 and Mrs. Indira Gandhi succeeded him as the next Prime Minister of India. Interestingly enough, immediately after assuming office, from March 27 to April 1, 1966, she paid a visit to the US and discussed at length as to how their bilateral ties could be bettered. The visit helped secure more food and developmental aid for India from the US. During this visit, in their bilateral talk, Mrs. Gandhi pragmatically relegated the Vietnam issue to the background. However, with the intensification of the US bombing in North Vietnam by 1966, India under Mrs. Indira Gandhi started to become more vocal about US activities, especially during her visit to the Soviet Union in July 1966, barely three months after her successful meeting with President Johnson in the US. The Soviet Union, under Premier Alexei Kosygin's leadership, pleased with her staunch criticism of the activities of the US under President Johnson's directives in its ally Vietnam's soil, announced a 970 million Rouble credit to India. Thus, with Mrs. Gandhi's accession to power, her growing proximity with the Soviet Union and her bitter and consistent criticisms of the US, India's relations with North Vietnam, once again started to improve and grow from strength to strength.

At this crucial juncture, the Cold War paraphernalia was being played out in the backdrop which was continuously shaping and re-shaping not only the destinies of these countries but also influencing their mutual ties to its utmost level. The unpredictability of the Cold War dynamics was leading to drastic and dramatic changes in the future course of actions and foreign policy decisions of all these countries. One such incident was the Sino-Soviet rift that started to surface from mid to the late 1960s. During this time, China under President Mao Tse Tung's leadership became extremely critical of the Soviet Union's policy of 'peaceful coexistence' with the US that was formulated and was being implemented under President Nikita Krushchev's leadership. Mao accused Krushchev of 'Marxist revisionism',[10] that is deliberately attenuating the fundamental tenets of Marxism. Moreover, the Soviet Union was not in concurrence with some of the radical policies followed by President Mao, such as going nuclear, the policy of 'Great Leap Forward', that is compulsory agrarian collectivisation, and its involvement in regional conflicts, such as the 1965 Indo-Pak War and pitting one country against the other. It is to be noted that it was not at all to China's liking when its ally, the Soviet Union, not only refrained from criticising India in the Indo-Pak War, but also brokered peace between these two countries at Tashkent. Or for that matter, China was also infuriated by the Soviet Union's disapproval of Chinese excesses in Tibet and its lack of criticism for the Tibetan uprising of 1959, and also by the soft posture increasingly taken by the Soviet Union towards the US under Krushchev's leadership, as exemplified by the Cuban Missile Crisis of 1962, where the Soviet Union clearly blinked the eyelid first. Moreover, the flaring up of China's border conflicts with the Soviet Union at Ussuri River, was yet another irritant in their bilateral ties by 1969. Therefore, with the clear crystallisation of the division in the Communist bloc, India, herself being a victim of Chinese aggressive postures, started to tilt more definitely in favour of the Soviet Union, and thus continued to criticise the acts of the US in Vietnam, now with renewed vigour.

As a result, China clearly started to move towards the US and the US responded by firmly laying the building blocs of an all-weather friendship with China and Pakistan in Asia, who were to become its key allies in the Cold War in the coming days. That is why, when in 1971, just a month before the India-Pakistan War, Mrs. Indira Gandhi visited the US and met President Nixon to convince them about the severe humanitarian crisis in East Pakistan, and the excesses committed by the Pakistan Army. But it all fell on deaf ears.

Meanwhile, with the proactive and positive role played by the Soviet Union buttressed by the Indo-Soviet Friendship Treaty of 1971, notwithstanding the limitations imposed by the hitherto followed non-aligned path, India played a very decisive role in the liberation of Bangladesh in 1971. The heroic victory of this War was followed by

Mrs. Gandhi's visit to Moscow in 1971. She once again discussed the Vietnam issue with the Soviet Union. She pledged India's support and commitment to fight for "the inalienable rights of all peoples, especially those of Vietnamese people, to national independence and freedom."[11] This statement was in concurrence with the speech of Swaran Singh delivered in the Lok Sabha on April 26, 1972, where he stated, "The liberation of Bangladesh was a great heroic event. The liberation of Vietnam will be an equally heroic and great event."[12] The Paris Peace Accord was signed on January 27, 1973, with the aim of putting an end to the protracted Vietnam War and to bring peace and stability in the country by ushering in the much-awaited reunification of the two Vietnams gradually on a peaceful basis, and India whole-heartedly hailed the decision.

To note finally, with the defeat of the West in Saigon, completion of the reunification process of the two Vietnams in January 1976 and creation of the Socialist Republic of Vietnam, Mrs. Gandhi remarked, "The West had not been able to assess the power of nationalism, even where forced to yield to it. This explains the paradox of West's involvement and failure in Asia in past two decades."[13] Therefore, India's relations with Vietnam during this period became one of closer proximity than ever before.

Turning over a New Leaf: The Saga of India's Role in Vietnam's National Reconstruction, 1976–1990

With the victory of the Communist regime in North Vietnam defeating the mighty US followed by the reunification of the two Vietnams, India's historical ties with Vietnam got a further boost, especially in the backdrop of worsening of the relations between Vietnam and China more particularly since 1975. With the intensification of the Sino-Soviet rift, Vietnam tilted more towards the Soviet Union, and not towards China, primarily owing to Vietnam's bitter memories of about one thousand years of Chinese colonial rule and also because of the fact that the Soviet Union was a superpower and embracing its policies and cultivating friendship with it would ensure Hanoi's security in the Cold War milieu. China was obviously extremely unhappy with Vietnam decisively moving towards the Soviet Union. Therefore, as a logical consequence to such displeasure, China decided to not pay any further heed to Vietnam's plea for economic assistance for its national reconstruction urgencies. On the one hand, while India started to generously help Vietnam in this regard, China on the other hand, despite its initial agreement to provide economic assistance to Vietnam, started to become more tight-fisted towards Vietnam with the gradual worsening of the Sino-Soviet rift. Finally it declared major reduction in economic assistance to Hanoi, and since February 1977 China refused any further fresh loan to Hanoi on the ground that China needed the money for its own internal development. This further worsened their bilateral understanding and pushed Hanoi decisively towards the Soviet Union and India. India on her part, besides providing handsome economic assistance amidst its own financial crunch, also actively started fighting for increased Vietnamese presence in the arena of global politics and staunchly demanded Vietnam's admission to the United Nations Organization, which finally happened in 1977.

In the meantime, since 1976, another development had started brewing in Vietnam's neighbouring country, Cambodia, which had had a major impact on Sino-Vietnam relations that further brought Vietnam closer to India and the Soviet Union during this phase. The triumph of the Communist government in Vietnam also brought about tectonic changes in the politics of Cambodia, with which China had established excellent ties, particularly since 1975 when the re-unified Vietnam's shift towards the Soviet Union became all too apparent. In Cambodia, throughout the Vietnam War, Prince Norodom Sihanouk had maintained largely a neutralist foreign policy posture, mostly opposed to any kind of intervention by the US. However, in connection with the ongoing Vietnam War, Cambodia too started to witness clandestine and covert Communist insurgent activities opposed to the established authority. In March 1970, following a brief period of complete chaos, General Lon Nol ousted Prince Sihanouk, and the Maoist guerillas overthrew General Lon Nol on April 15, 1975.[14]

Thereafter, the government headed by the Royal Government of the National Union of Cambodia was substituted in April 1976 by the Khmer Rouge government led by Pol Pot as the Prime Minister.[15] However, in the name of eradicating 'revisionists' (since the mid-1960s, China was accusing the Soviet Union of 'Marxist revisionism' by following the path of 'peaceful coexistence' with the Imperial West) the Pol Pot regime went on to exterminate about a third of the country's total population, which prompted Hanoi to extend support to the anti-Pol Pot communist groups, leading to further tensions between Vietnam and Cambodia (now renamed Kampuchea). Buttressed by its friendship with China, Kampuchea severed diplomatic ties with Vietnam on New Year's Eve of 1977.[16] By late 1977, while the Kampuchean crisis was at its peak, another incident was taking place simultaneously which further deteriorated Vietnam's ties with China. With the gradual worsening of Vietnam's ties with China, China started to vociferously condemn Vietnam's treatment of ethnic Chinese in Vietnam which constituted the minority population there. By early mid-1978, the mass emigration of Chinese came to notice and on 30 April 1978, the Head of the Overseas Chinese Affairs Office of the State Council in Beijing officially stated that owing to the expulsion of Chinese residents from Vietnam, about 40,000 of them had returned to China since April 1978. Infuriated, China immediately cancelled 21 Chinese mega projects that were underway in Vietnam then. Moreover, China cancelled additional 51 projects as it declared that caring for the expelled Chinese residents would not allow Beijing to extend any further financial support to Hanoi.[17]

Therefore, Vietnam with increased strains in ties with China, decided to come closer to the Soviet Union by joining the Soviet-led economic grouping, called the Council for Mutual Economic Assistance (CMEA) on June 28, 1978. Vietnam went further ahead by concluding a Treaty of Friendship and Cooperation with the Soviet Union on November 3, 1978. China severely reacted to these decisions taken by Vietnam to forge deeper understanding with the Soviet Union. With China standing in complete support of Cambodia and Pol Pot, and the worsening of the Sino-Vietnam relations, Vietnam in 1979 intervened in Kampuchea and replaced the Pol Pot-led government by the Heng Samrin government. Meanwhile the imposition of national emergency by Mrs. Gandhi in 1975, led to her being ousted from power. In 1977, the Janata Party, headed by Morarji Desai as the new Prime Minister, came to power in India. Adhering to its promised policy of 'genuine non-alignment', the Janata government decided neither to support the Pol Pot regime nor the Heng Samrin government.[18]

Meanwhile, Vietnam's action in Cambodia and placement of Heng Samrin as the Head of the State by replacing Norodom Sihanouk created severe tensions between Vietnam and China. For the Chinese Communist Party, this event led to severe commotion and humiliation , and as a result escalated hostility between Vietnam and Cambodia finally leading to a full-fledged military attack by Vietnam on Cambodia on December 25, 1978. China retorted by launching a corresponding attack along the land border between China and Vietnam on February 17, 1979, and justified it as an act of "self-defence" and to "teach Vietnam a lesson".[19] At this time, the then Foreign Minister of India, Mr. Atal Behari Vajpayee was touring China. Shocked by the news he immediately cancelled his visit owing to the 'insult' that China had inflicted on India by attacking her 'good friend' and ally, Vietnam. India herself being a 'victim' of 'Chinese aggression' completely stood by Vietnam. The Soviet Union too criticised the Sino-Vietnamese War. During this time President Alexei Kosygin had visited India in March 1979. India and the Soviet Union together demanded the complete and unconditional withdrawal of Chinese troops from the Vietnamese soil. India condemned China for always resorting to force while dealing with its neighbours to resolve outstanding issues.

In the meantime, keeping its promise to stand by Vietnam in its national reconstruction efforts, in April 1978, New Delhi extended its first commercial credit worth Rs. 300 million to Hanoi marking the beginning of bilateral trade on a large scale between the two countries and setting a glaring example of South-South cooperation. In late 1979, Vietnam set up the Institute for Rice Research in O Mon district in the Mekong delta of South Vietnam fitted with Indian laboratory equipment and farm machines, and a Buffalo Breeding Centre of Murrah milch buffaloes in Song Be province near Ho Chi Minh City. Indian scientists helped to build up a herd of Murrah buffaloes and also organised the cross-breeding programme through a number of artificial centres. In late February 1978, Prime Minister Pham Van Dong of Vietnam paid a seven-day visit to India. The striking features of this visit were the signing of four separate agreements on economic cooperation between New Delhi and Hanoi on February 26, 1978. According to these agreements, among other things, India agreed to provide Vietnam a credit of Rs. 100 million to buy railway equipment and such other goods besides livestock from India.[20]

Incidentally, India witnessed another major change of guards at the national level in January 1980, when Mrs. Indira Gandhi came back to power. With this development, India's ties with Vietnam and the Soviet Union marched ahead with more confidence and zeal. This was conditioned by the fact that, not only there was an ideological like-mindedness amongst these three countries, but also a genuine trust in each other's prowess and genuineness of intention. To renew the warmth in their bilateral ties after the reinstatement of Mrs. Gandhi to power in 1980, the Vietnamese Premier Pham Van Dong visited India in April 1980. During this visit, India extended whole-hearted support to Vietnam's proposal for the establishment of a Southeast Asian Zone of Peace, Genuine Independence and Neutrality. Reciprocally, Dong once again reiterated that Kashmir was an integral part of India, paid a visit to Srinagar and remarked that Pakistan and China 'will have to vacate the Indian territory which they have been occupying.'[21] This gesture of Vietnam was succeeded by the Indian government's decision on July 7, 1980, to recognize the Heng Samrin government of Kampuchea.[22] This was a stark departure from the previous Janata government's decision to not extend support to the Pol Pot regime and also not to the Heng Samrin government owing to its strict adherence to the policy of 'genuine non-alignment'. Following this event, India's relations with Vietnam became deeper. As an extension of this cordial understanding and considering the vulnerability of Vietnam's economic structure, India extended its whole-hearted economic support for Vietnam's national re-construction process. This resulted in the formation of the Indo-Vietnam Joint Commission for Economic, Scientific and Technical Cooperation, in 1982, during Mr. Nguyen Co Thach's second visit to India, the then Foreign Minister of Vietnam, for forging greater cooperation between Hanoi and New Delhi. The growing understanding between India and Vietnam gained momentum immediately after Mrs. Indira Gandhi came back to power. Before the Joint Commission was agreed upon, she had initiated a number of Indian incentives for Vietnam's economic reconstruction. The Industrial Development Bank of India gave a long-term credit of Rs. 150 million to Vietnam for purchase of machinery from India. And in the next month, New Delhi granted an interest-free loan of 50,000 tonnes of rice to Hanoi. At the same time, the Public Equipment Corporation (PEC) of India completed its consignment of 50 railway coaches to Vietnam. On May 26, 1981, a credit agreement was signed in New Delhi between the two countries. Under the agreement, India agreed to extend a loan of Rs. 100 million to the Government of Vietnam to import Indian textile fabrics for garments.

From February 12 to 15, 1982, the Minister of External Affairs of India, PV Narasimha Rao, paid an official visit to Hanoi. At the end of his visit, Rao announced India's decision to step up assistance to Vietnam, especially in the form of a Rs. 100 million loan to help rescheduling of recovery of earlier debts. All these developments during Mrs. Gandhi's tenure elevated their bilateral understanding to a high pedestal, with huge ramifications for these two countries. On July 3, 1984, Mr. Natwar Singh, the then Secretary (East) in the Ministry of External Affairs, signed an agreement in Hanoi for the grant of an Indian credit of Rs. 10 crores to Vietnam for buying diesel locomotives, equipment and services for the setting up of maintenance workshop for locomotives and for modernisation of the Nam Dinh textile mills. The modernisation of the rail yard at Ho Chi Minh City was among the specific projects in the programme. During his visit Mr. Singh also handed over the first three Indian diesel locomotives to Vietnam.[23]

When Le Duan, the then General Secretary of the CPV, visited India in 1984 to take stock of the state of ongoing bilateral cooperation between the two countries and to discuss the pressing issues of the region, *Nhan Dan* reported, "The identity of views of the two sides on many issues of bilateral cooperation and international and regional issues contribute to strengthening the existing solidarity between the two nations."[24]

However, this excellent growth in the trajectory of bilateral cooperation between India and Vietnam received a jolt when Mrs. Gandhi was assassinated in October 1984. There was official mourning in Vietnam for three days. Mrs. Gandhi was succeeded by her elder son, Rajiv Gandhi, as the new Prime Minister of India. He visited Hanoi in November 1985, only the second Prime Minister of India to do so, after Jawaharlal Nehru. Though the immediate reason of the visit was to receive Vietnam's highest civilian award, 'The Golden Star', posthumously conferred to Mrs. Indira Gandhi by the Vietnam government, Rajiv Gandhi pledged his support to carry on the legacy of his mother by putting in sincere efforts so as to build a deeper understanding and promoting all-round cooperation in political, economic, social and cultural development and unflinching support for each other's cause to strengthen peace and stability in Asia. In this regard, during his short stay at Hanoi, the second session of the India-Vietnam Joint Commission was held from November 23-26, 1985, and an agreement to extend a new line of Government-to-Government credit to Vietnam of Rs. 15 crores was signed. Moreover, India also decided to extend a commodity loan of one lakh tones of wheat over a two-year period: 1986 and 1987. Additionally, the Government of India agreed to help modernise textile mills in Vietnam and help it produce certain items such as oil, rubber and tin which could be exported to India.[25]

Meanwhile, amidst tectonic changes in global politics pursuant to Cold War dynamics since 1985 after President Gorbachev's ascendancy to power in the Soviet Union, his policies of 'Glasnost' and 'Perestroika' brought about considerable changes in the foreign policies of other countries as well. After getting the tacit message from the war and the debt-ridden Soviet Union that its allies and satellite countries must put in their best efforts to stand on their own feet rather than rely too much on the Soviet Union, which had started to show signs of crumbling, both Vietnam and India decided to bring in significant changes in their domestic and foreign policies as well. Therefore, in the Sixth National Party Congress of the CPV held in December 1986, Vietnam launched the policy of 'Doi Moi' or economic reconstruction. Once again, India extended its total support towards Vietnam for the successful implementation of this policy. High-level visits took place between the two countries, such as, the visit of General Vo Nguyen Giap, Deputy Prime Minister of Vietnam on April 10, 1989, and the visit of Nguyen Co Thach, Foreign Minister of Vietnam (who was pro-Soviet and pro-India and anti-China) for the discussion of bilateral and regional issues amidst the sudden emergence of flux in global politics. A delegation headed by the then External Affairs Minister, ND Tewari, visited Hanoi from January 9 to 12, 1987. An Indian credit of 100 million rupees to Vietnam was also declared. In addition, Prime Minister Rajiv Gandhi offered to Vietnam a gift of 10 million rupees for the purchase of urgently needed commodities. When Nguyen Van Linh, General Secretary of the Central Committee of the Communist Party of Vietnam, visited India as the principal foreign guest at the 39th Republic Day celebrations in January 1989, India once again extended a new Government-to-Government credit of Rs. 100 million to Vietnam in order to boost Hanoi's economic development at a time when it was in the grip of acute economic crisis.

From April 13 to 15, 1990, the Indian Minister of External Affairs, IK Gujral, visited Vietnam and once again reaffirmed New Delhi's commitment to Vietnam's national reconstruction. The important feature of this visit was the inauguration of the fourth meeting of the Indo-Vietnam Joint Commission by Mr. IK Gujral at Hanoi. In the meeting, New Delhi urged Hanoi to step up its imports from India which had an adverse balance of trade. India undertook to increase its imports from Vietnam. The Government of India also extended a credit of Rs. 100 million to Vietnam for import of capital and manufactured goods urgently needed by that country in its development program. Therefore, it is amply clear that the solidarity with the Vietnam cause that was a consistent feature of Indian foreign policy during the Second World War and the Vietnam War was carried forward in the post-1975 period largely under the leadership of Mrs. Indira Gandhi and subsequently by her elder son, Mr. Rajiv Gandhi.

To summarise, it is to be concluded that, India exhibited the highest form of friendship and camaraderie with Vietnam in the Cold War days and these ties of geniality were cultivated further by the common perception of 'China threat' during this phase as both these countries had faced Chinese wrath owing to their involvement in the Soviet security structure during the years of Sino-Soviet rift. By standing in unflinching political support of Vietnam during the Vietnam War, the re-unification process, and her national reconstruction drive, India during this phase had borne testimony to the fact that it was always Vietnam's greatest and truest friend in times of its economic needs, even at a time when India herself was reeling under domestic economic crunches and turmoil. For instance, to sum up India's major economic assistance to Vietnam in the post-1975 phase it can be stated that starting from 1978 when India offered the first line of credit to Vietnam worth Rs. 400 million, which was utilised for the import of 980 wagons, 1000 bogies and 50 coaches from India, genuine economic help continued, such as the setting up of the Joint Commission in 1982 for economic, scientific and technical cooperation between the two countries, offering the second Line of Credit to Hanoi in 1983 against which 15 diesel locomotives were supplied, followed by a third credit in 1984-85 which was utilised for the import of finished equipment and boiler for Nam Dinh Textile Mill and fabrics from India. The next credit in 1986 led to the supply of 300 coal hopper wagons for the Hon Gai and Cam Pha coal mines located in the northeast of Hanoi.[26] Moreover, India also assisted Vietnam in building the O- Mon Water Rice Research Centre and the Song Be Milk Buffalo Centre. It shared its experience in cross-breeding of a number of animals (milk buffalo, milk goat, fish and shrimp) and supplied Vietnam with several high-yielding seeds such as maize and cotton. Besides, between 1977 and 1990, Vietnam remained one of India's largest aid beneficiaries, receiving Indian credit assistance of Rs. 141. 15 crore on soft terms, with repayment being spread over 15 years at 5 percent rate of interest, for railway, telecommunication and sugar production equipment. India also treated Vietnam as a 'most favoured nation' in 1982 and signed an agreement for the setting up of a joint economic, scientific and technical commission which it had not negotiated with any other Southeast Asian country in the past.[27] In contrast, if we look at the scenario of China's economic assistance to Vietnam during the Cold War period, apart from two lean years in 1957 and 1962, Chinese aggregate aid commitments exceeded 200 million Yuan every year from 1955 to 1964, and amounted to 972 million Yuan in 1961 and 718 million in 1964. Although three Asian communist countries, notably North Korea, North Vietnam and Mongolia had received the bulk of China's military and economic aid in the period 1953–64; Burma, Indonesia and Pakistan had also obtained considerable amounts.[28] However, from the mid-1960s, China's economic aid to Vietnam started to dry up and eventually came to a halt as a result of the gradual intensification of the Sino-Soviet rift and the subsequent flaring up of discord between China and Vietnam, such as the mass emigration of resident Chinese from Vietnam, the Kampuchean crisis, border clashes and frequent flare-ups along the border during the 1980s (from 1979 up to August 1987 six major flare-ups were registered along the border),[29] emergence of disputed claims in the South China Sea and China's reluctance to provide economic assistance to Vietnam in her national reconstruction projects. All these issues and the positive and facilitating role played by the Soviet Union brought Vietnam closer to India and gave them an opportunity to build their ties on a concrete, unyielding and elevated pedestal right from the outset, marked by unflinching commitment and the promise of a brighter future.

Notes

1. Tridib Chakraborti, "India and Vietnam: The Historical Strategic Partnership in Asian Domain," in Arpita Basu Roy and Subhadeep Bhattacharya (eds.), *India and Southeast Asia: States, Borders and Culture*, Shipra Publications. New Delhi, 2015, p.123.
2. Jawaharlal Nehru, "Note on Visit to China and Indo-China," November 14, 1954, https://digitalarchive.wilsoncenter.org/document/121651.pdf?v=d7e143cb60346614a337c648500cf3a7 (accessed on November 16, 2016).
3. Suranjan Das, Tridib Chakraborti and Subhadeep Bhattacharya, *Indo- Vietnam Relations In The Emerging Global Order*, KW Publishers Pvt. Ltd, New Delhi, 2018, pp.10–11.
4. Tridib Chakraborti, "Three Stages in Indo- Vietnam Relations: An Overview," in Santimoy Ray and Tridib Chakraborti (eds.), *Vietnam: A Changing Horizon*, Chatterjee Publisher, Calcutta, 1992, pp.24–25.
5. Text of Speech of Mrs. Rameshwari Nehru, New Delhi, February 1958, collected from the Library of Indo-Vietnam Solidarity Committee, Kolkata.
6. Text of Speech of President Ho Chi Minh, New Delhi, February 1958, collected from Library of Parliament, Government of India, New Delhi.
7. Tridib Chakraborti, n.4, p.26.
8. On 15 September, 1965, Mr. B.K Nehru, India's the then Ambassador to the U.S told the National Press Club in Washington D.C, "What seems impossible to deny is that the Chinese and the Pakistanis are working in the closest possible co-operation to increase the military and economic pressure on India and to encourage internal disorder ….." Klaus P. Pringsheim, "China's Role in the Indo- Pakistani Conflict," *The China Quarterly*, No.24, October-December 1965, p.170.
9. Tridib Chakraborti, n.4, pp.27–28.
10. Joseph Camilleri, *Chinese Foreign Policy: The Maoist Era and its Aftermath*, Martin Robertson, Oxford, 1980, pp.63–64.
11. *Foreign Affairs Record*, Vol. XVII, September 1971. Also see, Tridib Chakraborti, n.4, p.30.
12. Ramesh Thakur and Carlyle A. Thayer, *Soviet Relations with India and Vietnam: 1945-1992*, Palgrave Macmillan, United Kingdom, 1992, p.237.
13. Tridib Chakraborti, n.4, p.31. For further details see, Indira Gandhi, *Aspects of our Foreign Policy*, Speeches and Writings, AICC, New Delhi, 1973, pp.89–90.
14. Suranjan Das, Tridib Chakraborti and Subhadeep Bhattacharya, n.3, p.19, also see, Arindam Sengupta, *The Survivors: Kampuchea, 1984,* Patriot Publishers, 1984, p.10.
15. Michael Vickery, *Cambodia: 1975-1982*, George Allen and Unwin, Sydney, 1984, p.146.
16. Ramses Amer, "Sino-Vietnamese Normalization in the Light of the Crisis of the late 1990s," *Pacific Affairs*, Vol.67, No.3, Autumn 1994, pp.357–83.
17. Ibid.
18. Tridib Chakraborti, *India and Kampuchea: A Phase in their Relations*, 1978-81, Minerva Associates, Calcutta, 1985, pp.62–63.
19. Xiaoming Zhang, "China's 1979 War with Vietnam: A Reassessment," *The China Quarterly*, Vol.184, December 2005, p.851.
20. Tridib Chakraborti, n.4, p.36.

21. *Indian and Foreign Review*, Vol.17, 15-30 April 1980, p.5.
22. Tridib Chakraborti, n.18, p.76.
23. *Annual Report: 1984-85*, Ministry of External Affairs, Government of India, New Delhi, 1985.
24. *Vietnam Information Bulletin*, Vol. XXIII, No. 19, 15 October 1984, p.2.
25. C. Ravindranatha Reddy, *India and Vietnam: Era of Friendship and Cooperation: 1947-1991*, Emerald Publishers, Chennai, 2009, p.43.
26. Shantanu Srivastava, "Four Decades of India- Vietnam Economic and Commercial Relations and the Way Forward," in Rajiv K. Bhatia, Vijay Sakhuja and Vikash Ranjan (eds.), *India- Vietnam: Agenda for Strengthening Partnership*, Shipra Publications and Indian Council of World Affairs, New Delhi, 2013, p.26.
27. Tridib Chakraborti, "From National Reconstruction To Market Economy: Space and Time Analysis of India's Look East Policy," in P. V. Rao (ed.), *India and ASEAN: Partners at Summit*, KW Publishers Pvt. Ltd, New Delhi, 2008, pp.319–35.
28. Joseph Camilleri, n.10, pp. 93–95.
29. Ramses Amer, n.16, pp.357–83.

TWO

India-Vietnam Economic Relations and China

The fall of former Soviet Union and the sudden collapse of its economy had a spillover effect on those countries which were previously partially or fully dependent on the Soviet Union. India, a traditional friend and ally, during that time maintained nearly 20 percent of her export market with the erstwhile Soviet Union and was also affected severely. This compelled India to not only try and find means to stand on her own feet but also to have better ties with her immediate and far eastern neighbouring countries, including China and Southeast Asia. Suddenly, this resulted in a dramatic change in the foreign policy priorities of India as the imperatives of Cold War politics ceased to be in play. The compulsions of post-Cold War dynamics led India to adopt the New Economic Policy (NEP) characterised by liberalization, privatisation and globalisation of the economy. The corresponding foreign policy that emerged in the early 1990s was the 'Look East' policy, whereby greater focus would now be given to the eastern neighbours, who was hitherto neglected on account of Cold War politics. It was realized that India could evolve to be a major player in the post-Cold War period, only if it can successfully tap the potentials of the Southeast Asian economies and beyond and make good use of their geostrategic location. It was historically not for the first time that India was engaging with this region. Trade and cultural interactions between India and Southeast Asia had also existed since time immemorial. Moreover, India did play a major fraternal role in the liberation history of this region from the

Western colonial powers. Unfortunately, during the Cold War period, there was an abrupt disengagement of India from the politics of this region. Now once again, the economic and strategic imperatives and challenges of the post-Cold War scenario, led to the adoption of India's 'Look East' policy and the overall mood that developed in the minds of the Indian foreign policy makers was of rapprochement with the countries of Southeast Asia and beyond.

As against such a backdrop, like India, both Vietnam and China had also embarked on the path of economic modernisation during this crucial juncture. This was another imperative that brought these three countries closer to each other in the post-Cold War years, than ever before. In 1978, after the death of Mao Zedong, Deng Xiaoping initiated the "Four Modernizations" program in China[1] for revamping the Chinese economy, with the aim of emerging as a global economic power by the beginning of the 21st century. Similarly, Vietnam too, initiated the 'Doi Moi' or renovation programme in 1986. This was started to reinvigorate the Vietnamese economy, which was then reeling under severe inflation owing to the ill-effects of command economy. The core of this strategy was liberation and deregulation of the economy and a realistic move towards the development of the private sector in the country and conducting massive reforms in the agricultural sector. The Sixth Party Congress of the Vietnam Communist Party heralded the reforms by changing the course of Vietnam's foreign policy and intensified the reforms in the economic sector. The course of action that 'Doi Moi' prescribed stressed on the market mechanism to allocate resources, deregulation of prices, reducing subsidies to state enterprises, and creating policies diverted towards the stabilisation and convertibility of currency. The Sixth Party Congress noted, "The bureaucratically centralized management mechanism based on State subsidies, which has been in force for many years now, far from creating a driving force for development, has weakened the socialist economy, limited the use and transformation of the other economic sectors, put a brake on production, lowered labour productivity, product quality and economic efficiency, put distribution and circulation in a state of chaos and given rise to numerous manifestations in our society. In that mechanism, the economy was managed mainly through administrative orders with detailed, legally enforceable plans and quotas handed down from higher levels. This was not at variance with the principle of democratic centralism".[2] It further made it amply clear that, "The guideline for renewing the economic management mechanism has been confirmed as follows: to abolish the bureaucratically centralised management based on State subsidies and to establish a new mechanism conforming to the objective laws and the level of economic development".[3] Hence, the aim of the 'Doi Moi' program was to initiate a 'socialist oriented market economy' in place of the command or state-controlled economy. It is interesting enough to note here that the Soviet Union too had adopted 'Glasnost' and 'Perestroika' under the leadership of Mikhail Gorbachev since 1985 and was trying to wrap up its engagement in the Afghanistan War, which it had been fighting since 1979. The economic crisis that had swelled up in the Soviet Union in the 1980s was also responsible for India and Vietnam to realise how important it is to increase the solvency of their own economies. This was the economic backdrop from where the destinies of these three countries would be written in the post-Cold War period. The purpose of the chapter is to analyse the economic relations that evolved between India and Vietnam in the post-Cold War years and their individual efforts in the same vein, to further strengthen their economic ties with the emerging economic giant, that is, China. This chapter also aims to study how their economic competition with China has led them to beef up their economic collaborative ventures in the new global order. For the convenience of study, this chapter has been divided decade-wise, i.e. 1991–99: the period of economic normalisation and pragmatism; 2000–09: the decade of strengthening of economic ties; and 2010–15: the years of economic bonhomie. Each phase gives a detailed discussion between India-Vietnam economic relations with the China factor as its crucial backdrop.

India-Vietnam Economic Cooperation: The Period of Normalization and Pragmatism, 1991–99

In India, the Tenth Lok Sabha elections were held in May 1991 and where the Congress (I) Party once again came to power by replacing the National Front government. The new Prime Minister, PV Narasimha Rao, continued the policy of friendship and cooperation towards Vietnam, much like his predecessors. Simultaneously though, India, at this juncture, initiated solemn rigorous efforts to recover the lost position in the Southeast Asian region in general and in Vietnam in particular and embarked on some important visits to Vietnam right at the beginning of the decade to further promote greater economic and political relationship. As a follow-up action of this understanding, the President of India paid an official visit to Vietnam from April 24 to 28, 1991. At the time of this visit, India agreed to assist Vietnam in establishing an industrial estate at an estimated cost of ⊠ 1 crore and was decided that talks on Civil Aviation and Banking would be held with the objective of establishing air links and opening a branch of the State Bank of India in Vietnam. The Civil Aviation talks were held in November 1991 and an Air Services Agreement providing for the establishment of air links between the two countries was initiated and was finally signed in May 1993. Following this agreement, India's economic relations with Vietnam continued unabated. In March 1992, the Foreign Minister of Vietnam, Mr. Nguyen Manh Cam, paid an official visit to India and both the countries agreed to develop better economic relations between them in the context of the then changing global and regional order. At the time of this visit, the fifth session of the Indo-Vietnam Joint Commission was held on March 24-25, 1992, which focused primarily on how to enhance cooperation in existing areas, especially in the field of trade and commerce as well as identification of new areas of cooperation.[4] As a follow-up of this visit, in September 1992, the General Secretary of the Vietnam Communist Party Du Muoi visited India. At the time of this visit, both the countries decided how to accelerate the implementation of the existing agreements and identified the areas and forms of future cooperation, namely joint ventures in the field of oil exploration, exploiting the process of minerals, small industry, agriculture and agro-based industries, hotel industry and marine products.[5]

Besides this, another significant event took place in the same year when the FICCI and ASSOCHAM from India and the Chamber of Commerce and Industry of Vietnam signed the agreement to form the Indo-Vietnam Joint Business Council on November 17, 1992.[6] Thus, all these concerted efforts clearly exhibit that both India and Vietnam were extremely serious and focused on strengthening their mutual ties, particularly in the economic sphere, to mitigate the losses caused with the fall of former Soviet Union, based on historical mindset of solidarity understanding.

Meanwhile, to accelerate the ongoing cooperation evolved between India and Vietnam, in February 1993, Shri Salman Kurshid, the then Minister of State for External Affairs visited Vietnam and identified the future economic areas for furthering cooperation including the ongoing energy sector, which was initiated during the Cold War period. Immediately after this visit, in July 1993, Minister of State for Petroleum and Natural Gas, Captain Satish Sharma visited Vietnam to review the progress of the offshore exploration of the ONGC (Videsh Limited) in Southern Vietnam and discussed how to strengthen the ongoing economic relations by exploring newer areas of cooperation. In the same year, the Vietnamese Vice Minister of Finance, Mr. Pham Van Trong, visited India in October 1993 and reiterated the measures for improving the course of India-Vietnam economic relations and how to make the Joint Commission Meeting more effective, which was scheduled to be held in Hanoi in early 1994. As a result of this visit, two Indian companies agreed to set up projects in Vietnam and among them KCP of Madras signed an agreement with a Vietnamese Company for setting up a sugar plant, and Harrison Malayalam set up a rubber plantation and processing project in Vietnam with a total investment sum of Rs 390 million.[7] Thus, it becomes amply clear that both these countries undertook serious concerted efforts right after the end of the Cold War to beef up their economic bilateral relations.

At this juncture, if we carefully analyse the two-way trade figures between Vietnam and India since the time when the first agreement was signed in 1956, we will find that annual trade turnover increased 20 times from US$ 5 million to about US$ 80 million by 1993.[8] Along with it, the export-import basket of the two countries also continuously expanded during this period and owing to the credit that the Government of India has been extending to Vietnam since 1970s for its national reconstruction, which played a major role in reinvigorating the Vietnamese economy to such an extent that, it could successfully expand and diversify its export and import basket by the early 1990s. During this period, Vietnam imported from India a large quantity of locomotives, passing coaches and a range of machineries, equipments and other capital goods for railway sector, textile mills, setting up tea, jute processing, leather tanning industries and exported coal, tin, raw silk, metal scrap, bean, cashew nut, groundnut, spices, in exchange for dyestuffs, cotton and polyester yarn and other commodities.[9]

Around this time, a significant development took place which had a spillover effect on Indo-Vietnam relations, not only immediately, but also in the coming decades. Just like Vietnam had done with China, similarly, it started warming up to the United States as well. As a result of concentrated and intense moves, finally, on 3 February 1994, the United States lifted the trade embargo on Vietnam and proposed the mutual establishment of liaison offices in the two countries. This was a very positive step as far as the economy of Vietnam was concerned and India, being a 'friend' of Vietnam, welcomed the development.[10]

The growing understanding between India and Vietnam economic ties was furthered strengthened when both the countries concluded the Double Taxation Avoidance Agreement on September 7, 1994. The real spirit of such an agreement was to avoid or eliminate double taxation of the same income in two countries. It came into force on February 2, 1995.[11] The 1994 Protocol was very important around this time because it provided for internationally accepted standards for effective exchange of information on tax matters including bank information between India and Vietnam.[12]

Thus, all these initiatives started having a positive effect on India's economic ties with Vietnam. As a result of India's definite focus on Vietnam in the post-Cold War years, during 1993–94, exports from India to Vietnam jumped by 60 percent to $27.8 million. Conversely, imports from Vietnam, on the other hand, declined by 28 percent to $43.8 million. However, India still continued to have an adverse trade balance with Vietnam. This mismatch of import-export figures between India and Vietnam was probably because the implementation of the process of 'Doi Moi' was still at a very nascent stage and India too, which was still in the flux of implementing the New Economic Policy, preferred to buy products from the developed Association of South East Asian Nations (ASEAN) economies than from Vietnam. Also the complementarities in the Indo-Vietnam bilateral export-import basket marred their bilateral trade.

Meanwhile, the sixth session of the Vietnam-India Joint Commission on Economic, Scientific and Technological Cooperation was held in Hanoi on April 15-16, 1994. The Vietnamese Government delegation was headed by Mr. Nguyen Manh Cam, Minister of Foreign Affairs of the Socialist Republic of Vietnam. The Indian delegation was led by Mr. NKP Salve, Minister of Power. The two sides reached agreements on repayment of principal, payment of interest of past credits and the utilization of new credit lines, discussed in detail measures to enhance trade, economic, scientific, technological cooperation between the two countries in the coming years. The two sides also decided to set up a Study Group with institutions of experts from both sides to oversee the bilateral interactions in all sectors, suggest measures to settle the problems and obstacles arising thereof in order to further promote cooperation.[13]

While keeping up the momentum of renewed vigour in strengthening their economic linkages, Prime Minister PV Narasimha Rao visited Vietnam in September 1994. He noted that although bilateral economic cooperation has been beefed up in recent years, it was still not up to par with the expectation of both the countries. This visit of Prime Minister Rao to Vietnam, was a reassurance of the continuity of India's policy of maintaining a warm and close relationship with Vietnam, particularly in the then changing environment. Both the sides recognized and appreciated the might of the bilateral relations, and at the same time they were of the opinion that the bilateral economic relations was nowhere near the satisfactory level. Thus, both sides pledged to upgrade their economic linkages, particularly in this changing global context where both these countries had initiated market reforms. Several new areas including trade in sugarcane cultivation and processing, dairy farming, rubber plantation and manufacture, vegetable oil production, leather processing, etc., was identified for intensifying economic collaborative efforts. At the time of this visit, four Agreements were signed and they were on Avoidance of Double Taxation, Facilitation of Visas, Defence Cooperation and Foreign Office Consultations. In addition, the visiting Indian business delegation signed six corporate agreements pertaining to investments and joint ventures in Vietnam in order to augment the ongoing economic initiatives.[14]

The height of economic initiative following this visit paid its dividend during the year 1994-95, when India's exports to Vietnam increased by 110 percent to $58 million; but imports from Vietnam increased just 1 percent to $44 million during the same period. Thus, for the first time in the previous five years, two-way trade turnover between India and Vietnam crossed $100 million as also India had a trade surplus with Vietnam.[15] During this time, main imports from Vietnam were rice, cashew nuts, wood, and wood products and major exports to Vietnam were drugs and pharmaceuticals, rubber products, machinery, iron and steel bars, electronic goods, etc. In continuation of the ongoing economic understanding, in August 1995, India set up a multipurpose industrial training centre in Hanoi at a cost of Rs 1.5 crore.

Similarly, during 1995-96, exports from India to Vietnam amounted to $123 million (a rise of 11.1 percent over previous year) and imports from Vietnam totalled $15 million (a fall of 65 percent). India, as a result, had a trade surplus of $108 million during the year. Moreover, to accelerate the bilateral trade between India and Vietnam, every year in November, Vietnam started organising an international

Trade Fair called Quang Trung International Trade Fair in Ho Chi Minh City. The prime scope of display at the fair covered all types of consumer goods, hand tools, chemicals, construction equipment, garments, pharmaceuticals, etc.[16]

In the meantime, the second meeting of the Indo-Vietnam Joint Working Group was held at Hanoi on 18 and 19 December 1995. The Indian delegation was led by Secretary (East) of the Ministry of External Affairs. This meeting identified concrete measures to promote trade, investment, banking and commercial relations between the two countries and also agreed that a new trade protocol would be signed at an early date. As a follow-up action of this meeting, the seventh Indo-Vietnam Joint Commission was held in New Delhi on February 23 and 24, 1996.[17]

The growing understanding between India and Vietnam to strengthen economic ties although started its journey but the level of economic cooperation was not satisfactory. This was clearly evident during 1996-97, when India's exports to Vietnam declined by 7 percent to $116.1 million. India's imports from Vietnam, on the other hand, declined by as much as 89 percent to $1.7 million during the same period. India, as a result, had a trade surplus of $114 million with Vietnam ($109 million previous year). While the two-way trade turnover between India and Vietnam declined to $118 million from $140 million recorded the previous year, trade surplus increased.

Therefore, by analysing these trade figures one can conclude that, despite renewed efforts to strengthen India's economic cooperation with Vietnam, it was not at all adequate or satisfactory and there were several lacuna which were impeding the development of better economic linkages between the two countries during this period. For instance, there was no direct shipping line between India and Vietnam and this was severely affecting the two-way trade because freight charges were becoming too high on account of transshipment at Singapore.[18] This proves that, at a time when the whole world was focusing its attention on Vietnam, Indian investment in various approved projects amounted to a paltry US$ 12 million. India thus ranked 40th out of 56 investing countries in Vietnam during this time.

Meanwhile, the Vietnamese Premier Vo Van Kiet visited India in March 1997, with the prime vision as how to accelerate the ongoing economic cooperation between both the countries. At the end of his visit, New Delhi and Hanoi concluded three important agreements: a) trade and economic cooperation (b) promotion and protection of investment and (c) credit agreement on India's supply of new credits to Vietnam, and a MoU on cooperation in environment and forests. Before leaving India, Premier Kiet expressed his satisfaction at the growth of bilateral trade which had crossed US$ 100 million mark on the period of 1994-95.[19]

Furthermore, on March 8, 1997, India and Vietnam concluded a Bilateral Investment Promotion and Protection Agreement (BIPPA). According to this agreement, each Contracting Party shall encourage and create favourable conditions for investors of the other Contracting Party to make investments in its territory and allow such investments in accordance with its laws and policy. Also, it was pledged that investments and returns of investors of each Contracting Party shall be at all times be accorded fair and equitable treatment in the territory of the other Contracting Party. In this Agreement, Article-4 pledged that the countries to accord national and Most Favored Nation (MFN) treatments to their investments in each other's territory.[20] Interestingly enough, Vietnam remained the second country in Southeast Asia with which India reached the agreement. Before that, India had signed this kind of agreement only with Malaysia on August 3, 1995.[21]

Shortly afterwards, in August 1997, the Eighth Session of Joint Commission was held in Hanoi. The Vietnamese Delegation was led by HE Mr. Nguyen Manh Cam, Minister of Foreign Affairs while the Indian Delegation was headed by HE Mr. Salleem I. Shervani, Minister of State for External Affairs. In this meeting, both the sides further discussed ways to improve their economic linkages and to keep up the pace of growing economic camaraderie between India and Vietnam. In continuation of this meeting, the fourth session of the joint working group meeting was held in Hanoi in April 1998. In this meeting, both the countries pledged to undertake new efforts to diversify their respective export of commodities to boost the quantum of bilateral trade for the desired growth target of US$ 200 million to be reached by the end of the 20th century. Further in this meeting, India agreed to consider the request of Vietnam for exploring possibilities of importing commodities from Vietnam, like raw silk, coal, crude oil, non ferrous metal and handicrafts items. It was also agreed by both the countries to upgrade and thereby strengthen economic and commercial relations through their respective companies in their mutual trade fairs.[22] However, it is to be noted in this context that in spite of the development of trade and economic cooperation between the two countries, there remained some hurdles, such as, fall in export from Vietnam to India at the time Vietnamese global exports were rising and the lack of information on goods and markets. To overcome these difficulties, the two Governments pledged to create favourable conditions for each other's business communities to visit and survey the market, to participate in the trade fairs and exhibitions and exchange products of high quality.[23]

If we analyse the trade statistics around this time, we can see that the downtrend in exports to Vietnam, which set in during 1996-97, continued unabatedly through 1997-98. During the first four months (April–July) of 1997-98, exports from India to Vietnam declined by 8 percent to $40.2 million from $43.7 million in the corresponding period in previous year. India's exports to Vietnam declined, while India's global exports increased by 2 percent during the same period. Imports from Vietnam, on the other hand, increased from $0.5 million to $1.9 million during the same period. As a result of increase in imports from and decline in exports to Vietnam, the trade balance, though continued to be in favour of India, declined from $43.2 million to $38.3 million.[24]

Interestingly enough, around this time, another very significant development was taking shape so far as India's economic relations with Vietnam were concerned. Vietnam got the approval to join Asia-Pacific Economic Cooperation (APEC) in 1998 and was getting nearer to gaining membership of the World Trade Organization (WTO). To integrate successfully, Vietnam had to reshape its economic policy in such a way that it would highlight the adjustments that would be required to become a member of the WTO, such as lowering tariff barriers, etc. That is why, the Government of Vietnam on January 1, 1998, made effective the Commercial Law of Vietnam. This new Law was designed to gradually emerge as instrumental in shaping an institutionalised trading relations with the market economy and where the role of the State in adjusting the market activities got modified.

As far as the trade statistics were concerned, during the first ten months (April–January) of 1997-98, exports from India to Vietnam declined by 3.6 percent, i.e. $91.3 million from $94.7 million in the corresponding period of the previous year. India's exports to Vietnam declined, while India's global exports increased by 2.4 percent during the same period. Imports from Vietnam, on the other hand, increased from $1.1 million to $6.1 million during the same period. As a result of increase in imports from and decline in exports to Vietnam, the trade balance, though continued to be in favour of India, declined from $93.5 million to $85.2 million.[25]

Immediately after the introduction of the new Commercial Law in January 1998, Vietnam announced another major decision in March 1998, according to which, the Vietnamese enterprises and joint venture enterprises no longer needed the sanction for export from the Ministry of Trade. The Vietnamese Government also lowered the number of items that required import permit from the Ministry of Trade. After this landmark decision, the Ministry of Trade controlled import of only ten items in Vietnam, such as petrol, fertiliser, construction steel, cement, sugar, etc.[26] All these steps were being taken so that Vietnam could successfully obtain its membership in APEC and WTO, which had definite ramifications for India's economic ties with Vietnam as well.

Shortly afterwards, Indian Deputy Foreign Minister, ET Devare visited Vietnam on April 25, 1998, to participate in the Fourth session of the Vietnam-India joint working group. In this session, the Indian side thoroughly stood in support of Vietnam's latest efforts to reform its economy and reviewed their work in sectors including agriculture, industry, education, fishery, transport and culture cooperation. It was felt that under the new Commercial Law introduced by Vietnam, both New Delhi and Hanoi governments were sincerely trying to advance their economic cooperation, despite the impact of the then regional and 1997 financial crisis. Unfortunately, their efforts still did not reach up to the mark and failed to tap the fullest potential of their bilateral economic space.[27]

As a fallout of this visit, more focus was given on correcting the sharp decline in the favourable balance of trade in favour of India vis-à-vis Vietnam. However, despite much focus on correcting the trade imbalance, during the first quarter (April˜June) of 1998-99, India's exports to Vietnam increased by 3.7 percent to $30.3 million from $29.2 million during the corresponding period last year. During the same period, India's imports from Vietnam recorded a sharp increase of 67 percent from $1.1 million to $1.8 million. As a result, trade balance, which was in favour of India, increased from $28.1 million to $28.5 million.[28]

In this phase, i.e. from 1991 to 1999, Vietnam mainly imported different products from India such as transportation equipment, machinery equipment for sugar plants and textile, telecommunication equipment, agro processing machinery, organic and inorganic chemicals, wheat flour, oil meals, etc. Vietnam in turn, exported to India many items such as, non-ferrous metal, spices, raw cashew nuts, rice, etc., and as the years advanced, a number of Indian companies started showing larger interest in investment in many economic sectors in Vietnam. In the sugar industry, the Nagarjuna group built around this time a sugar plant running well into production with the capacity of 3,500 tonnes sugarcane per day. By the late 1990s, there were six joint ventures and four ventures with 100 percent Indian investment of a total about US$ 165 million. This included the Nagarjuna group, the KCP Limited, the Dhampur Sugars, the KEC International Limited (manufacture of components for electrical transmission towers), SOL Pharmaceutical Limited (manufacture of pharmaceutical formulation), Ansal Group (to build apartments and office complex) and ONGC.

Meanwhile, the Ninth Session of the Vietnam-India Joint Commission was held in New Delhi from 29 January–3 February, 1999. The Vietnamese delegation was led by Mr. Nguyen Manh Cam, Deputy Prime Minister and Minister of Foreign Affairs of the Socialist Republic of Vietnam and Mr. Jaswant Singh, Minister of External Affairs of the Republic of India headed the Indian delegation. In the framework of the economic reform programmes that were being implemented successfully in the two countries, both the sides reiterated the need for further advancement of the multifaceted economic and commercial relations, so as to keep the economic tempo at par with excellent political relationship. Both sides discussed with each other the initiatives taken by them to develop their respective economies and exhorted each other to create conditions so that necessary steps could be taken for effective dissemination and exchange of business related information so that the business communities can better know the trade potentials in each other's country. The Session ended with the two sides signing the Agreed Minutes which covered issues such as bilateral trade, investment, education, telecommunication, property for the embassies and a new credit agreement worth 470 million Rupees. In this meeting, the then Minister of External Affairs, Shri Jaswant Singh said, "We are happy that bilateral trade has increased significantly in recent years. This is a trend which needs to be strongly encouraged since the volume of trade is well below its potential. The trade turnover between our two countries does not reflect either the strength of our political relations or the complementaries in our two economies. We would welcome discussion at this meeting and other forums on ways and means of diversifying and giving a boost to our bilateral trade...Participation of our oil company, ONGC, for the last ten years in an important natural gas exploitation project offshore in South Vietnam is a significant landmark in our bilateral cooperation."[29] The most striking event which took place during this phase was that the PetroVietnam signed an agreement with the ONGC Videsh Ltd. (OVL) on September 29, 1999. In this agreement, it was decided that OVL will shift 10 percent of its partaking interest to Petro Vietnam in the Lan Tray and Lan Do offshore areas discoveries.[30]

While summing up the major achievements of India-Vietnam bilateral economic relations in this phase, India offered a credit in 1993 which was used for tea machinery for Son La and Nghe An provinces and textile machinery for Vinh Phu province and Ho Chi Minh City. A complete sugar mill of 1250 TCD capacity was set up in Can Tho Province under another LoC, which was signed in the year 1995. Besides this, the Government of India in 1998 provided credit for the development of a fruit drink processing plant in Hanoi and a production line to manufacture adhesive tapes for packaging in Vinh Yen province.[31] In spite of this growing economic trade ties between the two countries which can be termed as a promising start, it is amply clear that the bilateral trade ties between the two countries during these years reached only more than US$ 165 million (see Table No. 1 below for details).

While assessing the trade relations between India and Vietnam during this phase, it is evident that the bilateral trade figure between these two countries compared to their overall global trade displayed quite nominal. The major reasons behind this slow growth in bilateral trade figure are as follows: **first,** the late entry of Vietnam and India in the ASEAN orbit and the former's newly inducted policy of Doi Moi and the latter's New Economic Policy, followed by the 1997 financial crisis severely affected their economies. **Secondly,** the lack of initiative from both the countries as how to increase their bilateral trade figure was clearly evident. **Finally,** India did not sign any Free Trade Agreement (FTA) with Vietnam during this phase that also slowed the bilateral trade progress. Therefore, the decade started on a very hopeful note with transformed vigour and expediency after the end of the Cold War and achieved some creditable landmarks, yet the high morale seemed to fizzle out by the end of the decade.

Table 1: India's Trade Relations with Vietnam (April 1991- March 2000)

Values in US$ Million

Year (April-March)	Export	Import	Total Trade	Balance of Trade
1991-1992	13.04	38.60	51.69	-25.6
1992-1993	16.43	57.36	73.79	-40.93
1993-1994	28.07	43.92	72.00	-15.85
1994-1995	58.71	44.2	102.92	14.51
1995-1996	123.38	15.49	138.88	107.89
1996-1997	118.07	1.70	119.77	116.37
1997-1998	126.60	8.73	135.33	117.87
1998-1999	125.43	9.14	134.57	116.29
1999-2000	154.37	11.52	165.89	142.85

Source: Prepared according to data available in Ministry of Commerce, Government of India, Annual Reports of Ministry of External Affairs, Government of India, Tridib Chakraborti, "From National Reconstruction to Market Economy: Space and Time Analysis Of India's Look East Vietnam Policy," in P.V Rao, India and ASEAN: Partners at Summit, K W Publishers Pvt. Ltd, New Delhi, 2008, pp.319–36 and General Statistics Office of Vietnam (Ministry of Planning and Investment, Government of Socialist Republic of Vietnam, Hanoi)

The China factor from the prism of India-Vietnam economic relations during 1991-1999

The commencement of economic reforms in both China and Vietnam, followed by the sudden fall of the former Soviet Union, led India's economic relations with these countries to gradually move in better direction. In fact, India's relations with China since 1962 was not at all cordial in nature. Realising fully well that particularly in the absence of the Soviet Union, China is going to play a major role in the affairs of the region, both India and Vietnam tried their best to normalise relations with China. It was felt that fostering greater economic cooperation would hold the key to mitigate the political and strategic tensions to a large extent, which both these countries had vis-à-vis China, owing to historical reasons. This state of relation of bitter experiences of the past gradually changed its discourse following Rajiv Gandhi's visit of China in 1988 (discussed in Chapter 2). Following this visit, India's relations with China gradually moved towards normalisation. However, this state of normalisation was further strengthened with the visit of R. Venkataraman, the then President of India to China in 1992. This was the first major visit from the Indian side to China after the end of the Cold War, where economic ties and the working of the Joint Working Group (JWG) between the two countries were consolidated for intensifying economic cooperation. The visit further laid emphasis to promote mutual Confidence Building Measures (CBMs) like mutual troop reductions and regular meetings of local military commanders.[32]

Consequently, in September 1990, General Secretary of the Vietnamese Communist Party Central Committee (VCPCC), Nguyen Van Linh, Chairman of the Council of Ministers Do Muoi, an advisor to the VCPCC Pham Van Dong went to Chengdu in China to meet their counterparts, Communist Party of China (CPC) General Secretary, Jiang Zemin and Premier Li Peng. This clandestine congregation smoothened the way for normalisation of relations between the two parties and two countries. Since then, economic ties between China and Vietnam expanded steadily.

As a result of this growing normalisation and intensification of their bilateral ties, by 1994, northern Vietnam and southern China emerged to be very similar markets, because in 1993 the China State Council had supported both Chinese and Hong Kong investment in Vietnam and added Hainan island to its plans to increase cross-border trade. When Hanoi hosted the Third Conference of Sub-regional Economic Activity, China attended to plan for adequate infrastructure and regulations to deal with increased trade. However, with the opening up of borders and liberalisation of economies, a problem soon emerged between China and Vietnam in this decade. China's less expensive products tended to flood Vietnamese markets and damage fledgling Vietnamese producers. In the 1990s, almost 20 percent of Vietnam's consumer goods used to come across the Chinese border; trade increased at the rate of more than 20 percent annually, and trade exchange in 1994 topped USD 500 million. To augment this activity, China in 1994 alone, invested more than USD 25 million in Vietnam.[33]

Meanwhile, continuing with the efforts to strengthen their bilateral economic ties, Permanent Politburo member of the Communist Party of China and Chinese Vice President Hu Jintao paid a visit to Vietnam in 1998 at the invitation of the Central Committee of the Communist Party of Vietnam and Vice President Nguyen Thi Binh. During his visit, Vietnam and China expressed their great pleasure at the fine development of the relationship between the two Parties and Governments since the two countries renovated relations. During this time, Vietnam and China signed an agreement on economic and technological cooperation, by which China pledged to provide Vietnam with 10 million Yuan as non-refundable aid for its development program.[34]

Since the normalisation of relations between Vietnam and China, bilateral trade and economic exchanges between them developed rapidly in this decade. In fact, trade figure increased during this decade from US$ 32.23 million to US$ 2.47 billion and the Chinese corporations had invested during the same period in over 80 projects in Vietnam with a contracted amount of almost US$180 million. The Chinese government also offered grant and interest-free loans to its Vietnamese counterpart amounting to US$45 million. The expansion of trade and economic exchanges was supported by the development of the transportation infrastructure. In spite of this growing trade figure between Vietnam and China, the Vietnamese government did not solely depend on China and its trade figures with Japan and ASEAN members were also high during this phase.[35]

Similarly, much like Vietnam, in 1991-92, India also took the initiative to open the first two border trade points in Uttarakhand and Himachal Pradesh with the hope that this route will become busier day by day with the pilgrims of Mansarovar and Kailash using this route.[36] Simultaneously, with the Indian government initiating economic reforms in 1991, India's market-oriented liberalisation and removal of Indian licensing and control policy, resulted in acceleration of GDP to about 6 percent a year since 1991, the fastest for any nation, but much lower than the Chinese pace of about 9 percent for the corresponding period, who had introduced reforms way back in 1978. Thus, the tussle and healthy economic competition between India and China, the two great giants of South Asia, started in the 1990s.[37]

Meanwhile, high level visits from India and Vietnam to China and from China to these two countries continued throughout the decade. For instance, the Commerce Minister of India visited China for the second session of the Joint Group on Economic Relations and Trade and Science and Technology in February 1991.[38] This was immediately after the end of the Cold War, with the definite aim to improve their economic ties. Some concrete steps were also taken by the Indian side to improve economic ties with China, such as, the resumption of border trade between Gunji (Pithorgarh District of UP) and Pulan in the Tibet Autonomous Region of China took place from June to September trading season in 1992.[39] Also, the border trade through Shipkila in Himachal Pradesh started on July 16, 1994. An agreement to open Shipkila for border trade had been signed at the time of Indian PM P.V Narasimha Rao's visit to China in 1993 with the focus on the economic content of their relationship with the expectation that these efforts would improve their trade scenario, which had been neglected to a large extent owing to Cold War compulsions. In the first nine months of 1994, the total volume of bilateral trade between India and China was US$ 593 million, an increase of 29.5 percent over the corresponding period in the previous year. To strengthen India's economic ties with China at this crucial juncture, the Vice President of India visited China in October 1994 with an emphasis on improving their economic ties.[40] As a result of all this; there was gradual improvement in the trade exchanges between India and China by the mid-1990s. For instance, the volume of trade in 1995 reached ⊠ 41.6 billion representing an increase of 30 percent over the previous year.[41]

Much like Vietnam, India too tried in its own way to woo China and engage with it economically as much as possible. Thus, gradually, India- China bilateral trade started to be viewed as the most agreeable and reliable pillar of mutual rapprochement. In fact, India- China trade ties progressively became the most positive aspect, barring the other sectors of their bilateral ties. A striking feature which is evident following the 1998 Pokhran II nuclear tests conducted by India, the trade figures between India and China continued to grow although as mentioned by George Fernandez that India blasted these bombs on account of a threat from an immediate nuclear neighbour. Though these nuclear tests were condemned by the world, including China, the economic parameters of India-China trade ties continued to improve. Perhaps, this is because of the fact that India's nuclear tests gave her a kind of parity in the power equations in the region and China did not want to lose the growing momentum of economic ties which it had accredited while keeping economic sector separate from other sectors. Thus, if we comparatively analyse Vietnam's trade figures with India and China in this decade, we will see that Vietnam's trade parameters with China were much ahead than Vietnam's trade figures with India. For a detailed and relative analysis, see **Table 2** below:

Table 2: Vietnam's Total Trade (1995-1999)

Values in US $Million

Year (Jan-Dec)	With India	With China	With World
1995	71.90	691.60	13,604.30
1996	97.55	669.18	18,399.50
1997	97.96	878.47	20,773.30
1998	121.26	955.09	20,859.90
1999	154.90	1419.50	23,283.10

Source: Prepared according to data available in Ministry of Commerce, Government of India, Annual Reports of Ministry of External Affairs, Government of India and General Statistics Office of Vietnam (Ministry of Planning and Investment, Government of Socialist Republic of Vietnam, Hanoi)

Therefore, it is amply clear that the 'China factor' did not play a very important role in influencing India's bilateral economic ties with Vietnam during this decade and Vietnam tried to engage economically with both India and China simultaneously, and intensify its trade ties with both these countries. Summarily then, it can be said that, Vietnam's trade with China during the end of this phase was US$ 1419 million, whereas with India it was US$ 154.90 million. The major rationale behind this asymmetrical trade figure of Vietnam with China and India were former's geographical proximity with similar political structures which put China, rather than India in an advantageous position. How far dis this trend continue in the next decade will be analysed subsequently.

India-Vietnam Economic Relations: The Decade of Strengthening Ties, 2000-2009

With the dawning of the new millennium, India's economic ties with Vietnam further deepened its roots following the Joint Declaration for Comprehensive Cooperation on the 21st century, which was promulgated in 2003. After signing several bilateral MoUs, this declaration clearly pledged greater efforts and commitment to improve their bilateral relationship, with particular focus on greater economic linkages through the effective implementation of several bilateral arrangements, like India-Vietnam Joint Commission, Joint Working Group, Joint Business Council, Trade Fairs and Exhibitions, etc.

After the end of the last decade in low spirits, meanwhile, in early 2000, certain important events took place which brought back the buoyancy of Vietnamese economy. These events included the implementation of an Enterprise Law that took effect on January 1, the US-Vietnam Bilateral Trade Agreement (BTA) on July 13, the opening of a stock exchange in Ho Chi Minh City on July 20, and the visit of US President Bill Clinton from November 16–21. This new Enterprise Law aimed to remove bureaucratic hurdles of the past years which Vietnam had been facing in its domestic investment sector. The dramatic decline in foreign investment in Vietnam around these years forced the then leadership to be more encouraging of the private sector, as a result of which the Enterprise Law made it much easier for small and medium enterprises to set up shop. The good results of this law started showing up very soon. For instance, by December, 12,000 new enterprises got registered under this new law, which was an exponential increase over the 600 in the entire period from 1995 to 1998. Similarly, the BTA concluded between Vietnam and the US during this year aimed that Vietnam-made goods would get access to the US market under the same low tariffs accorded to nations which have normalised trading relations with the United States. This displayed Vietnam's attraction to foreign investors and that was further amplified with the opening of the Ho Chi Minh City stock exchange immediately thereafter. Politically, all these incidents meant that the obstructive forces to economic liberalisation got moderated, and this ambience of greater liberalisation and opening up of the economy further provided an impetus to Vietnam's economic ties with India, which too had recently set out on the path of economic reforms.[42]

The fact that Vietnam has always been very serious to implement its reforms deeply, can be gauged from the fact that the new law on Foreign Direct Investment (FDI), that was introduced in Vietnam during the initial years of Doi Moi, in 1987, was time and again modified to keep pace with the fast changing global order. It was first amended in 1990, then in 1992, in 1996 and in 2000. On February 27, 1999, the Government disseminated Circular 02/CP on investment regulation under BOT (Build-Operate-Transfer), BTO (Build-Transfer-Operate) and BT (Build-Transfer). As per this, the foreign investors were allowed to open 100 percent foreign capitalised companies or enter joint ventures with a 70-80 percent of capital contribution. Since 1999, the Vietnamese Government allowed selling of shares to foreign investors, which is considered an effective measure of indirect investment. The amended laws and the government circulars have focused on the creation of a stable legal system on investment for a long period of time. From December 1987 to April 2000, Vietnam licensed more than 2405 foreign-invested firms with total USD 35, 964.74 million, of which 1,200 firms had reached an operational stage. This resulted in the contribution of foreign investments to the GDP of Vietnam that has been ascending from a mere 2 percent in 1992 to 7.4 percent in 1996 and 10.3 percent in 1999.[43]

This overall pro-investment atmosphere in Vietnam during 2000–2009 motivated several Indian companies, such as Godrej, Nagarjuna, Airhand oils, Rajshree and

Dhampur Sugar Mills to get actively involved in joint collaboration with the Vietnamese government projects. This congenial atmosphere facilitated the running of the government of India-owned company, ONGC Videsh Ltd., and private enterprises like Essar and Tata Steel in support of their investments in Vietnam. As a result of this, India moved up the ladder of global investors in Vietnam and became the sixth largest investor in Vietnam with USD 4.6 billion in 2007, its highest in any Association of South East Asian (ASEAN) country. Thus, concrete efforts in the direction of cementing Indo-Vietnam economic ties continued in this decade as well. They have come a long way since 1988, when as the first foreign company, the Oil and Natural Gas Commission of India (ONGC) signed a product-sharing agreement with Petro Vietnam, a project through which natural gas reserves of over 2 trillion cubic feet have been discovered in the Nam Con Son region. The government of India has since then attached major importance to this project and the Vietnam National Assembly has also regarded this project as one of the top three important projects of national importance.[44]

In the meantime, concerted efforts were undertaken by both sides in the economic sphere. Accordingly, a delegation of over 35 leading businessmen participated in the 4th meeting of the India-Vietnam Joint Business Council held in Hanoi concurrently with Prime Minister Shri Atal Bihari Vajpayee's visit to Vietnam in January 2001. During this visit, Memoranda of Understanding (MoU) were signed between ONGC and Petroleum Investment and Development Company (PIDC) of Vietnam, TCS and Transinco of Vietnam and FICCI and Indian Business Chamber (Vietnam). Moreover, Ranbaxy agreed to invest US$ 10 million in a production unit near Ho Chi Minh City during the same time.

To further accentuate the pace of economic cooperation between the two countries, in May 2003, Mr. Nong Duc Manh, Secretary General of the Communist Party of Vietnam visited India and signed the Joint Declaration on the Framework for Comprehensive Cooperation in the 21st century. As a follow-up action to this Declaration, in 2004,

Vietnam and India signed the Plan of Action for implementing the Joint Declaration in Hanoi. Due to these positive developments, trade relations between the two countries increased from US$ 50 million in 1991 to nearly US$ 697 million in 2005. The major items of Vietnam's export to India were pepper, tea, coal, machinery, cinnamon, rubber, coffee, etc., and its imports were animal feed, pharmaceuticals and medicinal plants, plastic, iron and steel, seafood, chemicals and chemical products, machinery and equipment, leather and leather garments, etc. Regarding investment, during this phase, India had about eleven FDI projects nearly US$ 230 millions mainly in production of sugar, edible oil, pharmaceuticals, office furniture, plastic production, oil and gas exploration, etc., in Vietnam. However, this rise in Indo-Vietnam economic relations failed to reflect the then excellent political relations between the two countries. Although during this period, Vietnam and India signed many cooperative agreements and participated in programs to identify the priority areas for cooperation, such as biotechnology in agriculture and healthcare, technology for new materials, IT and electronics, super computing, nuclear energy for peaceful use, science and technology, policy-making and administration, remote sensing, non-traditional energy, pharmaceutics, medicine, etc., the two-way trade just accounted for about one percent of the total trade of Vietnam and below 0.5 percent of the total trade of India and India ranked the 35th among 70 countries and territories investing in Vietnam. Not much interest in Vietnam could be elicited in the Indian minds during this time is evident from the fact that in tourism, in 2005, Vietnam received around 3.5 million foreign travellers, of which only about 13,000 were Indians.[45]

Perhaps as a result of the moral boost provided by the successive efforts from both sides, their bilateral trade ties started intensifying progressively and the Indian exports to Vietnam from January–November 2004 reached US$ 518.09 million registering an increase of over 30 percent vis-à-vis the corresponding period in 2003. The major items of trade during this period were animal feed (soya meal), drugs and pharmaceuticals, plastics, steel, textile and garment accessories, etc.

Several important trade promotional activities were undertaken in this period which included, a visit to Hanoi by a ten-member delegation from Basic Chemicals, Pharmaceuticals and Cosmetics Export Promotion Council (CHEMEXIL) in February 2004, organization of a Catalogue Show at the prestigious Vietnam International Industrial Fair in October–November 2004, catalogue-based participation at Vietnam International Agriculture Fair, ITPO sponsored visit of eight Indian companies to represent at the 14th Vietnam International Trade Fair (Vietnam Expo 2004) in April 2004, Vietnam's participation at the 24th India International Trade Fair in New Delhi in November 2004, visit of a six member Confederation of Indian Industries delegation to Ho Chi Minh City from 10–13 December 2004, participation by a six-member delegation from PLEXCONCIL in the Vietnam International Industry Fair at Hanoi from 1–4 December 2004. Moreover, a three-member delegation led by Shri SS Kapur, Joint Secretary, Department of Commerce visited Hue in Vietnam on 31 July 2004 to attend the 5th ASEAN-Senior Economic Officials Meeting (SEOM)- India Consultations[46] to beef up India's economic ties with the region in general and with Vietnam in particular, which can be gauged from the fact that India was inviting more investments from Vietnam at this time. Responding to India's plea, the Ministry of Planning and Investment of Vietnam sent an investment promotion delegation to India from 10–17 April 2005. Following this, India and Vietnam signed a very crucial agreement in August 2005 on Vietnam's accession to the World Trade Organization (WTO).[47]

In the meantime, in 2005 itself, the VCP passed the Enterprise and Investment Law to remove all the legal terms that discriminate between state-owned vs. private companies and domestic vs. foreign companies, so that further FDI could be invited. This had led to positive ramifications for the Indo-Vietnam trade ties as well.[48] As a follow-up measure of this new law, in April 2006, when the Tenth National Congress of the Communist Party of Vietnam was held, it was clearly pointed out that, as far as FDI to Vietnam was concerned, by the end of 2005, there were 6030 projects in effect with the total registered capital of more than $51.07 billion, of which the realized capital was $27.98 billion. By the end of 2005, there were 75 countries investing in Vietnam. The largest investors were from Asia itself, of which five countries (Singapore, Taiwan, Japan, South Korea and Hong Kong) made up 60.8 percent of the total registered capital. Thus, neither China nor India was in the list of top five trading partners of Vietnam during this time, and Vietnam was relying far more on Japan and other neighbouring Southeast Asian countries for her economic development and prosperity. However, China was in a comparatively stronger position than India as far as trade ties with Vietnam were concerned. Between 2004 and 2008, the trade volume between India and Vietnam recorded a steady increase. Eventually it crossed the US $1 billion mark in the year 2006-07. This was a major achievement, in the light of the fact that in 1994, the total trade was merely to the tune of US$ 102.6 million. While in 2002-03 the bilateral trade between India and Vietnam was US$ 366.57 million, it rose to US$ 448.56 million in 2003-04, US $642.46 million in 2004-05, US$ 822.06 million in 2005-06, US$ 1149.36 million in 2006-07. (**see Table 3 ahead**)

However, the most significant fact is, in spite of the steady increase in the bilateral trade volume, the total trade between India and Vietnam was extremely minuscule during this time compared to India's total trade. Between 2003-04 and 2007-08, the yearly percentage growth in total trade has increased from 0.32 to 0.37. This means, the rise in growth figures was not extraordinary and was much below its potential. By the middle of the decade, that is, during 2003-04, India constituted only around 1.6 percent of Vietnam's total export and was certainly not among the top ten trading partners of Vietnam. Another very important feature of India's economic relations with Vietnam which was much present even in this decade was that the balance of trade always went in favour of India. Despite concerted efforts, Vietnam could never correct the balance of trade scenario. In this decade too, the similarities in the export–import basket of India and Vietnam continued, which further contributed to the trade imbalance between the two countries and very slow growth of their bilateral trade. During this phase, both India and Vietnam exported garments, tea, rice, cashew, footwear, pepper, and marine products. Major items of India's exports to Vietnam in this period included food ingredients, ordinary metals, plastic materials, pharmaceuticals, steel of all kinds, leather and textile materials and pesticides. India's import basket from Vietnam contained crude oil, pepper, tea, rubber, cinnamon, coal, computer and electronic components. At this crucial juncture, Vietnam had been trying to woo more foreign investors and had thus introduced the "one stop shop" policy in licensing in order to attract more foreign companies to invest in Vietnam. Despite that, in this decade, there were only eight major investments in Vietnam from the Indian side, with a total registered capital of US$ 583 million. The major Indian investments were in sugar production, oil and gas exploration, edible oil, pharmaceuticals, office furniture and plastic industries. ONGC Videsh had invested US$ 162 million in off-shore oil and natural gas exploration. Essar Group, Godrej Limited and Ranbaxy were some of the important Indian companies that had invested in Vietnam. Although, the United Nations Conference on Trade and Development (UNCTAD) ranked Vietnam sixth among the most attractive destinations for FDI during this time, in 2006, India was investing globally to the tune of US$ 9676 million as FDI, whereas it invested only US$ 583 million in Vietnam. Thus, it can be argued that India's trade ties with Vietnam during this decade was absolutely not to the satisfactory level and could have performed much better had there been more political will and more specialised and prioritised focus on India's trade relations with Vietnam.

That is why, to add teeth to the ongoing economic cooperation, the Vietnam-India Entrepreneurship Development Centre (VIEDC) was launched on May 8, 2006, in Hanoi by Ambassador of India and Vietnam's Vice Minister of Planning and Investment Nguyen Ngoc Phuc and the first Entrepreneurship Development Program at VIEDC was conducted from May 8–June 16, 2006,[49] to discuss newer areas of economic cooperation and remedy the lacuna in the existing system. This VIEDC would function parallel to the existing India-Vietnam Joint Commission for Economic, Scientific and Technical

Cooperation, which was established in 1982, and organises meetings alternately in New Delhi and Hanoi. This is a purely government-to-government cooperative initiative and the Foreign Ministers of the two countries are joint co-Chairmen of this Commission. Apart from these two, there was another platform to converse on trade and business issues between India and Vietnam, that is, the Indo-Vietnam Joint Business Council, a body of the private business sectors in the two countries, coordinated by the FICCI on the Indian side and Vietnam Chambers of Commerce and Industry on the Vietnamese side. The first meeting of the Indo-Vietnamese Joint Business Council took place on September 6, 1993. These meetings try to promote various trade-related agreements between the companies of the two countries.[50]

The year 2007 was a landmark year in the bilateral relations between India and Vietnam. In this year, India entered into a strategic partnership with Vietnam, followed by the thirteenth meeting of the Joint Commission as well as, the fifth meeting of India-Vietnam Joint Business Council, which provided definite economic thrust to the bilateral areas. As a proof of seriousness of the Indian policy makers to augment her ties with Vietnam, a concessional Line of Credit of US$ 45 million for Vietnam was announced by India. Furthermore, India's TATA Steel signed an agreement for setting up an integrated steel mill in Vietnam with Vietnam Steel Corporation (VSC) in Hanoi on 29 May 2007. The proposed steel complex had an estimated capacity of 4.5 million tons per year and expected investment that was promised was to the tune of US$ 3.5 billion. Moreover, Tata Steel also had a stake of 30 percent in the Thach Khe Iron Ore Joint Stock Company in this decade, which was preparing itself at this time to undertake mining activities. As a follow-up action, on October 31, 2007, a MoU underscoring the partnership was signed between Tata Steel and VSC in Hanoi for setting up a cold rolled steel plant in Vung Ang Industrial Zone in Ha Tinh province. This was in addition to the Essar Steel's joint venture agreement of February 12, 2007, with VSC and Vietnam General Rubber Corporation (GERUCO) for setting up a hot strip mill in Vietnam with 2 million tons per annum capacity.[51]

Meanwhile, in October 2008, Ms Nguyen Thi Doan, Vice President of Vietnam, accompanied by a seventy-member high-powered business delegation visited India. It was of immense importance that despite global recession, bilateral trade between India and Vietnam in 2008 was US$ 2.5 billion and India emerged as the tenth largest exporter of items to Vietnam. In October 2009, India granted the Market Economy Status (MES) to Vietnam with the aim of providing a stimulus to their commercial ties and Vietnam responded by entering into the Indo-ASEAN Free Trade Agreement that India had signed with the other members of the ASEAN in August 2009. It is interesting to note that, Vietnam had set this granting of MES as a pre-condition for joining the Indo-ASEAN Free Trade Agreement. India complied with that promptly without any hesitation and the then Vietnamese leadership thanked the Indian government for its cooperative gesture. Granting of this MES was of vital importance during this time so that the existing bilateral commercial relations could be expanded by the aid of such legal framework which would empower the entrepreneurs from both countries to explore each other's market, and for making full use of the potential competitive advantages that the two nations had. With the aim of enhancing the then existing bilateral business ties, the two nations established Vietnam-India Business Forum in 2009 with the aim of facilitating meetings, exchange of information, business opportunities which would in turn boost investments and trade relations between the two countries.[52] While keeping up the momentum of such bilateral economic cooperation, a fifty-three-member delegation led by Federation of Indian Chambers of Commerce and Industry (FICCI) and Chemicals and Allied Product Export Promotion Council (CAPEXIL) paid a visit to Hanoi and Ho Chi Minh City in October 2009 to explore further business opportunities with Vietnam. In the same year, the Essar Exploration and Production Limited was awarded the oil and gas block 114 in Vietnam. Moreover, McLeod Russel, a leading producer of tea in India acquired Vietnam-based Phu Ben Tea Company. Simultaneously with all this, the Government of India extended to Vietnam a US$ 19.5 million line of credit with the aim of setting up three hydropower projects in Vietnam to address her needs of greater energy requirement.[53]

As a result of such cooperative measures, the bilateral trade statistics improved gradually. The trade between the two countries which was a paltry US$ 72 million in 1995 grew substantially to US$ 2.3 billion by 2010. In fact, in the period from 1995 to 2001, the bilateral trade between the two countries increased by 20 percent per annum that made the total trade volume close to US$ 400 million in 2002 from a low level of only US$ 75 million in 1995. From 2002 to 2009, the bilateral trade growth made its huge momentum as the trade volume sharply increased from US$ 376 million to over US$ 1 billion in 2006 and reached the peak close to US$ 2.5 billion in 2008 before witnessing a decline in 2009 to US$ 2.05 billion (-17.3 percent fall) due to the impact of the 2008 global financial crisis. During this period (2002–2008), the average annual two-way trade attained a rate of growth of 44.46 percent per annum. However, in spite of the growth registered in their bilateral trade turnover, Vietnam's trade share in the overall trade volume of India remained quite insignificant, even during this decade. Over the period of seven years, from 2002 to 2008, the share of Vietnam's trade with India in its total trade increased from 1.03 percent in 2002 to 1.73 percent in 2008. Thus, it can be understood that even though Vietnam-India trade volume was increasing, this rise was not at all commensurate with Vietnam's overall trade growth during the same period (from 16 percent to over 31 percent). On the other side, during the period 2002–2009, India's total trade volume with Vietnam constituted only about 0.32 to 0.49 percent of India's total trade.[54]

Table 3: India's Trade Relations with Vietnam

Values in US$ Million

Year (April-March)	Export	Import	Total Trade	Balance of Trade
1999-2000	154.37	11.52	165.89	142.85
2000-2001	225.90	12.39	238.29	213.51
2001-2002	218.17	18.91	237.08	199.26
2002-2003	337.39	29.18	366.57	308.21

2003-2004	410.43	38.21	448.64	372.22
2004-2005	555.96	86.50	642.46	469.46
2005-2006	690.68	131.39	822.07	559.29
2006-2007	985.69	167.38	1,153.07	818.31
2007-2008	1,610.09	173.68	1,783.77	1,436.41
2008-2009	1,738.65	408.66	2,147.31	1,329.99
2009-2010	1,838.95	521.81	2,360.76	1,317.14

Source: Prepared according to data available in Ministry of Commerce, Government of India, Annual Reports of Ministry of External Affairs, Government of India and General Statistics Office of Vietnam (Ministry of Planning and Investment, Government of Socialist Republic of Vietnam, Hanoi)

The China Factor from the mirror of India-Vietnam Economic Cooperation: 2000–2009

Both India and Vietnam continued to engage more and more with China economically in the new millennium, despite the fact that both of them continued to have political or strategic differences of opinion with China on several issues simultaneously. In fact, China's economic growth trajectory allured both India and Vietnam to engage with it with renewed vigour in the new millennium. China maintained a sustainable rate of growth of more than 9 percent per annum during the period 2002–2010. Particularly after its accession to the World Trade Organization in 2001, its rate of domestic expansion became all the more robust.[55] Thus, India tried to pursue further economic integration with China not only for ensuring her own economic prosperity but also to placate it or to further engage with it, so that differences of opinion in other spheres could be evened out. In that regard, in 2003, India and China signed a significant agreement at Bangkok, known as the 'Bangkok Agreement'. Under this agreement, both countries offered some trade preferences to each other. India provided concessions on 188 products exported from China. On the other hand, China provided preferences on tariff for 217 products exported from India. The main items China exported to India in this decade included petroleum, chemical, mechanical and electrical products and those China imported from India included iron ore and chromium mineral.[56]

At one point of time, India's bilateral trade with China was one of the most balanced among China's bilateral trading partners, which involved some kind of parity in the exchange of goods and services as well as capabilities to buy and sell in equal measure. However, increasingly in this decade, their trajectories of economic growth started going different ways and this balanced trade scenario became progressively more distorted. For instance, India's trade deficit with China crossed the figure of US$ 10 billion in 2007. This had huge ramifications for the Indian economy as the calls from India's domestic manufacturers to introduce non-tariff barriers against Chinese imports became stronger day by day. Also, the increase in trade volume between India and China did not substantially lead to the extension of mutual investments in each other's territory, primarily because of the trust deficit in their bilateral relations, which were amply clear to the world when it visualised their under-cutting activities while investing in third country assets, such as in oil fields of Africa and Syria. In spite of China and India both becoming major destinations for FDI and both increasingly expanding investment outflows, India's investments in China between 1996 and 2004 reached only US $965 million and China's investments in India between 1991 and 2004, according to India's Ministry of Commerce, stood at only USD 231.6 million. Thus, the dream of an 'Asian Century' was still not fructified as far as India-China economic relations in this decade were concerned. Therefore, in 2008, both these countries issued their Vision Statement for future course of their mutual economic cooperation. The Vision Statement stressed on the importance of supporting and facilitating the processes of regional integration which would provide mutually beneficial opportunities for growth, as an important feature of the emerging international system. This Vision Statement clearly reiterated the duty and the need of both India and China, the two Asian economic giants to support the needs and demands of other developing countries in international organizations, such as, the World Trade Organization. Thus, it is amply clear, in spite of the lacuna and the trust deficit which existed in their bilateral economic relations, a positive trend could be clearly perceived that a pattern of South–South cooperation started emerging as far as their economic leadership as Asian giants were concerned,[57] and this had very positive implications for their bilateral economic ties as well. Significantly enough, particularly during the closing years of this decade, when India was entering into strategic ties with Vietnam, simultaneously she was strengthening her economic ties with China as well. China gradually ascended to become the largest trading partner of India since 2008 by replacing the USA. The bilateral trade between them jumped nearly by twelve and half times during the period 2000–2010. During this decade, the exports of India to China grew at the rate of 39.0 percent per annum, and formed nearly 8.0 percent of the total exports of India in 2010.[58] In fact, China's economic relations with India is a more or less success story because they could resume their bilateral official trade in as late as 1978 after the major political differences of the Cold War years could be addressed to some extent. Even after according the Most-Favoured-Nation (MFN) status to each other in 1984, there was not much growth in trade ties which could be gauged from the fact that their bilateral trade was as low as US$ 2.92 billion in 2000. However, this decade witnessed real growth in their trade relations, which was unprecedented so much so that it reached US$ 61.7 billion in 2010. This positive growth trend of India-China economic relations in this phase was not lost on the Indian leadership. In fact, these two Asian giants bravely faced the 2008 financial crisis without being affected much, which proved the resilience of their economic structure. Thus, even Dr. Manmohan Singh, who remained the Prime Minister of India from 2004 to 2014, once remarked, "…the gathering momentum of India-China relations is visible in the expansion of our bilateral economic ties. The process of engagement in the Asian region has truly taken off."[59]

However, despite this intensification of economic ties, it still remained below its true potential. For instance, the third border trade post between India and China was opened in July 2006 in Sikkim (Nathu La) and the chief aim behind this initiative was to make an almost year-round access route, and the government on both side expected that the border trade between these two countries will shoot up immensely because of the opening of this route, so much so that it was expected that the bilateral trade value will reach Rs 120,000 million by 2015. But in reality, this remained a distant dream as the border trade continued to hover at just around Rs. 10 million till the end of this decade.[60]

Like India, Vietnam's trade relations with China intensified its mobility further during this decade. The main difference that lies in the trade patterns of Vietnam between 1991–99 and 2000–2009 is that in the 1990s, despite the fact that Vietnam's trade ties with China had started intensifying and growing further (the Sino-Vietnamese trade grew rapidly from US $32 million in 1991 to US $1.15 billion in 1996 and then US$ 2.81 billion by 2001), Hanoi relied more on Japan and other fellow ASEAN countries as its major trade partners than China. In the 1990s, Vietnam's trade volume was significantly more and comparatively diverse with Japan and other ASEAN countries than with China. However, in this present decade, that is, from 2000 to 2009, the scenario changed dramatically owing to China's phenomenal growth story, geographical proximity with Vietnam, improved means of transport and communication to facilitate higher growth, conclusion of land border and Gulf of Tonkin tensions and China's accession to the World Trade Organization (WTO) in 2001. Thereafter, in 2002, China offered Vietnam the Most-Favoured-Nation (MFN) status. In the same year, China made known its seriousness in engaging economically with this region for collectively realising the goal of economic prosperity by announcing its decision to establish an ASEAN-China FTA covering the six more developed ASEAN members by 2010 and in future extending the FTA to all the ten ASEAN members, including the four late entrants to the ASEAN grouping, if possible, by 2015 itself. For the lesser developed economies of the ASEAN, such as, Vietnam, Laos, Cambodia and Myanmar, China also offered an 'early harvest program' in 2004, with the aim of promoting and intensifying trade in agricultural and marine products. All these initiatives led to the economic integration of China with this region in general, and with Vietnam in particular.

Thus, by 2004, China emerged as the largest trade partner of Vietnam, surpassing Japan. With Vietnam's admission to the WTO in 2006, Sino-Vietnam trade ties improved further and by 2009, Vietnam's trade with China amounted to US$ 21.35 billion. However, despite the phenomenal growth, Vietnam's trade with China has been quite imbalanced just like its balance of trade with India or India's balance of trade with China. China's trade surplus vis-à-vis Vietnam continued to widen in this decade from US$ 10.57 million in 1991 to US$ 1.032 billion in 2002 and US$ 10.786 billion in 2008. That year, bilateral trade was only 0.76 percent of China's total trade but 13.57 percent of Vietnam's total trade. As far as the trade basket was concerned, obviously Vietnam traded more in mineral and agricultural products, whereas, China had a substantial comparative advantage in industrial products. The bilateral trade relationship thus followed the 'flying geese pattern' in this decade when China exported capital goods and key industrial intermediate products to Vietnam, while Vietnam exported finished products to the US and the European Union (EU). Despite greater flooding of Vietnamese markets with cheap Chinese products, Vietnam has not been keen to restrict imports from China, but to develop the horizons of its own export markets. Thus, as a result of China's keen interests in bettering economic ties with Vietnam, at the end of 2010, China's cumulative contracted investment in Vietnam reached US$ 3.185 billion. In 2010 alone, its actual investment amounted to US$ 0.365 billion, ranking 14th among Vietnam's investors.[61]

Progressively over the years in this decade, China became the chief source of Vietnam's machinery, computers, chemicals and textiles. Moreover, China sold three times more fruits, vegetables and agricultural products to Vietnam than it bought. Thus, this over-dominance of China in the Sino-Vietnamese trade relations has gradually led to an "asymmetric framework for the economic relationship" between the two countries".[62] Despite this, Vietnam more proactively continued to engage with China in this decade in the economic sector than in any other sector. For instance, in 2009 itself, the CPV held approximately 290 meetings with its Chinese counterpart. These meetings established

Vietnam's yearning to remain close to China for their continued economic relationship, even with its trade deficit of over $20 billion.[63] China, on their part, values its trade ties with Vietnam primarily because of its close proximity with the latter and mainly through its northern border provinces, since this region acts as a conduit or trading station for Chinese products reaching the rest of the countries of Southeast Asia.[64]

Table 4: Vietnam's Total Trade with India, China and the World (2000-2009)

Values in US $ Million

Year (Jan- Dec)	With India	With China	With World
2000	225.6	2937.5	30,119.2
2001	273.4	3023.6	31,307.2
2002	376.7	3677.1	36,451.7
2003	489.4	5021.7	45,405.1
2004	672.1	7494.2	58,453.8
2005	693.8	9127.8	69,208.2
2006	1018.1	10,634.1	84,717.3
2007	1536.7	16,356.1	1,11,326.1
2008	2483.3	20,823.7	1,43,398.9
2009	1955.7	20,814.3	1,27,045.1

Source: Prepared according to data available in Ministry of Commerce, Government of India, Annual Reports of Ministry of External Affairs, Government of India and General Statistics Office of Vietnam (Ministry of Planning and Investment, Government of Socialist Republic of Vietnam, Hanoi)

Therefore, after glancing at the trade figures mentioned in Table 4 above, it becomes amply clear that even at the end of this decade, Vietnam's total trade value with India was of no match compared to its trade volume with China. Despite the fact that in this decade Vietnam came convincingly closer to India as far as its political and strategic ties were concerned and this crystallised in the form of the 2007 Strategic Partnership Agreement, against the backdrop of the then Chinese 'aggressive' moves in the South China Sea, this understanding failed to create a footprint in the domain of India-Vietnam economic turf.

Summarily then, it can be said that, on the one hand, Vietnam was intensifying her political and strategic linkages with India to ensure latter's greater presence in the Southeast Asian region, especially with reference to the issue of the South China Sea as a bulwark against Chinese overtures, and on the other, Vietnam was beefing up her economic linkages with China to ensure its economic growth and development. Here, according to Vietnam's perception, India's role is necessary as a geostrategic balancer to keep away any external threat from its immediate neighbourhood.

India-Vietnam Economic Truss: The Period of Bonhomie, 2010–2015

The period from 2010 to 2015 can be termed as the bonhomie phase between India and Vietnam from the perspective of economic cooperation. During this period, Indo-Vietnam economic understanding reached its zenith as compared to the past years. The sign of cordial economic understanding was clearly reflected when the Government of India under the banner of Indian Business Association and VCCI organised a conference in November 2011. In this conference, the Indian entrepreneurs expressed their keen interest in commencing more and more joint ventures with Vietnamese companies as the production cost in Vietnam was much lower than in India. Nikhilesh Deshpande, Director, Mega Life Sciences, in this Conference reiterated that, Indian pharmaceutical companies have invested USD 2 million in Vietnam and Hiranandani Constructions Company agreed to expedite their plans to invest in real estate, hotels and health services in Vietnam.[65] Considering these on-going projects, Vietnam was gradually becoming one of the main destinations for Indian investments in Southeast Asia during this period. Most importantly, much to the delight of India, by this period, Vietnam had not only successfully integrated itself with the world economy but also started reaping benefits from membership in the global economic institutions such as, the WTO and the Asia-Pacific Economic Cooperation (APEC). Talking about the good effects that Vietnam has been obtaining from membership in various internal forums, Mr. Nguyen Minh Vu, Deputy Head of APEC body in 2017, said, "Vietnam's admission to Asia-Pacific Economic Cooperation (APEC) has made positive impact on the reform process as well as integration of Vietnam. This is a very important stepping stone for us to be able to participate in mechanisms of deeper integration in the global range. Vietnam joined APEC in 1998 and hosted the first APEC Summit in 2006, through which we could promote the implementation of the Bogor Goals and negotiations for WTO membership...we can see very clearly that in 2005, 2006 we had three FTA partners who are APEC members and the current number is thirteen out of sixteen FTPs in the Asia-Pacific region. In 2006, we had only two strategic partners, but now we have thirteen comprehensive strategic partners who are members of APEC. In 2005, 66 percent of the total foreign investment in Vietnam came from APEC economies and the current figure is up to 78 percent. Export revenue also rose from 65 percent to over 78 percent for countries from the Asia-Pacific region."[66] Thus, a stronger and a more resilient and integrated Vietnamese economy that emerged in this period was certainly to the best interests of India, which has always considered Vietnam to be a 'pillar' in its 'Look East' policy.

If we analyse the trade statistics of this period, we will see that, during 2010, India's exports to Vietnam increased only by 8 percent to $1762 million from $1635 million in 2009. India's imports from Vietnam, on the other hand, recorded a quantum jump and more than doubled to $992 million from $419 million during the same period. India's trade surplus with Vietnam, thus, declined to $770 million in 2010 from $1216 million in the previous year. In 2010, the then Prime Minister of Vietnam constituted the Vietnam-India Business Forum, whose main target was to regenerate the existing bilateral economic ties and building a strategic relationship with India. Moreover, as part of India-ASEAN Free Trade Agreement (FTA), India and Vietnam signed a FTA with effect from June 1, 2010, for which India would now require to slash duties on hundreds of products such as seafoods, chemicals, apparel and tyres, while trading with Vietnam. Additionally, Vietnam would also be required to reduce import duties, up to 70 percent in some cases, on Indian goods, including fruits, nuts and sea food. Meanwhile, the Global Competitiveness Report of 2010-11 of World Economic Forum evaluated that Vietnam was at the 4.3 competitiveness level, compared to 4.0 in the 2009-10 report. Along with this improvement, Vietnam's ranking in the global competitiveness list rose from 75 (2009) to 59. In the competitiveness report of the World Bank as a result of effective coordination with the International Finance Corporation (IFC), Vietnam jumped ten levels to conquer the number 78 spot, which further provided impetus to forge greater economic ties between India and Vietnam and contributed towards making Vietnam a more preferred destination of trade and investment in the Southeast Asian region. According to the report, Vietnam stood at number 4 in the ten most reformed economies of the world.[67] That is why, as a spill-over effect of these developments, during this year, India's FDI in joint ventures in Vietnam totalled more than $1 billion.

Therefore, during the years 2010 and 2011, there was a very sharp increase in Vietnam's exports to India, and that was further augmented on account of India-Vietnam bilateral treaty of 2007. Along with this factor, another factor which led to the promotion of the economic cooperation on a more solid basis was that both the countries were facing poor understanding with China relating to the South China Sea issue during this time. This perhaps motivated both India and Vietnam to strengthen their mutual bond in every sphere so that it could work as a bulwark against any kind of perceived Chinese aggression. During this time, Vietnam's exports share rose to US$ 1.55 billion or 39 percent of the total bilateral trade of US$ 3.90 billion in 2011. During the first 5 months of 2012, the trade was worth US$ 1.52 billion, out of which Vietnam's exports were US$ 0.59 billion or 39 percent of the total trade and India's exports were US$ 0.93 billion or 61 percent of the total trade. In this period, major items of export from India to Vietnam were engineering goods, chemicals, pharmaceutical formulations and raw materials, steel, non-ferrous metals, plastic resin, animal feed, agro-chemicals, textiles, cotton fibre and yarn, tobacco, maize etc and major items of export from Vietnam to India were black pepper, coffee, tea, cinnamon, cashew, rubber, sea food, coal, footwear, wooden furniture, mobile phones, computers, etc. During this phase, India offered Line of Credits (LoCs) worth US$ 27 million and US$ 45 million which were mainly used for making use of hydropower projects from India. These hydropower projects became not only highly successful but also created a large amount of visibility of Indian investment in Vietnam. Moreover, major Indian companies like NIIT, Aptech, R.K Marble, Alliance Mineral and Phillips Carbon Black, etc., were the chief investors from India in Vietnam during this time.[68] Besides this, in July 2011, financial assistance of US$ 57,500 was provided to Yen Bai Province in Vietnam for the development of their infrastructure projects. This Indian posture towards Vietnam amply demonstrated that Vietnam should not rely economically more on China.[69]

The growing economic understanding between India and Vietnam does not always reflect the sign of economic ties as expected. In December 2011, India had only 62 investment projects in Vietnam with total registered capital of US$ 234 million. This is despite the fact that, Indian companies have invested in oil and gas exploration, mineral exploration and processing, sugar manufacturing, agro-chemicals, IT, and agricultural processing in Vietnam. These include the Godrej plant for steel furniture, Mangalam Steel Limited for steel strips in Bing Duong province, JK Tyre, the Southern Rubber Industry Joint Stock Company (Casumina), Phillips Carbon Black, Venkateshwara Hatcheries Group, etc. Besides these, some joint ventures took place during this period, such as Marico, one of India's leading FMCG companies, picked up 85 percent equity in International Consumer Products Corporation (ICP) and Fortis Healthcare International bought 65 percent stake in Vietnam's Hoan My Medical Corp for US$ 64 million.[70] Thus, by this decade, the visibility of Indian investments in Vietnam was further heightened in the post-Cold War phase.

This trajectory of Indo-Vietnam economic relations failed to perform the expected result on account of certain projects which both the countries agreed in principle but could not implement, for example, the Tata steel project. By the onset of this decade, it became amply clear that the proposed Tata Steel project, which was put forth with much fanfare and promise of US$ 5 billion investment in setting up an integrated steel mill in Vietnam has run into severe difficulties particularly on two issues: first, the total amount of compensation for the acquisition of land estimated by Tata Steel is different from that sought by Ha Tinh province; and secondly, the Ha Tinh province expressed its inability to pay this amount due to lack of resources even though as per law, they were supposed to provide the amount towards compensation. They instead, requested Tata Steel to pay the same. Owing to the importance of the project and the severity of the crisis, this matter has repeatedly been taken up at the highest level for an amicable solution. For instance, during the visit by External Affairs Minister of India Mr. SM Krishna in September 2011, Prime Minister Nguyen Tan Dung of Vietnam proposed that the Government of India may consider extending Official Development Assistance of US$ 100 million to finance the compensation amount. Again, during the visit of President Truong Tan Sang to India, in October 2011, Prime Minister Mr. Manmohan Singh raised the issue of Tata Steel during delegation-level talks to which President Sang responded that this was a high priority project and Vietnam was prepared to offer Tata Steel a higher stake in the Thach Ke Iron Ore mine. However, nothing finally came out and the Tata project now is in a quagmire. Besides the private initiatives, the two governments continued the avenue of economic cooperation through LoCs and other ways. Since 1976, the Government of India extended 14 LoCs totalling Rs. 561 crores to Vietnam. This included a LoC of US$ 19.5 million in 2011 for setting up hydropower projects and US$ 45 million for Nam Chiem hydropower project which was being executed by BHEL. Moreover, India also agreed to an amount of US$ 100 million under the Buyers' Credit to provide Vietnam for the smooth running of the future project proposals.[71]

As against such growing economic cooperation discussed above, during the year 2011-12, trade and investment relations between the two countries continued to grow steadily. Bilateral trade increased to US$ 2.7 billion during JanuarySeptember 2011, with exports from

India accounting for US$ 1.67 billion and imports from Vietnam being US$ 1.03 billion. By the end of 2011-12 financial year, there were 76 Indian projects in Vietnam, with total investment of nearly US$ 750 million, including investments registered in third countries.

In the following year, that is during January–December 2012, trade turnover reached US$ 3.94 billion, an increase of 1.1 percent over the previous year. Indian exports saw a 7.9 percent decrease to US$ 2.1 billion and imports from Vietnam increased by 14.6 percent to US$ 1.7 billion. Thus, the trade deficit further lessened. Moreover, the Reserve Bank of India and the Vietnam State Bank signed an agreement which opened the way for Indian banks to apply for licenses to operate in Vietnam.[72] This was a very positive step for further cementing the commercial ties of the two countries.

Thus, efforts for increasing the bilateral trade between India and Vietnam continued its momentum very much in the next year as well. The total bilateral trade turnover between Vietnam and India reached US$ 2,592.1 million in the first six months of 2013, an increase of 40.3 percent from the same period in 2012, of which Vietnam's exports to India gained US$ 1,160.1 million, up 53.7 percent and Vietnam's imports from India gained US$ 1, 431.9 million, up 31.1 percent. In this period, Vietnam's main exports to India diversified over the years and now included mobile phones and accessories, computer hardware, electronic components, rubber, pepper, coffee, coal, wooden furniture, iron and steel products, chemicals, fibre, yarn, ores, textiles and garments, footwear, plastic, cashew nut, etc. On the other hand, Vietnam's main imports from India included cattle feed ingredients, pharmaceutical products, machines and equipments, maize, cotton, plastics, fishery products, chemical products, fibre, yarn, steel, chemicals, insecticides and raw materials, pharmaceutical materials, fabrics, cars, tobacco ingredients, steel products, paper, oil allied products, plastic products, fertiliser, etc.[73]

On July 11, 2013, the Fifteenth Meeting of India-Vietnam Joint Commission on Trade, Economic, Scientific and Technological Cooperation was held in New Delhi, where both countries called for early establishment of the Joint Trade Sub-Commission between Ministry of Commerce and Industry of India and Ministry of Industry and Trade of Vietnam, under the umbrella of the Vietnam-India Joint Commission, so that they could get a platform to discuss ways and means for enhancing the trade relations between the two sides. At this meeting, both sides made clear that they were also working for an early conclusion of India-ASEAN Free Trade Agreement in Services and Investment so that their economic ties could be boosted further, despite the fact that, by 2013 the investment by Indian companies with the total registered capital of about US$ 2,052 billion in 73 projects was underway in Vietnam in sectors such as oil and gas exploration, mineral exploration and processing, sugar manufacturing, agro-chemicals, IT, and agricultural processing. India ranked 12 out of 100 countries and territories investing in Vietnam. Likewise, Vietnam has three investment projects in India with the total registered capital of US$ 23.6 million and the most important investment project is Rothto Pharma (India) Private Ltd with the registered capital of US$ 22.8 million.[74]

While speaking to the media after the 15th meeting of the India-Vietnam Joint Commission about the details of Indian investments in Vietnam, the External Affairs Minister, Mr. Salman Khurshid remarked, investments by Indian companies total about $936 million in 86 projects in sectors such as oil and gas exploration, mineral exploration and processing, sugar manufacturing, agro-chemicals, IT, and agricultural processing. Further, Khurshid appreciated the Vietnam government's recent understanding with the Tata Power as the developer for a $1.8 billion 2X660 MW Long Phu 2 Thermal Power Project in Soc Trang province in southern Vietnam, despite strong competition from Korean and Russian companies, and mentioned that the Memorandum of Understanding between the two central banks—Reserve Bank of India and the State Bank of Vietnam—signed in 2012, would enable Bank of India and Indian Overseas Bank to upgrade their representative offices that they had opened in Ho Chi Minh City in February 2003 and March 2008, respectively, into full-fledged branches in the near future.

Moreover, he reiterated India's commitment to increasing trade with Vietnam and stated that India had so far, extended 17 Lines of Credit totalling $164.5 million, including a $19.5 million LoC for setting up Nam Trai- IV hydropower project and Binh Bo Pumping station and felt that these investments in Vietnam would further strengthen the ongoing economic cooperation and strategic partnership.[75] While mentioning the growing trade statistics between India and Vietnam he mentioned that the bilateral trade grew to 6.1 billion USD in 2012-13 and thus, both these countries were well on track to cross the target of 7 billion USD by 2015, the target that had been set by the two countries to achieve.[76]

While explaining the major rationale behind the growing economic ties between India and Vietnam especially since 2010, the fact remains that in June 2010, India signed a Free Trade Agreement (FTA) with the block of 10-member ASEAN countries of which Vietnam is a member. Signing of this FTA had positive effects on Indo-Vietnam trade ties as well. Thus, the total trade between Vietnam and India increased from US$ 3.45 billion in 2010 to US$ 3.90 billion in 2011, to US$ 3.94 billion in 2012, to US$ 5.23 billion in 2013, etc. As it became apparent, the increase in trade in 2013 was almost 33 percent and more remarkably, exports from Vietnam to India increased by almost 62 percent. In this year, Vietnam's trade with India became surplus because of the huge increase in their exports.[77]

Meanwhile, a Vietnamese delegation from Ho Chi Minh City participated in the India-CLMV (Cambodia, Lao, Myanmar and Vietnam) Business Conclave organised by Confederation of Indian Industries (CII) from 21-22 October 2013 in New Delhi, to further discuss the untapped potential areas for deepening their economic bonhomie with India.[78] In November 2013, the General Secretary of the Communist Party of Vietnam (CPV) visited India with a definite thrust to revamp the Indo-Vietnam economic cooperation. According to the joint statement issued by India and Vietnam on November 20, 2013, at the end of this visit, the leaders of both the countries agreed that the growing economic partnership was one of the main components of the strategic partnership evolved over the years between the two countries and revealed their satisfaction at the steady growth in bilateral trade, which was on way to meet the target of 7 billion USD by 2015. While expressing the growing upward mobility of economic ties, both the countries revised the trade target and set a new target of reaching bilateral trade of value 15 billion USD by 2020 and pledged to promote mutual investments especially in the areas of education, infrastructure, hydrocarbons, power generation, new and renewable energy, agriculture, textiles, information technology, and pharmaceuticals. Moreover, the leaders also agreed to work for the early signing and implementation of the India-ASEAN FTA in Services and Investments to build on the momentum created by India-ASEAN FTA in Goods. They further pledged to work together for early realization of Regional Comprehensive Economic Partnership (RCEP) so as to facilitate India's integration into the ASEAN Economic Community. The Vietnamese side welcomed new investments by Indian companies in oil and gas upstream and downstream projects in Vietnam. Moreover, the leaders noted with satisfaction that Vietnam's Oil and Gas Group (Petro Vietnam) offered new areas to India for oil and gas exploration. The leaders encouraged cooperation between the private sectors of both countries and reaffirmed their support to the Vietnam-India Business Forum and the activities of the Chambers of Commerce and Industry of both countries. The Vietnam government also agreed to actively support the 'ASEAN- India Business Council' as a gesture of Indo-Vietnam solidarity in the ASEAN platform. It was agreed by the leaders to strengthen physical connectivity through land, sea and air transport between India and Vietnam so as to make the transport of goods and people easier between the two countries. In this regard, they welcomed the signing of the Air Services Agreement that would promote cooperation in the civil aviation sector and they also appreciated the signing of the bilateral Maritime Shipping Agreement and proposed to initiate discussions, at the official level, on a sub-regional shipping agreement between India and CLMV countries. They highlighted the importance of extension of the road connectivity between India and Vietnam and welcomed India's suggestion to discuss soft infrastructure requirements to facilitate smooth movement of goods and services across economic corridors and initiation of discussions on an ASEAN-India Transit Transport Agreement (AITTA). The leaders further highlighted the important contribution of India to Vietnam in the form of capacity building and development partnership projects such as the establishment of a Vietnam-India English Language, IT training centre at the National Defence Academy in Hanoi, the Vocational Training Centre in Ho Chi Minh City and the operationalisation of the High Performance Computing Facility at Hanoi University of Science and Technology. They also agreed to explore new projects involving Lines of Credit from India. The Vietnamese side highly applauded the establishment of the India-CLMV Quick Impact Projects (QIPs) Fund under which short gestation projects would be undertaken with grant assistance from India, to directly benefit local communities in a visible and immediate manner in areas such as education, health, sanitation and community development. Furthermore, the leaders noted the strong cooperation in agriculture and related fields and agreed to further deepening of cooperation in research and development in agriculture, fisheries, aquaculture, animal husbandry and dairy. In this regard, they called for an early convening of the India-Vietnam Conference on Agriculture between the Indian Council for Agricultural Research (ICAR) and the Vietnam Academy of Agriculture Sciences (VAAS) and highlighted the immense scope for further collaborations. In addition to this, the two sides welcomed the establishment of a Pangasius breeding farm in India in cooperation with Vietnam and agreed to promote information exchange and research in Early Mortality Syndrome in shrimp industry.[79] Therefore, at this juncture, the economic ties between the two countries were developing at a steady pace.

The year 2013 remained an attractive investment destination for Indian companies in Vietnam. During this year, trade figures from Vietnam's Foreign Investment Agency clearly displayed that India had seventy three investment projects with total registered capital of US $ 252.21 million and Indian companies had investments in a wide variety of sectors such as, in oil and gas exploration, mineral exploration and processing, sugar manufacturing, agro- chemicals, IT, and agricultural processing. Vietnam on the other hand, had three investment projects in India with total investment of US $ 23.6 million. The major Indian companies that had invested in Vietnam included OVL, Essar Exploration and Production Limited, Nagarjuna Limited, KCP Industries Limited, Ngon Coffee Manufacturing, Venkateswara Hatcheries, Philips Carbon and McLeod Russell, CGL, etc. In the field of IT training, NIIT, Aptech and Tata Infotech by this time, could successfully open more than eighty franchised centres spread all across Vietnam. Moreover, Tata Power too revealed its plans to develop the US $ 1.8 billion Long Phu- II Thermal Power Plant in Soc Trang and a MoU was signed between Tata Power and Vietnamese Ministry of Industry and Trade during the visit of General Secretary of Vietnam to India in November 2013.[80]

An interesting point to be noted at this juncture is that before the ASEAN-India Trade in Goods Agreement (AITIG) came into effect, Vietnamese exports to India mainly included unprocessed goods and the range of Vietnamese exports to this market has diversified since AITIG was signed to include products with a high value, such as mobile phones, computers, electronic products and components, chemicals, plastic materials, products from plastics, and steel billets. Besides, traditional exports including pepper, rubber and footwear contributed to decreasing the imbalance of trade between Vietnam and India. Thus, by 2013, the AITIG started revealing its dividends on the Indo-Vietnam economic trade patterns. In continuation of the early year, the year 2014 clearly displayed the growing economic ties between the two countries. Continuing with high-level visits to boost their bilateral economic ties, in October 2014, Prime Minister of Vietnam Mr. Nguyen Tan Dung paid an official visit to India. During his visit, Prime Ministers of both sides approved to enhance economic and trade collaboration as a strategic objective and in this regard, the Prime Minister of India also offered US$ 300 million for the mutual cooperation in the textile sector. Both sides acknowledged that tariff and non-tariff barriers often acted as impediments to the development of bilateral trade, and agreed that there was a pressing need to address those issues for mutual interest. They also pledged to augment the trade flows between the two countries by minimising the application of trade barriers, and to gradually take concrete measures to remove or fully abolish trade barriers in accordance with the WTO rules and the Framework Agreement on Comprehensive Economic Cooperation signed between the Association of Southeast Asian Nations and the Republic of India.[81] Thus, to keep up the good spirit of PM Dung's visit, Prime Minister Narendra Modi announced India's willingness to provide a credit loan worth of 300 million USD for Vietnam to import materials. Incidentally, this move was motivated to a large extent by the fact that at that time these two countries were striving to increase their trade value to 7 billion USD in trade by 2015 and 15 million USD in a two-way trade by 2020. During this important visit, both sides identified certain sectors on which more stress would be given in the days ahead to bolster their trade value at a quicker pace. These were hydrocarbons, power generation, infrastructure, tourism, textiles, footwear, medicinal and pharmaceuticals, information and communications technology, electronics, agriculture, chemicals, machinery and support industries. Further, they noted that, by the time of this visit, as many as 68 Indian-invested projects with approximately 1 billion USD had been put into operation in Vietnam so far, mainly focusing on oil and gas exploration, mineral exploitation and processing, sugar production, agricultural chemicals, IT and food processing. Vietnamese companies have invested in a total of paltry three projects in India worth 23.6 million USD as well.[82]

Besides these, the two sides were apparently in an upbeat mood as they praised the increasing cooperation between the non-government and the private sectors between the two countries. They recognized and hailed the importance of Vietnam-India Enterprises Forum and the actions of the Chambers of Commerce and Industry of India and Vietnam. The Vietnamese side also collectively approved to give total support to the "Vietnam- India Enterprises Council". The two leaders expressed their resolute decision to expand the association between Vietnam and India in land, marine and air transportation. Further, the two sides once again reiterated the signing of the Agreement on Air Transportation with the aim to expand cooperation in the civil aviation sector and welcomed the signing of the Agreement on Marine Transportation. They also expressed to initiate that the official dialogue on the concord on the sub-region transportation network between India and Cambodia, Laos, Myanmar and Vietnam should take place at an earliest date. In this context, the two leaders highly treasured the worth of growing road connections between Vietnam and India and welcomed India's proposal to start discussions and negotiations on the requirement of the soft infrastructure so that the necessary environment for the transportation of the goods and services through the economic corridor could be created. It has thus been proposed that the India-Myanmar-Thailand trilateral highway should be extended to Cambodia and Vietnam as well, so that better economic connectivity could be generated not only with Vietnam but with the ASEAN region as a whole.

Thus, during this time, in India's efforts to strengthen her linkages with the ASEAN region, India intensified her dialogue and gradually expanded its engagement with the Cambodia, Laos, Myanmar, Vietnam (CLMV) countries through intensive discussion on issues of common interest and higher levels of assistance for projects, in accordance with their development priorities, in agriculture and water management, energy and transmission lines and Human Resource Development and capacity building. Accordingly, India started to engage with the CLMV through the India-CLMV Business Conclave and herself took the initiative of organising the second CLMV Business Conclave- "ASEAN- India Economic Engagement: The Way Forward" on December 11, 2014, in New Delhi, and clearly giving out the message that India was prioritising her economic ties with the countries of the region. In fact, India's negotiations with ASEAN picked up momentum in this decade on the prospects of realising the Regional

Comprehensive Economic Partnership (RCEP), as a part of the dream of establishing an ASEAN Economic Community, with the aim of promoting economic cooperation and regional integration.[83]

Like the past years, Indo-Vietnam economic ties maintained its upward growth trajectory in the year 2015 as well. As a follow-up action, the 2nd meeting of the Indo- Vietnam Joint Sub-Commission on Trade took place on January 20, 2015, in Hanoi. In this meeting, Mr. Rajeev Kher, Secretary, Ministry of Commerce, Government of India led the Indian delegation consisting senior officials from the Ministries of Commerce, Textiles and the Department of Pharmaceuticals along with export promotion councils and companies from the textiles, pharmaceuticals, engineering, agriculture and leather sectors and had a meeting with Vietnamese counterparts led by H.E Mr. Cao Quoc Hung, Vice Minister of Industry and Trade of Vietnam. During this meeting, both sides reviewed the progress made since the first meeting in November 2013 and expressed their happiness and content with the steady increase of bilateral trade, and discussed measures to enhance cooperation in textiles, pharmaceuticals, agricultural trade, investment, services and so on.[84]

The Ministry of External Affairs, Government of India in 2015 informed that the bilateral trade between India and Vietnam surpassed the target set for 2015 and both sides agreed on a new target of US$ 15 billion by 2020. In 2015, Vietnam had signed tax treaties with several countries, including with India, to provide relief from double taxation and India had almost hundred projects in Vietnam with an estimated total investment of about US$ 1 billion.[85] The major Indian companies that were operating in Vietnam included NIIT Limited, Ishan International Private Limited, ONGC Videsh Limited, Nagarjuna Limited, Venkateswara Hatcheries Private Limited, Essar Exploration and Production Limited, Reliance Industries Limited, Gimpex Group, TATA Group, Philips Carbon, Glenmark Pharmaceuticals Limited, Bank of India, and McLeod Russell, etc., and further, the potential sectors that have been identified by the leadership of both countries for trade and investments between them included, electricity, high-value manufacturing, electrical part production, steel manufacturing, high technology, entertainment complex development, seaport construction, hotel development, transport and urban development. Despite this, it can be argued that India has never been very proactive in investing in Vietnam, which can be assessed from the fact that there is no direct flight between India and Vietnam, which clearly indicates that Vietnam has not been on India's priority investment map for a very long time. Also, another problem that continued to pester Indo-Vietnam trade ties even in this decade, just like the previous decades that both these countries compete in the international market to sell the same set of products, namely textiles, pepper, tea and coffee, which created a major hurdle to augment their trade ties and affected the export sector as well as the total trade value.[86]

Therefore, in spite of growing trend of Indo-Vietnam economic ties, the bilateral trade between Vietnam and India was still much below their respective economic potential. Despite all efforts, India still could not be one of the top ten goods trade partners of Vietnam though India had by now become an economic superpower in Asia and the world, and time and again she has reiterated that Vietnam is a crucial 'pillar' of her 'Look East' or 'Act East' policy. In fact, from 1993 to 2015, the bilateral trade has mostly been in favour of India which has kind of given an asymmetric nature to their trade ties. Although over the years the two countries have signed several treaties and agreements related to trade and economic cooperation, and many meetings have been held at various levels that have discussed the issue of lowering tariff barriers between them, there is still much grievance in the Vietnamese diplomatic circles that the import tariff applied by the Government of India is much higher than that applied by Vietnam. Moreover, these two countries are at different stages of their economic reforms and they vary substantially in the degree of trade liberalization and openness which have affected the expansion of their bilateral trade. Besides these, till date, unfortunately, there has been no chief investment from Vietnam in India. Vietnam's only investment in India worth mentioning is by the FPT Corporation worth US$ 1,50,000 invested in an Indian technology development and investment project. However, on the brighter side, owing to several fiscal reforms and reforms in Vietnam's Foreign Investment Law, along with the introduction of advantageous policies especially for foreign investors, it has become easier for India and for other countries to invest in Vietnam now. That is why, FDI from India to Vietnam has been increasing sharply in the past 15 years with growing domestic market and export opportunities in Vietnam. For instance, till 2006, India's FDI in Vietnam was US$ 580 million. Since 2007, particularly with the signing of the Strategic Partnership Agreement between the two countries, there emerged considerable changes in India's FDI flows to Vietnam with Essar Groups MoU for setting up of a hot rolling steel mill worth US$ 527 million in Ba Ria- Vung Tau, and the Tata Steel's MoU to set up a mega project on steel complex in Thach Khe-Ha Tinh with estimated investment of US$ 3.5 billion. It was estimated that if all these projects come to operation, it would make India among the top ten investors in Vietnam, and Vietnam will become the largest receiver of Indian FDI in ASEAN. More recently, Vietnam's investment environment has become much more attractive with the implementation of 'one-stop-shop' policy licensing, and the introduction of favourable conditions for investors by reducing land rental, granting exemption and reduction in import duties, preferential profit tax, etc.[87] The overall trade figure between India and Vietnam during the year 2010–15 are as follows **(see Table 5)**.

Table 5: India's Trade Relations with Vietnam (April 2009–March 2016)

Values in US$ Million

Year (April-March)	Export	Import	Total Trade	Balance of Trade
2009-2010	1,838.95	521.81	2,360.76	1,317.14
2010-2011	2,651.44	1,064.90	3,716.34	1,586.54
2011- 2012	3,719.09	1,722.87	5,441.96	1,996.22
2012-2013	3,967.37	2,314.78	6,282.15	1,652.59
2013-2014	5,441.94	2,594.25	8,036.19	2,847.69

2014-2015	6,257.88	3,003.35	9,261.23	3,254.53
2015-2016	5,266.15	2,560.39	7,826.54	2,705.76

Source: Prepared according to data available in Ministry of Commerce, Government of India, Annual Reports of Ministry of External Affairs, Government of India and General Statistics Office of Vietnam (Ministry of Planning and Investment, Government of Socialist Republic of Vietnam, Hanoi)

Over the years, India and Vietnam have signed some important agreements and based on those agreements, the current state of their economic cooperation exists. The agreements which have direct economic implications are: Agreement on Science and Technology signed in 1976 and renewed in 1996; Bilateral Trade Agreement signed in 1978, which was amended in 1997; Vietnam-India Joint Commission for Economic, Scientific and Technical Cooperation, established in December 1992, is a very important mechanism for the two countries to review and promote cooperation in all fields, including economic cooperation; Consular Agreement signed in September 1994; Avoidance of Double Taxation Agreement signed in September 1994; Agreement on Science and Technology Cooperation signed in 1976 and extended in 1996; Agreement for Investment, Protection and Encouragement in 1997, Bilateral Investment Promotion and Protection Agreement (BIPPA) signed in March 1997; Agreement on Civil Aviation, which was signed in 1999 and amended in 2004; Memorandum of Understanding (MoU) between the Indian Oil and Natural Gas Corporation Ltd. (ONGC) and Petroleum Investment of Development Company (PIDC) of Vietnam signed in January 2001; MoU between Federation of Indian Chamber of Commerce and Industries (FICCI) and Vietnam Chamber of Commerce and Industries (VCCI) signed in 2001; Agreement on Tourism Cooperation in 2001; Joint Declaration on the Framework of Comprehensive Cooperation signed in May 2003; MoU on cooperation in the Field of Fisheries and Aquaculture signed in July 2007; Work Plan in the field of India-Vietnam Agriculture Cooperation signed in July 2007; MoU on Cooperation between Vietnam Steel Corporation and Essar Group signed in January 2007; MoU on Cooperation between Vietnam Steel

Corporation and Tata Steel Limited signed in July 2007; Vietnam-India Free Trade Agreement (VIFTA) in Goods signed in October 2009 under the ASEAN-India FTA (AIFTA). These agreements along with Agreements on Consular Affairs, Cultural Exchanges and Mutual Legal Assistance among others have facilitated the development of bilateral trade relations. Both countries have also established the Joint Commission for Economic, Scientific and Technical Cooperation in 1982, which meets twice a year. The Joint Business Council (JBC), the Joint Committee on Science and Technology and other mechanisms for cooperation in different economic areas and an Agreement on financial cooperation was signed in 2007. Moreover, the VIFTA, being a part of the AIFTA is thought to become extremely significant in boosting the Indo-Vietnam trade as this falls within India's overall drive to tap the markets of the Southeast Asian region.

Summarily then, it can be said that India-Vietnam economic relations are gradually gaining momentum but that momentum mismatches Vietnam's economic relations with China. The major impediments are as follows: **firstly**, lack of sufficient and affordable connectivity between the two countries; **secondly**, similar trade basket which have hampered their export revenue; **thirdly**, lack of sufficient knowledge about each other's market potentials; **fourthly**, bureaucratic inertia on both sides to implement the agreements proactively; **fifthly**, higher taxes levied by India on Vietnamese exports; **sixthly**, unwilling mindset among the business communities of both the countries on how to tap their market potentials and investment opportunities. Therefore, it has been opined by the governments of both the sides that India's connectivity with Vietnam should be further facilitated to tap the true potential of commercial exchange between them. In this regard, making Indo-Vietnam direct flights more frequent and more commercially viable, developing pan-Asia corridors, highways, road and rail routes, etc., should be prioritised in order to enhance bilateral trade between India and Vietnam. In fact, till 2010, there was no direct air connectivity between India and Vietnam which have adversely affected their linkages, not only in terms of commercial ties, but also the very important people-to-people contacts. Thus, Indians have visited other Southeast Asian countries, such as Singapore and Thailand, in large number numbers but not Vietnam to that extent and to increase their connectivity further, there are tangible suggestions to develop road connectivity between India and Vietnam, by linking and further extending the India-Myanmar-Thailand trilateral highway up to Vietnam. This proposal has been put forth specifically to boost the economic exchanges between the two countries. However, it is yet to be seen if this comes through.

Most importantly, besides bilaterally, India and Vietnam today is integrated with each through several regional and global organizations such as, the Mekong Ganga Cooperation (MGC), Association of Southeast Asian Nations (ASEAN), Asia-Europe Meeting (ASEM), Asia-Pacific Economic Cooperation (APEC), Asian Development Bank (ADB), UN Economic and Social Commission for Asia and the Pacific (UNESCAP), the World Bank and the International Monetary Forum (IMF). This gives both these countries ample opportunity to tap each other's potentials to the fullest extent and to amicably resolve any issue that might emerge between them. These institutions also motivate not only India and Vietnam, but also other developing and third world countries to nurture a feeling of solidarity with each other and to become a united force against discriminatory trade and fiscal policies.

Furthermore, Vietnam gradually developed to be an important destination for India as far as her trade relations were concerned particularly since the second half of the last decade mainly because, first, as compared to any other Southeast Asian country, India shares a special camaraderie with Vietnam owing to historical solidarity in its fight against imperialist powers. Their fraternal ties of the Cold War days permeated even in the post-Cold War years, and thus, India's generous economic assistance in Vietnam's reconstruction efforts provided a strong foothold to her trade ties with Hanoi in the post-Cold War days, which further intensified in the new millennium with the changing global situation. Another reason why India's economic relations with Vietnam have been on the rise is that India is highly approving and enthusiastic about Vietnam's sincere concerted efforts towards economic reforms and towards regular modification of investment laws to invite more foreign investments. After the intensification of their economic ties through the Strategic Partnership Agreement of 2007, by October 2009, India also recognized Vietnam as a full market economy. Moreover, owing to the frequent flare-ups in the South China Sea and Chinese 'aggression' in the Indian Ocean region, India realises that, Vietnam has several advantages due to its geostrategic location because the country is the gateway to the South China Sea and connects the pivotal route between Indian Ocean and Pacific Ocean, and lies on the important corridors to various potential markets in Southeast Asia and East Asia. Also, Vietnam's membership in various regional and international economic institutions has been an advantage for Indian investors. Besides, Vietnam's abundant natural resources and huge hydrocarbon reserves is an added attraction to Indian investors. In addition, India's political and strategic ties with Vietnam have always been good, and after the 2007 Strategic Partnership Treaty, it has further intensified, particularly at times when both these countries have resented Chinese moves in some regard. Thus, this good political and diplomatic relations have been having a very positive effect on their economic ties as well.

However, despite all this, both these countries have been trying to convert their economies into full-fledged market economies by bringing in more private economic players and FDIs,, but both of them still suffer from the drawbacks of centrally planned policies and their bureaucracies have not been very proactive in implementing the treaties and agreements that are being signed. In fact, both these economies are still suffering from the ill-effects of nepotism and red-tape which is hampering the very spirit of cooperation. Moreover, besides the above-mentioned reasons, several other reasons can be put forth while analysing why Vietnam's trade relations with India has not been very successful or commensurate with the existing excellent political and cultural ties that exist between the two countries. For instance, their underdeveloped economic structures, mutual ignorance of each other's domestic markets, etc. Besides this, over the years, in compliance with India's political and strategic relations with Vietnam, New Delhi provided number of economic initiatives to strengthen bilateral economic ties with Hanoi. However, given the then world economic structure and necessary economic structural adjustment of both the countries, led them to face severe hurdles to implement their bilateral economic understanding. In fact, India-Vietnam trade has been primarily hampered by the account deficit problems of Vietnam. India has provided considerable assistance to Vietnam through commodity loans as also through government-to-government credit transfers so that it can overcome the shortage of foreign exchange. The Vietnamese enterprises could not correctly assess the Indian markets and vice versa. The imperative for improving the institutional mechanism in both countries was underlined by the then Indian Prime Minister Vajpayee in an interview to the Vietnam News Agency, when he said, "I agree entirely that the present trade turnover between the two countries is totally incommensurate with the potential…we should diversify our trade basket. The one major thrust area is to improve the awareness within the business community and the bureaucracy in each country of the possibilities in the other. I consider the bridging of the 'awareness gap' the most important need to take our bilateral trade into a new order of magnitude."[88]

Therefore, as measures for improving their bilateral trade scenario, it is often suggested that there is urgent need to improve the economic infrastructure as well as to vigorously promote the untapped trade and investment potentials in both the countries. It is still a matter of concern that a vast majority in India and Vietnam are still quite unaware of the specialties of both the countries. For instance, Indians are familiar and obsessed with the coffee produced in Brazil, which is miles away, but have no idea about the beauty and aroma of Vietnamese coffee. That is why we need to more proactively promote our products in each other's territory.

Thus, if we look at the investment scenario, we will find that the value of Vietnam's exports to the Indian market has risen higher than the value of imports. For example, the total value of exports in 2006 was only $138 million, but by 2012 it increased to $1782 million, an increase of 13 times. In particular, the speed of growth reached 116 percent and 136 percent in 2008 and 2010 respectively, as compared with the previous year. Also, during this period, Vietnam has always been a net importer from India; however, this trend has decreased markedly in the current decade. In 2012, the trade deficit fell to $379 million, down to 50 percent as compared to $792 million in 2011. The ASEAN-India Trade in Goods Agreement (AITIG) under the Framework Agreement on Comprehensive Economic Cooperation, which was signed on August 16, 2009, and became valid from June 1, 2010, has spurred growth of exports in Vietnam, including a number of goods which have very high growth rates, such as rubber, telephones and components, etc. In the period between 1991 and 2005, Vietnam had an investment of about $100, 000 in India. But Vietnam now has three investment projects in India with a total investment of US$ 23.6 million, ranking 45th of 57 countries having capital investment in India up to January 2013. Specifically, regarding the industry structure, Indian projects are mostly focused on processing and manufacturing with 33 projects and a total investment of US$ 134.9 million (accounting for 49 percent of the total projects and 53.7 percent of the total investment). The next in line is the mining sector with three projects and a total investment of the US$ 86 million (accounting for 4 percent of the total projects and 34.2 percent of the total investment). Regarding investment areas, excluding three projects of oil and gas explorations, India has investments in 19 localities but invested capital is mainly used in the Tuyen Quang Province with Alliances mining projects and a total invested capital of US$ 15 million as well as in Ninh Thuan Province with Vietnam Dhampur's sugar production project. The total investment is US$ 22 million. Regarding investment forms, most of India's invested capital is in the form of 100 percent foreign capital with 49 projects (accounting for 72 percent of the total projects and 56. 5 percent of the total investment). The remaining capital is in the form of business cooperation contracts and joint ventures.[89]

China as a Factor in India-Vietnam bilateral economic relations, 2010-2015

Like India, Vietnam's trade with China during the years between 2010 and 2015, remained quite remarkable. Vietnam emerged to be the largest trading partner of China in the ASEAN while China became the largest trading partner of Vietnam.[90] The importance China attaches to the improvement of its economic ties with Vietnam can be gauged from the fact that, by the end of 2011, China had licensed 833 projects in Vietnam with a total registered capital of 4338.4 million USD, whereas during the same time, India had a paltry investment of 233.8 million USD in only 61 projects in Vietnam.[91] In fact, China's overdrive to better economic ties with Vietnam is a part of its overall plan to play an important role in the entire Southeast Asian region with its development interests as the guiding force. It has performed very well in the region in the economic front and has been involved in various collaborative infrastructural and connectivity projects with the countries of the region that will give China more economic leverage in the coming years. It has been particularly successful in establishing close trade ties with the ASEAN as a regional bloc. China has entered into a Free Trade Agreement with ASEAN in 2010 and has been participating in several sub-regional cooperative arrangements. Besides the economic benefits, there are definite geostrategic calculations that are influencing China's Vietnam and Southeast Asian economic policies. Southeast Asia has always been strategically very important and China has since time immemorial, considered it as its backyard of influence. Thus, China has been undertaking massive drives for the growth of its trade ties with Vietnam and other countries of the region. In Vietnam it has been coupled with massive up gradation and construction of infrastructural necessities such as important roads, bridges, railways, the lion share of which is funded by the Asian Development Bank and World Bank as part of the Greater Mekong Sub-region initiative. Through all these initiatives increasingly, mainland Southeast Asia is being linked to southwestern China and here Vietnam plays a very important role as these countries share a long land border. Thus, improving connectivity with Vietnam does not only have economic benefits for China, but will also give diplomatic and political leverages. That is why, China has been promoting with Vietnam, the concept of 'two corridors and one economic beltway' linking southern China, Hainan Island and northern Vietnam. Despite differences of opinion on several issues, Vietnam has not objected to this idea because this not only fortifies Vietnam's development needs, but also ensnares China and provides Beijing the required incentives for cooperative conduct with Vietnam.[92] In fact, Vietnam has officially endorsed China's 'One Belt One Road' initiative and became an active partner of the project.[93]

Thus, China emerged to be Vietnam's largest trading partner in this decade and Beijing supplies Vietnam with machinery, refined oil and steel. In return, Vietnam supplies China with unrefined oil, coal and rubber. However, just like the previous decade, in this decade too, the most important issue in the trade relationship between China and Vietnam is the imbalance in China's favour. In fact, trade surplus in favour of China has been increasing with passing years. Party and state leaders ofboth countries agree that effort should be made to make it more balanced. However, Vietnam has never thought of restricting Chinese imports to correct the imbalance because it believes that engaging with China in economic terms, will not only lead to its development, but also mitigate the other tensions in its relations with China because the more enmeshed China is with Vietnam in some form or the other, the lesser will be the chances of them conflicting on other issues. Thus, in case of any untoward incident, Beijing today cannot easily use punitive economic measures such as trade disruptions against Vietnam. This is because any such action will also adversely affect China, as its economy is becoming increasingly enmeshed with the Vietnamese economy. In fact, the disruption or suspension of bilateral economic ties would certainly do significant damage to the economies of China's southern provinces as well as those industries that have a large stake in maintaining their exports to Vietnam. For Vietnam, in effect, Vietnam's enhanced national security and defence capabilities achieved through its ongoing military modernisation program would have been impossible without the country's significant economic development under Doi Moi, due in part to expanded economic ties with China.[94] Furthermore, imports from China are critical inputs for Vietnamese manufacturing exports. Therefore, the Vietnamese supply chain is heavily dependent on China and the Chinese companies are the main contractors to Vietnam in the form of Engineering, Procurement and Construction (EPC) of many of the major projects in the power sector of Vietnam and are also present there in the civil work of several important highways.[95]

Moreover, coming more specifically to the trade and investment statistics, Vietnam has commercially become so integrated with China that the Chinese market today accounts for approximately more than 10 percent of Vietnam's exports and 28 percent of its imports.[96] At the end of 2010, China's cumulative contracted investment in Vietnam was $3.185 billion. In 2010 alone, its actual investment amounted to $0.365 billion, ranking 14th among Vietnam's investors. This was despite the fact that global financial crisis had taken place in 2008 and 2009. Their economic integration helped them to survive the crisis, almost unscathed. Interestingly enough, amidst this crisis, at the end of 2008, exactly like China, Hanoi announced an economic stimulus plan amounting to $6.9 billion for 2009, including about $1 billion in corporate tax relief and a four percentage point interest rate subsidy of medium and long-term loans for investment.[97] These measures contributed substantially to make the investment scenario in Vietnam more conducive to foreign investment. Thus, from $3.185 billion of Chinese investment in Vietnam in 2010, it rose to $4.8 billion in August 2015, with 915 valid projects. Most importantly, Chinese investments reach even the local provinces of Vietnam sharing borders with China, such as, Lao Cai, Lang Son, Cao Bang and Lai Chau. These projects mainly focus on mining raw materials.[98]

Both China and Vietnam are members of the ASEAN-China Free Trade Agreement. In this decade, they have involved themselves negotiating the RCEP, which is expected to further facilitate their commercial relations. Thus, to summarise the whole trade scenario between China and Vietnam, in the past 24 years, total trade turnover between Vietnam and China has increased more than 1,930 times, from $30 million in 1991 to $58.6 billion in 2014. In the past 15 years, Vietnam's trade deficit with China has risen from $190 million in 2011 to $28.8 billion in 2014 and up to $24.3 billion for the January-September period of 2015. T**able 6** below clearly shows that China-Vietnam trade figure during the year 2010–15. The growing trade figure between Vietnam and China has created several impacts in other economic sectors of Vietnam. Currently, China is now occupying the ninth position as a foreign investor. At present, the number of valid projects of China in Vietnam is about 1,180, with total registered capital of $8.5 billion. China's biggest project in Vietnam is the nearly-$2 billion Vinh Tan thermal power plant I. On the other hand, Vietnam had just 13 projects in China worth $16 million by 2014. Regarding Official Development Assistance (ODA), China ranked fifth among bilateral partners of Vietnam, with total ODA and preferential loans of over $395 million as of June 2015, mainly for the construction of the Cat Linh - Ha Dong urban rail in Hanoi.[99]

Thus, in 1991, when Vietnam and China re-established diplomatic ties, Vietnam's trade with China was estimated at $32.2 million. According to the World Bank, by the beginning of the present decade, China rose to be Vietnam's number one trading partner, making up 19 percent of Vietnam's total trade.[100]

Like Vietnam, China has emerged to be the largest trade partner of India since 2008-09. Interestingly enough, this was also the time when India was prioritising her relations with Vietnam after the 2007 Strategic Partnership Treaty. During the decade of 2000-2009, exports of India to China grew at an annual rate of 29.8 percent and by 2009 formed 7.7 percent of the total exports. However, India's exports to China have been highly concentrated and some of these dominant sectors are mostly resource-based and labour-intensive in nature, though some of them are partially technology-intensive sectors. But, India's bilateral imports are mostly concentrated in the manufacturing sector and four dominant sectors in this regard are chemicals, machinery, base metals and textile and clothing. As far as institutions for their bilateral cooperation is concerned, India and China have been cooperating with each other through the India-China Joint Economic Group on Economic Relations and Trade, Science and Technology (JEG), which is a ministerial level dialogue mechanism that was established in 1988 during the visit of former Prime Minister Rajiv Gandhi to China. At the beginning of this decade, to further intensify India's economic ties with China, the Strategic Economic Dialogue (SED) mechanism was initiated when Chinese Prime Minister Wen Jiabao visited India in December 2010, where India and China agreed to set up the Strategic Economic Dialogue (SED) mechanism. The SED is a forum for both sides to discuss strategic macro-economic issues impacting both nations as a result of the changing international economic and financial landscape, to share their individual best practices and in handling challenging domestic economic issues and to identify specific fields for enhancing cooperation, learning and experience sharing. The first India-China SED took place in Beijing from September 26-27, 2011. Most important issues that were discussed during the SED included introduction to the 12th plan priorities of the two countries, a discussion on each country's monetary and fiscal policies, investment policies of the two countries, policies on energy conservation and environmental protection, etc.[101] In continuation of the cooperative efforts to boost their trade ties, the third SED between India and China was held in Beijing on March 18, 2014. In this meeting, both the countries held discussions on bilateral trade, investment and economic cooperation and on the regional and global economic situation with the aim to enhance macro-economic policy coordination and bilateral cooperation in sectors like railways infrastructure, IT, energy and finance was emphasised.[102] Moreover, there are India-China Joint Economic Groups that function and meet regularly to further strengthen their economic cooperation.

The lacuna that is persistent in the Indo-China economic relations may be because of the discrepancies in their internal structures. For instance, China has mostly been a command economy which until in recent times had a small private sector, despite the economic reforms that were initiated by Deng Xiaoping way back in late 1970s. On the other hand, India, despite being a planned and heavily state-controlled economy from the Nehruvian era till almost about the mid-1980s, had set on the path of increasing liberalization and privatisation from late 1980s. Again, the Indian economy has been growing at a much slower pace than China. For instance, the Chinese economy has grown at an annual average rate of 9.8 percent for the last two and half decades, while India's economy has grown at around 5-6 percent during the same period. The higher growth in China essentially occurred because of the much higher rate of investment in China. The investment rate in China (investment as a share of GDP) has fluctuated between 35 and 44 percent over the past 25 years, compared to 20–26 percent in India. The critical role of infrastructure investment has been at an average of 19 percent of GDP in China, compared to 2 percent in India over the 1990s.[103] Thus, all these differences in their domestic economic situations also have led to severe repercussions in their bilateral economic relations and trade ties and thereby, contributed to the glaring imbalance in their trade value. Moreover, their domestic political structures are extremely different. On the one hand, India has institutionalised individual liberty, political pluralism, democracy and multi-party system; on the other hand, it suffers from mass poverty, red-tape, bureaucratic inertia, nepotism, mass-scale corruption, growing fiscal problems and an unsatisfactory physical infrastructure. Comparatively, China has much less poverty than India and has a superior physical infrastructure, more skilled labour, all of which have contributed towards the booming of China's manufacturing sector. In contrast to this, India has a vast pool of English-speaking people and a booming Information Technology sector. Moreover, Chinese belief in Confucian ethic, obedience to the authoritarian government, single party-rule, pre-dominance in the manufacturing and labour-intensive sectors have all contributed to its growth trajectory. India, unfortunately, has not been able to match up to China's economic growth rate and has not been able to tap the full potential of her trade with Beijing. Thus, by the end of 2015, India-China bilateral trade reached $100 billion US.

India's top five exports to China, mainly comprise primary or low value addition products—iron ore, plastic and linoleum, ores and minerals, marine products and drugs and pharmaceuticals and her imports from China are electronic goods, coal, coke, and organic chemicals, silk, medicinal and pharmaceutical products. India should move up the value-chain and export more IT-related products and pharmaceuticals as it has been doing recently.[104] Table 6 empirically analyses Vietnam's trade ties with India and China in this period (2010-2015).

Table 6: Vietnam-India-China Total Trade (2010-2015)

Values in US $ Million

Year (Jan- Dec)	Vietnam's Trade With India	Vietnam's Trade With China	Vietnam's Trade With World
2010	2753.6	27,946.5	1,57,075.3
2011	3900.3	36,479.7	2,03,655.5
2012	3942.7	41,871.0	2,28,309.6
2013	5234.0	49,404.2	2,64,065.5
2014	5621.7	58,575.9	2,98,066.2
2015	5128.8	66,608.0	3,27,587.1

Source: Prepared according to data available in Ministry of Commerce, Government of India, Annual Reports of Ministry of External Affairs, Government of India and General Statistics Office of Vietnam (Ministry of Planning and Investment, Government of Socialist Republic of Vietnam, Hanoi)

Therefore, we can clearly understand that Vietnam's trade volume with India was minuscule as compared to its total global trade volume. For instance, at the end of 2015, it was only 1.56 percent of its total trade volume, whereas with China, it was 20.33 percent. Moreover, the trade basket of Vietnam was much more diversified with China than India. Summarily then, it can be said that India's trade relations with Vietnam has come a long way since the nascent stage post the end of Cold War. Their economic relations have matured since the days of initiation of reforms and successive visits at the highest levels and concerted efforts from both sides have played a significant role in strengthening and boosting their bilateral economic ties. However, in this chapter, the findings and trade figures clearly reveal that India's trade volume with Vietnam has not been commensurate with New Delhi's excellent political and strategic ties with Hanoi. Vietnam's geographical proximity with China, low-priced Chinese goods, and similar political structures between China and Vietnam have been instrumental in cementing Vietnam's successful economic relations with China. The feeling of solidarity that has been proven to be present in Indo-Vietnam ties since the colonial era till the present day, has been conspicuously absent in their bilateral post-Cold War economic relations. In fact, India had a much more significant presence in Vietnamese economy in the days of their reconstruction period than in the post-Cold War phase. Despite the fact that New Delhi has time and again reiterated that Vietnam is a 'pillar' in its Look East and Act East policies, yet, the economic parameters prove otherwise. Today, India has prioritised her strategic ties with Vietnam rather than her economic ties which can be understood by her meagre investment in Vietnam and inadequate market for Vietnamese products in India, coupled with lack of adequate promotional activities of business opportunities and survey activities in each other's territories. Weak connectivity between India and Vietnam has also marred their trade prospects to an extent because Vietnam finds easier and cheaper to import a product from neighbouring China than from India. India has to walk the extra mile to offset this geographical disadvantage vis-à-vis Vietnam. Also, the Chambers of Commerce of both these countries have not been very active to tap the fullest potentials of their respective markets. Although China as a factor has not played any substantial role in shaping India's economic ties with Vietnam, both India and Vietnam have tried in their respective ways, to augment their economic relations with the economic superpower China, irrespective of their political and other differences with Beijing.

Notes

1. The 'Four Modernizations' Programme was initiated in 1977 by Deng Xiaoping to bolster China's economy, particularly in the sectors of agriculture, industry, national defense and science and technology, so that the Chinese economy can revive itself

from the ill-effects of various projects undertaken by Mao Zedong.

2. *85 Years of The Communist Party of Vietnam (1930-2015): A selection of documents from eleven Party Congresses*, The Gioi Publishers, Hanoi, 2015, p.645.
3. Ibid, p.646.
4. *Annual Report: 1992-93*, Ministry of External Affairs, Government of India, New Delhi, 1993.
5. Ibid.
6. *Indo-Vietnam Chamber of Commerce and Industry Newsletter*, Vol.4, No.3, January-March 1994.
7. *Annual Report:1993-94*, Ministry of External Affairs, Government of India, New Delhi, 1994.
8. *Indo-Vietnam Chamber of Commerce and Industry Newsletter*, Vol.4, No. 1-2, July–December 1993.
9. Ibid.
10. *Indo- Vietnam Chamber of Commerce and Industry Newsletter*, Vol.4, No.3, January–March 1994.
11. This Agreement was amended by a Protocol under Prime Minister Narendra Modi's leadership on October 7, 2015.
12. *Indo-Vietnam Chamber of Commerce and Industry Newsletter*, Vol.4, No.4, April–June 1994.
13. Ibid.
14. *Annual Report: 1994-95*, Ministry of External Affairs, Government of India, New Delhi, 1995.
15. *Indo-Vietnam Chamber of Commerce and Industry Newsletter*, Vol.5, No.4, April–June 1995.
16. *Indo-Vietnam Chamber of Commerce and Industry Newsletter*, Vol.6, No.3-4, January–June 1996.
17. *Annual Report: 1995-96*, Ministry of External Affairs, Government of India, New Delhi, 1996.
18. *Indo- Vietnam Chamber of Commerce and Industry Newsletter*, Vol.7, No.3-4, January–June 1997.
19. C. Ravindranatha Reddy, *India and Vietnam during Post Cold War Era*, Centre for Southeast Asian and Pacific Studies, Sri Venkateswara University, Tirupati, India, 2012, p.101.
20. *Indo-Vietnam Chamber of Commerce and Industry Newsletter*, Vol.8, No.2, October–December 1997.
21. Ibid.
22. Chu Van Chuc, "30 years of Vietnam- India Economic Relations," *Vietnam*, January 2002, p.32, for further details see, Tridib Chakraborti, "India- Vietnam Relations: A Time Tested Look East Friendship," *Jadavpur Journal of International Relations*, Vol.6, Issue 1, June 2002, pp.239–49.
23. "On the Occasion of the National Day, September 2, 1945- September 2, 1998," Publication of the Embassy of the Socialist Republic of Vietnam in India, New Delhi, 1998.
24. *Indo-Vietnam Chamber of Commerce and Industry Newsletter*, n.49.
25. *Indo- Vietnam Chamber of Commerce and Industry Newsletter*, Vol.8, No.3, January–March 1998.

26. *Indo- Vietnam Chamber of Commerce and Industry Newsletter*, Vol.8, No.4, April˜June 1998.
27. *Vietnam Information Bulletin*, Embassy of the Socialist Republic of Vietnam, New Delhi, June 1998.
28. *Indo- Vietnam Chamber of Commerce and Industry Newsletter*, Vol.9, No.1, July-September 1998.
29. *Vietnam Information Bulletin*, Embassy of Socialist Republic of Vietnam, New Delhi, October 1999.
30. Ibid.
31. Shantanu Srivastava, "Four decades of India-Vietnam Economic and Commercial Relations and the Way Forward," in Rajiv Bhatia, Vijay Sakhuja and Vikash Ranjan (eds.), *India- Vietnam: Agenda for Strengthening Partnership*, Shipra Publications, Delhi, 2013, pp.27–28.
32. Bashir Ahmad Dhar, "Bilateral engagements between India- China since 1988," in G. Jayachandra Reddy (ed.), *India and China Relations: Historical, Cultural and Security Issues*, ugc Centre for Southeast Asian and Pacific Studies, Sri Venkateswara University, Tirupati, India, p.35.
33. Clifford J. Shultz II and William J. Ardrey IV, "The Future Prospects of Sino-Vietnamese Relations: Are Trade and Commerce the Critical Factors for Sustainable Peace?," *Contemporary Southeast Asia,* Vol. 17, No. 2, September 1995, p.140.
34. *Vietnam Information Bulletin*, Embassy of Socialist Republic Of Vietnam, New Delhi, February 1999.
35. Joseph Y.S Cheng, "Sino- Vietnamese Relations in the Early Twenty-First Century," *Asian Survey*, Vol. 51, No. 2, March/April 2011, p.394.
36. Swaran Singh, "Limitations of India- China Economic Engagement," *China Report*, Vol.45, No.4, 2009, p.289.
37. Gautam Murthy, "Sino- Indian Economic Relations- Competition and Partnership-Convergence or Divergence?" in G. Jayachandra Reddy (ed.), *Dynamics of India and China Relations: Implications for New World Order*, UGC Centre for Southeast Asian and Pacific Studies, Sri Venkateswara University, Tirupati, 2016, pp. 82–83.
38. *Annual Report:1991*, Ministry of External Affairs, Government of India, New Delhi, 1991.
39. *Annual Report:1992*, Ministry of External Affairs, Government of India, New Delhi, 1992.
40. *Annual Report:1994-95*, Ministry of External Affairs, Government of India, New Delhi, 1995.
41. *Annual Report:1996-97*, Ministry of External Affairs, Government of India, New Delhi, 1997.
42. Russell Hiang-Khng Heng, "Vietnam: light at the end of the economic tunnel?" *Southeast Asian Affairs*, 2001, pp. 359–60.
43. "Special Issue on the Occasion of the 55th Anniversary of the National Day, September 2, 1945–September 2, 2000," Publication of the Embassy of the Socialist Republic of Vietnam in India, New Delhi, 2000.
44. Tridib Chakraborti, "From National Reconstruction to Market Economy: Space and Time Analysis of India's Look East Vietnam Policy," in PV Rao (ed.), *India and ASEAN: Partners at Summit*, KW Publishers Pvt Ltd, New Delhi, 2008, p.330.
45. "61st Anniversary of the National Day, September 2, 1945- September 2, 2006,"

Publication of the Embassy of the Socialist Republic of Vietnam, New Delhi, 2006.

46. *Annual Report:2004-05*, Ministry of External Affairs, Government of India, New Delhi, 2005.
47. *Annual Report:2005-06*, Ministry of External Affairs, Government of India, New Delhi, 2006.
48. "Law on Enterprises," Vietnam National Assembly, Decision No. 13-199-QH10, August 31, 1999, http://www.vietnamlaws.com/freelaws/Lw60na29Nov05Enterprises[10April06].pdf;LawofInvestment (accessed on May 5, 2017).
49. *Annual Report: 2006-07*, Ministry of External Affairs, Government of India, New Delhi, 2007.
50. Pranav Kumar,"India-Vietnam Economic Relations: Opportunities and Challenges," *Institute of Peace and Conflict Studies Special Report*, No.57, July 2008, p.4.
51. *Annual Report:2007-08*, Ministry of External Affairs, Government of India, New Delhi, 2008.
52. Nguyen Van Lich, "Prospects for India-Vietnam Economic Relations," in Rajiv Bhatia, Vijay Sakhuja and Vikash Ranjan (eds.), *India-Vietnam: Agenda for Strengthening Partnership*, Shipra Publications and Indian Council of World Affairs, Delhi, 2013, p.59.
53. *Annual Report:2009-10*, Ministry of External Affairs, Government of India, New Delhi, 2010.
54. Nguyen Huy Hoang, "India-Mekong Cooperation: Vietnam Perspective," in Prabir De (ed.), *ASEAN- India Deepening Economic Partnership in Mekong Region,* RIS, New Delhi, 2014, p.212.
55. Gautam Murthy, n. 66, p.83.
56. Srinivasulu Bayineni, "Economic Relations between India and China: Integration through Bilateral Trade," in G. Jayachandra Reddy (ed.), *Dynamics of India and China Relations: Implications for New World Order*, UGC Centre for Southeast Asian and Pacific Studies, Sri Venkateswara University, Tirupati, India, p.131.
57. Swaran Singh, n.65, pp.294–95.
58. Gautam Murthy, n.66, p.95.
59. Srinivasulu Bayineni, n.85, p.124.
60. Swaran Singh, n.65, p.289.
61. Joseph Y.S Cheng, n.64, p.394.
62. Brantly Womack, "Vietnam and China in an Era of Economic Uncertainty," *The Asia-Pacific Journal*, Vol. 36, No. 2, 2009. See, https://apjjf.org/site/view/3214 (accessed on November 16, 2017).
63. Le Hong Hiep, "Vietnam's Strategic Trajectory from Internal Development to External Engagement," *Strategic Insights*, No 59, Australian Strategic Policy Institute, 2012, p.6.
64. For details see, Oliver Hensengerth, *Regionalism in China-Vietnam Relations: Institution- Building in the Greater Mekong Subregion*, Routledge Contemporary Asia Series 19, Routledge, London, 2010.
65. M. Prayaga and V.Ramesh Babu, "India and Vietnam: Burgeoning Strategic Partnership," in S. Manivasakan (ed.), *Security Dynamics of India's Future Relations with Southeast Asian Nations*, Centre for South and Southeast Asian Studies, University of Madras, Chennai, 2012, p.169.

66. Interview of Mr. Nguyen Minh Vu, Deputy Head of the APEC 2017 National Secretariat's Standing Committee, APEC 2017: Opportunities and Challenges for Vietnam, *VietNam Net*, 15 December 2016, english.vietnamnet.vn/fms/special-reports/171142/apec-2017—opportunities-and-challenges-for-vietnam.html (accessed on May 10, 2017).
67. *Indo-Vietnam Chamber of Commerce and Industry Newsletter*, January-March 2011
68. Shantanu Srivastava, n.60, p.29.
69. *Annual Report:2011-12*, Ministry of External Affairs, Government of India, New Delhi, 2012.
70. Vikash Ranjan, "Strengthening India-Vietnam Trade and Investment Relations in the Current Global Financial Crisis," in Rajiv K. Bhatia, Vijay Sakhuja and Vikash Ranjan (eds.), *India- Vietnam: Agenda for Strengthening Partnership*, Shipra Publications and Indian Council of World Affairs, Delhi, pp.38–39.
71. "India-Vietnam Relations," Ministry of External Affairs, Government of India, January 2013, http://www.mea.gov.in/Portal/ForeignRelation/Vietnam_Feb_2013.pdf (accessed on March 3, 2013).
72. *Annual Report:2012-13*, Ministry of External Affairs, Government of India, New Delhi, 2013.
73. "On the Occasion of the 68th Anniversary of Vietnam's National Day: 2nd September, 1945- 2nd September, 2013," Publication of the Embassy of the Socialist Republic of Vietnam in India, New Delhi, 2013.
74. Ibid.
75. *The Hindu Business Line*, 11 July 2013.
76. "India issues statement on 15th Joint Commission Meeting," *Nhan Dan*, July 12, 2013, en.nhandan.org.vn/politics/external-relations/item/1858902-vietnam-laos-unite-to-promote-fine-artwork.html (accessed on December 3, 2013).
77. Welcome address by Mr. P R Agarwala, former President, Bharat Chamber of Commerce on 28 January, 2015, Kolkata.
78. *Annual Report: 2013-14*, Ministry of External Affairs, Government of India, New Delhi, 2014.
79. "Joint Statement on the occasion of the State Visit of the General Secretary of the Communist Party of Vietnam to India," Ministry of External Affairs, Government of India, 20 November 2013, mea.gov.in/lok-sabha.htm?dtl/22510/Joint+Statement+on+the+occasion+of+the+State+Visit+of+the+General+Secretary+of+the+Communist+Party+of+Vietnam+to+India (accessed on June 7, 2014).
80. "India-Vietnam Relations," Ministry of External Affairs, Government of India, December 2013, https://www.mea.gov.in/Portal/ForeignRelation/Vietnam_Dec_2013.pdf (accessed on May 5, 2014).
81 "On the Occasion of the 40th Anniversary of Reunification Day of Vietnam, 125th Birth Anniversary of great leader- President Ho Chi Minh, 70th Anniversary of Vietnam's National Day," Publication of The Embassy of The Socialist Republic of Vietnam in India, New Delhi, Special Edition, 2015.
82. Ibid.
83. *Annual Report: 2014-15*, Ministry of External Affairs, Government of India, New Delhi, 2015.
84. "On the Occasion of the 40th Anniversary of Reunification Day of Vietnam, 125th

Birth Anniversary of great leader- President Ho Chi Minh, 70th Anniversary of Vietnam's National Day," n.110.
85. *Annual Report: 2014-15*, Ministry of External Affairs, Government of India, New Delhi, 2015.
86. Pankaj K Jha , "India-Vietnam Relations: Need for enhanced cooperation, *Strategic Analysis*, Vol.32, Issue 6, November 2008, pp. 1092–93.
87. Nguyen Huy Hoang, n.83, pp.214–15.
88. Tridib Chakraborti, n.73, pp.333–34.
89. General Statistics Office of Vietnam (FDI).
90. *Xinhua*, June 15, 2017.
91. General Statistics Office of Vietnam (FDI).
92. Carlyle A. Thayer, 'The Tyranny of Geography: Vietnamese Strategies to Constrain China in the South China Sea, *Contemporary Southeast Asia*, Vol. 33, No. 3, 2011, pp. 353–54.
93. "Vietnam To Join China's One Belt, One Road Project," *Executive Intelligence Review*, 2 March 2017, https://larouchepub.com/pr/2017/170302_vietnam_obor.html (accessed on August 10, 2017).
94. Le Hong Hiep, "Vietnam's Hedging Strategy against China since Normalization," *Contemporary Southeast Asia*, Vol.35, No.3, 2013, pp. 345–46.
95. World Bank Report, July 2014, documents.worldbank.org/curated/en/641241468133544451/pdf./893100WPOP13240tock0July020140FINAL.pdf (accessed on August 10, 2017).
96. Dinh, Demombynes, and Badiani- Magnusson, "Taking Stock: An Update on Vietnam's Recent Economic Developments," The World Bank, Hanoi, July 2014, p. 21, www.worldbank.org/content/dam/Worldbank/document/EAP/Vietnam/Taking_Stock_July2014_EN_final.pdf (accessed on August 10, 2017).
97. Joseph Y.S Cheng, n.64, p.398.
98 General Statistics Office Of Vietnam (FDI).
99. "Vietnam-China economic relations after 25 years," *VietnamNet*, 6 November 2015, https://english.vietnamnet.vn/fms/business/145683/Vietnam---china-economic-relations-after-25years.html (accessed on August 11, 2017).
100. Joseph Y.S Cheng, n.64, p.392.
101. Srinivasulu Bayineni, n.85, p.126.
102. *Annual Report:2014-15*, Ministry of External Affairs, Government of India, New Delhi, 2015.
103. Gautam Murthy, n.66, pp.83–84.
104. Ibid, pp.97–98

THREE

China and the Politics of India-Vietnam Relations

With the end of the Cold War and the collapse of the erstwhile Soviet Union, India found itself all alone in the uni-polar global politics, surrounded by hostile neighbours. Moreover, it lost about 20 percent of her export market, which forced her to search for newer markets and liberalise her own economy. All these hastened the adoption of the New Economic Policy (NEP), characterised by Liberalisation, Privatisation and Globalisation of the economy, in 1991. In fact, India was suddenly jolted out of slumber to face the harsh realities and the gradual unfolding of events in global politics as the Cold War reached its abrupt end. The world now was left with the sole Superpower, the US, and India, with her legacy of bitter ties with the US owing to the Cold War compulsions, faced an acute financial crisis as an outfit of the Gulf War and 'Operation Desert Storm' during the early 1990s. The situation came to such a pass that, India's fiscal deficits rose to 8.4 percent of Gross Domestic Product (GDP) by 1990-1991, with inflation ranging over 12 percent and internal debt, escalating to 53 percent of GDP. On the other hand, external debt increased to US$ 72 billion from US$ 20.5 billion in 1980, making India the third largest debtor nation after Brazil and Mexico. By June 1991, foreign exchange reserves had declined to only US$ 600 million, or only two weeks equivalent of imports.[1] In such a situation, India had no other option but to launch her New Economic Policy (NEP), to salvage the economic situation of the country and to integrate India with the global economy by substituting the import-intensive, 'closed' and 'protectionist' economic policies with more export-oriented, 'open' and 'liberal' economic policies from this time onwards. Thus, in such a tumultuous political situation, India had to shape her 'Look East' policy out of her compulsions and exigencies.

The purpose of this chapter is to analyse the political relations that evolved between India and Vietnam in the post-Cold War years in the emerging global order and China's response. This chapter aims to study whether and to what extent the 'China threat' has influenced India and Vietnam to intensify their political ties and dependence on each other in the new world order. Therefore, for better analysis, this chapter has been divided decade-wise as follows: India-Vietnam Political Relations and the China Factor: From 1991 to 1999, India-Vietnam Political Cooperation and the China Factor: From 2000 to 2009, and India-Vietnam Political Conviviality and the China Factor: From 2010 to 2015.

India-Vietnam Political Relations and the China Factor, 1991 to 1999: The Period of Ups and Downs

The fall of former Soviet Union in the end of the Cold War was a historic event. This event occurred at a crucial time, when the world was undergoing tremendous unprecedented political changes, which had a severe impact on India too, both internally as well as externally. After years of considerable instability at the highest political level, in 1991, the General Elections were held in India for electing the members of the Tenth Lok Sabha. At this time, India was undergoing a politically tumultuous situation with successive change of governments, political unrest, assassination of the heads of the state, etc. Thus, after the dissolution of the Ninth Lok Sabha only after sixteen months since government formation, the Tenth Lok Sabha elections were held in 1991. In this election, no party could achieve a clear majority, the Indian National Congress (INC), which had obtained 35.66 percent seats, formed the government with the help of other parties, such as, the left parties and PV Narasimha Rao was proclaimed the Prime

Minister of the government and he could successfully complete the full five-year tenure of the government, thus bringing some stability in the political sphere of India. This also gave him the opportunity to take some bold steps as far as India's domestic and foreign policies were concerned. Thus, the NEP or the reforms in India's economic sector was supplemented with India's 'Look East' Policy in the realm of foreign policy. The thrust of Rao's foreign policy was based on his predecessor Rajiv Gandhi's foreign policy priorities, i.e. focusing more on our eastern neighbours and mending ties, even with China. Almost concurrent to the adoption of the NEP, as a natural prolongation of the NEP, the Government of India under Prime Minister PV Narasimha Rao's leadership started to 'Look East'. In fact, efforts in this regard had started in the 1980s itself under Rajiv Gandhi's leadership. However, the ASEAN then was not very willing to forge closer ties with India, because the Cold War was still on, the South East Asia Treaty Organization (SEATO) was effective, and the majority of ASEAN members was closely allied with the United States. India was politically and strategically in closer proximity with the former Soviet Union. Moreover, India's pro-Vietnam role in the Kampuchean Crisis was condemned by the ASEAN. However, now with the relegation of the Cold War imperatives to the background, India decided to give definite policy thrust to the ASEAN region and in this respect, India was essentially attracted to the booming economy of the Southeast Asian region at this time which was in stark contrast with India's domestic economic situation in early 1990s. In fact, a report titled "The East Asian Miracle: Economic Growth and Public Policy," contrasted India's slow and uneven economic performance with that of the nations of Southeast and East Asia.[2] Learning from his experiences as the External Affairs Minister under Mrs. Gandhi's leadership, Prime Minister PVN Rao could quickly and aptly judge the importance of the Southeast Asian region in the realm of India's post-Cold War foreign policy particularly in the wake of adoption of definite changes in India's domestic and foreign economic policies. India had to graze hard to achieve any success in her course-correction drives vis-à-vis the ASEAN and the Southeast Asian region. Luckily, at that time, India's efforts to 'Look East' coincided with the ASEAN's efforts to 'Look West' to tap newer markets in the post-Cold War milieu and to generate a fortification against security threats and against China's overtures in the region. The ASEAN was impressed by India's size, population, educated middle class, industrial base, military strength, technical capability, ancient cultural history and presence of overseas Indians are factors in its favour.[3]

Accordingly, India's active role in resolving the Cambodian crisis was well appreciated by the ASEAN members and India could successfully revamp her position in the psyche of the Southeast Asian countries as a neutral and benevolent South Asian power, which to a certain extent had got maligned owing to Indira Gandhi's staunch support to Vietnam initially in the Kampuchean crisis. Thus, such events during the Cold War are replete with examples where India had jeopardised even her own position to extend fraternal political and economic support to Vietnam. Therefore, India continued to strengthen her friendly ties with Vietnam and other Southeast Asian countries in the post-Cold War period. India's internal economic reforms and a liberal, global friend-seeking foreign policy, particularly vis-à-vis Southeast Asia through her 'Look East' policy was complimented with Vietnam's 'Look West' policy and its own internal economic reforms or Doi Moi after its Sixth Party Congress in 1986. Soon after the Cold War, to reinforce the importance that India attaches to her ties with Vietnam, the then President, R. Venkataraman paid a very important visit to Vietnam amongst other Southeast Asian countries, from April 24–28, 1991, and discussed the changing regional and global scenario and both countries committed their support to each other's cause. This visit of the President of India was significant as it took place after a gap of 32 years since President Rajendra Prasad visited Vietnam in 1959. The Vietnamese side appreciated India's role in bringing stability in Southeast Asia and her sincere efforts to establish a Zone of Peace, Stability and Friendship in the region. Following this crucial visit, India consented to provide an assistance of Rs 1 Crore to Vietnam for establishing an industrial estate.[4] In May 1991, a historic event took place in India when Rajiv Gandhi was assassinated. While extending Vietnam's condolences to this event, a delegation led by the Vice President of the State Council of Vietnam, visited India and took part in the funeral ceremony of the former Indian Prime Minister. At the time of this event, the Vietnam government highly acknowledged Rajiv Gandhi's contribution to strengthen Indo-Vietnam ties. Following this, in the same year, in November 1991, Shri Salman Khurshid paid a visit to the Ho Chi Minh City for inaugurating the Indian pavilion at the Quang Trung International Trade Fair in which about 57 Indian companies participated, and clearly gave a thrust to the economic aspect of the bilateral relations. It is to be kept in mind that the crucial year of 1991 was witnessing the process of rapprochement and normalisation of relations between both India and China on the one hand, and Vietnam and China on the other. The thawing of the Cold War bitterness between India and China in fact, started from 1988 during Rajiv Gandhi's visit to China, and Vietnam too, after dropping Nguyen Co Thach from the Politburo and the Central Committee in the Seventh Party Congress, went overboard in its efforts to normalize ties with China, especially after the fall of the Soviet Union. Thus, to consolidate Vietnam's efforts and to make known its intentions to normalise its ties with China, Nguyen Manh Cam, the newly appointed Foreign Minister of Vietnam, paid a visit to China in September 1991. This conducive environment finally paved the way for a high level summit at Chengdu in November 1991, in which their bilateral relations were officially fully normalised.[5] Thus, since 1991, both India and Vietnam started to strengthen not only their bilateral ties but also their political relations with other countries, including China, in order to make their post-Cold War foreign policy more multi-faceted, liberal and dynamic to meet the exigencies of the new global order.

Meanwhile, as a result of increasing realization on both sides of their mutual importance, India was rewarded with the Sectoral Dialogue Partner status by the ASEAN in January 1992 (which was officially initialed in March 1993). The Sectoral Dialogue Partner status was given to India to boost dialogue cooperation in areas of trade, tourism, investment, science and technology.[6] The Government of India welcomed the move and mentioned in the MEA Annual Report of 1991-92 that, "India's proposal to have sectoral dialogue with ASEAN in the areas of trade, technical and manpower development, technology and tourism was accepted by ASEAN in January 1992. This significant development would open up avenues of improving India's relations with ASEAN in economic and other fields."[7] Therefore, as an outfit of this measure, there gradually emerged greater interaction between government officials of India with their counterparts in ASEAN countries on a one-to-one basis and with the ASEAN Secretariat on a comprehensive manner.

Boosted by such developments, in March 1992, Nguyen Manh Cam, the Foreign Minister of Vietnam, visited India and had exhaustive discussions with the President, Vice President and the Prime Minister and the Minister of External Affairs. During his visit, the fifth session of the Indo-Vietnam Joint Commission was held in Delhi, which discussed possibilities of expanding and deepening the existing economic relations between India and Vietnam. At the time of this visit, Vietnam once again reiterated India's stand on the Kashmir issue and fully accepted that Kashmir was an integral part of India.[8] It is to be noted that, despite Vietnam's effort to strengthen its ties with China in the post-Cold War years, it did not budge from supporting India on the Kashmir issue even at the risk of inviting wrath from China as China continuing with the Cold War legacy, was further consolidating its ties with Pakistan in the post-Cold War days as well. Soon after, it became clear that despite Vietnam's best efforts to strengthen its ties with China, the differences of opinion in the political sphere remained lurking behind, which to a great extent, started shaping the Indo-Vietnamese ties. For instance, in May 1992, China entered into an agreement with the Crestone Energy Group, a US company, to engage in oil and gas exploration in a 10,000 square mile area in the South China Sea. It is to be noted that, this area earmarked by China for the Crestone Energy Group, was disputed by Vietnam, as it was located on

Vietnam's continental shelf, yet claimed by China as per its policy of 'nine dash/dotted lines'. This led to political discord in Sino-Vietnamese relations in 1992 and incidentally, when in September of that year, China began drilling in the disputed Gulf of Tonkin, Do Muoi, the then General Secretary of the Communist Party of Vietnam, visited India in the same month. Do Muoi's visit was a landmark incident as he was the highest ranking dignitary to visit India after President Ho Chi Minh's visit in February 1958. On that occasion, Prime Minister Rao remarked that a strong, prosperous and vibrant Vietnam was to the best interests of India and the very fact that Do Muoi had chosen to visit India, the first non-socialist country, immediately after coming to power, keeping aside invitations from several ASEAN countries, proved the importance that Vietnam attached to India in the post-Cold War years. Do Muoi's visit was extremely successful that ended in a joint communiqué and he urged both the countries to beef up their economic interaction to keep pace with the excellent bilateral political relations between them. Vietnam was definitely coming closer to India politically, than ever before, despite the increased level of economic ties growing more closer with China during this time. With the frequent flaring up of the South China Sea crisis, along with the disputed land border and the Gulf of Tonkin issues, Vietnam correctly assessed that India would be playing a major role in Vietnam's foreign policy in the coming years.

As a result, to keep up the momentum of India's relations with Vietnam, in February 1993, Mr. Salman Khurshid, Minister of State for External Affairs, paid a visit to Vietnam, especially to take stock of the current state of their bilateral relations and discussed some of the pressing regional and global issues. Following this, Vice President Shri KR Narayanan visited Vietnam in September 1993, when Do Muoi, once again gave complete support to India for her bid to obtain a permanent seat in the United Nations Security Council and reiterated Vietnam's support for India's stand on Kashmir. Thereafter, Vice Minister of Finance, Mr. Pham Van Trong paid an official visit to India in October 1993 to further deepen the then Vietnam's political and economic ties with India. To foster direct connectivity between India and Vietnam, an agreement on air service between India and Vietnam was signed in May 1993. Thus, overall, India and Vietnam maintained friendly ties with high-level visits throughout the year 1993 and maintained the solidarity of the past on the one hand. While on the other, Vietnam tried to settle its existing territorial disputes with China related to the land border and the Gulf of Tonkin area by exchanging delegates between both the countries. Like Vietnam, India too, during this time initiated the dialogue with China to resolve the long-drawn disputed land border issue and in 1993, when Prime Minster PV Narasimha Rao visited China, both the countries signed the "Agreement on the Maintenance of Peace and Tranquility" along the disputed Line of Actual Control (LAC). This agreement was instrumental in India's efforts to settle the border problem with China peacefully by initiating numerous Confidence Building Measures between them[9] and for setting up the India- China Expert Group to demarcate the LAC and discuss troop reduction.

With the gradual passage of time, India was increasingly trying to carve out a greater place for herself in the affairs of the Asia-Pacific region and Vietnam too, was trying its best to obtain an ASEAN membership and both these countries were supporting each other's foreign policy goals. For instance, when Prime Minister Rao again visited Vietnam in September 1994, the Vietnamese side remarked that Vietnam welcomes and highly appreciates India's efforts of participating in the activities of the community of the nations in the Asia-Pacific region in particular and the world as a whole and Vietnam whole-heartedly wished to see India play a greater role in the regional and global affairs.[10] This visit was successful enough as four crucial agreements on avoidance of double taxation, facilitation of visas, defence cooperation and foreign office consultations were signed. Thus, Vietnam's support to India's expanding role in Southeast Asia, Asia-Pacific and the world as a whole with enhanced position and activities in the United Nations was extremely significant from the perspective of India's national interest at a time when Vietnam was a candidate for

ASEAN membership during this time and thus, a gateway or a linchpin to India's enhanced profile in the Southeast Asian region. Such great political camaraderie between India and Vietnam perhaps, to a large extent, stemmed from Vietnam's increasing bitterness with China. For instance, in April 1994, Vietnam launched official protests against seismological surveys carried out by Crestone Energy Corporation in the 'Tu Chinh coral reef' area. On May 5, a spokesman for Vietnam's Foreign Ministry emphasised that the Tu Chinh area 'lies fully' within Vietnam's Exclusive Economic Zone (EEZ) and continental shelf, and that no area was disputed there. Following this, on May 10 a spokesman for China's Foreign Ministry was reported as saying that, "the Blue Dragon sea area belongs to the adjacent waters of the Nansha islands,"[11] i.e. the Spratlys. He also stated that an exploration contract signed between Vietnam and American Mobil Oil Company in the Blue Dragon oil field was 'illegal'. The following day Vietnam's Foreign Ministry reiterated that the areas of 'Tu Chinh' and 'Thanh Long' were located within its EEZ and continental shelf and that Vietnam "has the sovereign right to explore and exploit natural resources in these areas."[12] On May 12, the Chinese Foreign Ministry stated that any contract signed by Vietnam with oil companies for prospecting and exploiting oil deposits in waters around the Spratly islands would infringe on China's "rights and interests".[13] In an interview with *The Straits Times* (Singapore), published on May 19, Vietnam's Prime Minister, Vo Van Kiet, was quoted as reiterating Vietnam's position and refuting China's sovereignty claims to the 'Blue Dragon oilfield'.[14] Therefore, to lessen the bilateral tensions, Secretary General of the Communist Party of Vietnam (CPV), Do Muoi, immediately visited China in November 1994 to discuss the outstanding bilateral issues and both countries pledged to resolve the disputed issues of border and the Gulf of Tonkin by adhering to international law and through peaceful negotiations. Thus, Vietnam's lingering bitterness and political challenges vis-à-vis China, further provided the impetus to Vietnam to forge closer and multi-faceted ties with India. As far as India's ties with China in 1994 was concerned, China continued to engage through the

India-China expert group meetings, held in February and April 1994, to discuss ways of bringing peace and tranquility in the disputed border region, but not any significant progress could be made in this regard.

India for the first time was definitely prioritising her ties with the Southeast Asian region and that can be gauged from the fact that the Ministry of External Affairs Annual Report of 1994-95 mentioned Southeast Asia as 'an area of prime focus'. It further mentioned that, "as an immediate neighbour of Southeast Asia sharing common security concern, India desires to be associated with deliberations of the ASEAN Regional Forum (ARF). The general question of expanding ARF membership is under consideration of the ASEAN countries."[15] Therefore, India made it amply clear that it was sincerely trying to consolidate and further expand its ties with the ASEAN members during this time. In this regard, the 'Look East' policy was formally enunciated in September 1994 at the Institute of Southeast Asian Studies, Singapore when India's the then Prime Minister Narasimha Rao stressed on India's historical and cultural contacts with the Southeast Asian region and the importance of this region in the strategic calculus and economic development of India in the coming days.[16] As a follow-up to the speech, the Ministry of External Affairs Annual Report, 1995-96, for the first time used the phrase 'Look East' officially.

This conducive environment in India's political ties with Vietnam further got a boost in the following year, i.e. 1995. In July 1995, Vietnam was admitted to the ASEAN as its seventh member. India had wholeheartedly supported Vietnam's candidature as a member of the ASEAN. As fallout of PM Rao's visit to Vietnam in September 1994, India set up a Joint Working Group (JWG) with Vietnam under the aegis of the Indo-Vietnam Joint Commission to prioritize her ties with Vietnam and to further consolidate her relations by providing the podium of the JWG to discuss newer areas for bilateral cooperation. Accordingly, in August 1995, India decided to give Rs 1.5 Crore to Vietnam for setting up a multipurpose industrial training centre. Vietnam, at this time, was reaping handsome benefits from her open door foreign policy aimed at maximising friends at the global arena. Thus, not only by the mid-1990s, Vietnam had become a member of the ASEAN, but also it had successfully normalised its ties with the US, who withdrew its objections to the developmental assistance to Vietnam by the World Bank and the International Monetary Fund (IMF), and thus, trade and investment ties with the US were gradually bolstered. Moreover, Vietnam's foreign policy in the post-Cold War years helped it to make 163 non-communist states as diplomatic partners by 1995, as compared to a paltry 23 in 1989.[17] Therefore, Vietnam's emerging profile not only in the Southeast Asian region but also in the global affairs, certainly motivated India to further strengthen her ties with Vietnam.

Thereafter, as a result of continuous proactive diplomatic manoeuvres and negotiations, India was promoted to the level of Full Dialogue Partner at the ASEAN Summit in December 1995 at Bangkok, Thailand, and this further boosted India's relations with Vietnam. This incident was profusely appreciated and acknowledged by the Government of India and the Annual Report of the Ministry of External Affairs remarked: "The ASEAN Ministerial Meeting (AMM) held in Bandar Seri Begawan, Brunei Darussalam in July-August 1995 expressed satisfaction with the continuing Sectoral Dialogue with India. It was decided at the Fifth ASEAN Summit held in Bangkok (14-15 December 1995) that India would become a "Full Dialogue Partner" of ASEAN. As a result of this, hailing this development the Ministry of External Affairs Annual Report noted that, "As part of the full dialogue partnership process, India will be participating in the Post-Ministerial Consultations, India will also be interacting with ASEAN under the auspices of a Dialogue Committee"[18] Elevation of India's stature in the ASEAN to the "Full Dialogue Partner" level allowed India, for the first time, to enjoy holistic partnership with the ASEAN and involve itself in dialogue with the ASEAN in a wide gamut of subjects in the realms of Human Resource and Development, Science and Technology, Health, Enterprises, People-to-People contact and all other new areas expected to be mutually identified for bilateral cooperation, going beyond the limited focus on trade, investment, science and technology and tourism during the period of Sectoral Dialogue Partnership.

Meanwhile, as an outfit of the successful upward mobility of India in the ASEAN, India could join the ASEAN Regional Forum (ARF) in 1996. The ARF was formed in 1993 under the overall guidance and umbrella of the ASEAN as a regional security cooperation and dialogue platform based on deliberations in the ASEAN Post Ministerial Conference between the Foreign Ministers of ASEAN and its full dialogue partners. The ARF operates through a three-tier process: Track I, Track I ½ (activities approved by ARF and involving scholars and officials from member states acting in their personal capacity) and Track II (which provides a non-governmental forum for academics, scholars, researchers to interact in their private capacity with a view to developing structured regional processes).[19] In this regard, India was guided by the ARF Concept Paper of 1995, which was extremely significant as it clearly highlighted three broad areas, namely promotion of confidence building measures, development of mechanisms of preventive diplomacy and development of mechanisms of conflict resolution as the guiding principles of the organization.[20] Though the ASEAN was a divided body as far as India's membership in the ARF was concerned, some of the countries in the ASEAN, such as Singapore, Indonesia and the newly inducted Vietnam were staunchly in favour of India's induction in the ARF to balance the increasing presence of China in the region. India's membership in the Forum provided New Delhi with an unprecedented opportunity to involve itself in the crucial strategic and security issues of the region. This was a crucial development as the US too, during this time, was trying to increasingly re-engage in the Asia-Pacific region in the wake of China's increasing economic and military prowess and aggressive postures in the region owing to the South China issue and the conflicts in the Korean Peninsula. Therefore, India found herself to be in the midst of a major flux in the region and as a potential re-balancer of the Chinese overtures in the Asia-Pacific.

However, India in 1996 was herself undergoing tremendous tumult in her domestic political scenario. India conducted general elections for the Eleventh Lok Sabha in 1996. However, the result that emerged was that no party or alliance failed to obtain clear majority and it was hung Parliament. However, Bharatiya Janata Party (BJP) emerged as the single largest political party and the then President of India, Shri Sankar Dayal Sharma, invited BJP's Atal Bihari Vajpayee to be the tenth Prime Minister of India. Accordingly, he was sworn in and unfortunately, he resigned after 13 days on account of failure to obtain full majority. This paved the way for the United Front, a non-BJP, non-Congress coalition to come to power with HD Deve Gowda, leader of the Janata Dal, as the eleventh Prime Minister. However, his tenure too was short-lived and he resigned on April 21, 1997, barely eleven months after assuming office. He was followed by Mr. IK Gujral as the next Prime Minister, who too remained in office only for a year from April 1997 till March 1998. Therefore, this frequent political change and the ensuing flux in the government, did affect the implementation of India's foreign policy priorities and her image in the international arena. Nonetheless, these internal constraints within the domestic political scenario of India never touched the then existing relations between New Delhi and Hanoi and India continued to engage with Vietnam and the seventh Indo-Vietnam Joint Commission meeting was held in New Delhi in February 1996 to continue the momentum of bilateral economic collaboration. Interestingly enough, Vietnam, at its Eighth National Party Congress of June-July 1996, discussed the potential for cooperation even with nations under 'different political regimes'. Therefore, it could be clearly understood that by 1996, Vietnam was whole-heartedly leaving behind ideological considerations in designing her foreign policy priorities, particularly under the leadership of Prime Minister Vo Van Kiet, who was thoroughly in favour of reforms in Vietnam. However, despite best efforts, political differences between Vietnam and China continued unabated over the South China Sea issue even when they were engaging with each other through their bilateral cooperative mechanisms to resolve the land border and the Gulf of Tonkin issues peacefully. In April 1996, controversy erupted following the signing of a 'business' contract between Petrovietnam and Conoco Vietnam Exploration and Production B.G, a US company, for the exploration and exploitation of oil plots '133 and 134' in the South China Sea. China viewed the contract as an encroachment on its sovereignty and its 'marine rights and interests'. In fact, the spokesman for the Chinese Foreign Ministry claimed that the 'entire' area encompassed by the contract was located within the area of the Wan'antan Bei- 21 contract between the China National Offshore Oil Corporation and Crestone Energy Corporation.[21] India being involved in the joint exploration in the South China Sea since 1988 was obviously concerned about the unfolding of such events and staunchly stood in favour of Vietnam, without withdrawing from her exploration activities.

Meanwhile, in July 1996, India joined the ASEAN Post Ministerial Conference (ASEAN PMC) at Jakarta, Indonesia, as a 'Full Dialogue Partner' of ASEAN. This gave India a further leverage in the affairs of the region. It is interesting to note that along with India, China and Russia too joined the ASEAN PMC at Jakarta, with ASEAN clearly giving out the message that it was trying to garner political and strategic stability in the region through such measures. Furthermore, two months later, in September 1996, keeping up with India's gradual upward mobility and increasing involvement in the region, the then Minister of External Affairs, Shri Inder Kumar Gujral expounded the policy of a greater Asian-regionalism cutting across borders, which eventually came to be known as the 'Gujral Doctrine'. This policy highlighted the necessity to forge closer friendship with the smaller neighbours of India on the basis of sovereign equality and non-interference with 'non-reciprocal magnanimity' towards these countries.[22] Moreover, he remarked: "We are of Asia and the people of Asia are nearer and closer to us than others. India is so situated that she is the pivot of western, southern and south-east Asia. In the past, her culture flowed to all these countries and they came to her in many ways. Those contacts are being renewed and the future is bound to see a closer union between India and Southeast Asia. Immediately beyond the SAARC circle lays the ASEAN, which is truly a circle of growing prosperity, built upon successful regional cooperation. It has emerged as a major centre of economic and political power which has turned it into one of the most significant networks of financial, technological and commercial resources into which India can integrate. India has been a sectoral dialogue partner of the ASEAN for some years, and, last year, the relationship was upgraded to the status of a Full Dialogue Partner. India is thus embarked on building a development partnership with ASEAN, and is looking forward to membership of the organization for Asia-Pacific Economic Cooperation (APEC)."[23]

In the meantime, despite the domestic political upheavals in India, the high level visits between India and Vietnam continued in 1997. In March 1997, Vietnamese PM Vo Van Kiet visited India. This was incidentally, for the first time since Vietnam became a member of the ASEAN in 1995 and India became a full dialogue partner of the ASEAN in 1996 that both these countries were meeting at the top-most level. At the time of this visit, both the countries discussed in details important regional and global issues and analysed the future prospects for the interaction at the ASEAN platform. Three agreements and an MoU were signed: first, Agreement on Trade and Economic Cooperation; second, Agreement on Promotion and Protection of Investment and thirdly, Credit Agreement; and third, an MoU on Cooperation in Environment and Forests.[24] Following this visit, shortly afterwards in that year itself, Shri Salman Khurshid visited Vietnam to co-chair the Eighth session of the Indo-Vietnam Joint Commission meeting to discuss measures to improve the bilateral trade statistics. However, the smooth and friendly political relations of Vietnam with India was much in contrast to its political ties with China at this period of time as frequent unpleasant incidents in the South China Sea continued, despite their beefed up bilateral economic linkages and increased high level visits since the normalisation of their ties in 1991. For instance, in April 1998, Vietnam officially complained on three occasions about Chinese plans to use the Paracel islands for tourism and reiterated Vietnam's sovereignty claims to both the Paracel and the Spratly archipelagoes. In early May, Vietnam publicised its release of 53 crewmen from four Chinese fishing vessels which had been seized by Vietnamese naval forces off the coast of Quang Binh Province in late March 1998. On 20 May, a spokesperson from the Vietnamese Ministry of Foreign Affairs stated that the Chinese ship Discovery 08 was operating in the Spratly archipelago and even 'deeply' into the Vietnam's continental shelf, and this was a violation of Vietnam's territorial sovereignty. On May 21, Zhu Bangzao, spokesman for the Ministry of Foreign Affairs, replied that China had 'indisputable' sovereignty over the Spratly islands and their surrounding areas. He went on to say that the presence of Chinese ships in the waters 'for normal' activity was within China's sovereign rights.[25] All these further proved to be a motivating factor for Vietnam for strengthening its fraternal ties with India.

In the meantime, continuing with sincere efforts to bolster India's cooperation with the Southeast Asian region, India joined countries like Bangladesh, Sri Lanka and Thailand in the forming of a new sub-regional organization, BISTEC (Bangladesh, India Sri Lanka, Thailand Economic Cooperation) in 1997 to beef up economic cooperation in the region. Later that year, Myanmar joined the organization and it came to be known as the BIMSTEC.

Interestingly enough, the year 1998 was extremely crucial for India because India conducted general elections once again in 1998 after the collapse of the government elected in 1996. The result of the 1998 general election was that no party or alliance could get a clear majority, but the BJP supported by some other political parties like the All India Anna Dravida Munnetra Kazhagam (AIADMK), which resulted in Mr. Atal Bihari Vajpayee becoming the Prime Minister of India again for the second time. However, eventually, this government too, was short-lived as AIADMK withdrew support soon after and the government collapsed in the latter half of 1999. Amidst this political tumult, under the leadership of the then Prime Minister of India, Atal Bihari Vajpayee, in May 1998, India exploded its nuclear devices on May 11 and 13. However, India's burgeoning presence in the region got a sudden jolt when it conducted the series of nuclear tests on May 11 and 13, 1998, at Pokhran. At such a crucial juncture, Vietnam along with Singapore and Thailand stood strongly beside India in realising her regional threat perception which motivated her to conduct the nuclear tests. However, Malaysia and Philippines were highly critical of India's nuclear blasts and the then President of Philippines, Joseph Estrada denounced India for the nuclear blasts, at the Fifth Summit of the ARF at Manila in July 1998 for sparking regional arms race and instability. This ARF Summit was the first multilateral Summit in which India comprehensively elucidated its nuclear policy in front of the US, China, Russia, Japan and Australia. In order to explain its position clearly, India was represented at the ARF Summit by the then Deputy Chairman of the Planning Commission, Mr. Jaswant Singh. He clearly pointed out: "The two basic tenets of India's nuclear strategic thought are that India's, indeed the entire world's national security interests are best served through a global, non-discriminatory disarmament. In the absence of that, a second tenet is equal and legitimate security for all."[26] Therefore, Jaswant Singh's deft diplomacy at the ARF Summit helped to mellow down the harsh criticisms against India's nuclear tests and along with the tacit support of Singapore, Thailand and Vietnam, India could successfully convince her justification to the majority of ASEAN members and the overwhelming ASEAN opinion that emerged was that such an important multilateral forum should not be used for punishing participants, rather it should be used for constructive and holistic discussions on the emerging security threats in the region. Thus, despite their 'grave concern', the ASEAN stopped short of imposing punitive actions against India for the nuclear tests. This was hailed as a success of India's diplomacy and a concrete outfit of India's prioritisation of her ties with the ASEAN in the post-1991 period. Therefore, the then Minister of State for External Affairs of India, Smt. Vasundhara Raje observed, "At the recently held PMC and ARF meetings, we found in ASEAN an echo of our concern for complete and general nuclear disarmament. The ASEAN has understood our 'right aim' in conducting nuclear tests and has been assured about our not posing any threat to it or to regional peace and security."[27] Therefore, the initial shivers and concern that was felt by the ASEAN in the initial days of the nuclear blasts by India could be addressed successfully and fortunately, it remained only a minor hiccup and did not leave a major scar in the Indo-ASEAN post-Cold War relations. But most importantly, China bitterly and harshly criticised India for this move. It accused that India exploding nuclear device reflected "an outrageous contempt for the common will of the international community," it further accused India of seeking "hegemony" in South Asia and called on the international community that it should adopt a common position in strongly demanding India to immediately stop its nuclear development program."[28] China's "all-weather friend" Pakistan retorted by carrying out five simultaneous underground nuclear tests on May 28, 1998. The US, under the then President, Bill Clinton, rebuked India by imposing economic sanctions on her. Though the 1998 nuclear tests by India and Pakistan attracted international criticism and sanctions, but China categorically criticised India not only that it was "infuriated and deeply hurt, not as much by the tests themselves" but by the justification that India construed a growing 'China threat' behind conducting the nuclear tests. The People's Daily noted that the US "needs to rely on India to restrict China. India needs to show its value to the United States by flexing its muscle toward China so that it could gain U.S military support and help raise its international status."[29] Immediately after the Pokhran II (May 1998), China piloted a resolution of the UN Security Council calling on India to terminate its weapons development programme and sign the Comprehensive Test Ban Treaty (CTBT) and the Nuclear Non-Proliferation Treaty (NPT). The joint declaration of the Shanghai Five condemned India for starting the nuclear race in South Asia. This was reiterated by China while it was punctilious in avoiding India's offer of 'no first use'. China positioned itself as "the concerned P-5 nuclear weapon state." It had successfully mobilised US to denounce India's nuclear status as the July 2, 1998, statement called for "close coordination between China and the US in achieving the turning point set by the resolution".[30]

As against such a scenario, in July 1998, Minister of State for External Affairs, Vasundhra Raje visited Vietnam to make known India's reasons and justifications for the Pokhran tests. Vietnam completely supported India, which was well appreciated by India and India remained grateful to Vietnam for this show of solidarity at a critical hour, which further consolidated their ties. Nguyen Dy Nien, who was then Minister of State in the Foreign Ministry of Vietnam, assured Vasundhra Raje that Vietnam "fully understood India's intentions and was appreciative of India's desire to restore a semblance of a balance in the Asian region."[31] Meanwhile, in July 1998, Vietnam for the first time published a White Paper on defence, in preparation for a meeting of the ASEAN Regional Forum. The 33-page document, entitled "Vietnam- Consolidating National Defence, Safeguarding the Homeland," stated that relations in Southeast Asia had improved but there were "potentially destabilizing situations, among them the disputes in the East Sea."[32] This amply proves that Vietnam's entanglement with China in the South China Sea was a major political headache for Hanoi and it considered it to be a significant 'destabilizing' issue in the region.

In the meantime, important events took place in India's political sector, with substantive ramifications for both her domestic and foreign policies. The year 1999 proved to be very crucial for India mainly for two reasons. Firstly, after successive governments that failed with their premature fall, finally in the year 1999 national general elections were conducted once again and the National Democratic Alliance (NDA) headed by Shri. Atal Bihari Vajpayee, came to power, which would be staying in power for the next five years, bringing the much-needed stability to the Indian polity. Secondly, the Kargil War broke out between India and Pakistan along the disputed Line of Control (LoC) in May 1999 and continued till July 1999, where India defeated Pakistan convincingly. However, it is to be noted that, China not only failed to condemn the attacks of its 'all-weather friend' Pakistan on Indian soil, it in fact, provided tacit support to Pakistan in the garb of an official 'neutral stance'. For instance, Brigadier Surinder Singh, who was the commander of the 121-Brigade in Kargil during the war has remarked, "Before and during Kargil War, the Chinese had inducted and manned heavy artillery guns in the K2 gun position in Pakistan-occupied Kashmir (PoK), close to Kargil, and provided fire support to Pakistani Army during the war."[33] In contrast to this, Vietnam extended its support to India and has maintained throughout that Kashmir is an 'integral part' of India. This crucial moral support to India proved to be very significant in further intensification of India's bilateral ties with Vietnam. Thus, by the end of this decade, Vietnam became member of the ASEAN, APEC and the ARF, normalised its ties with the US for pragmatic reasons shedding its ideological affinities, and supported India on crucial controversial issues, such as the nuclear explosion or the Kashmir issue, proving to be a reliable partner and a genuine friend of India in the region. In contrast, with China, both India and Vietnam were trying to engage more on the economic sector, but they developed glaring differences of opinion with Beijing in some very crucial political and strategic issues, such as, the frequent flaring up of the South China Sea issue, the Gulf of Tonkin and the disputed land border issues in case of Vietnam and the controversial Line of Actual Control (LAC), the Kashmir issue and some other unfolding political issues in case of India. Therefore, the above-discussed incidents of these years further brought Vietnam and India closer to each other than ever before, especially in the backdrop of the 'China factor' as a major reason which shaped their bilateral genial ties.

India, Vietnam and China, from 2000 to 2009: The Areas of Cooperation and Conflict

At the turn of the new millennium, renewed stress was given on revamping the Indo-Vietnam relations in the new global order. Interestingly enough, besides nurturing its friendly ties with India, Vietnam made its best efforts to resolve its outstanding disputes with China as well. Thus, on July 6, 2000, the two countries exchanged instruments of ratification in Beijing and Land Border Treaty, which was signed on December 30, 1999, officially entered into force, putting an amicable resolution to their age-old differences of opinion regarding their bilateral land border. Soon after, on December 25, 2000, the two countries signed in Beijing, the Sino-Vietnamese Agreement on

Demarcation of Territorial Waters, Exclusive Economic Zone (EEZ), and Continental Shelf in the Gulf of Tonkin and the Agreement on Fisheries Cooperation in the Gulf of Tonkin, once again putting an amicable end to a major discord between the two countries, right at the outset of the new century. However, several inherent differences remained between them which were matters of deep concern for Vietnam. For instance, despite the fact that both countries regarded intensification of their bilateral border trade, Vietnam started gradually feeling the adverse effects of the uncontrolled flooding of cheap Chinese products that started to choke its own local industries. Therefore, in May 2001, in order to manage the border trade and to check smuggling, the Vietnamese Ministry of Trade issued a regulation declaring that import and export of goods between the two countries must be processed through designated gates or checkpoints that had been agreed upon by both sides.[34] Around this time, India along with Cambodia, Laos, Myanmar, Thailand and Vietnam formed the Mekong-Ganga Cooperation Initiative (MGCI) in November 2000 as an important sub-regional organization to cooperate on crucial issues of tourism, culture, education and transport connectivity for furthering mutual collaboration in the region under the tutelage of the ASEAN principles as the guiding force and thus, to elevate her 'Look East' policy to a higher pedestal. Furthermore, Vietnam conducted the Tenth session of the India-Vietnam Joint Commission for Economic, Scientific and Technical Cooperation, in Hanoi from November 6-8, 2000. The meeting was co-chaired by HE Mr. Nguyen Dy Nien, Minister of Foreign Affairs, from the Vietnamese side and Mr. Jaswant Singh, Minister of External Affairs from the Indian side. It is significant to note here that India at this time was undergoing a major transformation in her foreign policy priorities as it was gradually warming up to the US after the lull in their relations since the 1998 Pokhran tests conducted by India. In 2000, US President Bill Clinton paid a visit to India and the strategic goal of the trip was to stress that its policy in South Asia was no longer steered by cold war concerns, because now there were heavy issues of convergence between the two such as the problem of terrorism and the development of an equitable global economic order. Equally important was the message Clinton delivered in Pakistan warning Islamabad that the line of control could not be transformed by force, thus echoing India's policy that the LoC's sanctity should be upheld. The fact that Clinton spent only five hours in Pakistan as opposed to five days in India was also meant to convey the importance Washington accorded to India. The trip was largely symbolic with clues as to the direction the relationship may take in the years to come.[35] During this time, Vietnam was also warming up to the US as both of them were painstakingly negotiating the terms of the United States-Vietnam Bilateral Trade Agreement (BTA), as the US were trying to find its foothold in Asia once again, in the new millennium.

In the meantime, immediately after achieving some stability in the government after successive failed governments, the then Prime Minister of India, Shri Atal Bihari Vajpayee paid a visit to Vietnam in January 2001, thus revealing the importance that India has always attached to Vietnam. Both sides pledged to reinvigorate their ties after they had lost out on precious time owing to unstable internal politics in India in the major part of 1990s. Vajpayee's official visit to Vietnam was of four days and both sides signed documents of cooperation including a protocol for extending the cultural cooperation program, a Memorandum of Understanding (MoU) for atomic energy cooperation for peace and a tourism agreement. Vajpayee said India was always ready to share its experience with Vietnam in IT and pharmacy and hoped that the two countries would tighten cooperation at multilateral forums, such as the ASEAN Regional Forum and the UN. He pledged sincere efforts to enhance India's bilateral cooperation with Vietnam regarding concerted coordination in regional and international forums, including the Non-Aligned Movement (NAM), the ASEAN Post Ministerial Council and the ASEAN Regional Forum (ARF), for peace, stability and development in the Asia-Pacific region. Both sides pledged "a constant consolidation and development" of their comprehensive bilateral cooperative ties. He expressed his admiration for Vietnam's progress in renovation and said that the ongoing economic reforms in India and Vietnam would help both the countries to identify promising fields for further economic cooperation. In return, the Vietnamese side, led by Prime Minister Phan Van Khai assured the Indian leadership of Vietnam's whole-hearted support to India's efforts to join the UN as a permanent member of the Security Council and the APEC forum.

Meanwhile, on April 1, 2001, the very crucial Hainan Island incident occurred in the South China Sea, at a decisive time when both India and Vietnam were warming up to the US politically. This happened when a United States Navy EP-3E ARIES II intelligence aircraft and People's Liberation Army Navy's (PLAN) J-8II interceptor fighter jet collided with each other on the Hainan Island in South China Sea. It was reported that the US intelligence aircraft was intercepted by the PRC's fighter jet and it forced the US' intelligence aircraft to make an emergency landing and the crew was severely interrogated. This created a diplomatic row between the US and the PRC, the latter expressing its dislike over the increasing presence of the US in the disputed region.

In the intervening time, continuing with the momentum of increased high-level visits between India and Vietnam, a delegation led by Deputy Chairman of the Planning Commission, Shri K.C Pant attended the meetings of ASEAN PMC (Post Ministerial Conference), ARF and MGC held in Hanoi during July 24–28, 2001, where both sides utilised the opportunity to review bilateral relations, regional issues and other matters of mutual interest. Following this, the Minister of Foreign Affairs of Vietnam, Mr. Nguyen Dy Nien, paid an official visit to India from September 11–16, 2001. During the visit, both sides signed an Agreement on Cooperation between Doordarshan and Vietnam TV and an Agreement on Reciprocal Exchange of Plots of Land for the Embassies of the two countries. While the External Affairs Minister and the Vietnamese Foreign Minister were exchanging ideas of cooperation, they zeroed down on the necessary measures to further strengthen bilateral relations, particularly in the fields of trade, investment, credit, Information Technology as well as close and effective coordination within the framework of the

ASEAN, ARF and the MGC.[36] Simultaneously, the ASEAN was constantly negotiating the 'Declaration on the Conduct of Parties in the South China Sea' (DOC) with China and finally, signed the same in November 2002, which promised to lessen the spiralling tensions between the disputing parties in the South China Sea. As a result, for the time-being, both Vietnam and India could heave a sigh of relief as far as the South China Sea issue was concerned. Meanwhile, satisfied with the ongoing pace of 'Look East' policy, New Delhi decided to further upgrade its ties with the Southeast Asian region and therefore, it commenced the phase II of its 'Look East' policy in 2003, the aims and objectives of which got crystallised in the speech of the then External Affairs Minister Shri Yashwant Sinha at Harvard University on September 29, 2003, where speaking on the topic of "Resurgent India in Asia," he remarked: "A cooperative future global order will inevitably require full Asian participation. With its increasing weight in the world economy, Asia holds the key to collective global prosperity and security. Asia's contribution to world output has doubled since 1950. Both IMF and the World Bank consider that Asia will continue to power global growth in the coming years. We require, therefore, to advance the principles of democracy, development and dialogue, on the basis of respect for pluralism and national sovereignty, as the guiding principles of Asian and global progress… Guided by the vision, India is working vigorously to strengthen its relations with its Asian partners-with China, Japan, Southeast Asia, West Asian countries and Central Asian neighbours…Reaching beyond South Asia, East and Southeast Asia have remained a natural focus of India's foreign and trade policy. …we share land or maritime boundaries, not just with our South Asian neighbours and China, but also with several ASEAN countries, such as Myanmar, Thailand and Indonesia. Our historical and civilizational ties also extend to Japan. In the past, India's engagement with much of Asia, including Southeast and East Asia was built on an idealistic conception of Asian brotherhood, based on shared experiences of colonialism and of cultural ties. The rhythm of the region today is determined, however, as much by trade, investment and production as by history and culture. That is what motivates our decade-old 'Look East' policy. Already, the region accounts for 45 percent of our external trade. The first phase of India's 'Look East' policy was ASEAN-centred and focused primarily on trade and investment linkages. The new phase of this policy is characterised by an expanded definition of 'East', extending from Australia to East Asia with ASEAN at its core. The new phase also marks a shift from trade to wider economic and security issues, including joint efforts to protect the sea-lanes and coordinate counter-terrorism activities."[37] Moreover, right at the inception of India's 'Look East' phase- II, India signed the Treaty of Amity and Cooperation in the Second ASEAN-India Summit in Bali in October 2003, clearly giving out the signal that India was willing to participate in the affairs of the region in a peaceful and cooperative mindset.

Boosted by such developments, the high-level meetings between India and Vietnam continued this year and significantly enough, the General Secretary of the Communist Party of Vietnam (CPV), Mr. Nong Duc Manh paid a visit to India from April 29 to May 2, 2003. He was accompanied by a high level delegation and called on the President of India, met with the PM and participated in the delegation-level talks. During the visit, the two countries signed a Joint Declaration on the Framework of Comprehensive Cooperation for intensifying cooperation in the 21st century. Moreover, the PM announced recycling of the credit repaid by Vietnam up to US$ 20 million and softening of the repayment terms of the ongoing credit lines.[38] Interestingly, at this time, besides intensifying its cooperation with Vietnam and the US, India was trying to strike a balance in the power equations in the region by wooing China as well, particularly as the new leadership, Hu Jintao as the President and Wen Jiabao as the Prime Minister, assumed power in 2003. Accordingly, the then PM of India, Shri Atal Bihari Vajpayee went on to visit the new leadership in China from June 22-27, 2003. Both sides for the first time issued a signed Joint Declaration which laid down a roadmap to build a 'qualitatively new relationship' and build up a 'long-term constructive and cooperative partnership'. They were of the agreement that the then existing global geo-political situation demanded both India and China to work together for the stability and prosperity of the region. Another vital result of the visit was the decision to appoint Special Representatives from both sides to explore the framework of a boundary settlement from the political perspective of the overall bilateral relationship at an earliest date. Both India and China were of the opinion that these two South Asian giants should increasingly cooperate with each other on international podiums and explore possibilities of cooperation in regional and multilateral forums, on the basis of identified common interests and overlapping concerns on issues relating to WTO, energy security, environmental problems, etc., especially as the champions of the causes of the developing world vis-à-vis the developed countries.[39] Therefore, at this time, especially after the signing of the DOC in 2002, India's and Vietnam's relations with China started to warm up in 2003 and the promise of durable peace was hoped to be coming to fruition.

In the following year, that is in 2004, there was change of guards again at the level of national politics and the Indian National Congress-led United Progressive Alliance (UPA), headed by Dr. Manmohan Singh as the Prime Minister came to power in the month of May. Soon after, the then External Affairs Minister, Shri. K. Natwar Singh visited Hanoi from October 16-18, 2004, to commemorate the 50th anniversary of PM Pandit Nehru's visit to Hanoi in October 1954 after the liberation of Hanoi from French occupation and his meeting with President Ho Chi Minh on October 17, 1954. During this visit, both sides also signed a Plan of Action for 2004-06 for implementing the Joint Declaration on Comprehensive Cooperation Framework between India and Vietnam that was signed in May 2003 during the visit of the General Secretary of Communist Party of Vietnam to India.[40] At another level, in the Third ASEAN-India Summit of November 2004, India and ASEAN entered into the ASEAN-India Partnership for Peace, Progress and Shared Prosperity for bolstering their overall cooperation in the coming years. In fact, in 2004 Dr. Manmohan Singh participated in the 3rd ASEAN-India Summit at Vientiane, Laos, where the ASEAN acknowledged and highly appreciated the signing of the

"ASEAN-India Partnership of Peace, Progress and Shared Prosperity," India's accession to the Treaty of Amity and Cooperation in Southeast Asia, and the adoption of the ASEAN-India Joint Declaration for Cooperation to Combat International Terrorism. This reflected our determination and commitment to move the relationship forward in a substantive, comprehensive and purposeful manner contributing to regional peace and stability, and shared economic prosperity and development. Moreover, the ASEAN leaders expressed their appreciation to India for implementation of projects under the IAI, its support to establish an Entrepreneurship Development Centre (EDC) in each CLMV, aimed at promoting capacity building in the areas of entrepreneurship and skilled labour development and fostering SMEs, trade and investment in the respective countries and the region.[41] (The first EDC was opened in Vientiane during the 10th ASEAN Summit).

However, after the DOC of 2002, in early 2005, the South China Sea issue once again started to flare up when on January 8, it came to be known that the Chinese ships have fired upon Vietnamese fishing boats from Thanh Hoa province, in which nine people were killed and one ship with eight people was detained on the Hainan Island. Though the Chinese Foreign Ministry claimed that they were pirates, no such convincing proof could be obtained to substantiate such a claim. Interestingly, while the new leadership in China was getting embroiled in such conflicts with Vietnam, it was mending its ties with India at the same time, perhaps to wean away India from Vietnam's group of friends and allies in the South China Sea issue. For instance, China raised its relations with India to 'Strategic and Cooperative Partnership for Peace and Prosperity' in the year 2005 when Chinese Premier Wen Jiabao visited New Delhi in April 2005. The two Prime Ministers signed a Joint Statement on April 11, 2005. The Joint Statement reflected the consensus that India-China relations transcended bilateral issues and had acquired a global and strategic perspective. In this context, it was agreed to further develop and diversify bilateral relations and to resolve outstanding differences in a proactive manner without letting them come in the way of continued development of relations.[42] This clearly implied that the relationship had been upgraded from a merely bilateral level to a global level, signalling an important shift in China's policies towards India and at the same time, proving China's increasing recognition of India's big power status and growing influence in the region.[43] Therefore, the visit concluded with the signing of the 'Agreement on the Political Parameters and Guiding Principles for the Settlement of the India-China Boundary Question.' This marked the successful conclusion of the first phase of the work of the Special Representatives who were tasked to explore the framework of a boundary settlement from the political perspective of the overall bilateral relationship. Thus, the leadership of both sides at this time was revealing genuine concerted efforts to amicably resolve the outstanding bilateral challenges so that they could come together as a united force to take on the global challenges. This landmark visit and the pro-activeness of the Chinese leadership to reach out to the Indian leaders and resolve the outstanding bilateral disputes has to be interpreted with the changing geostrategic reality as its backdrop. This is because, in 2005, the Indian economy was on the upswing and its naval power appeared robust. Moreover, Delhi's relations with all major powers like Russia, Japan and the European Union were warm and its Look East policy was being gradually welcomed by China's small neighbours. In addition, India's relations with the US were at their apex: The US Secretary of State, Condoleezza Rice, on her maiden visit to India in March 2005, had announced that the US would help India become a major power (this eventually led to the signing of the July 2005 Indo-US joint statement whose high point was the civil nuclear deal).[44] Therefore, the PRC was definitely concerned about India's emerging profile and the growing Indo-US strategic partnership in the region. Also, at this time, India reached the next major milestone in India's 'Look East' policy when it joined the East Asian Summit (EAS) in 2005. The EAS is a unique Leaders-led forum of 18 countries of the Asia-Pacific region formed to further the objectives of regional peace, security and prosperity. Since being established in 2005, it has evolved as a forum for strategic dialogue and cooperation on political, security and economic issues of common regional concern and has been playing an important role in the regional architecture. Its members include the 10 ASEAN Member States: Australia, China, India, Japan, New Zealand, Republic of Korea, Russia, and the USA. EAS is an initiative of ASEAN and the concept of an East Asia Grouping was first promoted in 1991 by the then Malaysian Prime Minister Mahathir bin Mohamad. However, the final report of the East Asian Study Group in 2002, established by the ASEAN+3 countries (China, Japan, and RoK) recommended EAS as an ASEAN-led development limited to the ASEAN+3 countries only. Fortunately enough, the ASEAN Ministerial Meeting (AMM) held in Vientiane on July 26, 2005, welcomed the participation of ASEAN, China, Japan, RoK, Australia, India and New Zealand in the first EAS. USA and Russia were formally included as members of the EAS at the 6th EAS Summit held in Bali, Indonesia, on November 19, 2011. The relevance of EAS was aptly summarised by our PM, who in his speech at the 9th EAS, held in Myanmar in November 2014, stated, "No other forum brings together such a large collective weight of global population, youth, economy, and military strength. Nor is any other forum so critical for peace, stability and prosperity in the Asia-Pacific and the world."[45] The EAS has earmarked six priority areas of regional cooperation within its fold, namely Environment and Energy, Education, Finance, Global Health Issues and Pandemic Diseases, Natural Disaster Management and ASEAN Connectivity. Since India joined the organization, it has been playing a leading role and taking active interest in forging cooperation in each of these sectors.

However, despite best intentions, not much headway could be made and the areas of discord of Vietnam and India vis-à-vis China, such as the South China Sea issue in case of Vietnam and the disputed border issue in case of India, remained lurking behind waiting to be flared up any moment. For instance, in April 2006, a few months before President Hu Jintao's visit to India in November 2006, Sun Yaxi, the Chinese Ambassador in Delhi, created a stir by referring to India's Arunachal Pradesh as South Tibet and a part of China. This created uproar in the Indian Parliament for some time.

Therefore, in the meantime, India and Vietnam continued to strengthen their bilateral high-level visits, and in March 2007, the Speaker of the Lok Sabha of India, Shri Somnath Chatterjee paid a visit to Vietnam to take stock of the then existing political ties between the two countries. Both sides expressed the desire to further cooperate in more fields, moving beyond the traditional areas, and beef up bilateral cooperation in maritime industry, science and technology, software, education-training, and marine produce. Moreover, the Vietnamese side expressed their happiness about the emerging profile of India, particularly in the economic sphere and urged the leaders to intensify the cooperation of the two countries to a level commensurate with the potentialities. Shri. Somnath Chatterjee in return, thanked the Vietnamese leaders for their unwavering support to India and India's causes in the international podiums.

Around the same time in the year 2007, the ASEAN established another multilateral regional organization known as the ASEAN Defence Ministers' Meeting, with the prime motive of cooperating in the realms of humanitarian and disaster relief. Thereafter, the Second ADMM meeting in Singapore adopted the Concept Paper of the ADMM which was called for the establishment of the ADMM-Plus which would be developed as a platform of the ASEAN and its eight Dialogue Partners, to deliberate upon issues of defence cooperation for peace, prosperity and stability in the region. This was a positive development and of keen interest to India. Incidentally, the historic visit of the Prime Minister of Vietnam, Mr. Nguyen Tan Dung, to India took place from July 4-6 2007. During this visit, the two Prime Ministers signed a landmark Joint Declaration elevating the bilateral relationship to a 'strategic partnership.'[46] To divulge further details, it can be said that, India and Vietnam adopted a 33-point Joint Declaration on Strategic Partnership that mapped out cooperation in five major areas: political, defence and security cooperation; closer economic cooperation and commercial engagement; science and technology cooperation, cultural and technical cooperation and multilateral and regional cooperation. The Joint Declaration on Strategic Partnership set out six areas for political, defence and security cooperation: (1) strategic dialogue at vice ministerial level; (2) defence supplies, joint projects, training cooperation and intelligence exchanges; (3) exchange visits between their defence and security establishments; (4) capacity building , technical assistance and information sharing with particular attention to security of sea lanes, anti-piracy, prevention of pollution and search and rescue; (5) counter terrorism and cyber security; and (6) non-traditional security. Since 2007, defence cooperation has included high-level visits, an annual Defence Strategy Dialogue and naval port visits. Therefore, it can be convincingly argued that this "strategic cooperation" with India was planned by Vietnam. **First**, to elevate the time-tested and friendly ties between the two countries to the position which it actually deserved, and **second**, this "strategic cooperation" agreement would give Vietnam and India the necessary legitimate medium to intensify their cooperation in the wake of the increasing "aggressiveness" of China in the region, particularly in the South China Sea, so that this agreement could prove to be the necessary bulwark against any adverse change in the geopolitical scenario in the area.

Interestingly enough, in this decade, at a time when Vietnam was officially coming closer to India than ever before, it was warming up to the US to an unprecedented level as well, perhaps to counter the 'China threat' and to 're-balance' the region, which the US was trying to do officially and Vietnam along with India, far more tacitly. The renewed interest of the US in Asia was no longer a secret and its policy of "re-balancing," later re-coined as "pivot to Asia" policy under the Obama administration, was not taken nicely by China, who in turn, under the leadership of Hu Jintao, started to increasingly propagate the concept of "Asia for Asians". Not surprisingly though, the US started to appreciate greater involvement of India as a counter-force to China. Accordingly, both India and Vietnam did not hesitate to warm up its ties with the US, and as indelible proofs the historic Vietnam-USA Bilateral Trade Agreement (BTA) of 2001, which removed several trade barriers and intensified their trade ties, and the landmark Indo-US Civil Nuclear Deal of 2008, may be cited. Moreover, in 2007, both the United States and Vietnam expressed their wishes to elevate the bilateral relationship into a strategic level. In a web chat via the VietNamNet online newspaper in February, US ambassador to Vietnam Michael Marine noted that US-Vietnam relations had become ever more strategic in the last three years and the United States would support the building of closer ties with Vietnam. He also said of "the steady convergence of the strategic objectives of Vietnam and the United States" in a speech at the Chicago Council for Global Affairs in March. President Nguyen Minh Triet repeatedly said during his trip to the United States in June that "the Vietnamese people want to have solidarity (doan ket) and friendship with the American people." He emphasised that Vietnam regarded the United States as one of its most important partners and wished to build a friendly relationship with the United States on the basis of common long-term strategic interests.[47]

As these two countries were stepping up their engagement with the US much to China's dislike, several incidents started to happen which further soured up Vietnam's and India's ties with China. For instance, Sino-Vietnamese relations in 2007 were overshadowed by tensions related to territorial disputes in the South China Sea and Vietnam's conduct towards China. During Parliament chairman Nguyen Phu Trong's visit in early April, China lodged strong complaints against a US$ 2 billion gas pipeline project between Petro Vietnam and British Petroleum (BP) near the Spratlys that Vietnam said had been implemented since 2000 and lay within the bounds of its exclusive economic zones and continental shelf as well as Vietnam's plans to hold local elections on the Spratlys. Less than two weeks later Vietnam set up three administrative units on the Spratly Islands, while in June BP suspended its pipeline project due to the dispute. On July 9, just days after India and Vietnam declared that they were strategic partners, Chinese navy vessels fired on Vietnamese fishing boats in disputed waters near the Paracel Islands, causing one death and several injuries. Throughout the year, there were reports of several Chinese assaults on Vietnamese fishing boats in waters claimed by both nations. Furthermore, China pressured Vietnam to deny visa to a number of Taiwanese leaders and officials and vigorously protested against the Vietnamese media's reports on tainted food and counterfeit goods from China. Since China failed to act against other countries that granted visa to the very same Taiwanese and with the local media reporting the same stories, such moves reinforced the sense that China treated Vietnam as a second-class friend. Vietnam lodged verbal protests against China's planting of sovereignty markers and promotion of tourism in the Paracels (in January and August) and China's military drills and administrative plans in the South China Sea (in November). The last move—China's plan to create an administrative region to manage three archipelagoes, including the Paracels and the Spratlys—triggered a series of street protests in Vietnam.[48]

With India too, during this time, China chose to take a belligerent posture by denying a visa to then Chief Minister of Arunachal Pradesh on the basis of their argument that as the state of Arunachal Pradesh was in fact, a part of the People's Republic of China, the Chief Minister of Arunachal Pradesh would not require a visa to visit his own country. This created a major uproar in the diplomatic circles and in the Parliament of India, bringing back the bitter memories of Sun Yaxi's statement that had created a similar uproar in 2006. The government of India officially maintained that Arunachal Pradesh was an 'integral part' of India, but the protests refused to die and India's bilateral ties with China continued to nose-dive. Therefore, when the heinous terrorist attacks took place in Mumbai in November 2008, it was condemned by most countries of the world including Vietnam and the US, but China neither did throw its weight behind India in investigating the attacks, as was done by the US or France, nor did it strongly condemn Pakistan, its 'all-weather friend' in perpetrating such attacks on the Indian soil.

Interestingly enough, barely two days after the dastardly Mumbai attacks, the then President of India, Smt. Pratibha Devisingh Patil met with the Prime Minister of Vietnam, Mr. Nguyen Tan Dung, as she was officially visiting the country during the terrorist attacks. During her presence on the Vietnamese soil, on November 27, 2008, Vietnam's Ministry of Foreign Affairs spokesman Le Dung remarked that Vietnam was 'furious' over the vicious terrorist attacks and that, Vietnam was staunchly opposing all terrorist activities in any form, and most importantly he said that Vietnam sincerely felt India's loss. President Patil also remarked that as a part of India's 'Look East' policy, India had been endeavouring to forge closer ties with countries of the ASEAN, including Vietnam and that the friendship of these two countries was historical and traditional and that India had admired the phenomenal economic growth of Vietnam since the introduction of domestic economic reforms or Doi Moi since 1986. Furthermore, she expressed her desire to link Mumbai and Ho Chi Minh City as sister cities for further economic cooperation.

Early next year, that is, around March 2009, the South China Sea dispute once again flared up when the Pentagon reported that a US surveillance ship had been harassed by the Chinese ships. The report stated that the USNS Impeccable was 'aggressively maneuvered' by the Chinese ships while it was conducting routine operations in international waters and was asked to leave the place immediately by the Chinese ships. The US expressed concern about freedom of navigation according to international laws and condemned Chinese aggression, even flouting global norms. Thus, to boost Vietnam confidence, incidents of Chinese aggressive posture in the South China Sea were being increasingly reported by the Pentagon as well.

Therefore, continuing with the efforts to strengthen Vietnam's political and strategic ties with India as a fortification against Chinese advances, Vice President of Vietnam, Nguyen Thi Doan paid a five-day visit to India in September 2009 at the invitation of Indian Vice President Shri Mohammad Hamid Ansari. This visit further strengthened and developed its traditional and comprehensive partnership with India and the Vietnamese Vice President once again reiterated Vietnam's support for India's bid to run for a permanent seat at the UNSC. Moreover, she requested the Indian leadership to approve the granting of a market economy status to Vietnam, to which, the then Foreign Minister of India, Shri Krishna assured them in affirmative terms.

Soon after, that is in October 2009, Dr. Manmohan Singh paid a visit to Arunachal Pradesh, to which China raised their objections as the PRC continued to regard Arunachal Pradesh as a part of their territory. Moreover, it is to be noted that around this time, China had started the practice of issuing stapled visas, not regular visas, to those born in Arunachal Pradesh and Jammu and Kashmir which created a severe diplomatic tiff between New Delhi and Beijing. Further fuel was added to the fire when in August 2010, the Chinese government refused to issue visa to the Indian Army's Northern Command chief, Lieutenant-General BS Jaswal, who was about to visit China as part of a high-level military delegation. The official reason that was put forth by China for not giving visa to him was that he was the top Army Commander in Jammu and Kashmir, which according to China was a disputed region. As a result, waves of severe criticism lashed out in Indian diplomatic circles and as a fallout of this incident, India temporarily cancelled all defence exchanges with China and subsequently, refused to permit two Chinese defence officials to visit New Delhi, giving out a clear message of non-tolerance towards such vicious measures on the part of China. Therefore, it is evident that during this phase, unlike India-Vietnam relations, in which the China factor between these two countries brought them closer to each other, both India and Vietnam continued to have political differences with China, despite regular exchanges of ideas at the highest political level and the regular meetings of several bilateral cooperative frameworks. Whether this trend continued in the next decade or not, will be analysed in the following section.

India-Vietnam Conviviality and the 'China Factor': 2010–2015

At the very onset of the following decade, as a very bold gesture on Vietnam's part, it participated in the 'Milan' naval exercises which involve the countries of the United States, Japan and India as permanent members and several other countries like Australia and Singapore as non-permanent members, and it usually takes place off the coast of Malabar. This naval exercise started in 1992 and indulges in cooperative multilateral activities, including fighter combat operations, anti-piracy drills with the prime motive to secure the Indian Ocean region. Vietnam's participation in such a naval exercise led by the US and active participation of India, which had been complaining of Chinese encirclement in the Indian Ocean region through the "String of Pearls" theory, definitely antagonised China Nevertheless it was a landmark event in Indo-Vietnam bilateral political relations. Interestingly enough, another positive development was noted in this year when the first ADMM-Plus was convened in Hanoi, Vietnam, on October 12, 2010, and the meeting was chaired by General Phung Quang Thanh, Minister of National Defense of the SRV. Significantly enough, it was attended by the Defense Ministers and Representatives of Defence Ministers from ten ASEAN Member States and eight ASEAN Dialogue Partners (Australia, China, India, Japan, RoK, New Zealand, Russia, and the US). The Meeting emphasised that cooperation within the framework of ADMM–Plus should follow the ASEAN principles of respect for independence and sovereignty, non-interference in internal affairs of Member States, consultation and consensus. South China Sea should be resolved by peaceful means in conformity with the spirit of the Declaration on the Conduct of Parties in the South China Sea (DOC) of 2002 and recognized principles of international law, including UNCLOS 1982. Five areas for cooperation were earmarked for future collaboration, such as, humanitarian assistance and disaster relief, maritime security, military medicine, counter-terrorism and Peace-Keeping Operations (PKO). Therefore, this was a major achievement in India's 'Look East' Policy in its second phase, whereby India directed got involved in multilateral defence cooperation with the countries of the region and beyond.

Continuing with the efforts to further consolidate India's genial ties with Vietnam, Mr. Truong Tan Sang, President of Vietnam, paid a State visit to India from 11-13 October, 2011. It is extremely significant to note that President Sang chose India for his first official visit to a non-ASEAN country after assuming office and he was accompanied by the Deputy PM and several Ministers, besides a large number of business leaders. Significantly enough, during this visit, several agreements and

MoUs were signed, such as the Extradition Treaty, MoU on India-Vietnam Friendship Year 2012, Agreement on Cooperation between Petro Vietnam and ONGC Videsh Ltd, Cultural Exchange Program 2011-14 and Protocol of Cultural Activities in India-Vietnam Friendship Year 2012, MoU between Vietnam Airlines and Jet Airways for comprehensive cooperation including commencing direct flights in the near future.[49] Most importantly, during this visit, pacts between Indian and Vietnamese state-owned oil companies were concluded for further joint exploration and supply of oil and gas to these two countries. In this regard it is to be noted that since 1988, the ONGC Videsh Limited (OVL) had been involved in exploration in Vietnam in offshore Block 6.1. Moreover, since 2006, India has involved itself in Blocks 127 and 128, notwithstanding the severe wrath and criticisms of China. In 2011, once again, Beijing issued fresh warnings to OVL that its exploration activities off the Vietnam coast in the South China Sea was contrary to the peace and tranquility of the region and in contravention with international laws. China practically claims the entire South China Sea region as its own citing the 'nine dash/dotted lines', but Vietnam and India has summarily refuted China's claim that Blocks 127 and 128 in Phu Khanh Basin lie within its jurisdiction by highlighting the provisions of the United Nations Convention on the Law of the Sea (UNCLOS) III 1982, where the concepts of territorial waters, continental shelf, exclusive economic zone, high seas, etc., are clearly defined in unambiguous terms and as per the UNCLOS 1982 provisions[50] Blocks 127 and 128 certainly fall within Vietnam's jurisdiction. Following the visit of Mr. Sang, the Indian Prime Minister met with Chinese Premier Wen Jiabao in Bali in November 2011, and during this meeting, China raised its concerns on India's hydrocarbon exploration and exploitation projects in the South China Sea off the coast of Vietnam. The Indian Government clearly conveyed that such activity by Indian companies is purely commercial in nature. Thus, India's involvement in the disputed South China Sea region at the behest of Vietnam despite China's harshest criticisms and severest ire is certainly a reflection of India's renewed confidence not only in its own capabilities, but also in its relations with Vietnam in the second phase of her 'Look East' policy. Meanwhile, throughout 2011, Vietnam continued to clash with China in the South China Sea and as a result, their bilateral political ties reached the nadir. For instance, on May 26, 2011, Chinese maritime patrol vessels clashed with Vietnamese Binh Minh 02 oil and gas survey ship in the disputed waters and the Vietnamese remarked that the Chinese vessels had intentionally cut the Vietnamese survey ship's cables in Vietnamese waters and this incident led to severe demonstrations and protests against China in Hanoi and Ho Chi Minh City. Once again, on June 9, 2011, Chinese fishery patrol vessels clashed with a Norwegian-flagged seismic conducting ship hired by Vietnam's PetroVietnam, within Vietnam's Exclusive Economic Zone and Vietnam once again, alleged that the cables of the vessels have been deliberately cut by China. Such frequent news of clashes in the South China Sea flouting international norms and jeopardising freedom of navigation certainly made India, which regarded Straits of Malacca to be well within its sphere of influence, more concerned about the happenings in the region.

Meanwhile, the year 2012 was celebrated as the India-Vietnam Friendship Year to commemorate the fortieth anniversary of full diplomatic relations and the fifth anniversary of the establishment of Strategic Partnership. While continuing with its aggressive posture on South China Sea issue, the Central Military Commission of China made its decision in July 2012 of building military garrisons in the Sansha prefecture-level city in the Hainan province through which the PRC administers the disputed area. Since the entire area is disputed, the move drew criticisms from all quarters, including the United States, Vietnam, Philippines and India.

From 14-17 January 2013, Vice President of India Shri M. Hamid Ansari visited Vietnam in connection with the closing ceremony of the India-Vietnam Friendship Year 2012 and highlighted the traditional friendly ties shared by these two countries.[51] While such friendly intercourse between India and Vietnam were taking place, the Depsang Valley incident between India and China was gradually unfolding. In

April 2013, a contingent of Chinese PLA troops breached the Line of Actual Control (LAC) and set up camp in the Depsang plains, in Daulat Beg Oldi near the Akshai Chin-Ladakh area. The Indian side responded by setting up their own military camps nearby and following hasty diplomatic parleys between the two sides, the matter could be finally resolved and both sides withdrew ultimately. However, this incident shook up the Indian South bloc just days before Chinese Premier Le Keqiang's visit to India and was condemned by all quarters. China at that time did not officially remark about the incident but the Indian Government maintained that such incidents took place owing to 'differing perceptions of the LAC'. Thus, this incident once again reminded India of the grim realities of its relations with China. Incidents like these between India and China at regular intervals have proved to be reminders to the Indian side how important it is to cultivate better ties with other regional and even extra-regional powers, who are concerned about such a 'peaceful rise' of China. Following this incident, the General Secretary of the Communist Party of Vietnam, Mr. Nguyen Phu Trong, paid a State visit to India from November 19 to 22, 2013. During this visit, Prime Minister Dr. Manmohan Singh held delegation-level talks with the General Secretary. The General Secretary called on the President and met Vice President, Speaker of the Lok Sabha Smt. Meira Kumar, External Affairs Minister Shri Salman Khurshid and leaders of political parties. A joint statement issued on the occasion emphasised the strengthening and deepening of the Strategic Partnership between the two countries. Crucial documents were signed during the visit on Air Services Agreement; MoU for the setting up of the Indira Gandhi High tech Crime Lab (IGHCL) in Hanoi; Agreement on Protection of Classified Information between the Ministries of Finance; Cooperation Agreement between Hanoi National University and India Council for Scientific and Industrial Research; MoU on Cooperation between Indian Institute of Management Bangalore and HCM National Academy of Politics and Public Administration; MoU between Ministry of Industry and Trade and Tata Power Limited on Development of Long Phu 2 Thermal Power Project in Soc Trang, Vietnam.

Meanwhile, another event took place which further strained the relations between India and China and that was related to the Indian President's visit to Arunachal Pradesh on November 29-30, 2013. At the time of this visit, on November 30, 2013, Chinese Ministry of Foreign Affairs' spokesperson said that China's position on the dispute in the eastern section of China-India border is consistent and clear-cut and added that India should refrain from taking actions that complicate the boundary question.[52] In this regard, while answering to a question raised by Shri Neeraj Shekhar and Shri Yashvir Singh in the Lok Sabha, regarding whether China has expressed reservation on the visit of India's Head of State to Arunachal Pradesh and the government's reaction thereto, Smt. Preneet Kaur, Minister of State in the Ministry of External Affairs said, "the fact that Arunachal Pradesh is an integral and inalienable part of India was clearly conveyed to the Chinese at the highest level."[53] Thus, differing perceptions of the LAC and disputing territorial claims by China on the Indian soil, continued to mar their bilateral political relations at a time when Vietnam was clashing with China in the troubled South China Sea waters. This acted as an impetus for the two countries to strengthen their bilateral strategic and political cooperation.

The year 2014 was historic in the domain of Indian political process. The NDA government again came to power by replacing the UPA government and where the BJP captured the majority seats in the Parliament, with the promise as mentioned in the Election Manifesto, of reviving India's stature in the Southeast Asian region by creating a web of allies to mutually further India's interests, by adopting "proactive diplomacy" to spread India's soft power, focusing on the "spiritual, cultural and philosophical dimensions" of it, by reviving Brand India with the help of India's strengths of 5 Ts- Tradition, Talent, Tourism, Trade and Technology and working towards strengthening regional and global forums, namely the SAARC, the ASEAN, BRICS, G20, IBSA, SCO and ASEM.[54] Accordingly, after the new government assumed office in 2014, a new dimension of India's 'Look East' Policy was acquired and the 'Act East' Policy was declared as an enhanced

'Look East' Policy. This new phase in India's relations with the Southeast Asian region is characterized by a more pro-active and pragmatic approach to foreign policy with emphasis on concrete forms of cooperation in political, economic and cultural spheres, with definite timelines for implementation of projects. Continuing with the efforts to shore up India's bilateral ties with Vietnam, especially in times of political differences of opinion of both India and Vietnam vis-à-vis China, External Affairs Minister of India, Smt. Sushma Swaraj paid a crucial visit to Vietnam, as early as in August 25-26, 2014, the linchpin of her government's newly announced 'Act East' Policy, during which she held bilateral talks with Deputy Prime Minister and Foreign Minister of Vietnam Mr. Pham Bin Minh and met with the President and the Prime Minister of Vietnam to discuss the prevailing global and regional situation. During her visit, she inaugurated the 3rd Round Table of the ASEAN-India Network of Think Tanks (AINTT) with Deputy Prime Minister and Foreign Minister Mr. Minh. She also chaired the Regional Heads of Missions' Conference and met 16 Indian Heads of Missions from the region. Soon after Sushma Swaraj's visit, Indian President Pranab Mukherjee visited Vietnam during September 14-17, 2014. Interestingly enough, this trip took place just days before Chinese President Xi Jinping's visit to India. Thus, India's outreach to both China and Vietnam at a time when both India and Vietnam were facing some challenges in their relations with China was significant enough. This visit further led to the deepening of the Strategic Partnership between the two countries where both sides reminisced about the age-old traditional and friendly ties between the two countries and highlighted on the newer areas of bilateral cooperation in the 21st century. Following this, Prime Minister of Vietnam, Mr. Nguyen Tan Dung paid a very important visit to India in October 2014, at the invitation of Indian Prime Minister Narendra Modi. The two Prime Ministers welcomed the developments in recent years which have led to a continuous strengthening of the Strategic Partnership between India and Vietnam. The Prime Ministers agreed that a strong India-Vietnam partnership would lead to peace, prosperity and stability for people of both countries and in the wider region. Prime Minister Modi reaffirmed that Vietnam was an important pillar of India's Look East Policy. Prime Minister Dung welcomed a greater role for India in the regional and international arena. The two leaders noted that strategic partnership between the two countries was based on traditional friendship, mutual understanding, strong trust, support and convergence of views on various regional and international issues and called for more intensive exchanges at all levels under the established dialogue mechanisms and urged effective implementation of agreements concluded between both countries. Without naming the 'China threat', they made it amply clear that the two countries were extremely concerned about the aggressive stances and decisions that were being taken by China in the South China Sea and the Joint Statement issued by the two sides at the end of the visit, categorically referred to this concern. In the Joint Statement "the Prime Ministers reiterated their desire and determination to work together to maintain peace, stability, growth and prosperity in Asia and beyond. They agreed that freedom of navigation and overflight in the East Sea/South China Sea should not be impeded and called the parties concerned to exercise restraint, avoid threat or use of force and resolve disputes through peaceful means in accordance with universally recognized principles of international law, including the UNCLOS 1982."[55] They urged the disputing parties "to abide by and implement the 2002 Declaration on the Conduct of Parties in the South China Sea and to work towards the adoption of a Code of Conduct in the South China Sea on the basis of consensus,"[56] clearly giving out the message to China of a united front of Vietnam and India in the dispute. Thus, three consecutive visits in very quick succession clearly emphasised on the renewed importance that India attached to Vietnam, particularly with the coming of the new government and therefore, the implementation of the 'Act East' policy looked promising. In the meantime, Vietnam and China continued to clash in the South China Sea throughout the year. For instance, China unilaterally imposed a fishing permit rule in the South China Sea in January 2014, which led to severe protests by disputing countries such as Vietnam, the Philippines and even by the US. Again, in May 2014, China installed an oil rig in a disputed region in the South China Sea, where both countries lay claims and soon after a Vietnamese fishing boat sank near the oil rig after Chinese vessels collided with it. This led to severe diplomatic tiff between Beijing and Hanoi with the ASEAN urging both sides to exercise control and restraint. Such frequent violent political incidents between China and Vietnam, acted as a catalyst for Vietnam to develop a dynamic and liberal foreign policy of cultivating stronger ties with traditional friends like India and wooing other powers like Japan, Australia and even extra-regional powers like the United States, shunning ideological considerations to counter a fellow Communist country's hegemonic designs in the region. Therefore, Vietnam continued to renew India's exploration deals (Block 128) in the tense South China Sea region time and again, so that it could engage with India to balance China. India, in turn, despite the questions of viability of the exploration prospects in Blocks 127 and 128, continued to remain engaged in the disputed region at the behest of Vietnam, notwithstanding Chinese warnings and stressed on monitoring the Straits of Malacca on a regular basis to ensure freedom of navigation and anti-piracy drives.

Following the announcement of the new term 'Act East' by the NDA government, the newly appointed Prime Minister Mr. Narendra Modi paid a very crucial visit to Arunachal Pradesh for the first time in February 2015. China severely slammed Modi's visit to Arunachal Pradesh and the Chinese reaction this time was even severe than Dr. Manmohan Singh's visit to the state in 2009. Not surprisingly, China blamed India of complicating the boundary issue between the two countries and referred to Arunachal Pradesh as the "disputed area of eastern part of China-India boundary" and such actions by India would only obstruct the "good momentum towards the bilateral ties."[57]

Thus, by the end of 2015, India was facing several challenges with China despite assurances from both sides to build a closer developmental partnership and make it a core component of the bilateral relationship. For instance, during the visit of Prime Minister Modi to China in May

2015, the two sides emphasised the policy of attaching priority to the development of good-neighbourly and friendly bilateral relations on the basis of mutual respect and sensitivity to each other's concerns and aspirations. However, continued political differences marred their relationship to a great extent. Several such decisions and incidents that tested the patience of South bloc which happened during this period may be cited. For instance, despite India's repeated plea not to invest in Pakistan occupied Kashmir (PoK), China continued to give credence to Pakistan's presence in the disputed region and it regularly invests in the region too, which includes upgrading the Karakoram Highway, the Bunji and Bash dams, and the Kohala and Neelam-Jhelam hydroelectric projects, besides the fact that Beijing continues to bolster Islamabad's military capabilities and assist in supplying nuclear reactors. In this regard, while answering to a question raised by Shri KP Dhanapalan and Shri Gopinath Munde in Lok Sabha, regarding whether China and Pakistan have entered into an agreement for creation of an economic corridor through Pakistan occupied Kashmir (PoK) and whether China is developing basic infrastructure for its projects in Pakistan occupied Kashmir (PoK) and if so, the reaction of the government to that issue, Smt. Preneet Kaur, Minister of State in the Ministry of External Affairs replied that, "Government is aware that China is executing infrastructure projects in Pakistan Occupied Kashmir. Government has raised this issue with the Chinese side and has clearly conveyed India's consistent position that Pakistan has been in illegal occupation of parts of the Indian State of Jammu and Kashmir since 1947. China regards Kashmir as a bilateral matter to be settled between India and Pakistan. The Government of India has conveyed its concerns to China about their activities in Pakistan Occupied Kashmir, and asked them to cease such activities."[58] But till date nothing as such has happened.

With the increasing challenges in India's and Vietnam's political ties with China, both the countries have been seen upgrading their ties in this period with another Asian giant, Japan. For instance, immediately after coming to power, Prime Minister Shri Narendra

Modi paid an official visit to Japan from August 30 to September 03, 2014. It was his first major bilateral visit outside India's immediate neighbourhood. In this regard, while answering to a question raised by Dr. Arun Kumar, Smt. Jayshreeben Patel, Shri Yogi Adityanath, Shri Rattan Lal Kataria and Shri Y.V Subba Reddy in Lok Sabha, regarding the details of Prime Minister's visit to Japan, Gen (Dr.) VK Singh (Retd.), the Minister of State in the Ministry of External Affairs replied that the 'Tokyo Declaration for India-Japan Special Strategic and Global Partnership' was signed by the two Prime Ministers and 'Factsheet: India and Japan-Partners for Common Development' was issued at the end of this visit and generated substantive outcomes. On the economic side, a new India-Japan Investment Promotion Partnership was launched, under which Japan conveyed its intention to invest 3.5 trillion yen of public-private investment in India for a period of five years as well as to double the number of Japanese companies operating in India. Defence equipment and technology was identified as a new major area of cooperation. During the visit, the Japanese side also agreed to removal of six Indian entities from the Japanese foreign-end user list. The two sides agreed to strengthen their cooperation and collaboration in several areas including in energy, LNG, railways, infrastructure, smart cities, science and technology and in promoting people to people exchanges. The Memorandum on Defence Co-operation and Exchanges between Ministry of Defence of the Republic of India and the Ministry of Defense of Japan[59] was signed between the two countries to substantially upgrade their defence ties in the wake of renewed challenges in the region. Vietnam too, beefed up its defence cooperation with Japan in this period since entering into Strategic Partnership with it in 2006, particularly to counter the "China threat" in the Indo-Pacific region. Both these countries are now engaged in maritime security assistance, joint naval drills, port calls, coastguard cooperation, defence equipment and industrial cooperation. This perfectly coincides with Japan's Vientiane Vision that seeks to engage Southeast Asia as a collective region on defence issues.[60] This is a guiding principle formulated by Japan to shape its defence engagements with the ASEAN bloc in the coming years and to substantially reinvigorate the former's defence ties with the Southeast Asian countries in the 21st century. Without naming the 'China threat' the Vientiane Vision seeks to infuse confidence in the psyche of the ASEAN countries to deal with the challenges in the Indo-Pacific region. India too, though primarily involved in the troubled South China Sea region at the behest of 'good friend' Vietnam, who wants India to play a greater role in the region, nonetheless, India has become more vociferous in protesting Chinese assertiveness in the South China Sea by raising the issue at various regional settings like the India-ASEAN Delhi Dialogue in 2014 and 2015, the ASEAN Regional Forum in 2014, and the East Asia Summit in 2013 and 2014.[61] India herself has become victim of China's wrath when at least on two occasions, China objected to Indian ventures in the South China Sea. In July 2011, the INS Airavat, an amphibious assault vessel, while on its friendly visit to Vietnam was objected to by the Chinese naval forces as having entered into Chinese waters. Again in September 2011, when ONGC Videsh Limited, as per its three-year agreement with its counterpart Petro Vietnam started exploration operations in the South China Sea, China warned India of serious consequences.[62] In this regard while replying to a question raised by Dr. Thokchom Meinya in the Lok Sabha, regarding whether India's stand on South China Sea has annoyed China and the details of India's position vis-à-vis South China Sea, Gen (Dr.) VK Singh (retd.), Minister of State in the Ministry of External Affairs said, "India's position on South China Sea issue is consistent and has been reiterated bilaterally and in multilateral forums on several occasions. India supports freedom of navigation in and overflight above international waters while maintaining that sovereignty issues must be resolved peacefully in accordance with accepted principles of international law, including the United Nations' Convention on the Law of the Sea (UNCLOS) 1982. India has taken note of the 2002 Declaration of Conduct, adopted by the Foreign Ministers of ASEAN and China at the 8th ASEAN Summit in Phnom Penh in November 2002, which inter alia states that 'the Parties undertake to exercise self-restraint in the conduct of activities that would complicate or escalate disputes and affect peace and stability' and 'to resolve their territorial and jurisdictional disputes by peaceful means, without resorting to threat or use of force'. India welcomes the collective commitment by the concerned countries to abide by and implement the 2002 Declaration on the Conduct of Parties in the South China Sea and to work towards the adoption of a Code of Conduct in the South China Sea on the basis of consensus."[63]

Much like India, Japan too has become extremely forthcoming in this period in condemning Chinese aggressive postures in the South China Sea. For instance, during the Shangri-la Dialogue of May-June 2014, Japanese Prime Minister Shinzo Abe exhorted China to follow the "rule of law at sea." In fact, Japan can totally empathise with Vietnam and other disputing claimants of the South China Sea as it itself is embroiled in a similar imbroglio with China in the Senkaku/Diaoyu islands. Japan's political relations with China reached the nadir when in December 2012 China considered flights by Japan over the islands as a violation of its air space and in retaliation dispatched fighter jets to intercept the intruding aircraft. Tokyo accused the Chinese actions in its 2013 *Defence White Paper* of changing the status quo by "force based on its own assertion which is incompatible with the existing order of international law."[64] In a similar vein, China is accused of harassing the Vietnamese ships involved in fishing and oil exploration involved in the South China.

It is true that India and China today are cooperating with each other based on their common interests on several multilateral issues of global importance, like climate change, WTO, reform of the international financial institutions, etc. This is reflected in close cooperation and coordination between the two sides within the BRICS, G-20 and other forums, where these two sides are cooperating with each other and putting up a united fight against the Western world. Moreover, to deal with the challenges in their bilateral ties in a peaceful manner, External Affairs Minister (EAM) Smt. Sushma Swaraj during the visit to China from January 31 to February 03, 2015. In this regard, while replying to a question raised by Shri Ram Charitra Niishad in the Lok Sabha, regarding whether India has unveiled an ambitious agenda to elevate its ties with China and the details of that, Gen (Dr.) VK Singh (retd.), Minister of State in the Ministry of External Affairs replied that Smt. Swaraj during this visit "proposed that the two countries should follow (i) action oriented approach (ii) broad base bilateral engagement (iii) convergence of common regional and global interests (iv) develop new areas of cooperation (v) expand strategic communication (vi) fulfil common aspirations to usher 'Asian Century'."[65] However, outstanding issues in their bilateral political ties have only become complicated over the years. The issue of Arunachal Pradesh remains such an area of discord between the two countries, where India maintains that it is an "inalienable part of India"[66] and China claims it as part of their territory and vehemently opposes the visit of Indian dignitaries and officials in Arunachal Pradesh. In this regard, while answering to a question raised by Shri Jyotiraditya M. Scindia and Shri Pralhad Joshi in the Lok Sabha, regarding whether the Government's plan to construct a 1800 km long road along the Mc Mohan Line in Arunachal Pradesh had been strongly opposed by China, Gen (Dr.) VK Singh (retd.), Minister of State in the Ministry of External Affairs replied that the "Ministry of Home Affairs, Government of India is considering the examination of a concept/plan for construction of a lateral road from Tawang to Vijaynagar in Changlang District in the State of Arunachal Pradesh to provide livelihood and connectivity to the border population and for the development of border area. Government is also giving careful and specific attention to the development of infrastructure in all the border areas in order to meet its strategic and security requirements as also to facilitate the economic development of these areas."[67] Moreover, India decided in November 2011 to deploy a regiment of BrahMos surface to surface supersonic cruise missiles in Arunachal Pradesh, and thereby "making it India's first offensive tactical missile development against China."[68]

It is also an irony that India and China are not always on the same page as far as condemning terrorism is concerned. For instance, Home

Minister Shri Rajnath Singh visited China from November 18-23,2015. In this regard, while answering to a question raised by Smt. Vanaroja R. and Shri G. Hari in the Lok Sabha, about whether India and China had held discussions about counter terror collaboration recently, Gen (Dr.) V.K Singh (retd.), Minister of State in the Ministry of External Affairs replied that "the two sides strongly condemned the terrorist attacks in Paris and reiterated their resolute opposition to terrorism in all its forms and manifestations. They agreed to enhance cooperation in combating international terrorism through exchange of information, exchange of experiences and coordinating positions on anti-terrorism endeavors at regional and multilateral levels and both sides exchanged views about the spread of terrorism in different parts of the world and the efforts required to counter the menace. The importance of addressing the problem of terrorism through early finalisation of a Comprehensive Convention on International Terrorism (CCIT) under the auspices of the UN was emphasised by India. Chinese Government has conveyed that it would never support armed groups that are against the Government of India".[69] However, despite such tall promises, China has been taking a partisan approach in condemning Pakistan-based terrorist outfits which have been creating diplomatic tiff between Beijing and the New Delhi and deteriorating their political ties. Again, while answering to a question raised by Shri Hari Om Panday, Dr. Ratna De (Nag), Shri M. S. Rao (Avanthi), Shri V. Panneerselvam and Shri Chandra Pakash Joshi in the Lok Sabha, regarding whether the Government has proposed any plan to register official objection in the United Nations on China's negative stand on Masood Azhar issue in UNSC ban in the recent past, Gen (Dr.) VK Singh (retd.), Minister of State in the Ministry of External Affairs replied, "On 25 February 2016 Government requested the Security Council Committee, established pursuant to UN Security Council Resolution 1267 (now UNSCR 1267/1989/2253), to include Masood Azhar of the Jaish-e-Mohammad in the list of designated sanctioned entities. It was pointed out that while Jaish-e-Mohammad was designated by the Committee in 2001, its leader who is the group's chief financier, recruiter, and motivator had not been designated and continues to remain active in terror activities against India. The Committee, that takes its decision on the basis of the consensus amongst members, sought a six month period and subsequently has sought a further three months period to consider India's request. Government continues to take up the matter with all members of the Committee including China at the highest level. India's position has been conveyed that the working methods of the Committee are leading to a perception that the Committee adopts selective approach to combating terrorism. This does not help the international community to decisively confront the menace of terrorism. Government is firmly resolved to take all necessary measures to defeat terrorism, and ensure the security and territorial integrity of the nation."[70] Repeated Chinese veto on India's anti-terrorism move in the United Nations, thwarted India's plans to ban Masood Azhar, thus disappointing not only India but the world community as a whole who have been trying to fight the scourge of global terrorism. Thus, despite the fact the armies of India and China have launched 'hand-in-hand' or joint operations thrice so far—at Kunming, Belgaum and Chengdu—with counter-terror missions, China has not been on the same page with India as far as countering 'cross border terrorism' is concerned, specifically in relation to Pakistan. On this, Vietnam has staunchly stood by India throughout and both the countries strongly condemn terrorism in all its forms and manifestations and is resolved to increase cooperation in the common efforts of the international community in preventing this scourge in a comprehensive manner. Both the countries cooperate for an early finalisation of the Comprehensive Convention on International Terrorism, for which India had presented a draft at the United Nations in 1996.[71]

Moreover, China under the leadership of President Xi Jinping in this period has embarked on the implementation of some projects which are strongly objected by India. For instance, the Belt and Road initiative or the China-Pakistan Economic Corridor are certainly to India's dislike, having definite political ramifications in their bilateral ties. In 2013, President Xi unveiled his plan to jointly build the Silk

Road Economic Belt and the 21st century Maritime Silk Road (Belt and Road). The Belt and Road initiative will run through the continents of Asia, Europe and Africa. The Silk Road Economic Belt focuses on bringing together China, Central Asia, Russia and Europe; linking China with the Persian Gulf and the Mediterranean Sea through Central Asia and West Asia and connecting China with Southeast Asia, South Asia and the Indian Ocean. The 21st century Maritime Silk Road is designed to go from China's coast to Europe through the South China Sea and the Indian Ocean in one route and from China's coast through the South China Sea to the South Pacific in the other. On land, the initiative will focus on jointly building a new Eurasian Land Bridge and developing China-Mongolia-Russia, China-Central Asia-West Asia and China-Indochina Peninsula economic corridors by taking advantage of international transport routes relying on core cities along the Belt and Road and issuing key economic industrial parks as cooperative platforms.[72] Moreover, China has promised $57 billion in investment in projects along the China-Pakistan Economic Corridor, part of the Belt and Road initiative. The economic corridor, to be completed in three phases by 2030, will boost Pakistan's energy security and infrastructure and will help it attract more foreign investment. Moreover, Pakistan and China aim to build a network of rail, road and energy infrastructure as part of the Belt and Road Initiative and Pakistan has been one of the most enthusiastic supporters of the initiative, in part because many projects are for power plants to alleviate its chronic energy shortage that leads to frequent blackouts.[73] However, India has strongly objected to these projects as it impinges on the sovereignty of the host countries and the China-Pakistan economic corridor clearly runs through the PoK region which Pakistan is in illegal occupation of since 1965. Therefore, how these two Asian giants negotiate their political differences owing to India's objections to these projects, will to a great extent determine their future course of relations. Vietnam too, though officially has been taken on board by the Chinese as far as the OBOR is concerned, the former is quite reserved about it because, firstly, as the prospects of development for the host countries are not yet clear, and secondly, China is continuing to clash with Vietnam in the South China Sea. In such a situation how prudent will the decision be to join or not join hands with the Chinese on the OBOR project is not yet clear to the Vietnamese leadership.

Moreover, both India's and Vietnam's continuous improvement in relations with the United States since the 2010 ASEAN Regional Forum (ARF) meeting in Hanoi, where Secretary of State Hillary Clinton deftly announced that the United States is 'back in Asia' in support of Obama administration's 'Pivot to Asia' or a more benign 'Rebalancing in Asia' Policy, has been objected to by China. This has led to substantial policy readjustments and very intensive military build-up on the part of China, who itself has been propagating the concept of "Asia for Asians" under President Xi Jinping's leadership and treats the US as an extra-regional power with ulterior motives to disturb the peace and tranquility of the region, particularly since the AsiaPacific region economically marched substantially ahead of Europe after the 2008 financial crisis. The US is also assuming more responsibilities on conflicts in the South and East China Seas, coupled with increased military commitments. For instance, during his visit to Japan in April 2014, President Obama quickly stated that the Diaoyu/Senkaku Islands are covered by the US-Japan Security Treaty. Under the recently signed Enhanced Defense Cooperation Agreement with the Philippines, the US has restarted rotational deployment in five military bases in the country. It has also lifted its ban on arms trade to Vietnam. All these are indication that the U.S sees the Asia-Pacific as the priority in its global strategy in the 21st century.[74] Moreover, in 2013, Vietnam and the United States decided to upgrade their ties to the level of Comprehensive Partnership when President Truong Tan Sang paid a visit to the United States in the month of July. It included intensification of cooperation in the crucial areas of political and diplomatic relations, trade and economic ties, science and technology, education and training, environment and health, war legacy issues, defence and security, protection and promotion of human rights, and culture, sports, and tourism. Again, in October 2013, Vietnam and the United States reached an agreement on cooperation between the two Coast Guards and cooperation on the use of nuclear energy for peaceful purposes, and following this, in December 2013, Secretary of State John Kerry announced that the US would provide Vietnam with US$ 18 million to assist Vietnam enhance the capacity of its Coast Guard to conduct search and rescue, disaster and other maritime security missions.[75]

Similarly, the United States has been proactively improving its ties with India and welcoming a greater role for India in the Southeast Asia. This argument becomes clear when we analyse the speech of President Obama in the Indian Parliament in November 2010 where the "China threat" reverberated in his speech as well. He remarked, "India and the US can partner in Asia. Today, the US is once again playing a leadership role in Asia—strengthening old alliances; deepening relationships, as we are dealing with China; and we are re-engaging with regional organizations like ASEAN and joining the EAS organizations in which India is also a partner. Like your neighbours in Southeast Asia, we want India to not only 'Look East', we want India to 'engage East'- because it will increase the security and prosperity of all our nations."[76]

Vietnam has welcomed greater US involvement in the South China Sea to counter increasing assertiveness and has welcomed it when the US has raised concerns over it. For instance, during the Shangri-La Dialogue of May 2014, held in Singapore, Vietnam completely supported the US defence Secretary Chuck Hagel when he accused China of 'destabilizing' the South China Sea and its 'unilateral' actions are threatening the region's long-term progress. He further remarked that the US "would not look the other way" when countries flouted international rules.[77] Interestingly enough, on April 16, 2013, China released its eighth white paper on defence. Among other things that are of importance to this discussion, the most crucial feature of this paper was that, it declared that China will play a greater role in the global affairs commensurate with its international standing, and critiqued United States rebalancing postures in the Asia-Pacific. Moreover, not only did it term the South China Sea as its "core interest," which eventually led to 12 out of 27 countries criticising the move in the ASEAN Regional Forum, it also hailed and lauded the trailing incidents of USS Impeccable in 2009 and USS Cowpens in 2013 by the Chinese Navy in the South China Sea.[78]

Therefore, China has strong objections to Vietnam's increasing bonhomie with Japan and the US. Moreover, after Vietnamese Prime Minister Nguyen Xuan Phuc's visit to the US and Japan, the Global Times reported that Vietnam's ambitions may disturb regional cooperation and stir confrontation. Divulging further details of the visits and China's objections to their outcomes, the report further mentioned, "Political security formed an integral part of the meeting as both expressed 'deep concerns' over the developments in the South China Sea and urged all the parties to settle disputes through peaceful means with respect for diplomatic and legal process. Additionally, Japan will provide $350 million to help upgrade Vietnamese coastguard vessels and their patrol capability. Prior to his visit to Japan, Phuc's official visit to the US also generated tangible results. Phuc and US President Donald Trump issued a joint statement to enhance their comprehensive partnership. Regarding the South China Sea, both emphasized the importance of 'freedom of navigation and overflight' and the need for peaceful resolutions of disputes without the use of force or coercion. The US transfer of a Hamilton- class cutter to the Vietnam Coast Guard to enhance Vietnam's law enforcement capabilities represents another step to strengthen their defense cooperation. Successive visits to the US and Japan signify Vietnam's initiative to play a larger part in regional affairs. In the face of China's rise, Vietnam needs to woo other countries outside the region to contain China in the South China Sea and protect its vested interests…In view of this, Vietnam's frequent talks with the US and Japan about the South China Sea should not be viewed as benign. Japan's help to upgrade Vietnamese coast guard vessels is aimed at inciting Vietnam to confront China at sea."[79] Exactly in a similar way, China objects to the increasing strategic camaraderie between India and Vietnam and disapproves of India's involvement in the South China Sea. For instance, on the issue of Vietnam-India product-sharing joint exploration in the South China Sea, China Energy News published by the Chinese Communist Party's mouthpiece *People's Daily* carried a front page commentary calling upon the Chinese government to use force to disrupt Indian exploration in the South China Sea: "India is playing with fire by agreeing to explore for oil with Vietnam in the disputed South China Sea... Challenging the core interests of a large, rising country for unknown oil at the bottom of the sea will not only lead to a crushing defeat for the Indian oil company but will also most likely seriously harm India's whole energy security and interrupt its economic development".[80]

Owing to such developments, both India and Vietnam are increasingly expressing their deep concerns related to China with each other and also with the US, Japan and Australia, shunning all ideological affinities, to counter any untoward incident by the Communist China under the leadership of the all-powerful President Xi Jinping. That is why, the concept of Quad or the Quadrilateral grouping comprising the US, India, Australia and Japan, to ensure peace and tranquility in the Indo-Pacific region, has taken shape in this period. Thus, by the end of this period, it became amply clear that the US, Vietnam, India and Japan are progressively coming together against China and not only because of the strong foundation that was laid between India and Vietnam owing to liberation war solidarity, or South-South cooperation in the days of the Cold War, but also because of the perception of 'China threat' which is proving to be the arch-stone in India-Vietnam bilateral political relations in the 21st century.

Summarily then, it can be said that despite several water-shed events in global politics during 1991 to 2015, India's political ties with Vietnam have only been strengthened with each passing year as a crucial factor in the peace, stability and development of the entire Asia-Pacific region and overflowing the solidarity of the Cold War years, today India-Vietnam ties have blossomed into a "partnership that stands on its own merits."[81] Not only at the bilateral level, but presently, both the countries cooperate with each other on various platforms, such as the ASEAN, East Asia Summit (EAS), Mekong Ganga Cooperation

(MGC), and the Asia- Europe Meeting (AEM). Moreover, the Joint Commission Meeting at the Foreign Ministers' level also provides for a greater podium for bilateral cooperation while identifying concrete projects. Besides their focus to develop their bilateral ties in their own merit, their ties have also been conditioned during this period to a great extent by the fear of Chinese aggressive postures in the region, as was reverberated in the words of Dr. Manmohan Singh, when he stated that, "'India and Vietnam are maritime neighbors… facing common security challenges… We believe that it is important to ensure the safety and security of the vital sea lanes of communication… We have agreed to continue and strengthen our exchanges in these fields."[82] It is true that both these countries have an over-arching drive to tap the fullest economic potentials of trading with China, and for them, today, China has evolved as one of the greatest trade partners. It is amply clear that both India and Vietnam share the same concern with China and cooperate with Beijing on global issues, such as, restructuring of the International Monetary Fund (IMF), criticising the protectionist policies followed by the Western world, namely the US, Canada and Europe in their own domestic economies, whereas forcing open the economies of the third world in the name of structural readjustments as an essential condition for the Bretton Woods institutions, thereby depriving these countries of a level playing ground. In fact, it was because of the concerted and coordinated efforts of India and China, 5 percent of voting shares in the IMF and 3 percent in the World Bank were redistributed in favour of emerging and developing economies at the G20 Summit at Pittsburg in September 2009.[83] Thus, though India and China today are on the same wavelength politically and ideologically on most of the key global issues dividing the North and the South, such as global warming, environmental pollution, trade and tariffs, agricultural subsidies and food security, etc.,[84] yet fundamental differences in their bilateral ties have marred their political ties to a great extent and have created newer challenges and hiccups in the prospects of amicable solution. With the 'China dream' firmly as a guiding policy under Xi Jinping's leadership, both India and Vietnam are grappling to meet the challenges of Chinese expansionism in the 21st century. This common fear factor has brought these two countries closer to each other than ever before. How these two countries cooperate with each other to meet the challenges posed by China and how they will handle their political relations with other countries, such as the United States, Japan, Australia and such other disputes that have been drawn into the unfolding of events in the Indo-Pacific region in the present 'Asian Century', will to a great extent determine the peace, stability and prosperity not only of India and Vietnam but also of the entire region in the coming years.

Notes

1. Tridib Chakraborti and Mohor Chakraborty, *Expanding Horizon of India's Southeast Asia Policy: 'Look', 'Move' and 'Act' East*, KW Publishers Pvt. Ltd, New Delhi, 2018, p.25.
2. Text of the Report "*The East Asian Miracle: Economic Growth and Public Policy,*" The World Bank. See, documents.worldbank.org/curated/en/975081468244550798/Main-report (accessed on July 15, 2018). Also see, Mahendra Ved, "*India and Southeast Asia: Shedding Years of Mutual Neglect,*" SEAPS, Sri Venkateswara University, Tirupati, pp.33–34.
3. Tridib Chakraborti, "India's Look East Policy: Time for Stock-Taking," *World Focus*, November–December, 2009, Vol.XXX, p. 462.
4. *Annual Report: 1991-92*, Ministry of External Affairs, Government of India, New Delhi, 1992.
5. Ramses Amer, "Sino- Vietnamese Relations: Past, Present and Future," in Carlyle A. Thayer and Ramesh Thakur (eds.), *Vietnamese Foreign Policy in Transition*, Institute of Southeast Asian Studies, Singapore, 1999, p.74.
6. "ASEAN- India Dialogue Relations," ASEAN Secretariat, Jakarta, for details see http://www.aseansec.org/14802.htm (accessed on July 20, 2018).
7. *Annual Report: 1991-1992,* n.137.
8. VD Chopra (ed.), *Vietnam Today and Indo- Vietnam Relations*, Gyan Books Pvt. Ltd, New Delhi, 2001, p.19.
9. Bashir Ahmad Dar, "Bilateral engagements between India- China since 1988," *India and China Relations: Historical, Cultural and Security Issues*, UGC Centre for Southeast Asian and Pacific Studies, Sri Venkateswara University, 2016, pp.35–36.
10. Sridhar Krishna Swamy, "Scope for More Trade Ties with Vietnam," *The Hindu*, 6 September, 1994.
11. Ramses Amer, n.138, p.77.
12. Ibid.
13. Ibid.
14. Ibid.
15. *Annual Report: 1994-95*, *Ministry of External Affairs,* Government of India, New

Delhi,1995.

16. Text of Prime Minister Narasimha Rao's speech, *Institute of Southeast Asian Studies*, Singapore, September 30, 1994.
17. Carlyle A. Thayer, Vietnamese Diplomacy, 1975-2015: From Member of the Socialist Camp to Proactive International Integration, Presentation to International Conference on Vietnam: 40 Years of Reunification, Development and Integration (1975-2015), April 25, 2015, pp.1–27. For details see, https://auschamvn.org/wp-content/uploads/2015/04/Vietnamese-Diplomacy-1975-2015-by-Carl-Thayer_April-2015.pdf (accessed on May 10, 2016).
18. *Annual Report: 1995-96, Ministry of External Affairs,* Government of India, New Delhi, 1996.
19. "ASEAN Regional Forum," Ministry of External Affairs, Government of India. For details see, https://www.mea.gov.in/Portal/ForeignRelation/asean-regional-forum-august-2012.pdf (accessed on May 4, 2018).
20. "The ASEAN Regional Forum: A Concept Paper." For details see, aseanregionalforum.asean.org/files/library/Terms of References and Concept Papers/Concept Paper of ARF. pdf (accessed on June 12, 2018).
21. Ramses Amer, n.138, p.84.
22. Kanak Mani Dixit, "Gujral Doctrine for Modi darbar," *The Hindu*, 18 November 2015.
23. *IK Gujral's speech*, "India's Role in World Affairs: Retrospective and Prospects," Nehru Centre, Bombay, January 3, 1997, http://www.indianembassy.org/policy/Foreign_Policy/global(gujral).htm (accessed on June 3, 2015).
24. *Indo-Vietnam Chamber of Commerce and Industry Newsletter*, Vol.7, No.3-4, January-June 1997.
25. Ramses Amer, n.138, p.95.
26. Udai Bhanu Singh, "India and the ARF: The Post- Pokhran II Phase," Strategic Analysis, Vol.22, No.10, 1999, pp.1591–606 https://www.idsa-india.org/an-jan9-10.html (accessed on May 6, 2018).
27. Statement by Minister of State for External Affairs, Smt. Vasundhara Raje, on the occasion of the 4th Indo-ASEAN Eminent Persons Lecture Series, August 1998.
28. BR Deepak, *India China Relations in the first half of the Twentieth Century,* APH Publishers, New Delhi, 2001, p.22.
29. Dalbir Ahlawat, "The Convergence Dilemma: Mapping India- China Strategic Relations, India and China Relations: Historical, Cultural and Security Issues, UGC Centre for Southeast Asian and Pacific Studies, Sri Venkateswara University, Tirupati, p.228.
30. Snehalata Panda, "Bridging the Arroyo: China and India in the New Millennium," in M.R Biju (ed.), New Horizons of Indian Foreign Policy, Authors Press, New Delhi, 2007, p.129.
31. Aftab Seth, "Culture Binds India- Vietnam Relations," in Rajaram Panda (ed.), *India- Vietnam Relations: Retrospect and Prospect*, Northern Book Centre, New Delhi, 2016, p.56.
32. "Vietnam: Consolidating National Defence, Safeguarding the Homeland," Vietnam Ministry of Defence, 1998, pp.1–72. Also see, Stein Tonnesson, "Vietnam's Objective in the South China Sea: National or Regional Security," *Contemporary Southeast Asia*, Vol. 22, No. 1, April 2000, pp.199–220.

33. Ajay Sura, "China helped Pak during Kargil War: Brigadier," *The Times of India*, September 26, 2013.
34. Ang Cheng Guan, "Another Milestone and the Country Plods On," *Southeast Asian Affairs*, 2002, pp. 345–56.
35. Indu Singh, "India and the US: Issues of Convergence and Divergence," in Dr. (Mrs.) Annupurna Nautiyal (ed.), *Challenges to India's Foreign Policy in the New Era*, Gyan Publishing House, New Delhi, pp. 111–25.
36. *Annual Report: 2001-02*, Ministry of External Affairs, Government of India, New Delhi, 2002.
37. *Speech by External Affairs Minister Shri Yashwant Sinha*, Harvard University, September 29, 2003, https://www.mea.gov.in/Speeches-Statements.htm?dtl/4744 (accessed on August 10, 2015).
38. *Annual Report: 2003-04*, Ministry of External Affairs, Government of India, New Delhi, 2004.
39. Ibid.
40. *Annual Report: 2004-05*, Ministry of External Affairs, Government of India, New Delhi, 2005.
41. *Chairman's Statement of the 3rd ASEAN- India Summit*, aic.ris.org.in/chairman's-statement-3rd-asean-india-summit-vientiane (accessed on May 10, 2017).
42. *Annual Report: 2005-06*, Ministry of External Affairs, Government of India, New Delhi, 2006.
43. Zhao Hong, "India and China: Rivals or Partners in Southeast Asia?" *Contemporary Southeast Asia*, Vol. 29, No.1, April 2007, p.136.
44. Pravin Sawnhey and Ghazala Wahab, *Dragon on Our Doorstep: Managing China through Military Power*, Aleph Publishers, New Delhi, 2017,p.49.
45. "East Asia Summit," Ministry of External Affairs, Government of India, mea.gov.in/aseanindia/about-eas.htm (accessed on September10, 2018).
46. *Annual Report: 2007-08*, Ministry of External Affairs, Government of India, New Delhi, 2008.
47. Alexander L. Vuving, "Vietnam: Arriving in the World- and at a Crossroads," *Southeast Asian Affairs*, 2008, pp. 387–88.
48. Ibid.
49. *Annual Report: 2011-12*, Ministry of External Affairs, Government of India, New Delhi, 2012.
50. United Nations Convention on the Law of the Sea, 1982, https://www.un.org/Depts/los/convention_agreements/texts/unclos/unclos_e.pdf (accessed on May 10, 2016).
51. *Annual Report: 2012-13*, Ministry of External Affairs, Government of India, New Delhi,2013.
52. For details of the debate held in Lok Sabha, https://mea.gov.in/lok-sabha.htm?dtl/22889/Q+N03373+VISIT+OF+INDIAS+HEAD+OF+STATE+TO+ARUNACHAL+PRADESH (accessed on May 11, 2016).
53. Ibid.
54. Election Manifesto, Bharatiya Janta Party (BJP), 2014.
55. Joint Statement on the State Visit of Prime Minister of the Socialist Republic of Vietnam (October 27-28, 2014), Ministry of External Affairs, Government of India, New Delhi, October 28, 2014, https://www.mea.gov.in/bilateral-documents.

htm?dtl/24142/Joint+Statement+on+theState+Visit+of+Prime+Minister+of+the+Socialist+Republic+of+Vietnam+to+India+October+2728+2014 (accessed on May 4, 2015).

56. Ibid.
57. Dipanjan Roy Chaudhury, "PM Narendra Modi likely to visit Arunachal Pradesh to give a strong message to China," *The Economic Times*, January 3, 2018.
58. For details of the debate held in Lok Sabha, https://www.mea.gov.in/lok-sabha.htm?dtl/22016/Q+NO672+CHINA+IN+POK (accessed on May 15, 2015).
59. For details of the debate held in Lok Sabha, https://www.mea.gov.in/lok-sabha.htm?dtl/24340/Q_NO_584_INDOJAPAN_TIES (accessed on May 4, 2015).
60. Prashanth Parameswaran, "Japan- Vietnam Defense Relations in the Indo- Pacific Spotlight," *The Diplomat*, April 11, 2018, https://thediplomat.com/2018/04/japan-vietnam-defense-relations-in-the-indo-pacific-spotlight (accessed on May 14, 2018).
61. David Scott, "India's Incremental Balancing in the South China Sea," *E-International Relations*, July 26, 2015, https://www.e-ir.info/2015/07/26/indias-incremental-balancing-in-the-south-china-sea (accessed on May 13, 2017).
62. Dalbir Ahlawat, n.162, p.211.
63. For details of the debate held in Lok Sabha, https://www.mea.gov.in/lok-sabha.htm?dtl/26684/QUESTION+NO568+SOUTH+CHINA+SEA (accessed on May 5, 2017).
64. "Defense of Japan 2013," Japan Ministry of Defense, https://www.mod.go.jp/e/publ/w_paper/2013.html (accessed on May 12, 2016).
65. For details of the debate held in Lok Sabha, mea.gov.in/lok-sabha.htm?dtl/24961/Q_NO3677_STRENGTHENING_INDOCHINA_TIES (accessed on March 15, 2016).
66. For details of the debate held in Lok Sabha, mea.gov.in/lok-sabha.htm?dtl/24557/Q_NO4130_CONSTRUCTION_OF_ROAD_ALONG_Mc_MOHAN_LINE (accessed on March 15, 2016).
67. Ibid.
68. Dalbir Ahlawat, n.62, p.223.
69. For details of the debate held in Lok Sabha, https://www.mea.gov.in/lok-sabha.htm?dtl/26143/Q_NO1757_INDOCHINA_TERROR_PACT (accessed on November 10, 2016).
70. For details of the debate held in Lok Sabha, https://mea.gov.in/lok-sabha.htm?dtl/27712/QUESTION_NO2452_STAND_ON_MASOOD_AZHAR (accessed on February 5, 2017).
71. Joint Statement on the occasion of the visit of the President of Vietnam, October 12, 2011, https://www.mea.gov.in/bilateral-documents.htm?dtl/5341/Joint_Statement_ (accessed on June 12, 2016).
72. "Vision and Actions on Jointly Building Silk Road Economic Belt and 21st Century Maritime Silk Road," National Development and Reform Commission, Ministry of Foreign Affairs and Ministry of Commerce of the People's Republic of China, March 28, 2015, en.ndrc.gov.cn/newsrelease/201503/t20150330_669367.html (accessed on June 15, 2016).
73. "China-Pakistan corridor going smoothly despite challenges: minister," *Reuters*, June 28, 2017, https://www.reuters.com/article/us-china-pakistan-corridor-idUSKBN19J0B2 (accessed on August 12, 2017).

74. Yuan Xunhui, Zhang Juan and Shannon Tiezi, "A Chinese Perspective on Obama's Asia Policy," *The Diplomat*, November 9, 2016, https://thediplomat.com/2016/11/a-chinese-perspective-on-obamas-asia-policy/ (accessed on February 10, 2017).
75. Carlyle A. Thayer, n.158, https://www.c3sindia.org/environment-health/vietnamese-diplomacy-1975-2015-from-member-of-the-socialist-camp-to-proactive-international-integration-by-carlyle-a-thayer/ (accessed on February 10, 2017).
76. "Full text of Obama speech in Parliament," *India Today*, 8 November 2010, https://www.indiatoday.in/obama-visit/latest-updates/story/full-text-of-obama-speech-in-parliament-85230-2010-11-08 (accessed on October 15, 2016).
77. Chuck Hagel, "Beijing 'destabilising' South China Sea," *BBC News*, May 31, 2014, https://www.bbc.com/news/world-asia-27646223 (accessed on October 15, 2015)
78. Srikanth Kondapalli, "Changing Security Paradigm in China," *World Focus*, March 2008, pp 3-6.
79. Li Kaisheng, "Vietnam's ambition may disturb regional cooperation, stir confrontation," *Global Times*, June 18, 2017, www.globaltimes.cn/content/1052276.shtml (accessed on December 10, 2017).
80. *China Energy News*, October 16, 2011.
81. *The Hindu*, October 12, 2011.
82. Ibid.
83. A. Lakshmana Chetty, "BRICS and India- China Ties in the Asian Century," *Area Studies*, Vol. 6, No. 1, January–June 2012, pp.25–26.
84. B Ramesh Babu, "Peace through Containment and Prosperity through Cooperation: Continuing Challenge Confronting India's China Policy," *Area Studies*, Vol.8, No.1, January–June 2014, p.10.

FOUR

The Emerging Strategic Partnership Between India and Vietnam and the Chinese Response

India has always found a natural friend and ally in Vietnam, but the common perception of 'Chinese threat' has always played a very crucial role in bringing these two countries, ever closer to each other. As the years have progressed in the post-Cold War period, some issues cropped up instilling in them a fear of Chinese 'expansionism'. This has led them to upgrade their bilateral partnership to even greater heights at regular frequency. Despite the fact that both China and Vietnam have an ideologically similar political set up and they maintain a very cordial party-to-party interaction, Vietnam could never really erase from her memories the anguish of bitter historical experiences with China. As it has been discussed already, Vietnam found in India, a true friend and a supporter of her fight against the Western powers in the Cold War era. The initial ideological camaraderie between Vietnam and China soon faded away as the Cold War years progressed and India, time and again, through her constructive action, proved that she was a far more reliable partner of Vietnam than China. India too, in return, found Vietnam to be a very unfailing and important 'pillar' of her natural advance towards the East. Vietnam found in India a bulwark against Chinese 'aggression' and 'regional hegemony,' and India found in Vietnam a trustworthy voice that would support her on crucial issues in international forums and prove to be a fortification against

Chinese advances in the Southeast Asian region. If we analyse some very important issues which took place in the post-Cold War years that led India and Vietnam to come closer to each other against any kind of perceived Chinese aggressive posture, the picture will be clearer in the succeeding part of this chapter, where some of these strategic issues have been discussed.

Defence Cooperation: The New Vista of Understanding

India has always been supportive of Vietnam's defence capabilities and modernisation efforts and its abilities to counter the aggressions of relatively much stronger opponents, such as the United States and China. As part of exchange of high level military delegations, the then chief of the General Staff of the Indian Army General KV Krishna Rao, had even visited Hanoi in May 1983 after the Sino-Vietnam war of 1979 to learn more about Vietnamese defence abilities. In fact, the main purpose of Rao's visit to Hanoi in 1979 was to study how Vietnamese border troops defeated attacks by China.India's relations with Vietnam in the area of defence cooperation during the Cold War period were not in the limelight in the discourse of India-Vietnam relations. This lack of cooperation happened because Vietnam emerged as a political entity in the then global politics only after the unification of North and South Vietnam in 1976. During that time the Government of Vietnam was mainly concentrated on its economic reconstruction and never gave any priority to modernisation of its defence. After its intervention in Kampuchea in 1979 followed by the Chinese aggression in February 1979, Vietnam came closer towards the former Soviet Union and to the East European countries. This led the Vietnam government's defence industry to be solely based on Soviet assistance and a Treaty of friendship was signed with the Soviet Union in November. From this perspective, defence cooperation and collaboration between India and Vietnam never came into the limelight except some army personnel's occasional visits and counter-visits during the Cold War period. These visits were simply exchange of ideas of how to develop future defence cooperation between India and Vietnam. The end of the Cold War saw the disintegration of India's staunch ally, the erstwhile Soviet Union. New Delhi's defence relations with Hanoi developed slowly, in a limited manner. The sign of better understanding between India and Vietnam in the domain of the defence sector was reflected when Lt. Gen. Nguyen Huy Van led a four-member senior military delegation to India in July 1992. They held talks with the Chief of the Indian Army Staff, Gen. Rodriguez as well as others.

The cooperation in the field of defence between India and Vietnam gradually grew between 1991 and 2015. Even during the Cold War era, their relations were extremely affable but became more pronounced after the commencement of India's Look East policy in 1991. This policy led to India's rendezvous with the countries of Southeast Asia in general and with Vietnam in particular. Vietnam has been termed as 'one of the pillars of India's Look East policy and thus has remained an active partner of India in the post-Cold War period. India has displayed keen interest in ensuring the security and viability of the important sea lanes of communications and making the strategically important straits such as the Malacca straits, which are in the region, safe from aggression from other countries. This region is also important for India's energy security and it has definite proposals to secure oil and gas supplies from countries like Myanmar, Vietnam and Indonesia to meet her energy needs.[1] In the new emerging global order, India could no longer afford to remain lukewarm to defence cooperation with Vietnam. In the post-Cold War period, momentum gathered to consolidate their defence cooperation in the form of a very crucial defence cooperation agreement concluded in 1994.[2] It included provision for training of Vietnamese defence personnel and supplying military hardware spare parts. The defence agreement was signed by the two countries when Prime Minister Narasimha Rao visited Vietnam in September 1994. Actually, the main focus of this agreement was to promote cooperation between the defence establishments of the two countries on safeguarding and preservation of military equipment mostly supplied to Vietnam by the erstwhile Soviet Union. The agreement was not intended against any other country and the main focus was on military exchanges, visits and training. It was agreed that there would be frequent exchanges of visits by defence personnel and important information, and also transfer of relevant technologies and equipment as and when required. It was further agreed that the Hindustan Aeronautics Limited (HAL) will overhaul Vietnam's MiG-21 fighter aircraft.

Keeping up the momentum of this renewed vigour in India's defence ties with Vietnam, both countries continued with their high-level visits throughout the 1990s to bolster their defence ties and strengthen their defence cooperation commitments. For instance, a high-level delegation headed by the Vietnamese Vice Minister of Defence and Chief of the General Staff, Gen. Dai Din Luyen, visited India in 1995. The Director of Military Intelligence of Vietnam also visited India in September 1997.

Similarly, from the Indian side, the Director General of Military Intelligence of the Indian Army, Lt. Gen R L Sawhney visited Vietnam from November 10–13, 1998, and the Chief of the Army Staff of India visited Vietnam from February 23–28, 1999. In August 1997, the 8th Vietnam joint commission meeting was held in Hanoi, where India offered to supply spare parts to Vietnam and agreed to service Hanoi's Soviet origin defence equipment on a commercial basis. Both countries agreed to carry out intervallic exchange of defence personnel, information, and up gradation of defence equipment. It is interesting to note here that after the May 1998 nuclear tests, India became a nuclear weapon state, and thus demonstrated its ability to develop a variety of missiles, including ballistic missiles. At this crucial juncture when India came under strong criticism from most countries, including the United States and China, Vietnam staunchly stood by India. This further bolstered their bonhomie.

In the new millennium, serious efforts towards betterment of bilateral defence ties continued unabated. In March 2000, India's the then Defence Minister, George Fernandez visited Hanoi, the first ever visit by an Indian Defence Minister to Vietnam. A Defence Protocol was signed during this visit and India pledged her assistance to bolster Vietnam's naval capacity-building. As per this Defence Cooperation

Agreement, India further promised sale of advanced military light helicopters, assistance in repairs and overhaul of Vietnam's MiG-21 aircraft and training assistance for pilots and technicians. As the most remarkable facet of this visit, a fifteen-point agreement was signed between the two countries. The two Navies, the Indian Coast Guards and the Vietnamese sea-police agreed to cooperate with each other in combating piracy. At the end of this agreement, the Indian Defence Minister hailed Vietnam as India's 'most trusted friend and ally', and clearly mentioned that Hanoi 'stood by us after the nuclear tests because they understand that if (India) went nuclear there were good reasons for it,' and thereby implied that the 'China threat' was unmistakable. Finally, the Indian Defence Minister described the cooperation as the beginning of a 'periodical security dialogue,' and agreed to assist Vietnam in the process of setting up its DRDO (Defence Research and Development Organization) apart from paving the way for visit of Indian ships to Vietnam and more collaboration in naval exercises.[3] This was done keeping in mind that the DRDO could in future provide technical knowhow to Vietnam's nascent armament industry. Vietnam has been seeking to upgrade its air force. Therefore, the availability of cheaper Indian technology for refurbishing its ageing Russian Aircraft, setting up of small armed industry and purchase of equipment were crucial to Vietnam. Enhanced military capabilities enabled India not only to meet its own security concerns but also to project itself as a power to pursue the security affairs of the nations whose peace and security was a matter of concern for India. Thus, the Indian Defence Minister's visit in March 2000 gave a fillip to defence cooperation between the two countries by paving the way for greater military-to-military cooperation, sale of advanced military light helicopters, assistance in repairs, overhaul of Hanoi's mainstay MiG fighters and raising the level of military contacts between the two countries. The defence cooperation agreement moreover, elucidated the outline for periodical talks between Defence Ministers of the two countries and collaboration between the Indian Coast Guard and Vietnamese Sea Police in meeting challenge of the growing menace of piracy in the eastern seas. Defence Minister George Fernandez described the agreement as 'most significant'. Under this pact, Vietnam offered to admit Indian Armed Forces personnel for training in jungle warfare. The Vietnamese Army offered the training in Vietnamese language to Indian officers selected for warfare courses.[4]

The next major high point of their defence relations was the Strategic Partnership Agreement of 2007. This agreement was important as it took place amidst reports of growing assertiveness of China in not only the South China Sea region but also in its relations with neighbours such as India. For instance, in her relations with India, China became increasingly forceful and denied a visa to an Indian government official from Arunachal Pradesh to visit China around this time, arguing that since it considered the state as a part of China, the official would not require a visa to visit his own country. At this crucial juncture, the Prime Minister of Vietnam Mr. Nguyen Tan Dung paid a state visit to India from July 4-6, 2007. During this visit, the two sides resolved to strengthen mutual relations by establishing a New Strategic Partnership. They highly valued the important contributions made to bilateral cooperation by various existing mechanisms such as the India-Vietnam Joint Commission and the India-Vietnam Foreign Office Consultations. To further enhance cooperation and understanding in the context of the New Strategic Partnership established between the two countries, they agreed on a Strategic Dialogue at the level of Vice-Ministers in the Foreign Office. The two sides agreed that contracts and exchanges of visits between the Defence and Security establishments of the two countries should be further enhanced. Recognising that both countries have extensive maritime interests, the two sides agreed to work closely to enhance cooperation to effectively counter the China threat.[5]

Following this, the next important milestone in defence collaboration between the two countries was the visit of the Defence Minister of India, AK Antony to Hanoi in December 2007. This was a crucial juncture for defence negotiations between Hanoi and New Delhi as during this time the latter had started to actively engage in negotiations with the ASEAN after the formation of the ASEAN Defence Ministers' Meeting (ADMM) in 2006 and India could finally join the ADMM Plus in October 2010. This was a momentous event for India's 'Look East' Phase II, which further provided an impetus for Indo-Vietnam defence cooperation. Therefore, during this visit, Antony announced at the meeting with his counterpart General Phung Quang Thanh in Hanoi that India would transfer 5000 naval spares belonging to the Petya class of ship to Vietnam to make many of the ageing ships operational. The two sides agreed to set up a Joint Working Group to facilitate the signing of a Memorandum of Understanding (MoU) on defence cooperation. Antony congratulated Vietnam on being elected as a non-permanent member of the United Nations Security Council (UNSC) for a period of two years and said that New Delhi attached tremendous importance to the Strategic Partnership formed by the two Prime Ministers in July that year. He also announced the deputation of a four-member team to impart training on UN Peace Keeping Operations in the first half of the next year. General Thanh thanked India for providing training to their armed forces officers in various areas and said: "They are bringing back valuable knowledge and skills to their work areas."[6] He sought further Indian support in training of defence personnel, enhancing the exchanges of delegations, expanding training cooperation, an increase in the frequency of goodwill visits by naval ships, application of information technology and technical support for the Vietnamese navy. It is to be noted here that, India and Vietnam, as an important part of their institutionalised mechanisms for bilateral exchanges, has an annual Security Dialogue at Defence Secretary Level. In 2007 November, at the third India-Vietnam Security Dialogue meeting, the two countries agreed on a number of important decisions, like the exchange of visits for better appreciation of requirements and problems, greater cooperation in the field of training of Service personnel, particularly involving junior level officers, security dialogue at least once a year, sharing of expertise on issues of common concerns such as maritime security, border management and counter-insurgency. The dialogue parameter also included training for Vietnamese officers in the field of UN Peacekeeping operations, invitation to Vietnamese officers to Indian military exercises as observers, etc. All were aimed at providing greater impetus to their growing relationship.[7]

Throughout this decade, that is from 2000 to 2009, Indian and Vietnamese naval cooperation continued and was conditioned more by the 'China threat' perception than any other consideration. For instance, right from the beginning of the new millennium, with renewed vigour to step up their bilateral naval cooperation and to clearly give out India's message of support to Vietnam, in 2001, an Indian Coastguard vessel 'Sangram' paid a goodwill visit to Ho Chi Minh City from 7-9 June, after participating in the 'Coastguard Fleet Review' in Japan. This was the first ever stop over by an Indian Coast Guard ship in Vietnam. In the same year, two Indian naval ships 'INS Mumbai' and 'INS Jyoti' paid a three-day goodwill visit to Ho Chi Minh City from October 29-31.[8] In November 2004, three Indian naval ships, namely 'INS Ranvijay', 'INS Sukanya' and 'INS Kirch' paid goodwill visits to Ho Chi Minh City. This trip was commanded by Rear Admiral SK Damle, Flag Officer Commanding-in-Chief (FOC) of the Eastern Naval Fleet.[9] From June 9-13, 2005, the Indian naval vessel 'INS Magar' went on a goodwill visit to Vietnam.[10] From June 8-11, 2006, three Indian naval ships, 'INS Rajput', 'INS Kulish' and 'INS Kirpan', led by Rear Admiral D.K Joshi, FOC, Eastern Fleet visited Tien Sea Port at Da Nang City of Vietnam[11]. Two Indian Navy ships, namely 'INS Mysore' and 'INS Ranjit' and a Coast Guard ship 'ICGS Sagar' docked at a port in Ho Chi Minh City from May 7-11, and May 12-14, 2007, respectively, and India supplied free equipment to the Vietnamese Navy to repair its facilities.[12] On April 21, 2008, Flag Officer Commanding-in-Chief of the Indian eastern naval command visited Hanoi with two naval ships INS Kora and INS Kirpan.

Apart from the forums provided by the ASEAN, ASEAN Regional Forum, Mekong Ganga Cooperation and Asia Europe Meeting, an important 'track one' inter-governmental defence talk podium materialised in this decade, namely the 'Shangri-La Dialogue'. The Dialogue of Asia-Pacific states, is an initiative of an autonomous think-tank, i.e. the International Institute for Strategic Studies. This Dialogue is of immense significance as it is conducted every year and is attended by defence ministry personnel, military chiefs, legislators, journalists and the like. This Dialogue has been consistently held since 2002 and it is a forum where both India and Vietnam, along with China can participate and contribute in their own way to discussions on important security issues in the region. The fifth Shangri La Dialogue of 2006 was very significant. Here Mr. Pranab Mukherjee, emphasised the critical importance of the Strait of Malacca to Indian security, noting that more than 50 percent of India's trade passed through its waters, clearly and tacitly giving out the message to China that India is certainly concerned and will have to involve itself, if need be, in ensuring the safety and free rights of passage in the Straits of Malacca, as per international rules and regulations. On India's relations with China, Mukherjee remarked that India was engaged in a constructive dialogue with China to resolve outstanding border issues, and that through several confidence-building agreements of 1993, 1996 and 2005, tension had been reduced in the border areas along the Line of Actual Control (LAC).[13] Nonetheless, it remained a volatile issue in India's bilateral ties with China with the potential of flaring up any moment, with considerable ramifications for India-Vietnam relations.

The First Strategic Dialogue between the two countries was held at the fag end of this decade, on October 15, 2009, at New Delhi. Since then regular security dialogue have been held and institutionalised. Another important MoU was signed between the two ministries of defence according to which, India provided a concessional $100 million Line of Credit to Vietnam for procurement of defence equipment.[14] This was at a time when the South China Sea tensions were flaring up once again. Significantly enough, Vietnam released a Defence White Paper in 2009. In this White Paper, President Nguyen Minh Triet highlighted the steps to boost the defence industry, improve tactical skills and upgrade weaponry to counter the hi-tech weaponry and enhance military strength of Vietnam's enemies. Although in this White Paper, no particular reference was made to China, but the underlying theme was the need to counter the increasing pressure from Vietnam's bigger neighbour. In the Foreword to this Defence 2009 White Paper, the then Defence Minister General Phung Tuang Thanh wrote: "On the basis of the thorough grasp of the Party and State's guidelines of independence, self- reliance, peace, cooperation and development in external affairs and the foreign policy of openness, multi-lateralization and the diversification in International Relations, the Vietnamese People Army should enhance defence diplomatic activities; expand and consolidate ties and cooperation with all countries (first and foremost with neighbouring and regional ones, and other major partners.), and conduct deepened, effective, stable, sustainable, mutually confident international relations that contribute to the successful implementation of the party and state's foreign policy, and meet the needs of building the Vietnamese Army under new conditions."[15] In fact, the White Paper made only an indirect reference to China on the issue of military strategy, galloping defence expenditure, advanced weapon systems and technologies. It also laid emphasis on the increasing gap in defence capabilities between the major powers and developing countries and categorically listed Vietnam's major achievements in terms of demarcating the land borders and the settlement of maritime borders with China in the Gulf of Tonkin. The Paper furthermore, unambiguously once again reiterated Vietnam's sovereign rights over the South China Sea (East Sea), including the Spratlys and the Paracels. According to this White Paper, Vietnam was for expanding defence diplomacy and was actively participating in defence and security cooperation in the regional and international community to reinforce the friendship, mutual understanding, confidence building and conflict prevention. This is why, Vietnam has been trying to expand its defence and security cooperation with more and more countries and has been thus regularly engaging in joint naval exercises with India, China, United States, Australia, Japan, etc.[16] Coincidentally, in the same year, that is in 2009, India modified its maritime doctrine, which was originally formulated in 2004. According to the doctrine, areas of maritime interest to India not only include India's coastal areas and maritime zones, including the coastline, islands, internal sea waters, territorial waters, contiguous zone, Exclusive Economic Zone, continental shelf, and the Arabian Sea, Bay of Bengal, Andaman Sea and their littoral regions, but also the choke points leading to, from and across the Indian Ocean, including the Malacca and Singapore Straits, South and East China Seas and their littoral regions.[17]

In July 2010, General VK Singh paid a visit to Vietnam and met his counterpart, the Deputy Chief of the Vietnam General Staff Pham Hong Loi. This was the first visit to Vietnam by an Indian Army Chief in over a decade. Two areas were spotted by them for immediate cooperation. These were, firstly, training of military personnel and secondly, dialogue between experts on strategic affairs on both sides. Vietnam, which was then, chairing the ASEAN, invited India to the ASEAN Plus Eight Defence Ministers meeting.[18] India participated in the ASEAN Plus Eight Defence Ministers Meeting, held in October 2010 at Hanoi. Apart from the ten member states of the ASEAN, eight other countries, such as Australia, China, India, Japan, Republic of Korea, New Zealand, Russia and the United States of America participated as dialogue partners to discuss measures for improving the security architecture of the region. As a result of these positive and confidence-building efforts, India and Vietnam also began joint naval exercises. For example, in the 'Milan' of 2010, Vietnam was a successful participant with India. This event is held every two years, where navies of diverse countries from the Indian Ocean region carry out joint naval exercises in the waters of the Andaman and Nicobar islands.

However, a major hiccup in India-Vietnam relations during this period was India's apparent hesitations in delivering the BrahMos missile systems to Hanoi as was promised, during the tenure of the BJP government. This dithering led Vietnam to come closer to India's arch-rival Pakistan, and Vietnam procured 100 SMG-PK 9mm submachine guns and 50 sniper rifles in 2007. But India was quick to respond and in 2011, India entered into negotiations with Vietnam to sell its first BrahMos cruise missiles, which are capable of being launched from submarines, aircraft or land. This was for the first time that

India was entering into such a negotiation with any outside country. This purported to bolster Vietnam's defence abilities, particularly in the wake of re-ignition of the South China Sea issue and to combat China's assertiveness in the region. Another first was recorded in their bilateral relations when Indian naval warships were granted permission to anchor at the Na Trang port in southern Vietnam. This permission was granted to India by Vietnam, chiefly because Vietnam wanted a significant presence of the Indian navy in the South China Sea region, to counter the Chinese dominance in the Sea.[19]

Vietnam was likewise trying to come closer to the United States, particularly to thwart Chinese aggressiveness in the Southeast Asian and South China Sea regions. Strategic cooperation between Vietnam and the United States began in 2003. The perceived Chinese threat had drawn these two countries closer to each other. Vietnam wanted the United States to engage itself in the region more than ever before and contribute to its economic modernisation and security cooperation. Vietnam has vital interests and desires that the United States should remove restrictions on arms sale. The United States desires greater access to Vietnamese ports, so its warships could dock there and exert their presence in the region. Vietnam and the USA, keeping ideological differences and war experiences aside, have come a long way since the establishment of formal diplomatic relations on July 12, 1995, exchange of their Ambassadors in July 1997 and opening of the US Consulate General in Ho Chi Minh City and Vietnam Consulate General in San Francisco in November 1997. US Secretary of Defence W. Cohen paid a visit to Vietnam in March 2000 and Vietnam's Minister of Defence Pham Van Tra visited the US in November 2003. In June 2006, US Secretary of Defence D. Rumsfeld visited Vietnam. Since 2003, US naval ships have called on Vietnam's ports annually under a bilateral military cooperation framework. On December 29, 2006, together with the announcement of granting Permanent Normal Trade Relations (PNTR) for Vietnam, US President George Bush lifted the embargo on selling some non-lethal military items to Vietnam. Even during President Obama's tenure, positive developments took place for fostering greater camaraderie between the two countries. On September 2011, the US Deputy Assistant Secretary of defence for South and Southeast Asia and Vietnam's Defence Minister signed a MoU for advancing bilateral defence cooperation.

Vietnam welcomes the support of India and the United States on the South China Sea issue. In fact, the fear of Chinese belligerence in the region has drawn them closer to each other. The United States has released quite a few press statements condemning Chinese moves in the region. For instance, one such press statement was released by Patrick Ventrell, Acting Deputy Spokesperson, Office of Press Relations, Washington D.C on 3 August, 2012. According to the statement, "We are concerned by the increase in tensions in the South China Sea and are monitoring the situation closely...China's upgrading of the administrative level of Sansha City and establishment of a new military garrison there covering disputed areas of the South China Sea run counter to collaborative diplomatic efforts to resolve differences and risk further escalating tensions in the region."[20]

China's hard-line military modernisation and strategic proximity and support to Pakistan have drawn India, Vietnam and the United States closer to each other. While India stepped up its own military modernisation plan, Vietnam did the same almost exclusively driven by the threat of China. This is why, unlike any other country, Vietnam's publicly released defence budget has grown from $1.3 billion in 2006 to $4.6 billion in 2015, a 258 percent increase. Vietnam's arms imports stood at 34 percent of total ASEAN arms imports in 2015, the largest share among all other ASEAN countries.[21] Russia is the largest ally of Vietnam for procuring arms, despite the entry of the United States in this area.

Truong Tan Sang, President of Vietnam visited India from October 11-13, 2011. This visit was significant for bilateral defence cooperation. New initiatives were undertaken in the defence industry, Research and Development, and 'think-tanks'-related areas.[22] On April 18, 2012, at the peak of India and Vietnam's war of words with China over India's involvement in the disputed South China Sea at the behest of Vietnam,

India launched the Agni V missile to boost the country's rocket hitting capability to over 5000 kms. This two-stage missile, equipped with an advanced high-accuracy navigation system and guided by a novel state-of-the-art command and control system, is powered by a solid rocket propellant structure. The Chinese reaction was not favourable. The Global Times on April 19, 2012, wrote, "India should not overestimate its strength. Even if it has missiles that could reach most parts of China that does not mean it will gain anything from being arrogant during disputes with China. India should be clear that China's nuclear power is stronger and more reliable. For the foreseeable future, India would stand no chance in an overall arms race with China."[23]

Four Indian naval ships, including the indigenously built stealth frigate INS Satpura and fleet tanker INS Shakti, with a compliment of around 1200 officers and sellers, visited Da Nang from June 6-10, 2013. This was a friendly and cooperative gesture towards Vietnam, especially in the wake of reports of renewed Chinese militarisation in the South China Sea. Keeping up the momentum of improved defence ties with Vietnam, the high-level defence-related visits continued in the meantime. From the Vietnamese side, Lt. Gen. Do Ba Ty, Chief of the General Staff-cum-Vice Minister of Defence Senior, visited India from September 23-27, 2013. Mr. Pham Quang Vinh, Vice Foreign Minister participated in the Delhi Dialogue VI held on March 23-27, 2014. General Dalbir Singh Suhag, Chief of the Army Staff of India visited Vietnam from December 17-20, 2014. As part of the high-level defence engagement, Vietnam's Vice Defence Minister Lt. General Nguyen Chi Binh visited Delhi for the Security Dialogue with the Defence Secretary on January 16, 2015. In this crucial meeting, India offered $100 million Line of Credit to strengthen Vietnam's navy, clearly as an answer to greater Chinese arms twisting in the South China Sea region. Indian Naval Warship INS Shivalik (in August 2014) and coastguard ship Samudra Paheredar (in October 2014) went to Vietnam to display India's unwavering support to Vietnam in the face of the growing Chinese assertiveness.[24] Col Gen Do Ba Ty, Vice Minister of National Defence, Chief of the General Staff of Vietnam visited India and called on the Indian Defence Minister on September 24, 2013.

Continuing with the trend of bilateral visits to beef up their defence cooperation, in January 2015, Vietnam's Deputy Defence Minister Nguyen Chi Vinh visited India and together with India's Defence Secretary Shri R. K. Mathur convened the ninth Vietnam-India defence dialogue in New Delhi on January 16, 2015. In this meeting, the two countries agreed to continue sharing defence strategies and policies via visits and training courses for armies, especially naval forces. Following up this visit, in early April 2015, Indian national security advisor A. Doval paid a visit to Vietnam to discuss defence and security collaboration between the two countries.[25]

Thus, since 1980, when Vietnam and India for the first time, started exchanging Defence Attaché, they have traversed a long way. Today, the two nations are bound by various agreements, MoUs and protocols to guide their cooperative defence efforts, such as protocol on defence signed in April 1994, Memorandum of Understanding (MoU) on defence cooperation signed in November 2009, and a MoU on navy cooperation in June 2011. Vietnam and India signed a Mutual Legal Assistance Treaty in Criminal Matters in 2007, a Memorandum on Crime Prevention Cooperation in 2008, a MoU on Cooperation between Vietnam's Ministry of Public Security and India's Ministry of Home Affairs in September 2011.[26] Furthermore, since 1993 India has provided training to Vietnamese Army (20-30 trainees each year) and since 2009, India has deputed English teachers to teach Vietnamese trainees. On the other hand, Vietnam admits one Indian officer to Vietnam's Academy of Defence since 2008 and 1-2 Indian officers to Vietnamese language course at Vietnam's Academy of Military Science each year. The Indian Navy has been offering training in command and control, logistics and engineering, ship repair, military science and technologies, hydrography, foreign languages and computer skills to the Vietnamese Navy. The navies also cooperate in coping with non-traditional security issues like, counterterrorism, environmental pollution, natural disaster relief and prevention. Other areas of cooperation are: sharing information on developing maritime strategies and management; creating digital nautical charts, shipping, underwater sound and magnetic fields information; exchanging information about activities in the East Sea and Southeast Asian region.[27]

Taking strong offence to India's military modernisation moves and its growing defence ties with Vietnam, throughout this time China has been engaging increasingly with India's arch-rival, Pakistan, in the South Asian region. For instance, in July 2015 it was reported that China has built the world's largest single solar photovoltaic power plant in Bhawalpur in Pakistan's Punjab province. The 100 MW Quaid-e-Azam Solar Park has come up over 229 hectare land in the Cholistan desert in three months and cost $215 million. The project, named after Pakistan's founder Md. Ali Jinnah, gave a big boost to Prime Minister Nawaz Sharif, who was elected on the promise of solving the country's energy crisis. The Chinese media has linked the project with its Silk Road programme. Chinese President Xi Jinping had allocated $46 billion for a China-Pakistan economic corridor as a model project for Beijing's growing clout. Chinese officials say the corridor showcases efficacy of the Silk Road Programme, which they describe as 'One belt, One Road' programme.[28]

Incidentally, without paying much heed to the Chinese reservations about growing Indo-Vietnamese defence ties, the Indian Armed Forces got engaged with the capacity building of the Vietnamese Armed Forces, particularly the Navy. This is to ensure that the Vietnamese Navy is well-equipped to thwart all Chinese overtures in the South China Sea and particularly in the Straits of Malacca and it is of utmost importance to India that it remains in friendly hands with Vietnam. New Delhi has mainly focused on certain specific areas of cooperation, such as, training, repairs and maintenance support, exchanges between think-tanks, study tour and ship visits.[29] In fact, India and Vietnam bond over shared perception of the threat from China in intense defence cooperation. That is why India and Vietnam signed a five-year joint vision statement defence cooperation in 2015 to build closer strategic ties in the backdrop of an increasingly assertive China flexing its muscles in the South China Sea. Gen. Phung Quang Thanh, Vietnam Defence Minister visited New Delhi in May 2015 amid growing concerns over China's land reclamation project in the South China Sea, aimed at bolstering its territorial claims in the disputed area.[30] It is a fact that, China's claim of its 'peaceful rise', aggressive military modernisation drive in the new millennium and the 'Chinese dream' set as a goal for the Chinese people and nation, have sent awkward signals to the psyche of some of China's neighbours , including Vietnam. The latter has been beefing up its defence ties with India, the United States, Japan and some other countries so that it could acquire latest defence technologies, hardware, aircrafts and cruise missiles to counter Chinese advances effectively.

To sum up, it can be argued that defence collaboration between the two countries has witnessed proactive developments over the years, with the establishment of a deputy defence ministerial level strategic dialogue and acceleration of joint naval exercises The two sides reached a consensus on maintaining regular exchange of delegations, information sharing, and coordination with each other at relevant multilateral forums, including the ASEAN Defence Ministers' Meeting-Plus and the ASEAN Regional Forum.[31] Highlighting on the new field of cooperation in Vietnam-India defence cooperation, Vietnam's Deputy Minister of Defence, Nguyen Chi Vinh, during his visit to India on the occasion of the ninth Defence Dialogue between Vietnam and India in January 2015, remarked, "For a number of years, the two countries have been cooperating in various fields, namely regional strategic issues, defence industry, arms and services cooperation, education and training, science and technology, etc...Both sides are also interested in expanding to new cooperation fields, such as, cooperation in United Nations Peacekeeping cooperation and cooperation activities within ADMM Plus, Vietnam and India co-chair the Expert Working Group for Humanitarian Mine Action (EWG HMA). These are significant fields of cooperation for both countries with humanitarian nature and practical for maintaining peace and security of the region and appreciated by the international community. Another field of cooperation, which has been given great focus by both sides, is the defence industry, where some possibilities of cooperation are ship building, weapon system modernization and research and apply hi-tech for defence purposes. Recently, India has assisted Vietnam in establishing a Centre for Information Technology and English language within the University of Telecommunication and Signals, Ministry of National Defence of Vietnam. The centre is estimated to be inaugurated in the second quarter of 2015. Another field of cooperation is education and training. Vietnam appreciates India for training young Vietnamese officers in military engineering, language, Information Technology, etc in Indian military academics. This creates an important human resource for our military in the future."[32]

Science, Information Technology and Human Resource Development Programme: The New Space of Cooperation

Vietnam and India have been cooperating in science and technology since 1978, after the signing of the Agreement on Bilateral Cooperation in Science and Technology. This agreement pledged exchange of scientists, specialists and scientific information, joint research in areas of common interest and exchange patents and licenses[33] (this 1978 agreement was renewed in February 1996 with provision for joint research and exchange of scientists in various areas). As a follow-up, a three-member State Commission of Vietnam for Science and Technology visited India in July 1979 and identified the areas of cooperation in science and technology. Indian experts in drug research, virology, medicine and other scientific and technological fields visited Vietnam in 1980-81. In February 1982 India and Vietnam agreed to exchange documents on science and technical aspects prepared by international organizations.[34] When the India-Vietnam Joint Commission was established in December 1982, a plan of action for cooperation in science and technology was discussed. During 1979-80, India provided a credit of ⊠ 3.5 crore for purchase of railway rolling stock and also credit of ⊠ 20 crore for the year 1980-81 for the same purpose.[35] On July 27, 1979, India and Vietnam signed an agreement on scientific cooperation under which they agreed to cooperate in the field of technology of carriage fabrication, organisation in production of diesel engines, management and exploitation of automatic and semi-automatic signalling system and railway wire communication lines.[36]

In the post-Cold War period, a Joint Committee on science and technology was set up between the two countries in 1997 to analyse the ways of scientific and technological cooperation and to categorise the fields as far as collaboration in science and technology was concerned. This Joint Committee identified certain areas in which India and Vietnam were to expand their cooperation, such as, bio-technology, agriculture, material science, IT, electronics, computers, science and technology, management, atomic energy for peaceful purposes, ocean development and oceanographic resources, meteorology, health care, medical research and non-conventional energy. By the end of the 1990s, both these countries successfully completed about a decade of renovation programme and India emerged as 'software superpower' which provided the prospect for both these countries to develop a fruitful collaboration in the fields of science, IT and human resource development. Thus, in 1999, India and Vietnam signed a protocol on cooperation in the development of IT. The protocol was signed on August 12, 1999, by Ravindra Gupta, Secretary, Department of Electronics (Government of India), and Chu Hao, Vice Minister, Ministry of Science, Technology and Environment (Government of Vietnam). According to the protocol, the two sides agreed that the information technology and electronics sector is one of the dynamic sectors of global economy and there is an enormous possibility of cooperation in this sector between the two countries. Vietnam hailed the achievements of India in information technology development and it was agreed that both India and Vietnam would work together and pool their mutual resources in policy management sectors so that both could benefit from the achievements and opportunities in the field of IT and electronics. Moreover, it was also agreed that both these countries would exchange policy and technology related information on a regular basis and develop a Joint Website for the same so that information exchange is possible in real-time and online basis. Furthermore, it was decided by both sides to set up a Working Group to enhance collaboration in IT between New Delhi and Hanoi at an earliest date and it was pledged that this group would meet once a year alternatively in the two countries. The imminent necessity of definitive focus on collaboration between India and Vietnam in science and technology, human resource development and IT in the post-Cold War period was reverberated in the words of President Tran Duc Luong when he visited India on December 1, 1999. He said, "Marvellous achievements in science and technology have opened up unlimited opportunities for humankind and at the same time put the developing countries on a danger of lagging far behind the developed ones...Given the new context in the region and the world, greater importance is attached to the consolidation and strengthening of the well-rounded cooperation between Vietnam and India."[37] Thus, mutual cooperation and collaboration in this sector proved essential to foster greater South- South cooperation and to thwart against any imperialistic designs of a mightier power.

In August 1999, the Vietnam FPT company in association with Aptech opened training centres for Vietnamese nationals to become experts who would spread the learning of IT in Vietnam. At the turn of the century, Prime Minister of India, Mr. Atal Bihari Vajpayee visited Vietnam in January 2001 and he offered a soft credit of 100 million for setting up a software and training centre in Vietnam. In this context, the Vietnamese Prime Minister Pham Van Khai, once remarked, "The Indian Government has agreed to promote soft credits to Vietnam to assist the latter in establishing training centres and developing computer software. Vietnam hopes that early implementation of these projects will help strong IT development in Vietnam and constitute a new bright spot in our bilateral cooperation picture."[38] Furthermore, India has also borne the financial burden and the planning for setting up of the Advanced Resource Centre in IT in Hanoi. Moreover, going one step further, during 2001, a large number of IT training centres were set up in Vietnam by Indian IT companies like Aptech Limited, NIIT, Tata, Infotech and Redmond Institute of Coimbatore and by 2004 India became known and appreciated as a major source of HRD training for Vietnamese nationals. Particularly, under Indian Technical and Economic Cooperation (ITEC) programme, about 150 places were being offered annually to officials and trainees from Vietnam. Under the HRD programme, India sponsored about 30 scholarships each year to Vietnamese scientists for preparing in various fields of science and technology and, these scholarships were extremely beneficial to Vietnam. Fully paid scholarships were being offered annually for training in diverse fields including agriculture, fisheries, animal husbandry, management, foreign trade, small industry extension, science and technology, computer software/hardware, computer applications, pharmaceuticals, remote sensing, mass communication, English language, water resources, etc. Apart from these, as an outreach effort to address the needs of CLMV (Cambodia, Laos, Myanmar, and Vietnam) countries, India started the implementation of entrepreneurial development projects in each of these countries in order to prepare fresh entrepreneurs in these countries.

The next important landmark in India's bilateral cooperation with Vietnam in science and technology, HRD and ICT development happened when Vietnam's Prime Minister Nguyen Tan Dung visited India from July 4-6, 2007. This visit was extremely crucial as it elevated India's diplomatic ties with Vietnam to the Strategic level, in which cooperation in Science and Technology was given special focus. During this visit, India and Vietnam also signed a Memorandum of Understanding (MoU) for supporting augmentation of high performance computing in Vietnam. According to the MoU, the Indian government agreed to set up a state-of-the-art and modern upgradable supercomputing facility known as PARAM at the Hanoi University of Science and Technology at the cost of US$ 1 million. It was pledged that the India would train the Vietnamese to create a pool of skilled professionals for pursuing research and development in the area of High Performance Computing (HPC) and promote use of HPC systems in other applications and C-DAC was assigned the task to set up the Vietnam-India Advanced Resource Centre in information and communication technology in Hanoi.[39]

The next important milestone of bilateral cooperation in this context happened when President Truong Tan Sang of Vietnam visited India from October 11-13, 2011, and stressed on increasing collaboration in science and technology as a growing area of importance. Furthermore, he thanked the Government of India for taking initiatives in establishing the Advanced Resource Centre in Information and Communications Technologies (ARC-ICT). Following up this visit, in 2012, Vietnamese Deputy Prime Minister Nguyen Thien Nhan paid a visit to India in March 2012, especially with the aim of bolstering Vietnam's cooperation with India in areas of Science and Technology, HRD and ICT development. He revealed that Vietnam was moving forward with the aim of becoming a resilient power in IT by 2020, especially in areas of nano technology, biotechnology and oceanography. During this visit, the two sides signed nine MoUs on cooperation in application of biotechnology in agriculture, nano technology research and promotion of Indian and Vietnamese studies. Mr. Nhan said Vietnam was glad to have India's IT city of Bangalore as a partner in training IT human resources. In this regard, the then Indian Minister of Science and Technology Vilasrao Deshmukh said that science and technology was considered as one of the strong pillars of support for bilateral cooperation between these two countries.[40]

Another area where India and Vietnam have been trying to bolster their cooperation is space research. In 2006, Vietnam came out with an ambitious plan called 'Strategy for space technology research and applications until 2020' that reveals plans for developing communication and earth observation satellites. In fact, absence of a rocket science base in Vietnam motivated Hanoi to look for partners to tap its space research development. In this regard, Vietnam is being helped greatly by Japan, France and also by India.[41] For instance, within the framework of ASEAN- India space cooperation, India convened the meeting between space agencies of ASEAN and India at Bangalore in March 2012. The meeting focused on a project for establishing an Indian satellite centre for monitoring satellites, receiving and processing images in Ho Chi Minh City.[42] In fact, this is one area where there are huge prospects for India and Vietnam to collaborate with each other. India is way ahead of Vietnam in space research and can generously help Hanoi in providing training to Vietnamese experts in constructing and launching satellites, and by providing a handsome amount of Official Development Assistance (ODA) to Hanoi in this regard. (It is to be noted that in January 2018 MoUs were concluded by Prime Minister of India Narendra Modi and his Vietnamese counterpart Nguyen Xuan Phuc regarding the implementation arrangement between the Indian Space Research Organization (ISRO) and Vietnam's National Remote Sensing Department for the establishment of tracking and data reception station and data processing facility in Vietnam under the ASEAN-India Space Cooperation. This would enable remote sensing applications, including natural resources management, ocean development and disaster management by the ASEAN member states.[43] Vietnam has proposed to India to assist in the construction of a Science and Technology Park in Vietnam and India has responded positively. Thus, to sum up the major achievements in Indo-Vietnam cooperation in Science and technology, HRD and ICT development, by 2015, Vietnam has been participating actively in training programmes under the Indian Technical and Economic Cooperation (ITEC) programme. Presently, 150 ITEC slots are being offered to Vietnam every year along with 16 scholarships under the General Cultural Scholarship Scheme (GCSS), 14 scholarships under the Educational Exchange Programme (EEP) and 10 scholarships under the Mekong Ganga Scholarship Scheme. India has set up a US$ 2 million Vietnam-India Advanced Resource Centre in Information and Communication Technology (ARC-ICT) in Hanoi. The Vietnam-India Entrepreneurship Development Centre (VIEDC) and a Vietnam-India English Language Training Centre (VICELT) have been established with Indian assistance under the IAI (Initiative for ASEAN Integration) as well. Vietnam and India have signed two fresh(MoU on Information Technology in 2013 in a move hailed by India's the then Minister of Communications and Information Technology Kapil Sibal. The first MoU was between Vietnam's Authority of Radio Frequency Management and India's

Wireless Planning and Coordination Wing. The second was inked between the Vietnam Telecommunications Authority (VNTA) and the Telecom Regulatory Authority of India (TRAI). Both agreements were sealed during the visit to India by Vietnamese Minister of Information and Communications Nguyen Bac Son. During talks with Son in New Delhi on July4, 2013, Sibal described Vietnam as one of India's most important partners in Southeast Asia. Sibal praised Vietnam for the rapid development of its own Information Technology sector and suggested that network security and space technology are promising fields for bilateral partnership. Son remarked that the Vietnamese Government considered developing Science and Technology as a national priority as it aimed to become a modern industrialised nation by 2020. He stressed that Vietnam stood ready to bridge India with other Southeast Asian markets and with the Republic of Korea and Japan as well. The two sides proposed to set up a joint working group with three members from each country representing the postal, telecommunication, and information technology sectors. Son met with leaders of Tata Consultancy Services (TCS) and the Centre for Development of Advanced Computing (C-DAC). He suggested C-DAC help Vietnamese universities and research institutes with Science and technology research, especially applied Sciences and information safety, as well as Information Technology human resources development through training in both nations.[44] In this regard, it is to be noted that the Joint Committee on Science and Technology meets periodically to review the progress made in cooperation in science and technology. The very crucial ninth meeting was held in Hanoi in November 2012 at which the Programme of Cooperation in Science and Technology for 2013-14 was adopted by the two sides. The Programme of Cooperation agreed to by both the sides in this meeting provided for joint projects, seminars, workshops and exploratory visits of experts in the fields of biotechnology, material science, ICT, ocean development and oceanography research, pharmaceuticals and medical research. Furthermore, both sides have initiated a Joint Project for leather research and tannery waste recycling between Central Leather

Research Institute of India and the Vietnam Leather Research Institute. Important conferences and seminars are being regularly held to shore up their cooperation in this sector. For instance, a conference on Vietnam-India Biotechnology Cooperation was hailed in Hanoi on 27 February 2013 with participation of scientists from technology research and development institutes in both Vietnam and India.[45]

Interestingly enough, the 'China factor' in India's bilateral cooperation with Vietnam on this issue never acted as an impediment and Vietnam has progressed in an uninhibited manner in this regard to develop her own potentials in Science and Technology, HRD and ICT and continued its collaboration with India. However, this does not mean that China has always given a blank cheque to any foreign country, including India where its economic interests are actively involved. In recent times, China has put a commercial satellite into space for Sri Lanka and is setting up at least ten Continuously Operating Reference Stations there. Moreover, China is also reportedly collaborating with Afghanistan, Nepal and Maldives for space research and development partnerships.[46] These Chinese initiatives in some neighbouring countries of India may be interpreted as a psychological pressure on Government of India's initiatives towards Vietnam. However, in order to overcome the Chinese South Asia 'satellite diplomacy,' India in January 2016, announced her plans to set up a dual civilian-and-military use satellite tracking and imaging centre in southern Vietnam that will help Vietnam in obtaining pictures from Indian earth observation satellites that cover the region, including China and the troubled South China Sea region. This will have direct ramifications for New Delhi's and Hanoi's relations with Beijing because this project will satiate Vietnam's need for advanced intelligence and surveillance technologies in the disputed region besides the regular civilian use.[47] Therefore, there is much scope for India to share her rich experience with Vietnam in the sector of advances in Science and Technology, Space Research, HRD and ICT development and the true potential in this regard has not yet been tapped by New Delhi so far.

Indo-Vietnam Nuclear Collaboration: The Linking Bridge

Another issue which brought Vietnam closer to India over the years is the issue of nuclear cooperation. During India's first nuclear tests in 1974, Vietnam was fighting against the United States with total solidarity provided by the Soviet Union, along with India. Moscow has generally been supportive of India's plans for the peaceful application of nuclear energy,[48] whereas, Vietnam's reaction was not publicly available nor there was any official criticism of India's nuclear explosion in Pokhran. During India's second nuclear explosions in 1998, Vietnam staunchly stood by India, even when most countries of the world, along with China expressed their grave concern over India's nuclear stand. This support of Vietnam did not get lost on India's leadership who felt that Vietnam had rightly understood that if India had to go nuclear, there were good reasons for it. However, China has always criticised India's nuclear stand on grounds of increasing nuclear proliferation, despite the fact that, it has always helped Pakistan to build her nuclear capabilities. On the issue of disarmament and nuclear non-proliferation, Vietnam has been totally in sync with India's stand that it does not support such discriminatory mechanisms as Nuclear Non-Proliferation Treaty (NPT) without any binding commitment from the Nuclear Weapons States.[49]

In fact, the issue of nuclear cooperation between India and Vietnam remains a crucial area where India could display her sincere will towards its past historical solidarity ties with Vietnam. Despite having ideological affinity with China, Vietnam has always trusted India much more and the proof of it lies in the fact that way back in 1978, just four years after India herself became nuclear, Prime Minister of India Morarji Desai, during Pham Van Dong's visit to India in February, expressed the desire to help Vietnam develop her atomic research programme. Accordingly, in 1988, the Indian Atomic Energy Commission signed an agreement on peaceful use of atomic energy. On the basis of this agreement, over the years, many Vietnamese scientists have been trained by India. However, the process of nuclear cooperation once again got its momentum, when on April 23, 1999, the

Indian Atomic Energy Commission (IAEC), a part of the IDAE, and the Vietnam Atomic Energy Commission (VAEC) signed another agreement for cooperation in the field of nuclear power, exchange of scientists and assistance in setting up a training centre in Vietnam. Under this agreement, around 30 Vietnamese nuclear scientists have received training at the Bhabha Atomic Research Centre (BARC) in Mumbai and several Indian scientists have visited Da Lat in order to help Vietnam complete its nuclear energy programme at an earliest date.[50]

Meanwhile, during Atal Bihari Vajpayee's visit to Hanoi in January 2001, the two countries signed a Memorandum of Understanding (MoU) which further pledged Indian cooperation in this regard. Besides providing adequate training at Indian nuclear power plants, it pledged India's support for setting up a nuclear science laboratory in Vietnam. India has been instrumental in setting up a nuclear training centre in Da Lat in the year 2000. Vietnam is working on her plan to build its first nuclear plant in Ninh Thuan (construction to begin in 2020) province and India has been extending her sincere help to Vietnam in this regard. More recently, to further strengthen PM Narendra Modi's 'Act East' policy, India and Vietnam signed a civil nuclear cooperation agreement on December 3, 2016, when President of Vietnam's National Assembly Nguyen Thi Kim Ngar came to India. Vietnam plans to build eight nuclear power plants in five provinces by 2030 with a total capacity of 15 gigawatts, or 10 p.cnt of all electricity produced in the country.[51] In this pursuit, India is expecting to play a major role.

However, China has never been appreciative of India's nuclear support to Vietnam and has been extremely cautious about this issue. China has given this matter much importance, just to ensure that the status quo in Southeast Asia must not be disturbed and her immediate Southern neighbour does not come under India's overarching sphere of influence. However, China got a major jolt when Vietnam's efforts to improve ties with the United States led to the signing of the US-Vietnam Civil Nuclear Cooperation Agreement on October 10, 2013.

This permitted the industries of the United States to harness Vietnam's nuclear power market. This was a major strategic move which promoted Vietnam's ties with the United States to a completely different level. This move on the one hand, was a welcome decision as far as India was concerned. But on the other, this raised much tension in the Chinese diplomatic circles and China became even more cautious of United States' 'rebalancing' policies in Asia; China started propagating in various meetings, the idea of 'Asia for Asians' even more zealously.

The discussion on the nuclear issue would remain incomplete without a brief analysis of the issue of membership in the Nuclear Suppliers' Group (NSG) or Missile Technology Control Regime (MTCR). India, even during the 1990s, has shown aversion towards the working of these nuclear export control groups such as, the Australia Group, the NSG, the MTCR, etc., because India has always felt that these operate under the framework of discriminatory policies as propounded by the nuclear 'haves' countries, much in the same vein as she has protested against the NPT on the same ground. However, with the changing times, India has realized that it must integrate herself well in the global nuclear trade. That is why it is important to become members of such groups so that India can finally come out of her nuclear isolation.

In recent times, this issue of membership in the NSG has become a major bone of contention between India and China, which has once again brought Vietnam closer to India as it supports India's membership in the NSG. India is still not a member in the NSG and there are three ways for a country to become a member. **First**, after fulfilling all the necessary criteria for becoming a member, it can show its desire to do so to the present NSG Chair, **secondly**, by entering into a contract, and **thirdly**, even if some country has not fulfilled all the criteria for becoming a member, a Participating Government (PG) can recommend it for admission. Even if the country has not fulfilled all the criteria for becoming a member, based on its support for the nuclear non-proliferation regime and by analysing its nuclear track record, the PGs, by consensus, can admit the country. This third way of becoming a member of the NSG is very important for India because India does not fulfil a major criterion for membership in the NSG, i.e. becoming 'a party to the NPT'. Moreover, based on India's credibility, track record and responsible behaviour on nuclear non-proliferation, the United States has recommended and forwarded India's case for admission to the NSG. However, China has been constantly blocking the application of India, citing non-arrival of consensus in the group, despite the fact that, China itself has been engaging in nuclear commerce with Pakistan, in violation of the NSG Guidelines because the NSG Guidelines strictly forbid nuclear commerce between NSG members and those countries that do not have full scope for IAEA safeguards.[52] In this regard, while answering to a question raised by Kapil Moreshwar Patil in the Lok Sabha, regarding whether the government is aware of the nuclear deal that exists between India and Pakistan, Sushma Swaraj, the Minister of External Affairs of India said, India "is aware of the agreement to supply two additional nuclear power reactors, Chashma-3 and Chashma-4, by China to Pakistan. These reactors are under construction, in addition to Chashma-1 and 2, which are already in operation. Government is further aware of reports of an agreement for supply of additional reactors of Chinese origin to be built at Chashma, Karachi and a third site in Pakistan. Government has raised this issue in bilateral discussions with China. China maintains that its nuclear supplies to Pakistan are in accordance with its international obligations and are only for peaceful purposes. Government remains concerned about the impact of the deal on global non-proliferation norms. Government believes that all countries should abide by the commitments that they have undertaken in the field of nuclear non-proliferation."[53] India is extremely disappointed with China for repeated blocking of India's membership plea in the NSG and is engaging with all NSG members including China at the appropriate levels for an early decision on India's application for membership in the group. Despite India's best efforts, not much headway has been made in this regard and China remains persistent in her reluctance to admit India in the group. Meanwhile, India successfully obtained membership in the Missile Technology

Control Regime (MTCR) on June 27, 2016. Interestingly, China is not a member of the MTCR and hence, India's entry into the group has not been disrupted. The MTCR membership will provide India with the ease of access to high technology, particularly in the field of space programmes and the defence sector. With India's membership in the MTCR, China will now also have to depend on India's willingness to include China in the MTCR, much in the same vein, as India's membership in the NSG is dependent on China's reluctance or acceptance.[54] Therefore, we see, that the nuclear issue has so far played a very important role in pitting China and India against each other, and here again, we find that Vietnam, which has been beefing up its political, strategic, nuclear and defence cooperation with India, stands staunchly in support of India as a separate political entity in the emerging security architecture of Southeast Asia.

The Border Issue: The Point of Concord and Discord

In the annals of history, both India and Vietnam have shared experiences of war with China which has made the issue of border a very sensitive one. China has taken some concerted initiatives to resolve its border problems with Vietnam. However, the border remains a very crucial and an on-going burning issue with India. There has not only been procrastination as far as arriving at the final solution on the border issue is concerned, but also sporadic escalation of the problem from time to time. It has been opined that the final amicable solution has not been arrived at, simply to keep India, engaged and vulnerable, since India remains the main competitor of China in the security architecture of Asia-Pacific region.

Today, the border dispute remains a very complicated one and certainly, India's core concern. India's disputed border with China had its origin before India's independence and the takeover by the Communist government in China. Presently, the border is contested in two distinct sectors: the Western sector comprising India's Ladakh (Jammu and Kashmir) opposite Chinese Xinjiang and Western Tibet, and the Eastern sector is Arunachal Pradesh opposite Tibet. In the

Eastern sector, India's customary border, called the McMahon Line was drawn up by the Simla Agreement of 1914, but China never accepted it as it felt that it was a colonial Western construct and always challenged it. In the Western sector, China never had any disputed border with India. It so happened that after India got defeated in the 1962 border war with China; Pakistan decided to cosy up to China by offering it traction in Gilgit-Baltistan (Northern Areas), which has a 480 km common border with China's Xinjiang province. The boundary settlement was reached on March 2, 1963, following which China got a foothold on the Karakoram and a stake in the Kashmir dispute between India and Pakistan. India protested against what it called Pakistan's illegal gifting of Kashmiri territories to China as it felt that the area belonged to it following the Instrument of Accession signed by the Jammu and Kashmir ruler on October 26, 1947. To this, China reacted by saying that its border agreement with Pakistan was 'provisional'. Peking clarified that it would re-negotiate its 1963 border agreement after the settlement of the Kashmir dispute with whichever country would possess it. China also said that it would remain neutral in the Kashmir dispute. However, in less than a year after the 1963 agreement, work started on the Karakoram highway between China and Pakistan.[55] Interestingly enough, China's stand on the Kashmir dispute fluctuates from time to time. Over the years, China mentions that the Kashmir problem is a bilateral problem between India and Pakistan, and sometimes it has also offered to act as a third party to resolve the problem. However, India disagrees to such an arrangement as it violates the very basis of the 1972 Simla Agreement that was signed between Mrs. Indira Gandhi and Zulfiqar Ali Bhutto. Currently, on account of China's 'One Belt One Road' (OBOR) initiative, it is whole-heartedly and indirectly supporting Pakistan on the Kashmir issue.

With this, India's border problems with China worsened further. Over the years, despite the institutionalisation of several mechanisms to resolve the border issue by both sides, such as the China Study Group, the Joint Working Groups, or the appointment of Special Representatives, the truth is that the Indo-China border remains neither delimited nor demarcated. As a result, the border remains a severely disputed area since both the countries have varying perceptions of the issue. Despite China's strong protests, India under Indira Gandhi as Prime Minister, passed the 38th Amendment Bill on April 23, 1975, and annexed Sikkim as the 22nd State of the Union of India. Again, Rajiv Gandhi, despite his best efforts to thaw relations with China, did not hesitate to grant full statehood to Arunachal Pradesh, undeterred by the staunchest criticism from the Chinese side. Despite the fact that some very concrete political parameters and guiding principles have been concluded between India and China over the years, the dispute remains unresolved. In this regard, while answering a question raised by Shri R. Dhruva Narayana and Shri Sanjay Haribhau Jadhav regarding whether India's border with Arunachal Pradesh is disputed by China and whether any agreement has been arrived at between the two countries on the border issue, Gen (Dr.) VK Singh (retd.), Minister of State in the Ministry of External Affairs replied that "in recent years, following agreements related to India-China border have been signed between the two countries: Agreement on the maintenance of Peace and Tranquillity along the Line of Actual Control in the India-China border areas, signed in September 1993, Agreement on Confidence Building Measures in the military field along the Line of Actual Control in the India-China border areas, signed in November 1996, Protocol on modalities for the implementation of Confidence Building Measures in the military field along the Line of Actual Control in the India-China border areas, signed in April 2005, Agreement on the Political Parameters and Guiding Principles for the Settlement of the India-China Boundary Question, signed in April 2005, Agreement on the establishment of Working Mechanism on Consultation and Coordination on India-China Border Affairs, signed in January 2012, Border Defence Cooperation Agreement, signed in October 2013,"[56] and such other documents have been institutionalised. Despite this, the truth remains that, time and again, there have been transgressions into the Indian territory leading to many days of stand-off between the armies of the two countries. For instance, in more recent times, there have been border infiltration and many days of stand-off between the PLA and the BSF in the Depsang Valley, Chumar area, Demchok region and most recently, in Doklam. The Government of India officially maintains that, "China disputes the International Boundary between India and China. There is no commonly delineated Line of Actual Control (LAC) in the border areas between India and China. Government regularly takes up any transgressions along the LAC with the Chinese side through established mechanisms including border personnel meetings, flag meetings and diplomatic channels".[57]

Vietnam, itself a victim of border issues with China completely empathises with India's situation and has staunchly stood in support of India's stand on Jammu and Kashmir in all international forums, including in the United Nations. Vietnam has fought a border war with China in February 1979, when China initiated an attack on the Vietnamese soil as a reaction to Vietnam attacking Cambodia in December 1978 to remove the Chinese-supported Khmer Rouge government in Cambodia. Despite the bloodshed and the heavy damage inflicted by the Chinese on Vietnam, China could not succeed in forcing Vietnam to withdraw completely before 1989. However, both these countries stationed several hundreds of thousands of their army men to monitor their sensitive and vulnerable border. Finally, after they normalised their ties in 1991, both the sides started negotiating an amicable resolution of the Gulf of Tonkin and the land border issue. In this regard, the first expert-level discussion was held in October 1992. As a fallout of this meeting, land border and Gulf of Tonkin disputes were separated and each assigned to a specialist joint working group. Thus, the joint working group on land issues first met in February 1994 and concluded successfully in December 1999 after sixteen meetings. As a result of this, on December 30, 1999, China and Vietnam signed a land border agreement during the visit to Hanoi by Premier Zhu Rongji. Both sides ratified the treaty in 2000 and the process of placing stone markers along the border was completed at the end of 2008. In the meantime, the joint working group on the Gulf of Tonkin first met in March 1994 and held seventeen meetings before concluding.

So, as a result, in December 2000, Vietnam and China signed the agreement on the demarcation of waters, exclusive economic zones and continental shelves in the Gulf of Tonkin and the agreement on fishing cooperation in the Gulf of Tonkin.[58] Vietnam has not forgotten how India, along with the Soviet Union, staunchly stood by Vietnam during the Cambodian crisis, even by relegating her own importance in the ASEAN and by facing international condemnation and flak for standing by Vietnam in this incident. It is true that India has always supported Vietnam during her land border and Gulf of Tonkin negotiations with China in the post-Cold War days. Thus, the common issue of border dispute with China has certainly played a crucial role in the history of these two countries in consolidating their ties.

The Issue of Terrorism: An Emerging Issue

This is another area where India has been locking horns with China, and expectedly, once again, has found Vietnam empathising with India's point of view. All the three countries—China, India and Vietnam—have voiced their deep concerns time and again, in several international forums about fighting the scourge of terrorism tooth and nail. In fact, when Home Minister of India Shri Rajnath Singh visited China in November 2015, the two sides even pledged to enhance cooperation in combating international terrorism through exchange of information, exchange of experiences and coordinating positions on anti-terrorism endeavours at regional and multilateral levels and the Chinese Government conveyed that it would never support armed groups that are against the Government of India. However, in practice, it has been found that China is adopting a partial stance as far as Pakistan-based terrorists are concerned. China had been repeatedly vetoing India's bid at the UN to list Maulana Masood Azhar, Chief of Pakistan-based Jaish-e-Mohammad (JeM), as a global terrorist. Masood Azhar has been the mastermind behind several heinous terrorist attacks in India including the Mumbai attacks. While answering to a question in Lok Sabha on April 27, 2016, raised by Lallu Singh and others regarding China's veto against India, Gen (Dr.) VK Singh (retd.), the then Minister of State in the Ministry of External Affairs replied, "UN Security Council Resolution 1267 regime is an important building block of the UN Global Counter Terrorism Strategy that should aim to protect all member states and their citizens from the activities of terror groups such as Jaish-e-Mohammed (JeM) and its leader Mohammed Masood Azhar....We have forcefully taken up with international community that while the Pakistan-based JeM was listed in UN Security Council Committee established under UNSCR 1287/1989/2253 as far back as 2001 for its well known terror activities and links to the Al Qaeda, the designation of the group's main leader, financier and motivator has been put on a technical hold."[59] In the same debate, the Minister further added that the Government of India has raised serious doubts regarding such "selective approach to combating terrorism"[60] will yield no substantial result ever as these groups operate across borders and pose a common threat to the entire mankind and thus needs concerted effort moving well beyond narrow political and strategic concerns. China remains unfazed even when the United States, the UK, France and Russia have strongly supported India's move. China has lashed out at the India media for terming Pakistan 'safe havens' of terrorists and even refused to discuss the issue of Pakistani terrorism at the BRICS Summit in 2017. In fact, China has even gone to the extent of hailing Pakistan for its sacrifices in fighting terrorism! Thus, India has been finding itself stuck in a quagmire as far as fighting terrorism is concerned because of China's 'dualism' and persistent blocking of India's proposals to counter global terror. However, Vietnam has steadfastly stood by India on the counter-terrorism issue and shares with India a similar zeal to uproot the menace of global terrorism.

The Issue of Hydro-Politics: An Emerging Burning Issue

This is one critical issue which is emerging to be very important in both India's and Vietnam's relations with China in the post-Cold War years. This is because the Mekong River originates in China and passes through lower riparian countries like Myanmar, Laos, Thailand, Cambodia and ultimately Vietnam, before it joins the South China

Sea. Therefore, any activity by China as the upper riparian country will have direct spillover effect on these Southeast Asian countries. Over the years, China has built not less than seven hydropower dam projects in the upper Mekong basin and many more dams have been planned to be built by China in the near future. China, with its single party rule and with the 'China dream' in its eyes and developmental goals in its policies, has not hesitated to commission more dams in the Mekong River. This has caused severe crisis in Vietnam's water reserve as the Mekong has always been its lifeline. These mainstream dams have created decreased water flows from the upstream, thereby aggravating the salinity of the Mekong River in Vietnam and generating anxiety in the Vietnamese government to provide adequate fresh water supplies to its population. Apart from difficulties in providing freshwater, the government is also very worried about the ecological diversity, the agricultural output and the ecological balance in the Mekong Delta. It therefore does not come as a surprise that in the year 2016, Vietnam had to face a major drought situation. About 80 percent of Vietnam's total rice produced for export comes from the Mekong Delta and China has been one of the largest importers of Vietnamese rice. Therefore, China's activities in the upper Mekong have started showing repercussions lower stream and affecting the geopolitics of the region.

Similarly, India as a lower riparian country like Vietnam is extremely worried about China's dams in the Brahmaputra River. The Brahmaputra originates in Tibet and is known as Yarlung Tsangpo before entering India. The added dimension of the geopolitics here lies in the fact that China has been exemplifying a tendency to link it with its relations with Pakistan, its 'all-weather friend'. For instance, very shortly after India announced plans to emphasise its rights as per the Indus Water Treaty in 2016, China announced its plan to build a dam in the tributary of Yarlung Tsangpo. Also, Chinese overdrive to build dams in this region not only severely affects the ecological equilibrium of the region; it also allows China to have a strong presence near the Arunachal Pradesh region. India and China are treaty bound to cooperate with each other on the hydrological issue and provide data on water levels and rainfall twice a day from June 1 to October 15. During the visit of Indian Vice President Hamid Ansari to China from June 26-30, 2014, the two Governments signed an Implementation Plan on Provision of Hydrological Information of Brahmaputra River in flood season by China to India.[61]

Despite this, India is suspicious of this Chinese stress on building more and more dams on the Brahmaputra as the water can become very crucial during times of armed conflicts. The 'Outline of the 12th Five Year Plan for National Economic and Social Development of the People's Republic of China' has clearly indicated that three more hydropower projects on the main stream of the Brahmaputra River in Tibet Autonomous Region have been approved for implementation by the Chinese authorities. While replying to a question asked by Shri Neeraj Shekhar in Rajya Sabha on 3 December 2015, Smt. Sushma Swaraj, Minister of External Affairs, Government of India, answered, "As a lower riparian State with considerable established user rights to the waters of the River, India has conveyed its views and concerns to the Chinese authorities, including at the highest levels of the Government of the People's Republic of China. India has urged China to ensure that the interests of downstream States are not harmed by any activities in upstream areas."[62] She further added in her reply, "During the visit of Prime Minister Sh. Narendra Modi to China in May 2015, this matter was discussed. The two sides agreed to further strengthen cooperation on the provision of flood-season hydrological data and emergency management, and exchange views on other issues of mutual interest through the Expert-Level Mechanism."[63] Therefore, both India and Vietnam are not only fighting the ecological challenges that have emerged due to the dams built by China in the Brahmaputra and the Mekong respectively, they are also very cautious owing to the geopolitical and strategic implications of this issue.

The South China Sea Dispute: A Cockpit of Power Struggle

This is an issue which has clearly brought India and Vietnam closer to each other over the years against the threat of 'China factor' looming in the backdrop. Though the dispute of sovereignty in South China Sea (SCS) has been very much prevalent in the Cold War era, it has flared up more in the post-Cold War years and Vietnam, being at the centre of this dispute with China, has found in India a potential re-balancer in Asia in this quandary. Though India has no territorial claims in the South China Sea region, it has direct interest in keeping the Straits of Malacca in friendly hands to ensure uninterrupted commerce and freedom of navigation. It is true that India has got herself involved in the region at the behest of 'good friend' Vietnam, but it is also true that India has definite strategic interests in the region, particularly in the wake of renewed policy thrust towards the Southeast Asian region owing to Prime Minister Narendra Modi's 'Act East' policy. The South China Sea is a moderately enclosed sea, about 3.5 million square kilometres in area, extending from the Singapore Strait to the Taiwan Strait. It is strategically located between the Pacific Ocean and the Indian Ocean, and about one-third of the world's shipping takes place through its waters. It is situated in the South of the PRC and has the islands of Taiwan and the Philippines in its east. It has Vietnam and Cambodia towards its west and has Singapore, Malaysia and Brunei in its south.[64] The South China Sea issue has been flaring up at regular intervals from the latter half of the previous century because eight states have been claiming sovereignty to these islands. Singapore and Malaysia has disputing sovereignty claims over Pisang Island and Pulau Batu Puteh. China, Taiwan and Vietnam contest each other's claims to sovereignty over the Paracels, a group of 15 islets and several reefs and shoals scattered over a 200 km area in the northern South China Sea. Today China is in possession of all the islands in the Paracels as it had captured those from South Vietnam in 1974. Taiwan also contests China's claims to Pratas Island and Macclesfield Bank. Seven states assert their claims on the Spratly archipelago. Whereas China, Taiwan and Vietnam claim the entire archipelago, Indonesia, Philippines, Malaysia and Brunei claim sovereignty over portions of it. Except Brunei and Indonesia, all the others have established a military presence in the Spratlys.[65] In fact, the People's Republic of China has been claiming their complete sovereignty over the entire South China Sea region, citing the presence of historical documents that apparently prove Chinese interaction with this region from time immemorial and China has put forward the concept of 'nine dash/dotted lines' extending over the entire South China Sea region as its sovereignty claims. Vietnam too, has claims over the entire South China Sea region. Accordingly, at the Seventh Plenary Session of the United Nations General Assembly in 1951, the then Prime Minister of Vietnam Tran Van Huu said, "...we affirm our right to the Spratly and Paracel Islands, which have always belonged to Vietnam."[66] Vietnam and China has already had two armed skirmishes with each other in 1974 and 1988 on the South China Sea issue and continues to be embroiled in regular scuffles on this issue. Though these countries are bound by the United Nations Convention on the Law of the Sea (UNCLOS III), 1982, and ASEAN's Declaration on the Conduct of Parties in the South China Sea (DOC), 1992, based on the principles of peace and tranquillity in the region as per the Treaty of Amity and Cooperation (TAC), there have been frequent untoward incidents leading to loss of lives, owing to their sovereignty claims in the region. Time and again,'aggressive' postures have been reported, such as the Chinese Navy building artificial island on the Mischief Reef in the Spratlys, deploying Romeo-class conventional submarines in the disputed region, Chinese ships firing on Vietnamese fishing boats in the South China Sea, Chinese plans to begin tourist cruises to Paracels, China placing boundary markers on the Paracels, China creating a country-level city called Sansha in the Hainan province to administer its claims in the South China Sea, China cutting the exploration cables of Binh Minh 02 seismic vessel of Vietnam National Oil and Gas, etc.[67] Though under increasing international pressure, China has agreed in principle to work with other disputing claimants towards establishing a 'Code of Conduct' to mitigate tensions in the South China Sea, it however, is suspect of the desired neutrality of the ASEAN as several members of the ASEAN are themselves disputing claimants. Therefore, China has been advocating a bilateral approach, rather than the multilateral approach in resolving the crisis, which is not acceptable to the ASEAN members. This divided nature of the ASEAN has rendered it ineffective to a large extent, in addressing the issue. Perhaps this explains why, besides discussing the South China Sea issue in various summits, meetings and programs of the ASEAN and the ASEAN Regional Forum, Vietnam has been warming up to India, and to the United States, Japan and Australia as well, to thwart Chinese belligerent postures in the South China Sea. India, on her part, believes that the events in the South China Sea have a direct repercussion on the Indian Ocean region, as indicated by the Indian Maritime Doctrine of 2007 and of subsequent years. India's ONGC Videsh Limited, acting on Vietnam's offer, has been involved in the exploration activity in South China Sea since 1988. At that point of time, China did not object to India's involvement in the region. In 2006, the OVL signed a contract with Petro Vietnam to jointly explore sectors 127 and 128 in the Phu Khanh Basin. Later, in September 2011, it signed three deals to jointly explore oil and natural gas in these blocks. This time however, China has vehemently protested against India's exploration activity in the region. However, India chose to turn a deaf ear to Chinese protests and went ahead with consolidating her ties with Vietnam. In 2014, Vietnam extended the licence of exploration by ONGC Videsh Ltd. in these blocs for a period of two years and offered two additional blocs to India in the region. Thus, at present, the ONGC Videsh Limited is involved in exploration activity in five blocks. India officially maintains that it supports freedom of navigation in the South China Sea and hopes that all parties to the dispute will abide by the 2002 Declaration of Conduct in the South China Sea. While replying to a question in the Lok Sabha on 17 August 2012, asked by Shri K. Sudhakaran and Shri Anant Kumar Hegde, "whether the Government of India has taken note of the Chinese claim over a Vietnamese petroleum block under exploration by an Indian entity," Shri S.M Krishna, the then Minister of External Affairs remarked, "India has on several occasions reiterated its position that it supports freedom of navigation, right of passage and access to resources in accordance with accepted principles of international law."[68] The United States also appreciates India's presence in the region as a great balancer to China and has beefed up defence and maritime cooperation with Vietnam and other disputing countries to convince them of its seriousness in the 'pivot to Asia' or 'rebalancing in Asia' policy, as initiated by President Obama. China has been vociferous about US moves to 'militarize' the disputed region and have even intercepted US reconnaissance aircraft and have demanded the US to stop their navy and air force forays in waters in the troubled waters. Nonetheless, this sovereignty dispute in the South China Sea has further cemented the Indo-Vietnam bilateral strategic relations in the post-Cold War days.

It must be noted that there are four types of island groups that make up the islands in the South China Sea. They are Pratas, Macclesfied Bank, the Paracels and the Spratlys. The Paracel archipelago (Vietnam termed as Hoang Sa and Xisha by China) is a group of 50 islands and several sand banks and reefs. This group is located less than 150 nautical miles from China's Hainan islands and about 240 nautical miles from Danang in Vietnam. This archipelago is scattered over an area of 1500 sq kms and is divided into two clusters; the eastern cluster of An Vinh and the western cluster of Luoi Liem. The last group of islands, the Spratlys (known as Troung Sa by Vietnam and Nansha by China) is a group of more than 230 islets, reefs, shoals and sand banks scattered over a sea area of about 1, 60,000 to 1, 80,000 sq kms, situated in the southern part of South China Sea. The coast point of the Spratly archipelago is about 250 nautical miles from Yulin (Hainan island of China). It is not less than 100 nm from the Philippines' Palawan and Malaysian Borneo and about 400 nm from Paracels.[69] Freedom of navigation through the South China Sea, particularly through the chokepoints of the Taiwan Strait in the north and the Strait of Malacca in the south, remains essential to the region's geostrategic role in linking North East Asia's seaborne trade with the rest of the world. Even so, the South China Sea's significance has been recently highlighted, not just for its strategically important commercial and military sea lanes, but for also furnishing living and mineral resources to the littoral states. Almost 50 percent of the protein requirement of the population bordering the South China Sea is met by the abundant fishing activity in the region.[70]

The beginning of the South China Sea dispute is a contentious one, with some disputing claimants, such as the People's Republic of China (PRC) and Vietnam situating their claims on historical reasons and some others, such as the Philippines and Malaysia referring to the provisions of international law to claim their territories in the disputed region. Eight states currently claim title to these islands. Singapore and Malaysia dispute claims over Pisang Island and Pulau Batu Puteh. China, Taiwan and Vietnam challenge each other's claims to sovereignty over the Paracels. Taiwan also disputes China's claims to Pratas Island and Macclesfield Bank. As for the Spratlys, seven states assert their claims. Whereas China, Taiwan and Vietnam claim the entire archipelago, Indonesia, Phillippines, Malaysia and Brunei claim sovereignty over portions of it. Apart from Brunei and Indonesia, everybody else has established a military existence in the Spratlys.

Since the People's Republic of China has been claiming their complete sovereignty over the entire South China Sea region, and in fact, till sometime in the chronicles of history, they were even willing to share their exploration rights with other countries of the region, but never did they feel the necessity to negotiate sovereignty rights with those countries vis-à-vis South China Sea. In addition to claiming that it was the first to discover the South China Sea and its various island groups, Beijing contends that it was the first to name, map, study, use and patrol the South China Sea and its islands under the jurisdiction of a national and/or local government, and the only government to have accepted the Japanese surrender at the end of the Second World War and retaken sovereign control of the area. Based on accepted norms of the time, it is argued that these actions entitle China to the entire South China Sea and all of its constituent features, which include the Spratly archipelago.[71] As Vietnam too claims total sovereignty over the area based on 'historical right' to the region, its government has always maintained that in modern times since the 1800s, the Spratly archipelago was totally under the administration of the Vietnamese emperors. They have also claimed to be in possession of maps depicting Spratlys under the effective administration of Vietnam.[72]

As Vietnam attained independence from France by defeating France in the Battle of Dien Bien Phu (1954), territories of Vietnam that were under the French control during the colonial period, were returned to Vietnam and Vietnam claims that it has regained its rights to the Spratlys. During the Second World War (1939–45), particularly during the latter half of the war, Japan completely dominated the South China Sea waters. Japan occupied the Spratlys and the Paracels in 1939 and set up several military bases across the region, such as the military bases on Woody and Pattle Islands in the Paracels and Itu Aba in the Spratlys. As per the 1954 Geneva Accords, the division of Vietnam along the 17th parallel led South Vietnam to inherit all the French Indochina's Vietnamese territories under the 17th parallel. According to the Vietnamese sources, since the Spratlys and the Paracels lay below the 17th parallel and were important parts of the French Indochina since 1933, they could now enjoy total sovereignty over the region. In fact, it was South Vietnam rather than North Vietnam which actively pursued its policies in the South China Sea since 1950s. This was because North Vietnam geographically lacked control of any coastline except in the Gulf of Tonkin and its main harbour was Haiphong, in the Gulf of Tonkin itself. It was South Vietnam under whose administration most of the coastline lay and its coast had important harbours such as Saigon and Da Nang and naval bases in Cam Ranh Bay. This is why the questions of safety and security of the South China Sea became extremely important to South Vietnam. Simultaneously though, the People's Republic of China under the leadership of Zhou Enlai became increasingly vociferous about China's 'lawful' claiming the region, and on September 4, 1958, China published 'Declaration of the government of the PRC on China's Territorial Sea' (nine-dotted line/11 dash line), practically extending its claim over the entire South China Sea.

China and Vietnam clashed in the South China Sea in 1974. It so happened that South Vietnam was trying to fortify its claims in the Spratlys by reportedly placing settlers there and driving Chinese fishermen out from the south western Paracels. It was not accepted by the Chinese and they inflicted defeat on the Vietnamese naval forces, and thereby extending its effective control on the entire Paracels. "South Vietnam's response to the loss of the western Paracels was to rush to permanently occupy several Spratly islands, using the same troops that had been driven out of the Paracels. In 1975, even before the final conquest of Saigon, a North Vietnamese task force arrived in the Spratlys and command of the Vietnamese garrisons there.. Since then, Vietnam has gradually expanded its garrisons on the Spratlys and has always occupied more reefs and islands than any other power. Finally, the UNCLOS III of 1982 decided that every coastal state could claim a continental shelf out to the same limit as the Exclusive Economic Zone (EEZ) 200 nautical miles, regardless of the depth of the sea (and to a maximum of 350 nautical miles if the shelf was naturally prolonged that far."[73] In 1974, China enforced its claim upon the Paracel Islands by seizing them from Vietnam. China refers to the Paracel Islands as the Xisha Islands and included them as part of its Hainan Island province in 1988. The Chinese began moving into the Spratlys in July 1987. Two Islands were occupied in January 1988 and on March 14, 1988, Chinese naval vessels clashed with Vietnam naval units near Johnson (Chigua) Reef. These Vietnamese naval vessels were sunk and there are reports of up to 80 Vietnamese sailors having lost their lives. By April, Vietnam had garrisoned a further 15 reefs, bringing its total to twenty-one. At this point the Spratly Islands conflict was in the main a symptom of Cold War rivalry between China and Soviet-backed Vietnam. By May 1989, China had occupied seven islands and by 1992 a total of nine islands, giving it a presence in the area where previously it had none. From the late 1980s, PRC started building military structures in the SCS Islands, including Huayang, Chigua, Nanxun, Donmen, Zhubi and Yong Xing.

Though India does not have any claim in the disputed region, it has always played a constructive and positive role in the dispute. For instance, India had played a major role in the negotiations leading to the

Agreement related to implementation of Part- XI of the Convention deep sea-bed mining and exploration, which was adopted unanimously by the resumed forty-eighth session of the United Nations General Assembly in June 1994.[74] Finally, the United Nations Convention on the Law of the Sea (UNCLOS) entered into force on 16 November 1994.

By the mid-1990s, it was revealed that the Chinese navy had successfully built an artificial island on Mischief Reef in the Spratlys. This created tensions in the diplomatic circles of countries such as Vietnam, India and Philippines. This circular Mischief Reef area was disputed by the Philippines as the Philippines claimed that this region was well within the EEZ of the Philippines. In 1992, China announced that it will give concession to the US Crestone Company for oil exploration and deployed three Romeo-class conventional submarines to patrol the area, which raised alarms among the ASEAN states that had just called for the non use of force in resolving the Spratly Islands dispute in the Manila Declaration on the South China Sea.

In February 1995, China constructed 'steel supported structures' on Mischief Reef. The reef lies well within the Philippine claim and lies close to the Philippine island of Palawan. The Chinese action was in contravention of the Manila Declaration. It created alarm amongst the ASEAN members because this was the first time that China had unilaterally changed the status quo at the expense of a claimant other than Vietnam and had covertly established its presence in these waters and in an area claimed by the Philippines as falling within its Exclusive Economic Zone.[75] Moreover, the United Nations Convention on the Law of the Sea of 1982, which came into force in 1994, identified the territorial sea, contiguous zone and the exclusive economic zones as regions where a coastal State can exercise its sovereign rights. It is clearly stated in Part II, Article 2, that the sovereignty of a coastal State exceeds beyond its land territories and internal waters and, in the case of an archipelagic State, its archipelagic waters, to an adjacent belt of sea, described as the territorial sea and this sovereignty extends to the airspace over the territorial sea as well as to its bed and subsoil and every state has the right to establish the breath of its territorial sea up to a limit not exceeding 12 nautical miles, measured from baselines.[76] The Convention further mentions in Part-II, Article 33, "In a zone contiguous to its territorial sea, described as the contiguous zone, the coastal State may exercise the control necessary to first, prevent infringement of its customs, fiscal, immigration or sanitary laws and regulation within its territory or territorial sea and secondly, punish infringement of the laws and regulations committed within its territory or territorial sea."[77] It also stipulates that the contiguous zone may not extend beyond 24 nautical miles from the baseline of the coastal states. Moreover, Part V of the Convention deals with exclusive economic zones. Part V, Article 55, states, "The exclusive economic zone is an area beyond and adjacent to the territorial sea, subject to the specific legal regime established in this Part, under which the rights and jurisdiction of other States are governed by the relevant provisions of this Convention." Article 56 of this Convention states, "In the exclusive economic zone, the coastal State has, first, sovereign rights for the purpose of exploring and exploiting, conserving and managing the natural resources, whether living or non-living, of the waters superjacent to the seabed and of the seabed and its subsoil, and with regard to other activities for the economic exploitation and exploration of the zone, such as the production of energy from the water, currents and winds and secondly, jurisdiction as provided for in the relevant provisions of this Convention with regard to (i) the establishment and use of artificial islands, installations and structures (ii) marine scientific research (iii)protection and preservation of marine environment."[78] Furthermore, Article 57 says, "The exclusive economic zone" shall not extend beyond 200 nautical miles from the baselines from which the territorial sea is measured."[79]

Under escalating stress from all quarters, by late 1995, China agreed in principle to establish bilateral 'codes of conduct' with Vietnam and the Philippines in the Spratly islands.

After such repeated skirmishes in the South China Sea, at the initiative of disputing countries, particularly of the Philippines, the

ASEAN started negotiating a 'Code of Conduct' with the disputing countries to bring enduring peace in the region. China too agreed in principle to negotiate with the ASEAN, and started negotiations in the year 2000. On 4 November 2002, China signed the Declaration on the Conduct of Parties in the South China Sea, based on the principles of peace and tranquillity in the region, as per the Treaty of Amity and Cooperation (TAC). It was a momentous event as it was the first concrete political document signed between China and ASEAN, guiding its behaviour in the region on the disputed issue. However, the desired neutrality of the ASEAN in the issue is circumspect in Chinese eyes as many of its members, such as Vietnam and the Philippines are themselves the disputing claimants and even after signing the document, the PRC knows that the ASEAN is a divided body as far as the issue is concerned and it will not be possible for the ASEAN to put up an effective fight against the aggressive behaviour of the Chinese.

However, despite the goodwill expressed from both sides to resolve the dispute peacefully, skirmishes continued to take place in the disputed area, for instance, on January 8, 2005, the Chinese ships shot two Vietnamese fishing boats in the South China Sea, killing nine people and detaining one ship with eight people on Hainan Island. This created furore in the diplomatic circles of Vietnam. The Chinese foreign ministry claimed that they were pirates operating in the troubled waters and obtained confession from the arrested members. Simultaneously though, as a result of the Declaration on the Conduct of Parties (DOC) in South China Sea of 2002,various Confidence Building Measures (CBMs) were being undertaken mostly at the bilateral level. For instance, 'in September 2004, the Philippines and China agreed to conduct joint explorations for oil and gas in the contested waters'. In March 2005, Vietnam agreed to partake the tripartite Joint Marine Seismic Undertaking (JMSU). However, since 2007, three episodes greatly increased tension between Vietnam and China. First, China accused Vietnam in April 2007 of violating its sovereignty by allowing a consortium of energy companies led by British Petroleum (BP) to develop two gas fields in the Con Son Basin,

230 miles off Vietnam's Southeast coast. Vietnam rejected China's protest by claiming the project was well within its EEZ. Second, in early 2007, China placed boundary markers on the Paracel islands, which was vociferously protested by the Vietnamese authority and the Chinese naval patrol vessels fired on a Vietnamese boat in July 2007, killing one sailor. In August 2007, China proclaimed plans to begin tourist cruises to the Parcels, leading Vietnam to reaffirm its sovereignty claims over the archipelago. Finally, the Chinese National People's Congress had passed a law in early 2007 creating a county-level city in Hainan province called Sansha to administer China's claim in the South China Sea, including the Paracel and Spratly Islands.[80] In mid-November 2007, PLAN exercises near the Paracels angered Vietnam again, who staged a diplomatic protest. Again, the China's National People's Congress (NPC) decided in 2007 to create the Sansha county-level town in Hainan province with administrative responsibility over three archipelagos in the South China Sea, including the Paracel and Spratly islands. News of the NPC's actions provoked anti-China student demonstrations in Hanoi and Ho Chi Minh City on 9 and 16 December 2007. All these incidents angered Vietnam beyond words and brought Vietnam's diplomatic relations with China to its nadir.

However, once again, in May 2009, China announced a unilateral three-month moratorium on fishing in the South China Sea (above the twelfth parallel) from May 16 to August 1 in order to preserve fish stocks, prevent illegal fishing and protect Chinese fishermen. This was the height of the Vietnamese fishing season. Eight modern Chinese fishery administration vessels were dispatched to enforce the ban. Vietnam, once again, was infuriated and lodged a diplomatic protest again China's decision. In May 2009 itself, China tabled a protest with the United Nations Commission on the Limits of the Continental Shelf (UNCLCS) when submissions on extended continental shelves were presented jointly by Malaysia and Vietnam and by Vietnam in a separate submission.[81] In the meantime, Chinese 'aggressive' actions continued. As per the media reports in Vietnam, about 33 Vietnamese fishing boats and 433 Vietnamese crew members were detained by China in 2009.[82]

It was not only the regional powers that were being affected by the increased Chinese assertiveness. Even extra-regional powers, such as the United States was being increasingly drawn into the dispute and countries like Vietnam and the Philippines were actually in favour of increased US presence in the region to effectively counter the China factor in the South China Sea issue. In March 2009, it was reported by the Pentagon that the US surveillance ship USNS Impeccable was harassed by Chinese ships while it was conducting routine operations in international waters. Five Chinese vessels shadowed and aggressively manoeuvred dangerously close to USNS Impeccable. Perhaps because of these developments, on July 23, 2010, the USA signed the Treaty of Amity and Cooperation (TAC) at the ARF meeting in Hanoi and became a direct part taker in the affairs of the region.

Again, on May 26, 2011, there was a clash between the Vietnamese and Chinese vessels, when a Chinese surveillance vessel allegedly 'cut the exploration cables of Binh Minh 02 seismic vessel of Vietnam National Oil and Gas Group.' There was an unprecedented uproar in Hanoi and Ho Chi Minh City as Vietnam alleged that China has cut the exploration cables in the Vietnamese waters whereas Beijing responded by saying that Vietnam's explorations 'had undermined China's interests and jurisdictional rights in the South China Sea area.[83]

Once again, on June 9, 2011, there was another clash between Vietnam and China in the South China Sea when a Norwegian-flagged ship hired by Petro Vietnam clashed with three Chinese fishery vessels within, allegedly, the EEZ of Vietnam. Vietnam, once again, reported that its exploration cables of a 3-D seismic exploration vessel have been cut by a Chinese fishing vessel.[84] China gave a different version of the same events in a report carried by the official news agency, *Xinhua.* Chinese Foreign Ministry spokesman Hong Lei said that Chinese fishing vessels were driven away by armed Vietnamese ships. As the boats were driven out, they got entangled in the underwater cables of the Vietnamese ship. They subsequently got caught in the area and two Chinese ships had to come to free the vessels. China reacted to this incident by stating that Vietnam should not take actions that would further add or complicate the issue.[85]. On October 10, 2011, Vietnam and China agreed to a new set of principles on settling maritime disputes.

However, it is to be noted that despite all these repeated occurrences, the ASEAN's role in resolving the problems remained quite ineffective. This is because the ASEAN remains a divided platform with some of its members such as the Philippines, Vietnam and Brunei having disputes with China over the sovereignty issue in South China Sea, whereas others like Malaysia, Cambodia, Singapore are in very good terms with China. Cambodia, for instance, has been hugely benefited by billions of dollars of Chinese assistance in its national development, and perhaps this is why, the role of extra-regional powers, such as that of the USA, Japan and India has increased substantially. This led to constant efforts both from the side of China and the pro-China ASEAN countries, such as Cambodia, to portray these incidents and differences of opinion as essentially bilateral in nature and not encompassing the views of the ASEAN as a whole. This could be the reason why, during various ARF meetings (such as the one held in Phnom Penh in July 2012), when the Philippines and Vietnam desired to include their latest naval skirmishes with China in the South China Sea, Cambodia offered strong objections and reiterated that this issue has been essentially bilateral and not to be interpreted as a China-ASEAN issue. They are also against the American interference in the dispute as they consider it to be an essentially regional problem, and the United States being an extra-regional power should not get itself embroiled in it. China further believes that the internationaliation of this issue will only further complicate the problem.

The United States however, mentions that like any other nation, it has a national interest in freedom of navigation, open access to Asia's maritime commons and respect for international law in the South China Sea. The United States has discussed the SCS issue with China at various fora. Hillary Clinton in an article 'America's Pacific Century' in *Foreign Policy* stated, "And over the past year, we have made strides in protecting its vital interests in stability and freedom of navigation and have paved the way for sustained multilateral diplomacy among the many parties with claims in the South China Sea, seeking to ensure disputes are settled peacefully and in accordance with established principles of international law."[86] At the back of this Asia-Pacific pivot lays an economic impetus vis-à-vis the SCS. Almost USD 1.2 billion of the US trade crosses the Western Pacific and Indian Ocean through the SCS.

Here India is seen by the United States as a strong factor to level Chinese growing assertiveness in the region. The Indian Maritime Doctrine suggested in 2007 that the events in the SCS have a bearing on the Indian Ocean region. Exploration of oil and petroleum is just one of the many interests India has in the SCS. India has taken the position that it supports the freedom of navigation in the SCS under the Declaration of Code of Conduct, 2002. Almost 55 percent of India's trade with the Asia-Pacific transits through the SCS. In 2006, OVL signed a contract with Petro Vietnam to jointly explore sectors 127 and 128 in the Phu Khanh Basin. Later, in September 2011, it signed three deals to jointly explore oil and natural gas in these blocks. These two blocks have been at the centre of a diplomatic uproar between India, China and Vietnam, grabbing the limelight when India withdrew from them. Apart from these two blocks, OVL had already signed a gas exploration contract with Vietnam in 1988. This gives access to Lan Tray and Lan Do fields in Block 06.1, off the coast of Vietnam in the SCS. India would continue to engage in the Nam Con Son basin (close to Natuna Sea) that OVL was awarded as a goodwill gesture to India. Currently, OVL has 45 percent stakes in these blocks. Thus, India is one of the major stakeholders in the strategic waterways but certainly does not claim any island in the region.

On November 17, 2011, President Obama made a policy announcement to Australian Parliament about the US pivot, that is, the new thrust area of the US foreign policy is the Asia-Pacific region. In July 2012, the National Assembly of Vietnam passed a law segregating Vietnamese sea borders to include the Spratly and Paracel Islands. In the same month, China reiterated by restating their absolute sovereignty over the region. The Central Military Commission of China decided to establish the Sansha garrison in the region and this decision was heavily criticised by the Philippines and Vietnam. China launched a programme on September 23, 2012, to increase the number of UAVs monitoring the Scarborough Shoal, Paracel Islands, Spratly Islands and East China Sea, which follows a national marine zoning program approved by the State Council in 2011 as a part of China's twelfth five year plan. In December 2012, Admiral Joshi of the Indian Navy remarked that the Indian Navy is prepared to operate in the South China Sea, which was welcomed by countries like Vietnam and the Philippines. On May 2, 2014, Vietnamese naval ships and Chinese vessels collided in the South China Sea. The incident occurred as China set up an oil rig in an area to which both nations have been extending their claims. On May 26, a Vietnamese fishing boat sank near the oil rig, after colliding with a Chinese vessel. On this incident, ASEAN leaders expressed 'serious concerns' over the tensions, calling for self-restraint and peaceful acts from both sides. In December 2014, the United States State Department released a report concluding that China's nine-dash line claim does not accord with the international law of the sea. Next year, that is, in April 2015, it came to light that China is transforming Mischief Reef into an island. On October 27, 2015, US destroyer USS Lassen navigated within 12 nautical miles of the emerging land masses in the Spratly Islands as the first in a series of 'Freedom of Navigation Operation'.

On this issue, Vietnam has been putting in all its efforts to strategically engage both the United States and India as a fortification against an increasing aggressive posture of the PRC. The relations between the United States and Vietnam are at its peak currently and both these countries have been strengthening their ties since the 2013 bilateral Comprehensive Partnership Agreement.

In connection with this understanding, two bilateral engagements of Vietnam with the United States is noteworthy here, namely the agreement on civil nuclear energy and a seismic shift in defence policy resulting in the partial lifting of a decades-old arms embargo with respect to lethal military assistance specifically referring to maritime defence and security. Under the United States-Vietnam Comprehensive Partnership, building maritime capacity has a two-pronged goal to enhance Vietnam's third party logistics competences, reduce trans-shipment needs through building larger and more modern ports to manage greater throughput, and to strengthen Vietnam's offshore patrol capabilities while leveraging sentinels in the South China Sea for the United States. Vietnam is courting various countries embroiled in maritime disputes with China, including the Philippines and Japan. Vietnam has voiced support for the Triple Action Plan.[87]

Also, on his third visit to India, Vietnamese Prime Minister Nguyen Tan Dung cemented an evolving alliance between the two Asian countries by inking new defence and energy deals. This deal pledged a $100 million line of credit to the Vietnamese for the purpose of purchasing four offshore naval vessels to be used to patrol Vietnamese-claimed energy assets in the South China Sea.[88]

The growing camaraderie between the United States and Vietnam has angered China, who has been publicly voicing concern about the growing presence of the United States in the disputed South China Sea. Beijing accuses the United States of 'militarising' the South China Sea by staging patrols and joint military drills there, ramping up the rhetoric. China has repeatedly urged Washington not to take sides in the escalating maritime dispute over the area, where the Asian giant stepped up its creation of artificial islands, alarming neighbours and provoking US criticism. China has been angered by the forays of the United States navy and air force through waters it claims as its own, especially when US navy admiral Scott Swift said he joined a routine surveillance flight. The United States has also stepped up military contacts with regional allies such as the Philippines.[89]

Similarly, China has been angered by the increasing solidarity between Vietnam and India on the South China Sea issue and has been thwarting India's efforts in various directions, whether it is in her United Nations Security Council reforms bid or in her desire to be a Nuclear Suppliers Group (NSG) member. Moreover, throwing caution to the wind, despite the hue and cry about China's militarisation of the South China Sea, China has spent years building military outposts on a group of contested islands in the South China Sea. First, there was the dredging in which ships sucked sediment from the sea bed and pumped it atop formerly barren reefs. Then came the buildings—once said to be for civilian purposes but which analysts now say are military installations—followed quickly by international uproar. But the building continued. Now, some of the islands, part of the group known as the Spratlys, where China began large-scale development in 2013, have been transformed from barren reefs into military outposts. The Chinese focus has changed from dredging and reclaiming land to building airstrips, radar and communications facilities and hangers. On Mischief Reef, which was once largely underwater, 1,379 acres have been developed by China with a nearly 2-mile runway and concrete building.[90] Moreover, since 2013, China has commissioned 17 new vessels in the South Sea Fleet to focus on the South China Sea region. PLAN has also commissioned a 051 A multi-role warship, 056 light warships, 052 C destroyer and a 903 A supply ship in the region. Constant attempts are also being made to revitalise the South Sea Fleets, whose area of operation is between North of the Taiwan Strait to the south, to the James Shoal. This area covers the Paracel and Spratly islands as well as Macclesfield Bank.[91]

Vietnam officially maintains that Vietnam and India share the same viewpoint, which is turning the East Sea and Asia-Pacific into a stable, cooperate and developed region. Any country, which goes against this trend, would be condemned by regional countries and the international community has raised their voice to express concern and show a common trend of maintaining an equal relation among countries, resolving disputes on the basis of international law, no use of force or threat of the use of force. Amidst all the skirmishes, both China and Vietnam have been trying to lessen the tensions in South China Sea. For Instance, Vietnam's General Secretary Nguyen Phu Trong paid a state visit to China from April 7-10, 2015. At the talks, the two sides exchanged opinions on sea-related issues in a sincere and straightforward manner, stressing the serious implementation of the Agreement on basic principles guiding the settlement of Vietnam-China sea-related issues; effectively utilising the Government-level negotiation mechanism on Vietnam-China boundary and territorial issues.[92]

However, not much headway has been made in bringing durable peace in the region, simply because of the lack of genuine political and goodwill. Despite all these efforts to reduce tensions, on July 28, 2015 "China conducted a massive live firing drill in the disputed South China Sea with over 100 naval ships and dozens of aircraft. The exercise aimed to improve maritime combat ability involved more than 100 naval vessels, dozens of aircraft, several missile launch battalions of the Second Artillery Corps, as well as unknown number of information warfare troops. The drill tested the navy's air defence and early warning system and improved its ability to react quickly."[93]

To sum up, it can be argued that the South China Sea remains such an issue that has strengthened the historical ties between India and Vietnam. The perceived common threat of 'China factor' is very much visible in this issue. The dispute is further unfolding and taking a new turn each day and India and Vietnam are working hand-in-hand to bring comprehensive peace and tranquillity in the region. Interestingly enough, in July 2016, in a case brought by Philippines against China, the International Court of Justice "delivered a sweeping rebuke of China's behaviour in the South China Sea, including its construction of artificial islands. The tribunal rejected China's argument that it enjoys historic rights over most of the South China Sea."[94] Both India and Vietnam had welcomed the ruling. However, China did not agree to the ruling and though this ruling is legally binding, there is no mechanism to enforce it. Therefore, the future course of Chinese activities in this regard will be decisive as to how the South China issue will be shaped in the future decades and to what extent it will continue to bring New Delhi closer to Hanoi's strategic planning in the disputed waters.

Indian Ocean: New Conflicting Turf of New Delhi-Beijing-Hanoi

The Indian Ocean spreads over 28 million square miles, comprising 30 littoral States, 11 land-locked States and 12, 181 islands, encompassing one-fourth of world area, one-third of population, two-third of strategic minerals and three-fourth of oil reserves. This proves how strategically important this region is, and that remains the major reason why both India and China have been locking horns in this area in the post-Cold War period. Over the years China has taken a number of initiatives to keep its presence felt in the Indian Ocean Region (IOR) and has taken certain strategic moves to encircle India and some other South Asian countries. Some very important issues in the IOR that have cropped up in recent years, and are elevating Indo-Vietnam cooperation to a higher level, are discussed below.

China's 'String of Pearls' Strategy in the Indian Ocean Region

India has always considered this region to be its backyard of influence and regarded herself a natural leader of South Asia. However, China has been making a very fast and effective intrusion in this region, and spreading its influence over smaller neighbours by collaborating with them on economic, defence, capital investments, technology transfers, connectivity and infrastructure development projects in these countries with huge geostrategic ramifications for India which has put India's standing in this region in the face of serious challenge. This has reignited global interest in this region, with Vietnam, itself being a challenger of China's aggressive intrusion in the South China region, completely stands by India on this issue as well. The United States through it 'pivot to Asia' policy and Japan itself being a contender of China in the East Sea regarding Diaoyu/Senkaku Islands, have been appreciative of India's role in the region and consider India to be a bulwark against China's aggressive advance in the Indian Ocean region.

China has been accused of increasingly encircling India in the Indian Ocean by building ports and naval bases in her neighbouring countries, such as in Myanmar (Coco Islands and Sittwe), Bangladesh (Chittagong), Sri Lanka (Hambantota), Maldives (Harao), Pakistan

(Gwadar), having huge implications for India's security concerns. This process has been theorised, first by the U.S consulting firm Booz Allen Hamilton in 2005, as the "String of Pearls"[95] through which China has been building important sea lines of communication that will link China's mainland with the ports in these neighbouring countries for uninhibited trade. Also, building ports and naval bases in these countries have given an added advantage to China to monitor India's presence in the region and an additional leverage to undercut India's efforts in case of an armed conflict in the IOR. Moreover, these sea lines of communication run across several important choke points in the Indian Ocean, such as, the Strait of Mandeb, the Strait of Malacca, the Strait of Hormuz, and the Lombok Strait. Thus, exerting its dominance in these areas, China has exalted itself to a supreme position as far as global trade and free flow of goods and essentials are concerned, to such an extent, that the fear looms large that it might become uncomfortable and difficult for India and some other smaller nations in the region which are not very friendly with China, in case of an untoward incident.

China's 'Belt and Road' Initiative: Reactions of New Delhi and Hanoi

Besides encircling India in the Indian Ocean, China has been going overdrive in trying to build a global economic system with China at its core, according to which, China is trying to revive the 'maritime silk route' which is the maritime portion of the historic Silk Route. This idea was formally first announced by Chinese President Xi Jinping in his speech when he visited Central Asia and Southeast Asia in September and October 2013 and he raised the initiative of jointly building the Silk Road Economic Belt and the 21st Century Maritime Silk Road (Belt and Road) in the Indonesian Parliament and once again at the China-ASEAN Expo in 2013, Premier Li Keqiang highlighted the necessity to build the Maritime Silk Road directed towards the ASEAN and to generate deliberate propellers for neighbourhood development.[96] The proposed Maritime Silk Route will run through and connect China's Fujian Province, Guangdong, Guangxi, Hainan, the Malacca Strait, Kuala Lumpur, Kolkata, Colombia, passing through the rest of Indian Ocean it will connect Nairobi, Horn of Africa, Red Sea, the Mediterranean, and Venice and then will finally connect with the land segment of the Silk Route.[97] The Belt and Road, therefore, will run through continents of Asia, Europe and Africa. The Silk Road Economic Belt focuses on bringing together China, Central Asia, Russia and Europe; linking China with the Persian Gulf and the Mediterranean Sea through Central Asia and West Asia; and connecting China with Southeast Asia, South Asia and the Indian Ocean. It will connect China with Europe through the South China Sea and the Indian Ocean in one way, and in another direction, it will connect China with the South China Sea and the South Pacific.[98] Thus, it is an extremely ambitious project joining several countries and continents with China's provinces and the Indian Ocean has an extremely prominent role in it. Many of the host countries, therefore, are in dilemma over extending support to China on this project. India clearly has withheld her support towards China on this, citing threat to sovereignty issues. Vietnam too, much like India, has not been very forthcoming in welcoming this project, because this project, once materialised, will definitely increase China's presence in the South China Sea which is disputed between Vietnam and China. China has been trying its best to make this project look lucrative to host countries and has thus termed this initiative to be 'harmonious and inclusive', fostering 'a multi polar world' with 'open regional cooperation' and they have been actively promoting this proposal by visiting countries and garnering support in this regard so that the concept of 'peaceful rise' of China do not take a beating.[99]

As far as Vietnam's official reaction to this project is concerned, in May 2017, Vietnamese President Tran Dai Quang attended the Belt and Road Forum for International Cooperation in Beijing. Speaking at the Forum, Mr. Quang welcomed the Belt and Road along with efforts to promote economic and regional connectivity. He also proposed principles for the implementation of the Initiative. Specifically he emphasised that cooperation within the Initiative "must ensure sustainability, effectiveness and inclusiveness, to be based on the principles of consensus, equality, voluntariness, transparency, openness, mutual respect and benefits and compliance with the UN Charter and international law."[100] Following this, during President Xi Jinping's visit to Hanoi in November 2017, the two countries signed a MoU promoting connection between the "Two Corridors, One Belt" (TCOB) Framework and the Belt and Road Initiative. The two economic corridors (proposed by China in 2003 to promote economic cooperation) namely the Kunming-Lao Cai-Hanoi-Haiphong-Quang Ninh corridor and the Nanning-Lang Son-Hanoi-Haiphong-Quang Ninh corridor, were designed to improve connectivity between Yunnan and Guangxi with 12e cities and provinces in North Vietnam. It took two years to negotiate the MoU, implying that there were some disagreements. Vietnam has kept the two initiatives separate and TCOB is independent of the BRI.[101] Vietnam is treading a cautious path as far as the BRI is concerned and is vigilant about the debt trap in which increasing number of countries are finding themselves to be in, after accepting soft credits from China for infrastructural development to concretise the BRI projects in the host countries.

However, India was the only country in the eight-nation Shanghai Cooperation Organization Summit in Qingdao, China on June 10, 2018, which refused to endorse Belt and Road Initiative. In his address Prime Minister Modi said, "Any mega connectivity project must respect sovereignty and territorial integrity."[102] India is particularly against this Initiative because, the US$ 50 billion China-Pakistan Economic Corridor, part of the Belt and Road Initiative, passes through Pakistan occupied Kashmir (PoK).[103]

The Quadrilateral Security Dialogue and Vietnam's Position

China's emerging global mobility with the help of a number of initiatives such as String of Pearls concept, the BRI, maritime silk route projects, China-Pakistan Economic Corridor, etc., have created suspicion and anxiety, directly or indirectly to many countries including India. As a reaction to these Chinese initiatives, India has been joining hands with other countries such as, Japan, Australia, the United States and France to come together to thwart Chinese advances in the Indian Ocean region, because any occurrence in this region will have direct bearing on India's security structure and this region has been mentioned as India's 'immediate' sphere of influence in her maritime doctrines. Thus, India has been appreciative of the US's 'Pivot to Asia' policy in the 21st century as a re-balancer in the region. France is the largest resident power in the Indian Ocean with the largest amount of real estate, including about 11 million sq km of Exclusive Economic Zone, particularly in the Mozambique Channel with over 10 islands as part of French overseas territories. For France's military bases in Djibouti, Abu Dhabi and Reunion Islands, India regards France as an attractive strategic partner in the Indian Ocean region[104] and a major stakeholder in the security of the sea lanes of communication and critical choke points. Japan too has challenged China's sovereignty claims in the Senkakau/ Diaoyu Islands and Australia being an Indian Ocean littoral, too, shares India's concerns of unhindered materialisation of Chinese projects in this zone. In fact, the PLA's announcement in November 2013 of an Air Defence Identification Zone (ADIZ) over the East China Sea zone that overlapped the Japanese, the South Korean and Taiwanese zones was a momentous development in this context[105] which angered Japan significantly. Therefore, since 2007 and particularly since the time of announcement of the Maritime Silk Road project by China, India, the United States, Japan and Australia have been holding talks and discussions to collaborate and come together on a single platform and they could finally do so by forming 'the Quad' or the 'Quadrilateral Security Dialogue (QSD)'. It is to be noted that these countries also regularly collaborate with each other to perform joint naval exercises, known as the Malabar exercise, which is normally held in the Malabar Coast off Bay of Bengal and which has been protested by the Chinese government. Interestingly enough, France has expressed its support to the Quad and the Vietnamese Navy has successfully taken part in the Malabar exercise of 2010, clearly giving out the signal that it is in support of India's naval initiatives to check China's hard-line advances in the region. India has always been a zealous advocate of the 'open regionalism' concept in the Indian Ocean. That is why, it has pursued this idea in IORA (Indian Ocean Rim Association), previously known as IOR-ARC (Indian Ocean Rim Association for Regional Co-operation), the only comprehensive multilateral body in the Indian Ocean, comprising the coastal states of the Indian Ocean. It has 21 countries and India has been playing a leadership role in it to uphold the issues and challenges of this region, but the body has not been unanimous and vociferous about China's projects in the area.

Though Vietnam is not a member of the Quad, but is significant to note that, in recent years with the increasing politico-military assertive posture of China in the South China Sea, Vietnam has upgraded her political and defence ties with each of the Quad members, thereby getting labelled by China as a 'shadow member' of the Quad. Thus, the Indian Ocean is slowly becoming the theatre of rift between India and China, with Vietnam once again proving to be a staunch ally of India in this regard. The China factor in the Indian Ocean issue is clearly a major area of convergence between India and Vietnam and this challenge has the potential to further their bilateral bonhomie by leaps and bounds in the coming days.

India's Project 'Mausam', Vision 'SAGAR' and Vietnam's Reaction

Inundated with several Chinese projects in its backyard, the South Bloc has been going overdrive to tackle the situation and with Prime Minister Modi's ascendancy to power, certain projects have been named so far in the 'Indo-Pacific' region, such as Project 'Mausam' and Vision 'SAGAR', two of his pet projects. Though both these are in very nascent stages and the modalities for their implementation have not yet been clearly understood, nonetheless these should be mentioned for its future prospects. Project 'Mausam is to be implemented by Indira Gandhi National Centre for the Arts (IGNCA), New Delhi as the nodal coordinating agency with support of Archaeological Survey of India and National Museum as associate bodies with aims to showcase a Transnational Mixed Route. The Project was launched at the 38th World Heritage Session at Doha,

Qatar on June 20, 2014. Focusing on monsoon patterns, cultural routes and maritime landscape, Project 'Mausam' is examining key processes and phenomena that link different parts of the Indian Ocean littoral as well as those that connect the coastal centres to their hinterlands. Broadly, it aims to understand how the knowledge and manipulation of the monsoon winds has shaped interactions across the Indian Ocean and led to the spread of shared knowledge systems, traditions, technologies and ideas along maritime routes. At the macro level, it aims to reconnect and re-establish communications between countries of the Indian Ocean world. At the micro level, the focus is on understanding national cultures in their regional maritime milieu. Vietnam, China, Myanmar, Iran supported this project to revive the historic 'Spice Route.'[106]

Much similar to Project 'Mausam', Prime Minister Modi is increasingly talking of the 'Vision SAGAR' in the 'Indo-Pacific' region. The speech delivered by Sushma Swaraj, External Affairs Minister at the 2nd Indian Ocean Conference on August 31, 2017, explained the crux of the vision that India has adopted under her 'Act East' policy. The Minister says, "India is, and has always been, a maritime nation. It is home to some of the oldest seaports in the world and historically has had extensive maritime links with Africa, Gulf, Mediterranean, South East Asia and the Far East. The waters of the Indian Ocean have not only carried commerce but have borne India's culture, religion, and ideas far and wide. India's location at the very centre of the Indian Ocean has linked us with other cultures, shaped our maritime trade routes, and influenced our strategic thought. This vision was enunciated by Prime Minister Modi in March 2015 when he put forward the concept of SAGAR – "Security and Growth for All in the Region." This is a clear, high-level articulation of India's vision for the Indian Ocean.[107] She further said, "SAGAR has distinct but inter-related elements and underscore India's engagement in the Indian Ocean. These are enhancing capacities to safeguard land and maritime territories & interests; deepening economic and security cooperation in the littoral; promoting collective action to deal with natural disasters and maritime threats like piracy, terrorism and emergent non-state actors; working towards sustainable regional development through enhanced collaboration; and, engaging with countries beyond our shores with the aim of building greater trust and promoting respect for maritime rules, norms and peaceful resolution of disputes. The principles enshrined in SAGAR provide us with a coherent framework to address some of the challenges relating to economic revival, connectivity, security, culture and identity, and India's own evolving approach to these issues. The challenge before us is to ensure intra-ocean trade and investment, and the sustainable harnessing of the wealth of the seas, including food, medicines and clean energy."[108] Moreover, in this speech she pointed out, "A related aspect is the emergence of the 'Blue Economy' as a promising new pillar of prosperity in the region, with immense economic and employment potential. We are already engaging our neighbours in Blue Economy initiatives, particularly in the areas of marine bio-technology, exploration and sustainable exploitation of ocean mineral resources, sustainable fishing practices, and harnessing of ocean energy. In India, we are implementing targeted programmes for re-energising economic activity in our islands and our coastal areas. There is also a renewed focus on strengthening marine research, developing eco-friendly marine industrial technologies, promoting sustainable fisheries and, ensuring the protection of the maritime environment. We remain committed to extending port connectivity among the littoral states of the Indian Ocean and beyond. This is the objective behind the Sagarmala initiative, which aims to establish new ports and modernise old ones. It is only natural, therefore, that connectivity is one of the major themes of Prime Minister Modi's 'Neighbourhood First' policy'."[109]

Along with these projects, India and Vietnam have beefed up their bilateral naval cooperation to secure their maritime and strategic interests in the 'Indo-Pacific' region. The concept of 'Indo-Pacific' has gained such popularity in the new millennium, that it may be argued, the new concept has replaced the usage of the idea of 'Asia-Pacific' in all practical purposes, and from the geo-strategic lexicon of several world leaders and strategists in recent years. It is interesting to note that an Indian scholar has been officially credited with the coinage and popularisation of the term 'Indo-Pacific'. Dr. Gurpreet S. Khurana, presently, executive director of the National Maritime Foundation, New Delhi and a Captain in the Indian Navy, published a paper titled "Security of Sea- Lanes: Prospects for Indo- Japan Cooperation" in IDSA's journal titled "Strategic Analyses" in January 2007, in which he discussed the concept of 'Indo-Pacific,' especially in the context of highlighting the transfer of the world economic epicentre towards the Asian Continent in the 21st Century. The main motive behind the genesis of such a concept by Dr. Khurana was to analyse China's growing "politico-military assertiveness"[110] in the region. As a concretisation of the apprehension, a US think-tank first propounded the concept of 'String of Pearls' strategy in 2005, in which it revealed how China was building bases and developing ports in crucial and strategically located countries off the Indian Ocean, and practically encircling India from all sides. As a result of such enunciation, anxieties gripped not only the South Bloc, but also other countries in the region which faced challenges in their relationships with China, such as Japan. That is why, immediately after the 'String of Pearls' strategy was propagated, India and Japan started sharing strategic assessments and intensified their discussion on beefing up their bilateral cooperation in crucial strategic areas, such as, protection of energy lifelines in the Indian Ocean. Against such a backdrop, the 'Indo-Pacific' concept as analysed by Dr. Khurana highlighted how and why the maritime region of Asia and Indo-Pacific should be considered a singular and a continuous geo-political entity, so that that the unexplored tremendous geo-economic opportunities can be tapped to the optimum level and the huge security challenges therein, can be better analysed.

Thereafter, in August 2007, when Japanese Prime Minister Shinzo Abe paid a crucial visit to India to deepen their bilateral strategic and political cooperation to meet the growing regional challenges, he provided adequate support to the 'Indo-Pacific' concept. Addressing the Indian Parliament, he delivered a speech titled "Confluence of the two Seas". He remarked, "We are now at a point at which the

'Confluence of the two Seas' is coming into being. The Pacific and the Indian Oceans are now bringing about a dynamic coupling as seas of freedom and of prosperity. A 'broader Asia' that broke away geographical boundaries is now beginning to take on a distinct form. Our two countries have the ability and the responsibility to ensure that it broadens yet further and to nurture and enrich these seas to become seas of clearest transparence."[111]

In 2010, the US officially recognised the 'Indo-Pacific' concept for the first time. Speaking at Honolulu, US Secretary of State, Hilary Clinton spoke about "expanding our work with the Indian Navy in the Pacific, because we understand how important the Indo-Pacific basin is to global trade and commerce. Following this, in 2013, Australia released its Defence White Paper, which carried the first government articulation of the 'Indo-Pacific' concept. This Defence White Paper discussed in detail, the ongoing strategic shift to the region of Asia-Pacific and the Indian Ocean Rim, particularly the shift of economic weight to the region and the US re-balance to the region.[112]

In this context, it is interesting to note that, the genesis of the 'Indo-Pacific' concept has been to the advantage of India, because, India was not a part of the 'Asia-Pacific' concept which related to that part of Asia that was in the Pacific Ocean. There were three major constituents of Asia-Pacific, namely Northeast Asia, Southeast Asia and Oceania (Southwestern Pacific). However, India perceives the 'Indo-Pacific' region to consist of the Indian Ocean and the Pacific Ocean, and the landmasses that surround the coast of East Africa, across Indian Ocean to Western Pacific, including countries like Japan and Australia. Moreover, whereas the 'Asia-Pacific' concept was predominantly economic in nature, the 'Indo-Pacific' strategy is both a strategic as well as an economic policy, especially concerned with maritime security and cooperation as it comprises important sea-lanes of communication connecting the littoral countries of the Indian and the Pacific Oceans.

Coming specifically to the genesis of the 'Indo-Pacific' strategy in the US psyche, it can be argued that the first intricate articulation of this concept could be found in Obama administration's 'Asia Pivot' policy. The then Secretary of State highlighted the importance of the region when she spoke of "America's Pacific Century" that was published in *Foreign Policy* in October 11, 2011. She said, "The Asia-Pacific has become a key driver of global politics. Stretching from the Indian subcontinent to the western shores of the Americas, the region spans two oceans — the Pacific and the Indian — that are increasingly linked by shipping and strategy. It boasts almost half the world's population. It includes many of the key engines of the global economy, as well as the largest emitters of greenhouse gases. It is home to several of our key allies and important emerging powers like China, India, and Indonesia." She called it a "forward-deployed diplomacy" which will ensure America's continued presence as a resident power in Asia.[113]

The fact that the US is sincere in its 'Indo-Pacific' strategy was made known when it conceptualized the idea of the "Indo-Pacific Economic Corridor" during the US- India Strategic Dialogue of 2013 where Secretary of State John Kerry referred to the potential of the Indo-Pacific Economic Corridor for trade and transit between the economies of South and Southeast Asia. He declared that the US is "cooperating to realize the potential of the Indo-Pacific Economic Corridor, which can spur development and investment as well as trade and transit between the dynamic economies of South and Southeast Asia." Indo-Pacific Economic Corridor once materialised, will link India with South Asia, Southeast Asia and East Asia through Myanmar. Moreover, the US in its 'Asia Pivot' policy, has firmly found Japan which through its PQI (Partnership for Quality Infrastructure) Initiative, that includes plans for large-scale infrastructural projects in South and Southeast Asia, desires to be an important player in the 'Indo-Pacific' region in the coming days. In fact, the "Joint Statement on India and Japan Vision 2025" aims to synergize India's 'Act East' Policy and Japan's 'Partnership for Quality Infrastructure.'

Meanwhile, highlighting on the importance of the region to US's geostrategic policy formulations in the 21st Century, Hillary Clinton remarked in Vietnam in 2010, "The US has a national interest in freedom of navigation, open access to Asia's maritime commons, and respect for international law in the South China Sea. The US supports a collaborative diplomatic process by all claimants for resolving the various territorial disputes without coercion. We oppose the use or threat of force by any claimant. While the United States does not take sides on the competing territorial disputes over land features in the South China Sea, we believe claimants should pursue their territorial claims and accompanying rights to maritime space in accordance with the United Nations Convention on the Law of the Seas. Consistent with customary international law, legitimate claims to maritime space in the South China Sea should be derived solely from legitimate claims to land features.[114] Therefore, without naming China, Clinton made an oblique reference to its and its assertive behaviour in the region, particularly in the South China Sea, providing justification for US's re-engagement with the region as the US feels it is its "national interest" to do so.

Once again, US President Donald Trump's speech at the East Asia Summit in November 2017 highlighted the importance of 'Indo-Pacific' region in America's strategic calculus during his tenure at the White House. Again, immediately after returning from his historic 12-day trip to Asia, he remarked at the Diplomatic Reception Room, White House, that, it was one of the core goals "to strengthen America's alliances and economic partnerships in a free and open 'Indo-Pacific' made up of thriving, independent nations, respectful of other countries and their own citizens, and safe from foreign domination and economic servitude."[115]

However, the most concrete articulation of US's 'Indo-Pacific' strategy was made in the US National Security Strategy of 2017. It says, "A geopolitical competition between free and repressive visions of world order is taking place in the Indo-Pacific region. The region, which stretches from the west coast of India to the western shores of the United States, represents the most populous and economically dynamic part of the world. The US interest in a free and open Indo-Pacific extends back to the earliest days of our republic. Although the United States seeks to continue to cooperate with China, China is using economic inducements and penalties, influence operations, and implied military threats to persuade other states to heed its political and security agenda. China's infrastructure investments and trade strategies reinforce its geopolitical aspirations. Its efforts to build and militarise outposts in the South China Sea endanger the free flow of trade, threaten the sovereignty of other nations, and undermine regional stability. China has mounted a rapid military modernisation campaign designed to limit the US access to the region and provide China a freer hand there. China presents its ambitions as mutually beneficial, but Chinese dominance risks diminishing the sovereignty of many states in the Indo-Pacific. States throughout the region are calling for sustained US leadership in a collective response that upholds a regional order respectful of sovereignty and independence."[116]

Meanwhile, the US has prioritised its ties with India in the region as it truly believes that India can play the role of a balancer against China, and can thus ensure a congenial environment for the successful realization of its 'Indo-Pacific' strategy. Briefing reporters on the Trump administration's Indo-Pacific strategy and India's 'key role' in it, the Deputy Assistant Secretary of State for East Asian and Pacific Affairs, Alex Wong has said, "India as a nation has invested in a free and open order. It is a democracy. It is a nation that can anchor free and open order in the Indo-Pacific region. And it's our policy to ensure that India does play that role and that it becomes over time a more influential player in the region." "India plays a key role" and "India for sure has the capability and potential to play a more weighty role."[117]

India too, on its part has been highlighting the 'Indo-Pacific' concept, especially under Prime Minister Narendra Modi's 'Act East' policy. Prime Minister Modi during his speech at the Shangri La Dialogue, Singapore, in June 2018 said, "Oceans have an important place in Indian thinking since pre-Vedic times. Thousands of years ago, the Indus Valley Civilization as well as Indian peninsula has maritime trade. Oceans and Varuna—the Lord of all Waters—find a prominent place in the world's oldest books—the Vedas. The Indian Ocean has shaped much of India's history. It now holds the key to our future. The Ocean carries 90 percent of India's trade and our energy sources. It is also the lifeline of global commons. The Indian Ocean connects regions of diverse cultures and different levels of peace and prosperity. To the East, the Malacca Strait and South China Sea connect India to the Pacific and to most of our major trade partners-—ASEAN, Japan, Republic of Korea, China and the Americas. Our interests in the region are vast, and our engagement is deep. We are also helping build economic capabilities and improve maritime security for our friends and partners. We promote collective security through forums like Indian Ocean Naval Symposium."[118] He further said, "We have more trade agreements in this part of the world than in any other. We have Comprehensive Economic Partnership Agreements with Singapore, Japan and South Korea." He highlighted the fact that, "India (n) Armed Forces, especially our Navy, are building partnerships in the Indo-Pacific region for peace and security as well as humanitarian assistance and disaster relief. They train, exercise and conduct goodwill missions across the region."[119] Moreover, "More than anywhere else, our ties will deepen and our presence will grow in the region. The Indo-Pacific is a natural region. India does not see the Indo- Pacific Region as a strategy or as a club of limited members. Nor as a grouping that seeks to dominate. And by no means do we consider it as directed against any country."[120] He, in this speech, highlighted certain elements of the 'Indo-Pacific' concept. For instance, first, "It stands for a free, open, inclusive region, which embraces us all in a common pursuit of progress and prosperity."[121] Secondly, "Southeast Asia is at its centre. And, ASEAN has been and will be central to its future."[122] Thirdly, "Such an order must believe in sovereignty and territorial integrity as well as equality of all nations, irrespective of size and strength."[123] Fourthly, "We should all have equal access as a right under international law to the use of common spaces on sea and in the air that would require freedom of navigation, unimpeded commerce and peaceful settlement of disputes in accordance with international law."[124]

With the aim to curb China's growing military influence in Southeast Asia, India and selected ASEAN countries have begun holding joint military exercises. The Indian Navy has conducted regular joint military and naval exercises with Vietnam along with Singapore,

Japan, South Korea, Indonesia and Malaysian navies to ensure the safety of the strategic water ways in the region such as Straits of Malacca and Isthmus Kra. India and Vietnam have also engaged in the PASSEX Naval exercises that includes signal drills, surface manoeuvres and communications. China has always regarded the Asia-Pacific Region as vital to its security and any Indian attempt to intrude into this region displeases Beijing. Since the time the US made known its plans of re-engagement in the region in the 'Asian Century,' China has been highly critical of the US's presence in the region, particularly to counter China's growth and to thwart Beijing's economic and political predominance in the region. Chinese President Xi Jinping has thus, on a repeated instance, tried to popularise the 'Chinese Dream' and his aim to see 'Asia for Asians' obliquely referring to the US and other western powers as "extra-regional powers." As far as US's 'Indo-Pacific' strategy is concerned, many people believe that apart from renaming US Pacific Command as Indo-Pacific Command in May (2018), Washington has made little substantial progress in its Indo-Pacific strategy. However, from the prospective of military deployment, the general outline and structure of US military presence is being shaped. Such military presence includes materials and equipments, military exercises, military exchanges and the establishment of military bases, which can enable US troops to flex their muscles. The establishment of the Indo-Pacific Command indicates that the strategic position of the Indian Ocean has thus been elevated. Guam in the Western Pacific, Darwin Harbour in Northern Australia and Diego Garcia in the central Indian Ocean will provide support for the new Indo-Pacific strategy. Military presence at the three spots will be key to the future of the US Indo-Pacific strategy. The roles of the three places are different. Guam and Diego Garcia will be hubs of military operation and Darwin Harbour will be a support centre.[125] As far as India's role in the 'Indo-Pacific' strategy is concerned, China believes that Washington has declared New Delhi a "major defense partner"[126] in May (2018), putting India on a par with the closest allies and partners of the US. The same month the Pentagon renamed the Pacific Command the

Indo-Pacific Command, signalling the growing importance of India to the US. Due to its geopolitical position and status as an emerging country, India is considered by many US strategists as the best choice for the US to counter-balance China. China is hopeful that New Delhi is unlikely to take sides between China and the US. The neutrality is of course determined by its own political, economic and security interests. As two emerging powers, China and India share more common interests than differences. They should ponder how to better cooperate especially in the face of pressure from Washington. Beijing and New Delhi should enhance coordination so as to develop more balanced relations with Washington. Coordinated Sino-Indian ties are essential to the stability of Asia.[127] Furthermore, it believes that the Indian quest for strategic autonomy means it won't be bound by US military pacts to join a war waged by the US against a friendly country while requesting for the US technology, which is obvious from the Logistics Exchange Memorandum of Agreement inked between the two in 2016. In this part, India clearly states that it will not allow the stationing of US troops on Indian soil and won't extend support in the event of US military action against friendly countries. India is ambitious to play a leadership role rather than being subservient to the US in containing China in the Indian Ocean Region and beyond.[128] Meanwhile, US Commerce Secretary Wilbur Ross designated India as a Strategic Trade Authorization-1(STA-1) country, which "acknowledges the US-India security and economic relationship," and is comparable to trusted NATO allies. The US will ease its export controls on defence and other hi-tech products to India,[129] which is of concern to China.

However, China is not only critical about the 'Indo-Pacific' strategy, but is also not stopping short of ridiculing it and has questioned US's commitment and sincerity in the implementation of such a strategy. In July 2018, when US announced US$ 113 million in new infrastructural initiatives in the region (new technology, energy, and infrastructural initiatives), Secretary of State Mike Pompeo said, "These funds represent just a down payment on a new era in US economic commitment to peace and prosperity in the Indo-Pacific region." To which China retorted, "Imperialism is deeply rooted in Western countries' political thinking" and "not engage in power games with massive investment."[130] Furthermore, an editorial in the *Global Times* remarked, "What is the Indo-Pacific strategy? Many complain about its vagueness. Its most innovative part may be the name itself. Washington probably hopes the rest of the world would stop asking questions, tacitly understand Washington's interests and firmly gather around the US after a few exchanges of glances and together begin to counter China's rising influence." "When ASEAN was first founded, countering China's "Communist expansion" was one of its main purposes, but the regional situation has changed. China's reform and opening- up has fundamentally transformed ASEAN countries' relations with Beijing. China has become the largest trading partner of almost all ASEAN countries" It also said, "What ASEAN saw was the Trump administration's withdrawal from the TPP, which the US had already agreed to and the White House's full-blown trade war. ASEAN members are worried about being caught in the crosshair or hit by Trump's trade tariff "bullets". Both Singapore and Malaysia lowered their GDP growth expectations for 2019 amid the trade war. ASEAN members are not sure what the US Indo-Pacific strategy entails. The US announced only an investment of US$ 113 million, which also includes India. The amount seems only sufficient to build an overpass perhaps in the centre of Mumbai. Washington is using a strategic gimmick. Indo-Pacific strategy should be consecrated as the "best geopolitical jargon." If it is used to counter China's serious strategy in the ASEAN, the US will eventually find out that it has no supernatural power and that it will bump into an invisible wall."[131]

Moreover, Beijing believes that it is a 'trap' by the Western world to stunt the growth of China and India, two Asian giants to drive a wedge between the two countries. An editorial in the *Global Times* will throw light in such perspective which is prevalent in Beijing now. It says, "The Westerners hold a complicated feeling viewing the development of China and India. Western opinion currently favors India, a result of temporary geopolitical calculation. With India's continuous economic success, antipathy toward New Delhi will emerge in the West sooner or later. India is enjoying smooth diplomacy at the moment, but it won't last very long. For Washington, driving a wedge between China and India is its best Asia policy. Two possible scenarios can unfold in Asia. China and India might be dragged by the US into an exhausting dispute with the rise of the two delayed, or China and India can resolve or shelve disputes to promote their own development with Asia as a whole embarking on modernization. The Indo-Pacific strategy is a trap set by Washington to bury the rise of China and India."[132]

Therefore, in this context, India's 'Look East' Policy launched in 1991 primarily due to economic reasons, has now taken an added security dimension following its maritime doctrine announced in 2004 and 2009. This Indian maritime doctrine also coincided with the release of Vietnam's defence white paper, depicting certain commonalities of interests between the two countries in regional matters. With the dawning of the 'Asian Century,' India and Vietnam began to regularly engage in naval visits not only as goodwill visits, but also as a concrete proof of growing naval cooperation between the two countries in the region. Vietnam has participated in the MILAN naval exercises in 2010 and 2018, a multi-nation naval exercise in the Indian Ocean, much to the chagrin of China. It is important to note that, without paying much heed to China's wrath in this regard, in May 2018, India and Vietnam conducted their first ever joint naval exercise, a further significant step in their 'naval diplomacy'. Therefore, it can be said that, like the Cold War years, Indian Ocean has again emerged as a centre of power struggle among the littoral States along with other extra-regional powers. The centre of gravity of power struggle in this region is now mainly confined to China on the one hand and US, Australia, Japan, France, India and Vietnam on the other.

Summarily then, it can be argued that, after the analysis of some very important strategic issues, such as, the South China Sea, defence cooperation, collaboration in Science and technology, human resource development and Information Technology, nuclear cooperation, border issue, the issue of hydro-politics, terrorism and the Indian Ocean, it may be concluded that in the post-Cold War years, the rising and more assertive 'China factor,' is largely perceived as a major security threat in the emerging Asian architecture and has led India and Vietnam to come closer to each other than the past years. The feeling of solidarity that was evident in the Cold War days is finding its truest materialisation in the strategic front in the post-Cold War years. Most importantly, these two countries are coming together on various regional and global platforms to voice their unanimous opinion against Chinese 'excesses' in this regard. And significantly enough for them, they are getting the tacit support of some extra-regional countries, such as the USA and even some European countries in their united fight on many issues in this emerging Asian global order.

Notes

1. Tridib Chakraborti, "India and Vietnam: Sprouting Strategic Partnership," *World Focus*, October 2011, p.895.
2. Shantanu Chakrabarti, "Evolving India- Vietnam Relations," in Rajiv. K. Bhatia, Vijay Sakhuja and Vikash Ranjan (eds.), *India- Vietnam Agenda for Strengthening Partnership*, Shipra Publications, New Delhi, 2013, p.9.
3. Tridib Chakraborti, n.218, p.898.
4. C. Ravindranatha Reddy, India and Vietnam during Post Cold War Era, Centre for Southeast Asian and Pacific Studies, Sri Venkateswara University, Tirupati, 2012, pp.66–67.
5. "India- Vietnam Relations," Ministry of External Affairs, Government of India, https://mea.gov.in/Portal/ForeignRelation/India-Vietnam_Relations.pdf (accessed on September 12, 2016).
6. Baladas Ghoshal, "India's Look- East Policy and Vietnam," *Mainstream Weekly*, Vol. XLVII, No.40, 19 September 2009, www.mainstreamweekly.net/article1639.html (accessed on June 15, 2018).
7. Tridib Chakraborti, n.218, p.899.
8. *Annual Report: 2001-02*, Ministry of External Affairs Government of India, New Delhi, 2002.
9. *Annual Report:2004-05*, Ministry of External Affairs, Government of India, New Delhi, 2005.
10. *Annual Report:2005-06*, Ministry of External Affairs, Government of India, New Delhi, 2006.
11. *Annual Report:2006-07*, Ministry of External Affairs, Government of India, New Delhi, 2007.
12. *Annual Report:2007-08*, Ministry of External Affairs, Government of India, New Delhi, 2008.
13. "The Fifth Shangri- La Dialogue," IISS Shangri-La Dialogue, https://www.iiss.org/

en/publications/conference.proceedings/sections/shangri-la-aa36/the-shangri-la-dialogue-2006-9f22 (accessed on October 12, 2016). For further details see http://www.iiss.org/conferences/the-shangri-la-dialogue (accessed on October 12, 2016).

14. "Agreements/MoUs signed during the State Visit of Hon'ble President to Vietnam," Ministry of External Affairs, Government of Indiawww.mea.gov.in/bilateral-documents.htm?dtl/23996/AgreementsMoUs_signed_during_the_State_Visit_of_Honble_President_to_Vietnam_15_September_2014 (accessed on November 3, 2016).
15. "Vietnam National Defence," Ministry of National Defence, Socialist Republic of Vietnam, Hanoi, December 2009, https://www.files.ethz.ch/isn/155222/Vietnam2009.pdf (accessed on May 15, 2016).
16. Tridib Chakraborti, "Rising India- Vietnam Ties in the Emerging Security Architecture of the Asia-Pacific Region," in Rajiv K. Bhatia, Vijay Sakhuja and Vikash Ranjan (eds.), *India- Vietnam Agenda for Strengthening Partnership,* Shipra Publications and Indian Council of World Affairs, New Delhi, 2013, pp.95–132.
17. "Indian Maritime Doctrine," Ministry of Defence (Navy), Government of India, New Delhi, 2009, www.indiannavy.nic.in/sites/default/files/Indian-Maritime-Doctrine-2009-Updated-12Feb16.pdf (accessed on November 10, 2016).
18. P.S. Suryanarayana, "India, Vietnam agree to firm up defence ties," *The Hindu*, July 28, 2010.
19. Tridib Chakraborti, n.218.
20. Patrick Ventrell, "South China Sea," Press Statement, U.S Department of State, August 3, 2012, www.state.gov/r/pa/prs/ps/2012/08/196022.htm (accessed on October 16, 2016).
21. Zachary Abuza, Nguyen Nhat Anh, "Vietnam's Military Modernization," *The Diplomat*, 28 October 2016, https://thediplomat.com/2016/10/vietnams-military-modernization/ (accessed on November 3, 2016).
22. *Annual Report:2011-12,* Ministry of External Affairs, Government of India, New Delhi, 2012.
23. "India being swept up by missile delusion," *Global Times*, April 19, 2012, www.globaltimes.cn/content/705627.shtml (accessed on August 20, 2016).
24. *Annual Report:2014-15,* Ministry of External Affairs, Government of India, New Delhi, 2015.
25. "On the Occasion of 40th Anniversary of Reunification Day of Vietnam, 125th Birth Anniversary of Great Leader- President Ho Chi Minh, 70th Anniversary of Vietnam's National Day," A Publication of The Embassy of The Socialist Republic of Vietnam, New Delhi, 2015.
26. Ibid.
27. Nguyen Hong Quan, "Evaluation of Vietnam- India Defence Cooperation," in Rajiv K. Bhatia, Vijay Sakhuja and Vikash Ranjan (eds.), *India- Vietnam Agenda for Strengthening Partnership*, Shipra Publications and Indian Council of World Affairs, , New Delhi, 2013, pp.158–61.
28. Saibal Dasgupta, "China builds massive solar power station to help Sharif in Pakistan," *The Times of India*, July 29, 2015.
29. *Annual Report: 2013-14,* Ministry of External Affairs, Government of India, New Delhi, 2013-14.
30. Elizabeth Roche, "India, Vietnam ink 5-year defence pact amid Chinese naval expansion," *Livemint*, May 26, 2015, https://www.livemint.com/Politics/

bUWnCvNDTwKT513o51TodP/India-Vietnam-ink-5year-defence-pact-amid-chinese-naval-ex.html (accessed on September 15, 2017).

31. "On the Occasion of 40th Anniversary of Reunification Day of Vietnam, 125th Birth Anniversary of Great Leader- President Ho Chi Minh, 70th Anniversary of Vietnam's National Day," n.242.
32. Dipanjan Roy Chaudhury, "India, Vietnam exploring avenues of cooperation in a host of areas: Vietnam minister," *The Economic Times*, January 17, 2015.
33. *Asian Recorder*, Vol.24, No. 15, 9-15 April 1978, p. 14257.
34. *Asian Recorder*, Vol.28, No. 27, 2-8 November 1982, p.16673.
35. *Annual Report: 1981-82*, Ministry of External Affairs, Government of India, New Delhi, 1982.
36. *Foreign Affairs Record*, Vol.25, No.7, July 1979, p.155.
37. K. Raja Reddy, "India-Vietnam Relations: Enhanced Cooperation in IT, Science and Technology," in Rajiv K. Bhatia, Vijay Sakhuja and Vikash Ranjan (eds.), *India-Vietnam: Agenda for Strengthening Partnership*, Shipra Publications and Indian Council of World Affairs, New Delhi, 2013, pp.169–70.
38. C. Ravindranatha Reddy, n.221, p.135.
39. K. Raja Reddy, n.254, pp.172–73.
40. "Vietnam, India look towards stronger IT development," *The Voice of Vietnam*, 30 March 2012, English.vov.vn/politics/Vietnam-india-look-towards-stronger-it-development-234780.vov (accessed on May 4, 2018).
41. Ajay Lele, "India- Vietnam Space Cooperation: Looking For New Frontiers", *Society for the Study of Peace and Conflict*, 14 September 2011, www.sspconline.org/opinion/IndiaVietnamSpaceCooperationNewFrontiers_14092011 (accessed on June 15, 2015).
42. Pham Hoang Ha, "India's Potential in Science and Technology: Scope for Cooperation," in Rajiv K. Bhatia, Vijay Sakhuja and Vikash Ranjan (eds.), *India-Vietnam: Agenda for Strengthening Partnership*, Shipra Publications and Indian Council of World Affairs, New Delhi, 2013, p.181.
43. "India, Vietnam sign MoUs on I &B, space cooperation," *Business Standard*, New Delhi, 25 January 2018, https://www.business-standard.com/article/news-ani/india-vietnam-sign-mous-on-i-b-space-cooperation-118012500008_1.html (accessed on May 4, 2018).
44. "On the Occasion of the 68th Anniversary of Vietnam's National Day: 2nd September 1945- 2nd September 2013," A Publication of the Embassy of the Socialist Republic of Vietnam, New Delhi, 2013.
45. "India-Vietnam Relations," Ministry of External Affairs, Government of India, New Delhi, https://www.mea.gov.in/Portal/ForeignRelation/Vietnam_Dec_2013.pdf (accessed on March 6, 2016).
46. Sudha Ramachandran, "Chinese and Indian Competition in Space Heats Up," *China Brief*, Vol.17, Issue 13, October 20, 2017, https://jamestown.org/program/chinese-indian-competition-space-heats/ (accessed on December 25, 2017).
47. Sanjeev Miglani and Greg Torode, "India to build satellite tracking station in Vietnam that offers eye on China," *Reuters*, January 25, 2016, www.reuters.com/article/us-india-vietnam-satellite-idUSKCN0V30B3 (accessed on March 3, 2016).
48. Ramesh Thakur and Carlyle A. Thayer, *Soviet Relations with India and Vietnam*, Palgrave Macmillan, United Kingdom, 1992, p.151.

49. *Annual Report:1995-1996*, Ministry of External Affairs, Government of India, New Delhi, 1996.
50. Tridib Chakraborti, "India and Vietnam Relations in the 21st Century: From Solidarity Friendship to Comprehensive Strategic Partner," *NAM Today*, Vol. LVXXIV, No.01, January 2018, New Delhi, p.11.
51. Ibid.
52. G. Balachandran, India and NSG: Approaches to Indian Membership, *Institute for Defence Studies and Analyses Issue Brief*, 23 May 2013, p.126.
53. For details of the debate held in Lok Sabha, https://mea.gov.in/lok-sabha.htm?dtl/24540/QNO343NUCLEAR+DEAL+BETWEEN+CHINA+AND+PAKISTAN (accessed on July 5, 2018).
54. For details of the debate in Lok Sabha, https://www.mea.gov.in/lok-sabha.htm?dtl/27051/QUESTION+NO605+MISSILE+TECHNOLOGY+CONTROL+REGIME (accessed on December 14, 2016).
55. Pravin Sawhney and Ghazala Wahab, "*Dragon on Our Doorstep*," Aleph Publishers, New Delhi, 2017, p.38.
56. For details of the debate held in Lok Sabha, https://mea.gov.in/lok-sabha.htm?dtl/24344/Q_NO_645_BORDER_DISPUTE_WITH_CHINA (accessed on July 15, 2015).
57. For details of the debate held in Lok Sabha,mea.gov.in/bilateral-documents.htm?dtl/16723/Q3517+Border+dispute+between+India+and+China (accessed on May 4, 2014).
58. Carlyle A. Thayer, "Vietnam And Rising China The Structural Dynamics of Mature Asymmetry," *Southeast Asian Affairs,* 2010, pp.399–400.
59. For details of the debate held in Lok Sabha, https://www.mea.gov.in/lok-sabha.htm?dtl/26677/QUESTION+NO544+CHINAS+VETO+AGAINST+INDIA (accessed on July 15, 2016).
60. Ibid.
61. "India to pay China Rs.82 lakh annually for Brahmaputra flood data," *RediffNews*, 1 July 2014, https://www.rediff.com/news/report/india-to-pay-china-rs-82-lakh-annually-for-brahmaputra-flood-data/20140701.htm (accessed May 14, 2015).
62. For details of the debate held in Rajya Sabha, https://mea.gov.in/rajya-sabha.htm?dtl/26106/Q_No52_DAM_ON_BRAHMAPUTRA_BY_CHINA (accessed on June 10, 2017).
63. Ibid.
64. Tridib Chakraborti and Subhadeep Bhattacharya, South China Sea Imbroglio: Problems, Outcome and India's Stand, *Policy Brief*, The Institute of Foreign Policy Studies, The University of Calcutta, No.5, December 2012, p.2.
65. Raman Puri and Arun Sehgal, "The South China Sea Dispute: Implications for India," *Indian Foreign Affairs Journal*, Vol.6, No.4, October–December 2011, p.438
66. Xavier Furtado, "International Law and the Dispute over the Spratly Islands: Whither UNCLOS?" *Contemporary Southeast Asia*, Vol.21, No.3, December 1999, p.391.
67. Carlyle A. Thayer, "Vietnam and Rising China: The Structural Dynamics of Mature Asymmetry," *Southeast Asian Affairs*, 2010, pp.401–04.
68. For details of the debate held in Lok Sabha, https://www.mea.gov.in/press-releases.htm?dtl/20381/Q+102+Dispute+over+Petroleum+block (accessed on July 10, 2016)

69. Tridib Chakraborti and Subhadeep Bhattachaya, n.281.
70. Raman Puri and Arun Sehgal, n.282, pp.437–38.
71. Xavier Furtado, n.283, pp.388–89
72. Stein Tonnesson, An International History of the Dispute in the South China Sea, EAI Working Paper No 71, 16 March 2001, pp.1–24.
73. Ibid.
74. *Annual Report:1994-95,* Ministry of External Affairs, Government of India, New Delhi, 1995.
75. Teshu Singh, China and the South China Sea: Recent Developments, *World Focus*, September 2012, p.33.
76. Text of the United Nations Convention on the Law of the Sea of 10 December 1982, www.un.org/depts/los/convention_agreements/texts/unclos/UNCLOS-TOC.htm (accessed on August 13, 2017).
77. Ibid.
78. Ibid.
79. Ibid.
80. Tridib Chakraborti, China and Vietnam in the South China Sea Dispute: A 'Creeping Conflict- Peace- Trepidation' Syndrome, *China Report*, Vol.48, No.3, Sage Publication, December 2012, p.290.
81. For details see, official website of UN Commission on the Limits of the Continental Shelf (CLCS), http://www.un.org/Depts/los/clcs_new/clcs_home.htm (accessed on December 16, 2017).
82. Carlyle A Thayer, The Tyranny of Geography: Vietnamese Strategies to Constrain China in the South China Sea, *Contemporary Southeast Asia,* Vol.33, No.3, 2011, p.357
83. Tridib Chakraborti, n.297, p.291.
84. Ibid.
85. Teshu Singh, n.292, p.35.
86. Hillary Clinton, "America's Pacific Century," *Foreign Policy*, October 11, 2011, https://foreignpolicy.com/2011/10/11/americas-pacific-century/ (accessed on July 15, 2016).
87. On 8 August 2014, the Foreign Affairs Secretary Albert F. Rosario at presented the Philippine proposal of Triple Action Plan in the 47th ASEAN Foreign Ministers' Meeting, held in Nay Pyi Taw, Myanmar. The TAP is aimed at reducing and managing tension in the South China Sea until a settlement of the dispute may be obtained. The TAP contains immediate, intermediate and final approaches to address the provocative and destabilizing activities in the region without prejudice to existing territorial claims. (For details see, Department of Foreign Affairs, Republic of the Philippines, http://www.dfa.gov.ph/dfa-releases/3789/philippines-presents-triple-action-plan-at47th-asean-foreign-ministers-meeting-in-nay-pyi-taw+&cd=1&hl=en&ct=clnk&gl=in, accessed on October 10, 2017).
88. Melissa S Hersh, Dr. Ajay Lele, "Why Vietnam is an important ally for India," *Rediff News*, 2 December 2014,www.rediff.com/news/column/why-vietnam-is-an-important-ally-for-india/20141202.htm (accessed on January 15, 2016).
89. "US warns Beijing for militarizing South China Sea," *The Times of India*, May 4, 2018.
90. Megan Specia & Mikko Kotakkunen, "How South China Sea is fact turning into Beijing's military outpost," *The Times of India*, February 10, 2018.

91. Jagannath Panda, "Maritime Silk Road and the India-China Conundrum," *Indian Foreign Affairs Journal*, Vol.9, No.1, January-March 2014, p.30.
92. "On the Occasion of 40th Anniversary of Reunification Day of Vietnam, 125th Birth Anniversary of Great Leader- President Ho Chi Minh, 70th Anniversary of Vietnam's National Day," n.242.
93. *The Times of India*, July 29, 2015.
94. Jane Perlez, "Tribunal Rejects Beijing's Claims in South China Sea," *The New York Times*, July 12, 2016, https://www.nytimes.com/2016/07/13/world/asia/south-china-sea-hague-ruling-philippines.html (accessed on August 16, 2018).
95. Suhasini Haidar, "Zheng and Now," *The Hindu*, December 5, 2017, https://www.thehindu.com/opinion/op-ed/zheng-and-now/article21261349.ece (accessed on February 6, 2018).
96. "Vision and Actions on Jointly Building Silk Road Economic Belt and 21st Century Maritime Silk Road," National Development and Reform Commission, Ministry of Foreign Affairs, People's Republic of China, March 2015, en.ndrc.gov.in/newsrelease/201503/t20150330_669367.html (accessed on August 15, 2018).
97. Rajeev Ranjan Chaturvedy, "The 21st Century Maritime Silk Road," *Observer Research Foundation Brief*, 10 February 2017, https://www.orfonline.org/research/the-21st-century-maritime-silk-road/ (accessed on August 10, 2018).
98. "Vision and Actions on Jointly Building Silk Road Economic Belt and 21st Century Maritime Silk Road," n.313.
99. *The Economic Times*, August 27, 2018.
100. Le Hong Hiep, "The Belt and Road Initiative in Vietnam: Challenges and Prospects," Institute of Southeast Asian Studies, Singapore, 29 March 2018, p.3, https://www.iseas.edu.sg/images/pdf/ISEAS_Perspective_2018_18@50.pdf (accessed on August 11, 2018).
101. Ibid.
102. "India refuses to endorse China's Belt and Road Initiative: PTI," *The Hindu*, June 10, 2018.
103. Ibid.
104. "After quad meet, France-India to deepen ties in Indian Ocean Region: PTI," *The Times of India*, November 15, 2017.
105. Jagannath Panda, n. 308, pp.29–0.
106. Project Mausam, Ministry of Culture, Government of India, https://indiaculture.nic.in/project-mausam (accessed on August 11, 2018).
107. Speech of External Affairs Minister, Government of India at the 2nd Indian Ocean Conference, August 31, 2017, mea.gov.in/Speeches-Statements.htm?dtl/28907/Address+by+External+Affairs+Minister+at+the+2nd+Indian+Ocean+Conference+August+31+2017 (accessed on August 16, 2018).
108. Ibid.
109. Ibid.
110. Mercy A. Kuo, "The Origin of Indo- Pacific as Geopolitical Construct," *The Diplomat*, January 25, 2018, https://thediplomat.com/2018/01/the-origin-of-indo-pacific-as-geopolitical-construct/ (accessed on August 5, 2018).
111. Speech of Prime Minister of Japan at the Indian Parliament, August 2007, https://www.mofa.go.jp/region/asia-paci/pm/0708/speech-2.html (accessed on August 5, 2018).

112. "Defence White Paper 2013," Department of Defence, Australia, www.defence.gov.au/whitepaper/2013/ (accessed on August 5, 2018).
113. Hillary Clinton, n.86.
114. Speech of Hillary Rodham Clinton, US Department of State, National Convention Center, Hanoi, July 23, 2010, https://2009-2017.state.gov/secretary/20092013.clinton/rm/2010/07/145095.htm (accessed on August 10, 2018).
115. Speech of Donald J. Trump, Diplomatic Reception Room, White House, November 15, 2017, https://www.whitehouse.gov/briefings-statements/remarks-president-trump-trip-asia/ (accessed on August 10, 2018).
116. "US National Security Strategy of the United States of America," December 2017, pp.45–46, https://www.whitehouse.gov/wp-content/uploads/2017/12/NSS-Final-12-18-2017-0905.pdf (accessed on August 12, 2018).
117. "India can play a more weighty role in Indo-Pacific region: US," *The Hindu*, 3 April 2018, https://www.thehindu.com/news/international/india-can-play-a-more-weighty-role-in-indo-pacific-region-us/article23421165.ece (accessed on August 10, 2018).
118. Prime Minister Narendra Modi's Keynote address at Shangri La, Singapore, June 1, 2018, https://www.mea.gov.in/speeches-statements.htm?dtl/29943/Prime+Ministers+Keynote+Address+at+Shangri+La+Dialogue+June+01+2018 (accessed on August 11, 2018).
119. Ibid.
120. Ibid.
121. Ibid.
122. Ibid.
123. Ibid.
124. Ibid.
125. Han Xudong, "US intensifies military presence in Indo-Pacific," *Global Times*, July 24, 2018, www.globaltimes.in/content/1112119.shtml (accessed on August 12, 2018)
126. Yu Jincui, "China, India need to coordinate in face of US pressure," *Global Times*, 3 September 2018, www.globaltimes.in/content/1118176.shtml (accessed on September 15, 2018).
127. Ibid.
128. Zhang Hualong, "India, US interests don't align on Indo-Pacific," *Global Times*, August 30, 2018, www.globaltimes.in/content/1117703.shtml (accessed on September 15, 2018).
129. Long Xingchun, "Indo-Pacific strategy more a geopolitical military alliance," *Global Times,* August 7, 2018, see, www.globaltimes.cn/content/1114280.shtml (accessed on September 15, 2018).
130. Shailaja Neelakantan, "After US announces big Indo-Pacific investment, Chinese media warns it against 'imperialism', 'power games' ." *The Times of India*, August 1, 2018.
131. "Indo-Pacific strategy unpopular in ASEAN," *Global Times*, August 3, 2018, www.globaltimes.cn/content/1113773.shtml (accessed on August 16, 2018).
132. "Indo-Pacific strategy a trap by Washington," *Global Times*, May 31, 2018, www.globaltimes.cn/content/1105064.shtml (accessed on August 16, 2018).

FIVE

India-Vietnam Cultural Relations and China: Complex Interactions

India has rich and deep cultural contacts with Vietnam since the prehistoric time. The cultural heritages, relics, inscriptions, artefacts, steles all bear testimony to the fact that India had a vibrant and direct presence in Vietnam for about fourteen hundred years. China too, being a neighbouring country of Vietnam and through one thousand years of direct imperial rule over Vietnam, has an indelible presence in the Vietnamese society and culture. The purpose of this chapter is to highlight the major facets of India's cultural relations with Vietnam, which are most prominently found in the tangible heritages of the Cham civilisation, Buddhism, India's modern 'soft power' in Vietnam and finally, the governmental efforts to beef up India's cultural cooperation with Vietnam. Under these sub-headings, the 'China factor' are simultaneously discussed where the role of Chinese culture is significant and relevant to the discussion. Thus, important edifices of India's cultural ties with Vietnam are analysed below in details.

The Cham Kingdom: Symbol of Historical Heritage

The greatest and the most intense revelation of the rich cultural contact between India and Vietnam was the existence of the Cham Kingdom, proven by the ruins of the architectural heritages and artefacts of that period. The Champa Kingdom was located in central part of Vietnam, stretching well into the southern part and existed between the 2nd and 15th centuries AD. Today, based on archaeological evidences and historical records, there is unanimity among researchers on the India-Vietnam cultural ties that in the 2nd century BC, convoys of maritime traders originating from India's Champa region (Bhagalpur, Bihar), eventually joined by traders from Odisha and Bengal, reached Vietnam at Tien Sa port and at Hoi An near Da Nang. Thus, initially India and Vietnam were related through maritime trade ties and the Da Nang area was the epicentre of such Indian traders to rest and reside. Eventually, they started residing there permanently, married local Vietnamese women, mixed gracefully and peacefully with the local natives and gradually, with the consensus of the local people, a Hindu Kingdom was established there. Since the first group of traders originated from Champa, they began to be known as the Chams. Even while maintaining their own identity, they assimilated beautifully with the Vietnamese society and their Indian artefacts, steles, inscriptions and other tangible objects of their Indian cultural heritage made an indelible mark on the Vietnamese society, which is visible even today. The most striking fact about this Champa Kingdom is that, there was no warfare or bloodshed to establish this kingdom. There is no historical record of any violence in this regard. There were several capitals in this kingdom, such as Amaravati, Panduranga, Sri Vyaya, Kauthara, etc., and many Hindu dynasties ruled over it from these different capitals.[1] The kingdom was founded by Sri Mara in Central Vietnam but the first King who established the Cham Temple Towers was King Bhadravarman. The peaceful Hindu rule in Vietnam continued for about 1400 years. The Champa kingdom though adopted and assimilated well with the Vietnamese society, retained Indian customs, traditions, language, food habits, religion, script, dance and musical forms to a very large extent. For instance, the Cham had introduced the Indian technique of rice cultivation during the 4th and 5th centuries or even before that, which was prevalent in India then and had not been introduced anywhere in Vietnam then.[2] Their textiles, jewelries, sculptures, food habits all bore striking resemblances to the Indian ones. For instance, dance and music played a very significant role in the lives of the Chams, and Indian musical instruments such as the Mridang, Drum, Shahnai, etc., were all used to enrich their renditions. Even today, these instruments are used in cultural programs and Indian apsara dances are very popular in Vietnam, which are performed for entertaining the tourists at the Cham heritage sites to reminisce India's rich cultural links with Vietnam. Moreover, the Chams initially conversed through the Sanskrit script, however, overtime, the dialect and the script underwent modifications and changes.[3] Today, the Cham population is spread across Vietnam and numbers about 1,61,729 according to Vietnam's 2009 census and are mostly settled in Quang Nam, Binh Dinh, Phu Yen, Ninh Thua, Binh Thuan, Tay Ninh and An Giang provinces.[4] The Chams are mostly Hindus, but some of them converted to Islam as well, but are extremely liberal in nature. The Chams, following their traditional customs, still worship their ancestors and have idols of Hindu deities in their household and follow the Saka calendar.[5] In this regard, it is important to note that, between the 7th and 14th centuries AD, several Hindu temples were built which are known as the Cham Temple Towers. The oldest inscriptions that have been found in these temple towers were all in Sanskrit, thereby proving the strong influence of Indian culture in their daily lives, even after settling down in Vietnam. In subsequent years, people and traders from various places of India went to Vietnam for trade purposes and settled down in the Champa kingdom and they all came to be known as the Chams. Though there are Cham Hindus and Cham Muslims, they all live together in the most liberal way and celebrate festivals together.

My Son was the first temple city of the Champa kingdom that was established by King Bhadravarman, who ruled from the years 349 to 361 AD. My Son was previously known as Simhapura and is located at 68 kms from Da Nang. The My Son Sanctuary is situated in the mountainous border of Duy Xuyen District in the Quang Nam Province in central Vietnam. It is surrounded by a ring of mountains and here lies the point of origin of the Thu Bon River, which the Vietnamese regard to be very sacred. The river meanders by the monuments in the My Son region and passes through the heartland of the Champa Kingdom, and finally drains into the South China Sea. My Son is in a narrow, isolated valley about 2 km in diameter, surrounded by a range of high mountains. The sanctuary is located under the foot of the holy mountain of Mahaparvata. A stream originating there flows north through the site to join the Thu Bon River. This was lost in oblivion after the decline of the Hindu kingdom in the 15th century, when Da Viet dynasty took over. Finally, in 1898, MC Paris rediscovered it and sometime later two French scientists L. Finot and H. Parmentier researched and wrote about this area and its glorious past in great detail. On December 1, 1999, UNESCO declared this My Son area to be a World Heritage Site. In My Son, Lord Shiva was revered as the presiding deity though, in the temples, one can find the installations of idols of other Hindu gods and goddesses like the Brahma, the Vishnu, etc. The Chams constructed their monuments in fried brick with stone pillars and decorated those with sandstone bas-reliefs and carvings of ed Hindu mythology scenes. From these we understand that they had developed very sophisticated engineering and architectural skills with meticulous iconography that aptly reveal the content and growth of religious, social and political beliefs and thoughts of the Chams. The Sanctuary in the My Son was developed over a period of ten centuries. Presently, eight groups of seventy one standing monuments are existing in the My Son Sanctuary, and therefore for safeguarding these monuments and the entire property, the Vietnam government has passed Decision 1915/QD-TTg, for providing budgetary assistance to implement the Master Plan for 2008 to 2020 for conservation and promotion of tourism in the region.[6]

Besides this, in the central city of Nha Trang, one can find the Po Nagar Temple Tower complex. The Po Nagar Temple Tower is located in Kauthara. It is dedicated to Yan Po Nagar, the goddess much akin to goddess Durga or Mahishasuramardini of Hindu culture. It is located on Cu Lao Mountain and has three tiers or levels. The main tower is about 25 metres high and the Yan P Nagar, the main goddess of the Po Nagar Temple Tower can be found sitting cross-legged with ten hands holding various symbolic religious items. Also, in the Phan Thiet region, one can find the Pho Hai Towers or Po Shanu Towers, which has been listed by the Government of Vietnam as a 'National Monument' by its decision number 1371/QD dated August 3, 1991. Unfortunately, a major portion of the Po Shanu stone-spired Cham towers have already been lost due to failure in adequate preservation. Nonetheless, there one can still find two pointed towers and a third building adjoining the two towers. Moreover, in the small village of Bang An, 30 kms near Da Nang, one can also find several temples in dilapidated conditions, which were built by King Bhadravarman II. Furthermore, there is another group of temple towers which are known as Chien Dan Towers, built during 11th-12th centuries located 60 kms South of Da Nang. More specifically, it is situated in the Tam An Commune, which is about 5 km from the city of Tam Ky, that is in Quang Nam Province. It is a group of three towers, dedicated to three deities: Brahma, Vishnu and Shiva. Presently at the site of the Chien Dan Towers, a showroom has been erected to display Cham artefacts, statues, etc.[7] Moreover, there is another Champa Tower group on the hill of Dai Loc, Phoc Hiep commune, Tuy Phuoc District in the central province of Binh Dinh, known as Tho Son, Thi Thien or Banh It.

From these sites, various inscriptions and statuettes have been excavated over the years which clearly depict Hindu mythological characters like Rama setting the strings of his bow; marriage ceremony of Rama and Sita; Rama's army of monkeys; Krishna playing flute under a tree; Indra flocked by dancing apsaras; Garuda devouring a snake; Mahisasuramardini Durga killing buffalo-headed demon; four-headed Brahma; Bishnu reclining over Sheshnag; Saraswati; Lakshmi; Sivalinga and Yoni. Thus, the Hindu settlers had definitely summoned Indian artisans to these sites to construct these temples along with the idols, statuettes and inscriptions.

Therefore, Indians were mainly concentrated in and around the Da Nang and India's relations with the Da Nang area are about two millennia old. Moreover, much later, only about two hundred years ago, the Indians also started settling in the Ho Chi Minh City area (erstwhile Saigon) when the Chettiyars, who were the trading community from South India, started trading with and settling down in this area and they too built temples in this area, such as the Subramanyam Swamy Temple, the Mariyamman Temple, the Chetty Temple and the Ganesha Temple. Besides this, in this area there are at least two Gurudwaras built by the Sikhs. Many idols of Hindu deities, statuettes, steles and rock inscriptions have been recovered through excavations in the Mekong Delta region as well. All the tangible symbols of the Cham cultural heritage are on display in various museums of Vietnam, while the Da Nang Museum of Cham sculpture is the unique and the biggest of its kind.

Even today, more discoveries are taking place through new excavations. For instance, in the year 2000, the Hon Chuong Tower was discovered on the top of 727 metres high Mount Ba in Chanb Danh village of An Nhon District, Binh Dinh District, about 50 kms Northeast of Qui Nhon. In the year 2001, another small brick temple, My Khanh was discovered in Phu Dien village of Phu Vang district, Thira Thien-Hue Province, about 35 kms Southeast of Hue. This is a unique example of a Champa temple built on a beach during the 8th century. In 2002, the archaeologists discovered yet another complex of ruins in Thap Long, Tam Ky town, Quang Nam Province, that included the remains of a gate-tower and a mandapa built during the 12th and 13th centuries. In the spring of 2001, the archaeologists from the Quang Nam Museum unearthed the foundations of South Towers. The sandstone high reliefs depict a theme of the Ramayana. More recently, at Phong Le, 10kms from the Da Nang City, a new site has been discovered where some structures have been excavated, which is believed to be the 'gopuram' or the 'gate temple' of a group of Cham temples.[8]

The famous Khanh Van and Chanh Lo towers are still in place even today. It has been widely agreed that the Champa kingdom was divided into five regions. For instance, Indrapura or the present-day Donh Duong served as the religious centre of the kingdom, and Simhapura, currently known as Tra Kieu was the political capital; Amaravati in the north is the present day Quang Nam province; Vijya in the central is now Cha Ban; Kauthara is the modern Nha Trang; and Panduranga in the south is known today as Phan. These were the main provinces of the Hindu kingdom. Prof. RC Mazumdaar argues that there is a strong semblance between the temples of Mamallapuram (Tamil Nadu in India) and the temples of the Chams as the spires of Champa temples replicate the Ratha of Dharmaraaja and Arjun of Mamallapuram and the overall architectural details are strikingly similar.[9] While analysing the inscriptions on various temples, one can find songs of fame of the Champa Kings inscribed in Sanskrit from which we are able to decipher further details of the period. It is mentioned in the inscriptions that King Bhadravarman was well versed in the four Vedas. King Indravarman knew the six system of Philosophy, including Mimamasa and Buddhist philosophy, the grammar of Panini, and the Aakhyaana and the Uttarakalpa of the Saivas. King Sri Jayavarmadeva was versed in Grammar, Astrology, philosophical doctrines like Mahayana and Dharmasutras, notably the Naradiya and the Bharggviya.[10]

The interesting part is that, when during the 15th century the Da Viet king defeated the Champa kings to establish his kingdom, despite their defeat the Chams were not thrown out or enslaved. They gradually assimilated in the mainstream society and were never considered as foreigners. The Chams were never harmed by the Vietnamese, whereas, the Chinese, who despite their thousand years of rule, from the 1st to 10th centuries in northern Vietnam were looked down upon by the Vietnamese with contempt as invaders and had to face intermittent armed conflicts with the Vietnamese. It is a fact that many Vietnamese have laid down their lives and have become martyrs while fighting the Chinese during this period, whereas the interface between the Chams and the Vietnamese was the most peaceful one. That is why the Vietnamese people have taken a keen interest in preserving the various artefacts, steles, inscriptions and idols that have been excavated at various sites in central Vietnam. The Danang Museum is the biggest museum outside India that has on display more than two thousand Indian artefacts. It was not only in ancient times that the Chams used Sanskrit and Pali as their languages, even today, the vowels and consonants in the Cham language and their pronunciation is very similar to those of Sanskrit and Hindi and the Saka calendar is still being followed by the Chams despite they being an integral part of the Vietnamese society.

The difference between the Chinese and Indian presence in the Vietnamese soil can be aptly summarised in the following words: "Sporadic contact with the two great powers of Asia, India and China, became increasingly frequent and important over the centuries. While keeping their cultural identity, the peoples of Southeast Asia bore the preponderant influence now of China, now of India, depending on shifting geopolitical conditions. The Chinese expansion towards Southeast Asia was carried out by armed force. Beginning in the 2nd century BC, almost all the lands to the South of the Yangtze were annexed to become the southern part of the Chinese Empire, their peoples completely Sinicized. The embryonic Vietnamese State Au Lac was first conquered in 179 B.C., and literally colonised for a millennium, from 111 BC until 938 AD. Other Southeast Asian people who lived south of the Yangtze left the Chinese territory to move south. Indianization came through commerce and religion, supported by a political strategy of assimilation. From the bases in the parts of South Indian, commercial enterprises launched expeditions that led to the creation of outposts in Southeast Asia. These merchant colonies became centres for cultural and religious diffusions, grafting themselves onto the indigenous populations to create Indianized kingdoms."[11] In fact, several Sanskrit inscriptions can still be found along important rivers of Vietnam, for instance, one can still find Sanskrit riverside inscriptions of this period along the Da Rang River.

Moreover, another proof that the Vietnamese and the ethnic Chams shared excellent ties in Vietnam can be understood if it is contrasted against conditions of ethnic groups in other neighbouring countries. There is no evidence that there has been any mass exodus of ethnic Chams from Vietnam ever. They have lived most peacefully centuries after centuries in Vietnam and some Chams inhabited the Khmer Kingdom too. They maintained their identity by changing their religion. They accepted Islam after the fall of Champa and they could protect their identity successfully during the French colonial period. However, with the Khmer Rouge's ascendancy to power in Cambodia in 1975, they were driven out by Pol Pot who treated them as foreigners. Just like Vietnamese refugees, there were many Cham refugees who were persecuted and driven out of Cambodia between 1975-78.[12] However, in Vietnam, they have always lived their own lives without being driven out or needing any affirmative action from the government. They have assimilated serenely with the Vietnamese society over the years.

It is interesting to note that, the study of the Cham inscriptions was inaugurated in the 19th century by the great French Sanskrit scholar Abel Bergaigne. He prepared the first editions and translations of Champa inscriptions, which were published a few years after his death, in 1893. Studies of the inscriptions in Sanskrit and Cam language made significant progress in the first two decades of the 20th century, mainly due to the efforts of George Coedes, Edouard Huber and especially Louis Finot. Another scholar, Antoine Cabaton, a university professor in Paris, is credited with the creation of the dictionary of modern Cam language, compiled together with Etienne Anymonier and published in 1906.[13] The earliest inscription of the Chams is in Sanskrit. During the early centuries of the production of inscriptions, the language of inscriptions was always Sanskrit. However, after a period of several centuries during which Sanskrit was used as the only language used for inscriptions and mutual communications, from the 9th century onwards Sanskrit had to share space with the Cam language, which gradually evolved owing to changing circumstances. In the inscriptions during the Indrapura dynasty, Sanskrit was still clearly the dominant language, but in the 11th century, we see only a minor part of inscriptions reserved for a perfunctory opening in Sanskrit, while the more substantial part was now done in the Cam language. And in the following centuries, the use of Sanskrit disappeared completely. In fact, the later Sanskrit inscriptions of the Chams were lesser meticulous in nature, using only simple vocabulary and disrespecting rules of grammar. The Sanskrit inscriptions are found most commonly composed in verse form.[14] Therefore, it can be concluded that the thriving of the Cham civilisation for 1400 years bears the testimony to the fact that India shared one of her deepest cultural bonds with this Southeast Asian country, and the ruins till date stand witness to the glorious past.

Buddhism: The Linking Philosophy

Buddhism has always bonded India and Vietnam together in the common thread. Till date, India is revered by the Vietnamese people as the land of the Lord Buddha, and there is no doubt that Buddhism had come to Vietnam directly from India because, as one of the evidences suggests that in Haiphong, 60 miles from Hanoi, there is a commemorative tower of King Ashoka that was built by the local Vietnamese Buddhists as a token of gratitude to King Ashoka. In the 3rd century BC, he had organised the Third Buddhist Council at Pataliputra in India, and after the Council, he sent nine Buddhist monk-delegations to preach Buddhism in the foreign shores. One such delegation, which was led by Shona and Uttara, reached Vietnam to spread the message of Buddhism. The commemorative plaque at Haiphong is to reminisce about this event.[15] Moreover, the Hoang-Gia-My's genealogy register of the region also recorded an Ashoka tower at Do Son.[16] Also, the Champa kingdom had Theravada Buddhism from as early as 3rd century B.C.[17] Thus, it is generally accepted that in the 2nd century AD, (AD 168-189), Buddhism became popular in Vietnam and flourished with the contribution of three great Buddhist monks who came from India: Marajivaka, K'ang Seng Houei, Tchi Kiang Liang and a local scholar, Mecu-Fo. However, as a result of about one thousand years of Chinese rule in Vietnam (111 BCE-939 CE), the Chinese Buddhist influence in Vietnam was eventually far more substantial and enduring than Indian Buddhist influence. Chinese political domination and culture exerted a more direct and profound impression on Vietnam than on any other Southeast Asian culture. The first recorded instance of a Chinese missionary in Vietnam is Mou Po, who propagated Buddhism in northern Vietnam in the 2nd century CE. However, Mahayana Buddhism from China really became dominant and widespread beginning in the 5th century CE.

Buddhism in Vietnam, as in China, existed throughout its long history alongside, and sometimes in competition with, Confucianism, Taoism and ancestor worship.[18] The prosperity of Buddhism in Vietnam reached its highest glory during the rule of Ly and Tran dynasties that existed in Vietnam from the 11th to the 14th century, when Buddhism was recognized as the state religion. And thousands of pagodas and Stupas were built across the country. Hanoi became the capital of Vietnam under the Ly kings and emerged as a prominent Buddhist centre as the seaport near Hanoi was used by Indian monks to arrive in Vietnam and disseminate Buddhist teachings. Some important Indian names such as Mahajivaka, Kalyanaruchi and Vinitaruchi stand out in Vietnamese history as revered monks in Buddhist teachings. By the end of Tran dynasty, Buddhism lost its influence. After the Chinese Ming invasion in 1440, Dai Viet again became Chinese vassal. The Ming rulers started a rule of oppression against the Buddhists for promoting Confucianism. Even after the fall of the Ming rulers, Buddhists could not regain their past position and all efforts to do so, fall flat owing to beginning of French colonial domination.[19] In Vietnam today, though the majority of Buddhist believers follow Mahayana Buddhism, and only a minority follow Theravada Buddhism, it is actually Theravada Buddhism that is the most conservative and traditional branch of teachings of Lord Buddha and is the closest to the preaching of the Indian Buddhist monks who travelled to foreign shores to propagate Dhamma. The language of the canonical texts of Theravada Buddhists in Vietnam was Pali, clearly the proof that its origin was from India. Whereas, the brand of Buddhism that spread to northern regions from India such as, China, Tibet, Taiwan, Mongolia, etc., was the Mahayana branch of Buddhism, whose main language for scriptures was Sanskrit and not Pali. Moreover, Mahayana Buddhism being less conservative than Theravada Buddhism, also started to incorporate local customs of each country, such as, it adopted Tantrism in Tibet. Though the core beliefs in both Theravada Buddhism and Mahayana Buddhism are the same, yet there are some fundamental differences in their teachings (the detailed analysis of these differences is not within the scope of my study). Thus, due to Chinese predominance in Vietnamese culture and society owing to over 1000 years of direct rule and many more years of indirect exchanges as a neighbouring country, the branch of Buddhism that was propagated by them was Mahayana Buddhism and not Theravada Buddhism. Therefore, the most original and the purest brand of Buddhism that travelled from India to Vietnam was Theravada Buddhism, and later on, China popularised Mahayana Buddhism in Vietnam, that had definitely deviated from the original teachings of Lord Buddha by allowing interferences from Taoism, Confucianism and other local beliefs.

Nonetheless, Buddhism remains the strongest link between India and Vietnam today, and several Vietnamese tourists visit India to visit Bodhgaya, the abode of Buddhism and the place of Buddha's enlightenment site.

Soft Power as a means of Connectivity between India and Vietnam

Joseph S Nye Jr, an American scholar, was the first person to coin the word 'soft power' and defined it in 1990 as a 'co-optive power' or 'when one country gets other countries to do as it wants'. Later, he described the determinants of 'soft power' as growing out of a country's 'culture;...out of our values—democracy and human rights, when we live up to them.'[20] In 2006, he elaborated it further as the ability to alter the behaviour of others to get what you want, and that there are basically three ways to do that: coercion (sticks), payment (carrots) and attraction (soft power)'.[21] It is well accepted that India has always lagged behind countries like the US, China, etc., as far as hard military power is concerned, despite its modernisation drive over the years. In contrast, India stands a much better chance to woo other countries and nationals through its trump card of soft power. India's rich cultural heritage, civilisational links with Vietnam, her rich democracy, thriving pluralist society, her active civil society, her legacy of social movements for various sections of her population, her vibrant entertainment industry, her fashionable apparels, her wide gamut of culinary spread, her multilingual, multi-religious, multi-caste society, her right to freedom, her enumeration of fraternal ties among various communities, her excellence in education, English language, Information and Communication Technology, her peace-loving foreign policy all have elevated her to such a high pedestal in the psyche of Vietnamese people that over the years the Vietnamese youth have been greatly drawn towards India. These above-mentioned tools act as a major means of 'soft power' for India to integrate its relations with Vietnam more on a strong foothold. In recent times the fruits of Indian 'soft power' means are getting its dividend when we see that there is an increase in the footfall of Vietnamese tourists in India. For instance, according to Vietnam's Ministry of Culture, Sports and Tourism's data, in the five years from 2010 to 2014, the number of Indian tourists to Vietnam increased by 344 percent from 16,000 arrivals in 2010 to nearly 55,000 arrivals in 2014.[22] A major reason for an increased number of Vietnamese tourists in India is because of enhanced connectivity between these two countries and because of the realization on the part of the youth to learn the English language and the software technology, in which, India has ample expertise. Today, therefore, we see that, a considerable number of Vietnamese students are enrolled in different courses, in different Indian Universities. For advancement in higher research between the two countries, the Institute of Indian and South West Asian Studies, in the Vietnam Academy of Social Sciences was inaugurated in 2012 in Hanoi and likewise, the Vietnam Centre has been opened in New Delhi in 2018. Moreover, Vietnam book corner was established in Jadavpur University Central library and in National Library at Kolkata in 2015, which was published as a significant move forward in Vietnamese newspapers, fostering greater people-to-people contacts. Moreover, India's plans for the revival of the age-old Nalanda University as an international University par excellence has been supported by ten countries from the East Asian Summit (EAS) and one non-EAS country and Vietnam has extended its whole-hearted support to the Project.

In the face of increased bitterness in the arena of hard politics, owing to resistance by China on various fronts and in several efforts of India to better her ties with Vietnam, (such as, in the joint Malabar exercises, in the joint exploration of the South China Sea, or in the arena of defence cooperation and modernisation) India has been stressing on greater people-to-people contacts, an easier visa regime and greater cultural exchanges and programs to further enrich their friendly bilateral ties.

It is interesting to note that the Indian Ayurvedic products are much in demand, especially the ones for cosmetic and medicinal purposes. Though Vietnamese markets are flooded with cheap Korean and Hong Kong's products, the Ayurvedic products are hailed to be of superior quality. It is important to note that, in recent years, there is a boom in the opening of several Ayurvedic salons, Ayurvedic detoxification (Pancha Karma) centres with well-defined training courses and sessions are held regularly in places like Hanoi, Ho Chi Minh City, Da Lat, Chu Chi, etc. Moreover, yoga has emerged to be a very important Indian influence on the Vietnamese society. The health-conscious Vietnamese youth are glued to practising yoga on a regular basis and as a result, there is the mushrooming of yoga retreats, courses, studies, classes, centres and ashrams all along the length and breadth of Vietnam. Vietnam has started hosting and celebrating the International Yoga Day on every year. The Indian Embassy and the Ministry of Culture, Sports and Tourism of Vietnam co-hosts the event every year and in 2018, about 1200 Vietnamese participated in the event.[23] Thus, it is one area where further stress should be given to promote India's 'soft power' among the Vietnamese youth.

Another major area of tapping India's 'soft power' is through the "Buddhism diplomacy". For instance, the increase of Vietnamese tourists in India is largely because of visiting Bodhgaya and in recent years, top-level Vietnamese leaders such as the General Secretary of the Communist Party of Vietnam, the President of Vietnam, the Prime Minister of Vietnam and the Speaker of the National Assembly of Vietnam have all visited Bodhgaya to woo more Vietnamese tourists in India as their drive to strengthen the Track II diplomacy between them. There is a Vietnamese Buddhist pagoda in Bodhgaya and also a number of Buddhists from Vietnam travel there on pilgrimage, thus enriching the spiritual tourism between the two countries. From the Indian side as well, especially after Prime Minister Narendra Modi came to power in 2014, there is an extra drive to project Buddhism as a great cultural link between India and Vietnam, which can be gauged from the fact that after President Rajendra Prasad in 1959, Narendra Modi was only the second Indian topmost level leader who addressed the Vietnamese Buddhist monks at Hanoi's Pagoda Temple on September 3, 2016. He remarked, "Some people came here with the objective of war. We came here with a message of peace, which has endured."[24] This was directly a reference to their common enemy, China, without naming it. Moreover, India has announced special annual scholarships for Vietnamese students in advanced Buddhist studies at Masters/Doctoral level, to increase the inflow of Vietnamese students in India in the coming years.

Another major instrument of India's efforts to assuage its 'soft power' is her film industry. The Vietnamese population is well aware of the very vibrant and prosperous Bollywood and the Vietnamese government officials are inviting Bollywood film makers to go to Vietnam and check out its exotic locations for setting up bases for shooting and film production purposes. According to Nguyen Van Tuan, "Bollywood is the most effective tool to market Vietnam as a tourist destination to Indians."[25] In recent years, several Bollywood movies, such as *Ek Tha Tiger*, *Zindagi Na Milegi Dobara*, *Cocktail*, *Heroine*, etc., have been released in Vietnam and have lapped up appreciation from the Vietnamese audience. Moreover, several popular Hindi serials, dubbed in Vietnamese, are regularly shown on Vietnamese entertainment channels, thereby giving a feel of India's culture to the Vietnamese youth and women. For instance, the serial *Balika Badhu* was quite a hit in Vietnam. In this regard, it is to be mentioned that, a high-level film delegation from India visited Vietnam in December 2015 at the invitation of Vietnam National Administration of Tourism and found certain locations in Vietnam quite spectacular for shooting purposes. More concerted and consistent efforts are required in this direction to tap the true potential of Vietnam for catering to our huge and flourishing entertainment industry.

As far as the Indian Diaspora in Vietnam is concerned, there are about 2500 Indians living in Vietnam today, mostly concentrated in the Ho Chi Minh City area and are predominantly engaged in working in Indian companies in Vietnam or Multinational Companies (MNCs) in Vietnam. They are extremely vibrant and organised and celebrate Indian festivals like Holi and Diwali with much enthusiasm. They contribute very appreciably in propagating India's culture in Vietnam in a very subtle but significant way. Moreover, the Indo-Vietnam Chamber of Commerce and Industry has been working tirelessly since July 14, 1989, to beef up India's economic cooperation with Vietnam.

As far as the popularity of India's literature in Vietnam is concerned, not much work has been done in this regard so far. In 1958, the year when Ho Chi Minh paid a historic visit to Delhi, the first Asian Writer's Conference was held in Delhi and revered poet Xuan Dieu came to Delhi. Following this visit, poet Xuan Sanh came to India who had translated Kalidas's *Meghdoot* into Vietnamese. Subsequently, *Mahabharata* and over a dozen works of Tagore have been translated in Vietnamese. In more recent years, Indian story collection of modern authors, such as Mulk Raj Anand and three books of Geetesh Sharma, namely *Vietnam Liberation War: Role of Calcutta*, *Traces of Indian Culture in Vietnam* and *India-Vietnam Relations: First to Twenty-first Century* have been translated in Vietnamese, Moreover, over the years, several Vietnamese literary works have been translated into English and these, though unavailable in Indian book markets, may be procured or read online. Some of these important books for instance, are as follows: *Spring Essence: The Poetry of Ho Xuan Huong*, *The Tale of Kieu*, *Lament of the Soldier's Wife*, *The Sorrow of War: A Novel of North Vietnam*, *The Stars, the Earth, the River*, *Behind the Red Mist*, *Against the Flood*, *The Cemetery of Chua Village*, *An Insignificant Family*, *Green Rice*, *Crossing the River*, to name a few. However, these names are not very popular to the Indian youth, and there is not much demand of the Vietnamese literature in India. Despite this, in both International Book Fairs, those organised annually in Kolkata and New Delhi, Vietnam remains a prominent participating country and Vietnam pavilions are set up so that the

Indian readers can experience Vietnamese literature. As against this, owing to Chinese predominance in the Vietnamese society during 1000 years of imperial rule and also due to China's meteoric economic rise as an Asian giant, a large number of Vietnamese youth are interested in learning the Chinese language and thousands of Vietnamese students go to China as part of academic exchange programs. That is why, from 2009 to 2013, in these four years only, a total of 841 Chinese book titles were translated and published in Vietnamese.[26] Chinese literary books are found almost in every nook and corner of Vietnam, especially in the northern part of Vietnam, and the famous "Book Street" in Hanoi displays Chinese literatures in very prominent shelves, owing to their much popularity among Vietnamese readers.

China's 'soft power' in Vietnam is exerted through the legacy of one thousand years of their imperial rule in Vietnam and its impact on various aspects of Vietnamese society. China's culture, societal structures, values of family and kinship, language, calligraphy, culinary spread have all made an indelible impact on Vietnamese society, especially in the neighbouring northern region. The southern region of Vietnam, being the epicentre of western occupation during the colonial and Cold War years is much more westernised than the northern region. Thus, since historic times, the Vietnamese language itself has been influenced by the Chinese language and the Chinese calligraphy that several Chinese words have seeped into the Vietnamese language and are being used as its own. In the northern part of Vietnam, there are several Buddhist pagodas which have inscriptions in the Chinese language since ancient times, and the majority of Vietnamese people were well-versed in the Chinese language, though in recent years, one can find greater efforts on the part to Vietnam to use more of Vietnamese language and other indigenous dialects. The old Vietnamese script was greatly inspired by Chinese characters, which were known as Chu Nom. Even till date, Vietnamese architectural designs and its pagodas bear striking resemblances with those found in China. In Vietnamese clothing as well, there remains some influences of the Chinese clothing style, such as the Ao dai is largely based on the clothing style that was prevalent during the Ming dynasty in China.

Moreover, Confucianism and Taoism have, over the years, seeped into Vietnamese societies and have garnered Vietnamese followers to such an extent that, Confucian temples can be found in Hanoi and in other parts of Vietnam and Confucian schools were established, especially in northern Vietnam. The Mahayana branch of Buddhism, that was followed by the majority in Vietnam was popularised by China, whereas, Indian monks had preached the message which was more akin to the Theravada branch of Buddhism. Furthermore, though Vietnam has witnessed for past two thousand years the growth of Confucianism, that was brought to Vietnam by China, the common people of Vietnam has been increasingly resenting to the growth of Confucian institutes on their soil, for they believe that these institutes by teaching Chinese language and promoting Confucianism, actually is realising China's 'soft power' on Vietnamese soil. It is not that they fear the growth of China's 'soft power' in their country, nor do they abhor learning Chinese language, but the display of China's hard power in different phases of their history, that has made the Vietnamese youth more cautious about any form of dependence on China. That is why, when in 2013, Vietnam's the then Prime Minister Nguyen Tan Dung announced the decision to establish the first Confucian Institute at Hanoi University, Vietnamese youth and intellectuals protested the decision and voiced their concerns.[27]

Therefore, when the Confucius Institute was finally established at Hanoi University on December 27, 2014, in the presence of Nguyen Thien Nhan, Politburo Member and President of Vietnam Fatherland Front Central Committee, the concerns were still being raised by the Vietnamese citizens.[28] However, India takes a far more conservative and rigid stand on the question of Confucius institutes in India as it considers such a move as a 'benign outreach' of China's 'soft power' with a huge gamut of ramifications in future days. China has opened its first Yoga College under Yunnan University in 2015, still India is extremely cautious, much more than Vietnam, about the spread of Confucius on its soil, owing to its challenging political relations with Beijing. Nonetheless, Vietnam's festivals are similar to that of Chinese festivals

, such as the Tet, the mid-Autumn Festival, and the Dragon Boat Festival are all celebrated in Vietnam and China alike, with common customs such as giving out red envelopes in New Year festivities and eating moon cakes during mid-Autumn festivities. Chinese literature, Chinese fairytales, legends of past Chinese emperors and warriors are well-known to Vietnamese people. For instance, the Tang poems are very popular in Vietnam. Much like their love for Bollywood, the Vietnamese people love Chinese movies and music. For instance, Chinese movies like, "the journey to the West," "Three Kingdoms," "The Swordsman," "All Men are Brothers," etc have been very popular in Vietnam. Moreover, the largest number of foreign tourists in Vietnam comes from China. For instance, in 2014, a paltry number of 55,000 Indian tourists arrived in Vietnam,[29] whereas, a whopping number of nearly two million Chinese tourists visited Vietnam in the same year.[30] Thus, it becomes amply clear that, India has immense prowess as far as her "soft power" credentials in Vietnam is concerned, but she has not been able to harness her capabilities to the fullest potential so far.

Initiatives at the Government level to enhance India's Cultural Ties with Vietnam

India had always wished to revive her ancient cultural ties with Vietnam but the imperatives of Cold War politics and Vietnam's involvement in the protracted war with the United States did not allow a conducive environment in this context. Thus, immediately after the US-Vietnam War got over and the North and South Vietnam were reunified, India signed a Cultural Relations Agreement with Vietnam in Hanoi on 18 December 1976. The agreement incorporated provision for exchange of visits, scholarships, recognition of degrees and diplomas of the two countries and also for the formation of friendship associations, etc. It was to be renewed for every five years. The agreement provided for exchange of letters, packages, parcels, and telecommunication services, and for routing mail to third countries through either of the countries.[31] Following the agreement, air mail and parcel services and telecommunication links in accordance with international practice were established. This agreement provided the much-needed formal scaffolding for establishing and continuing the growth of Indo-Vietnam cultural relations at the official level in the Cold War days.

With the onset of the new millennium, the Government of India has been taking special measures to deepen and strengthen her cultural ties with Vietnam. For instance, presently, 150 Indian Technical and Economic Cooperation (ITEC) slots are being offered to Vietnam every year along with 16 scholarships under the General Cultural Scholarship Scheme (GCSS), 14 scholarships under the Educational Exchange Program (EEP) and 10 scholarships under the Mekong Ganga Cooperation Scholarship Scheme (MGCSS).[32] These are coveted opportunities for Vietnamese students to study and pursue research in India. Moreover, India's capabilities and her success story in Information and Communication Technology is well known in Vietnam and the government in both the countries have been stressing on putting efforts this aspect of her ties to reap maximum benefits in cultivating India's benign and friendly image in the psyche of the Vietnamese people. This is why, a US$ 2 million Advanced Resource Centre in Information and Communication Technology (ARC-ICT) was inaugurated by EAM in Hanoi in September 2011.[33] The Centre has been set up by Centre for Development of Advanced Computing (CDAC) and it imparts training to students and government officials in various areas such as web designing, network systems, GIS applications, e-governance, etc. In this regard, it is interesting to note that, India has gifted the 16-node cluster high-performance computer with basic visualization laboratory and a 5-node Grid Computing facility at an estimated cost of Rs. 4.7 crore on November 12, 2013.[34] It must be noted that this is the highest configuration of supercomputer ever gifted by the Indian Government to any foreign country till date.

Furthermore, the Vietnamese youth realises that they must learn English and their lack of expertise over this language is a major reason for their unsatisfactory global visibility in today's world. It is here that Vietnam is collaborating with India in a major way. For instance, India has set up the 'Vietnam-India Centre for English Language Training' in Danang in July 2007, the Vietnam-India Entrepreneurship Development Centre in Hanoi in May 2006 and the "Vietnam-India Centre for English Language Training" at the Technical University in Nha Trang has also become quite flourishing.[35]

The Institute of Indian and South West Asian Studies, Hanoi and the Vietnam Centre, New Delhi is also collaborating to produce high-quality research work related to India's bilateral relations with Vietnam. Most importantly, Sri Venkateswara University in Tirupati, Andhra Pradesh, India, launched the Area Studies Programme in 1966 under the leadership of Prof. VM Reddy, which became a full-fledged independent department in 1990. Subsequently, the Centre for Studies on Indochina and South Pacific Studies was established in 1976. The Area Studies Centre, now officially rechristened since 2005 by the UGC as "Centre for Southeast Asian and Pacific Studies" is making great strides in original research in this area. Moreover, the Centre for Indian Studies (CIS) at the Ho Chi Minh National Academy of Politics, Hanoi, which was inaugurated in 2015 in the august presence of the then Indian President Shri Pranab Mukherjee, is also active in interacting with scholars and research think-tanks in India to enrich original research in this regard.[36] To further educational cooperation between these two countries, the Government of India has also funded the construction of several primary/kindergarten schools and hostels for children in remote areas of Vietnam. Moreover, to attract a larger number of Vietnamese tourists to India, the Festival of India was organised by the Embassy of India in Vietnam from March 5-15, 2014, in three cities of Vietnam-Hanoi, Ho Chi Minh City and Danang. The Festival showcased classical dance recital by Sangeet Natak Academy, Buddhist Festival by Central Institute of Himalayan Cultural Studies, Food Festival, Folk dance performances by Kalbelia Group, mehendi sessions and yoga performances. The event was such a major success that it motivated the Government of India to organise the first ever Indian Film Festival (IFF) in Danang, Hanoi and Ho Chi Minh City from December 12-23, 2015. During the festival, eight Hindi films with Vietnamese subtitles were screened and were much appreciated by the Vietnamese audience. Buoyed by the positive feedback by the Vietnamese audience, a seminar on "Collaboration in Film Making and its role in promotion of Tourism" was arranged on December 19, 2015, in Hanoi. This event too, was a major success. This is the reason why India was invited as a participating country in the Hanoi Film Festival of November 2016, where several Indian films were screened during the Festival with a warm response from the Vietnamese audience. All these events promise the greater promotion of film tourism between these two countries in the coming years. Moreover, 'Buddhism diplomacy' has been put to good use in recent years and in 2017, a major four-day event called "Buddhist Festival-Days of India" was organised by the Indian Embassy in Tay Thien, Tam Dao District, Vinh Phuc Province of Hanoi. Moreover, in recent years, to commemorate India's contribution to the world in the form of yoga, Vietnam celebrates the International Yoga Day with much fanfare. Similarly, the Government has also started regular youth exchange programs between the two countries. For instance, the Indian youth delegation visited Vietnam fromJuly 21-28, 2017 and the Vietnamese youth delegation visited India during March 27–April 5, 2017.[37] Moreover, in various government functions, efforts are being increasingly put to showcase India's rich mythological heritage through the organization of plays, theatres or dance recitals based on the *Ramayana*, the *Mahabharata* and other historical stories. For instance, in November 2017, when the East Asian Summit (EAS) was held in Manila, Philippines, a musical play based on the Ramayana was organised in the opening ceremony and was warmly welcomed the participating dignitaries of all countries.

With renewed vigour under Prime Minister Narendra Modi's 'Act East' policy, conservation and restoration of the World Heritage Site of My Son, Quang Nam Province, Vietnam has been undertaken and in this regard a Memorandum of Understanding has been signed. The Memorandum of Understanding took after receiving the plan of the Government of the Socialist Republic of Vietnam to get India's proficiency and support in reinstatement of Group of Temples at the World Heritage Site of My Son, Quang Nam Province of Vietnam and the subsequent 'Initial Conservation Report and Project Plan' of Archaeological Survey of India (ASI) of May 2011. The Project is projected to be around 16 crore Rupees, and is to be funded by the MEA, Government of India. The project would be implemented by the ASI on behalf of the Indian government. Moreover, a Centre for English Language and Information Technology Training at the Telecommunications University, Ministry of Defense in Vietnam has been decided to be set up very soon for instructing in English language training and IT for increasing the average level of aptitude of trainees in these matters. Additionally, the Cultural Exchange Programs are regularly framed and updated to allow strengthening cultural cooperation through organising art exhibitions, exchanging cultural and art troops, organising folklores, art performance activities in both countries. These programmes make exchange of records on classical, traditional and folk music and dance, photographs, pictures and publications on performing arts, sharing of information and expertise in the field of cultural heritage protection and promotion possible. Also, at another level, we have framed the cooperative framework between the Prasar Bharti and the Voice of Vietnam in the field of broadcasting through exchange of programs in matters of culture, education, science, entertainment, sports and news.[38] The Indian Council for Cultural Relations (ICCR) is steadfastly working to foster greater cultural interaction between the two countries by inviting Vietnamese delegates, officials and participants and organising several cultural festivals throughout the year. It must be mentioned in this context that the 'Indian Cultural Center' has been opened in Hanoi in the year 2017 and they have started organising multifarious activities for closer cultural cooperation between the two countries. Similarly, Vietnam should also think of setting up a similar kind of cultural centre in India, which will popularise Vietnamese cultural aspects in India.

Summarily then, it can be argued that, it is not at all difficult for India to more proactively propagate the 'cultural' aspect of her ties with Vietnam, particularly because they share an excellent political and strategic relation, whereas with China, Vietnam has several differences of opinion in the political sphere, horrific memories of Chinese invasion and about one thousand years of Chinese imperial rule, events of war and armed conflicts in modern history over the South China Sea issue and an asymmetrical power equation. All of these give India an excellent opportunity to be more proactive in highlighting her cultural and civilisational linkages with Vietnam and particularly tap her "soft power" capabilities and propagate those in Vietnam, especially as a means of growing understanding with Vietnam in the wake of renewed political and strategic tensions with China. If India truly considers Vietnam to be a 'linchpin' or a 'pillar' in India's 'Look East' or 'Act East' policy, then definitely India has to put stress on renewing her cultural contacts with Vietnam, so that it can work as a bulwark against the southern expanse of Chinese 'soft power' through its diplomatic manoeuvres and lenient economic aid policies in the Southeast Asian region. The cultural aspect of India's relations with Vietnam thus, will definitely play a major role in the coming years and how India plays her cards in this regard will surely hold the key to many a challenges not only in the destinies of these two countries but also in the politics of the Southeast region and in global politics of the 21st century as a whole.

It is interesting that Rabindranath Tagore, during his visit to Saigon, on June 21, 1929, in a speech at the Municipal Theater observed that he was profoundly touched by returning to the land where "the heart of India had once beaten under a sun sky on this shore." He moreover added, "Please know that before human joys and human miseries, my heart always beats with the same rhythm as that those of my predecessors who in the most distant past lived among you. My voice always expresses man's aspiration toward light, love and liberty. It is always for the triumph of the divine martyr over all that is basely cruel and meanly selfish. I bring you the greetings of that radiant India, who lavished her light of this land as well as the message of sympathy and brotherhood of present India who lives separated from you by geographic distance and by the dead solitude of her own darkness."[39] It is the need of the hour that the governments, intellectuals, scholars and common people of both these countries make the best possible efforts to come out of their slumber and re-ignite that old flame of love, compassion, solidarity and cultural cooperation between both these countries, which is still flickering in these two Asian peoples. For doing so, India will have to more proactively promote her diaspora, English language skills, yoga, classical music, rich cuisine, dance, religion, festivals, Bollywood movies, TV serials, painting, literature, etc., and can thereby nurture the civilisational linkages that we have lost in modern times.

Notes

1. C. Ravindranatha Reddy, *India and Vietnam: Era of Friendship and Cooperation, 1947-1991*, Emerald Publishers, Centre for Southeast Asian and Pacific Studies, Sri Venkateswara University, Tirupati, 2009, pp.58–62.
2. Geetesh Sharma, *Vietnam 1982-2017: Ruins To Incredible Progress*, Banyan Tree Books Pvt. Ltd, New Delhi, p.106.
3. Ibid, p.107.
4. Ibid, p.108.
5. Geetesh Sharma, *Traces of Indian Culture in Vietnam*, Banyan Tree Books Pvt. Ltd, New Delhi, 2009, p.47.
6. "My Son Sanctuary," UNESCO- World Heritage Convention, https://whc.unesco.org/en/list/949 (accessed on December 3, 2017).
7. "Chien Dan Towers," Vietnam National Administration of Tourism, www.vietnamtourism.com/en/index.phptourism/items/1628 (accessed on December 3, 2017).
8. Geetesh Sharma, n.351, p. 179.
9. For further details see, R. C. Majumdar, *Champa: History And Culture of an Indian Colonial Kingdom in The Far East 2nd- 16th Century A.D.*, Gyan Publishing House, 2008.
10. Vijay Shankar Shukla, "Chams: A Study of Social Harmony with Special Reference to Champa," proceedings from the International Conference titled *The Cham Art Heritage of Vietnam: Ecological, Cultural and Art Historical Traditions*, Indira Gandhi National Centre for the Arts, New Delhi, April 25-26, 2014.
11. Huu Ngoc, *Wandering through Vietnamese Culture*, The Gioi Publishers, Hanoi, 2012, cited in Geetesh Sharma "Cultural Bond between Vietnam and India," in Rajaram Panda (ed.), *India- Vietnam Relations: Retrospect and Prospect*, Indian Council for Cultural Relations and Northern Book Centre, New Delhi, 2016, p.30.
12. Ganganath Jha, "The Ethnic Profile of the Chams," proceedings of the international conference titled *The Cham Art Heritage of Vietnam: Ecological, Cultural and Art Historical Traditions*, Indira Gandhi National Centre for the Arts, New Delhi, April 25-26, 2014.

13. Arlo Griffiths, Amandine Lepoutre, William A. Southworth and Thanh Phan, *The Inscriptions of Campa At The Museum of Cham Sculpture in Da Nang*, VNU-HCM Publishing House, Hanoi, 2012, p.177.
14. Ibid, p.189-90.
15. Do Thu Ha, "India and Vietnam: Cultural Contacts Through Buddhism," in Rajiv K. Bhatia, Vijay Sakhuja and Vikash Ranjan (eds.), *India- Vietnam: Agenda for Strengthening Partnership*, Shipra Publications, Delhi, 2013, p.194.
16. Thic Duc Nghiep, *Phat Giao Vietnam Buddhism in Vietnam*, Hanoi, Hanoi Publishing House, 1988, pp. 28–29.
17. Skilton Andrew, *A Concise History of Buddhism*, Windhorse Publication, Birmingham, 1994, p.160.
18. Do Thu Ha, n.364, p.199.
19. Ha Thanh Ngoc, "India and Vietnam: Role of Buddhism and Hinduism," in Rajaram Panda (ed.), *India-Vietnam Relations: Retrospect and Prospect*, Indian Council for Cultural Relations and Northern Book Centre, New Delhi, 2016, p.151.
20. Joseph S. Nye. Jr., "Soft Power," *Foreign Policy*, No.80, Autumn 1990, pp.153–71, https://www.jstor.org/stable/1148580 (accessed on December 3, 2017).
21. For further details see, David M Malone, "Soft Power in Indian Foreign Policy," *Economic and Political Weekly*, Vol. XLVI, Issue No. 36, September 3, 2011, p.35 https://www.epw.in/journal/2011/36 (accessed on November 10, 2017).
22. "Vietnam taps potential of Indian tourism market," Vietnam National Administration of Tourism, Ministry of Culture, Sports and Tourism, Hanoi, 25 May 2015, www.vietnamtourism.com/en/index.php/news/items/9402 (accessed on June 10, 2017).
23. "Vietnam marks International Yoga Day," *Voice of Vietnam*, June 17, 2018, vovworld.vn/en-US/spotlight/Vietnam-marks-international-yoga-day-2018-653850.vov (accessed on October 10, 2018).
24. Dipanjan Roy Chaudhury, "Vietnam ties Buddhist knot with India, not China," *The Economic Times*, September 10, 2016.
25. Satya Prakash, " Vietnam invites Bollywood to attract Indian tourists," *The Hindustan Times*, May 6, 2015.
26. Wang Jian and Zhao Yanrong, "Chinese literature scores a hit with Vietnamese," *China Daily*, November 5, 2015, www.chinadaily.com.cn/culture/2015-11/05/content_22376261.htm (accessed on October 10, 2017).
27. Huynh Thuc Vy, "Vietnam's Confucius Institute Distraction," *The Diplomat*, November 24, 2018, https://thediplomat.com/2013/11/vietnams-confucius-institute-distraction/ (accessed on December 24, 2017).
28. "Confucius Institute established at Hanoi University," *Nhan Dan*, December 27, 2014, en.nhandan.org.vn/society/education/item/3039102-conficus-institute-established-at-hanoi-university.html (accessed on January 2, 2018).
29. "Vietnam taps potential of Indian tourism market," n.22.
30. Ibid.
31. *The Hindustan Times*, December 13, 1976.
32. "India-Vietnam Relations," Ministry of External Affairs, Government of India, https://www.mea.gov.in/Portal/ForeignRelation/Bilateral_Relations_Website_Sept_17_.pdf (accessed on December 20, 2017).
33. Ibid.
34. Ibid.

35. Ibid.
36. "President at Inauguration of India Study Centre in Ho Chi Minh National Academy of Politics", Centre for Indian Studies, Ho Chi Minh National Academy of Politics, April 7, 2015, cis.org.vn/artcle/7/president-at-inauguration-of-india-study-centre-in-ho-chi-minh-national-academy-of-politics.html (accessed on November 2, 2018).
37. "India-Vietnam Relations," Ministry of External Affairs, Government of India, n.381.
38. Melissa S. Hersh and Dr. Ajay Lele, "Why Vietnam is an important ally for India," *Rediff News*, 2 December 2014, www.rediff.com/news/column/why-vietnam-is-an-important-ally-for-india/20141202.htm (accessed on December 10, 2017).
39. Speech of Rabindranath Tagore, Saigon, June 21, 1929, cited in Tridib Chakraborti, "India- Vietnam: Strategically Close, Culturally Distant," in Rajaram Panda (ed.), *India- Vietnam Relations: Retrospect and Prospect*, Indian Council for Cultural Relations, Northern Book Centre, New Delhi, year, p. 191.

SIX

Recent Developments in India-Vietnam-China Relations

India continued on the path of consolidating her friendly ties with Vietnam during the 2016–19 period as well. However, their ties with China remained mired in disputes despite consistent and constructive efforts to establish enduring peace. To begin with, bilateral trade between India and Vietnam has grown substantially by the year 2019 and India emerged to be the seventh largest trading partner of Vietnam, and Vietnam grew to be the fourth largest trading partner of India and the third largest export destination for India among the ASEAN countries. By the end of 2019, India had about investments worth US$ 1.9 billion in Vietnam. According to Vietnam's Foreign Investment Agency, as of 2019, India has 255 valid projects with total invested capital of US$ 922.34 million, ranking 26th among countries and territories investing in Vietnam.[1] As of 2019, Vietnam has six investment projects in India with total estimated investment of US$ 28.55 million.[2] Compared to this, China is the largest trading partner of Vietnam and the most important economic partnership of Hanoi. By March 2017, the cumulative Chinese FDI stood at a whooping US$ 11.9 billion for about 1616 active projects.[3] As far as India's economic relations with China during this period is concerned, the Development Research Centre of the State Council of China held four rounds of dialogue with the NITI Aayog of India. There were six rounds of Strategic Economic Dialogue (SED) between New Delhi and Beijing to promote bilateral economic and trade cooperation. Furthermore, both sides have held nine rounds of financial dialogues dealing with cooperation under multilateral frameworks as well as bilateral investment and financial cooperation. Besides these, they have held eleven sessions of China-India Joint Group of Economy and Trade to constantly deepen bilateral cooperation on economy and trade in goods, services and investment. Indian companies have a cumulative investment of nearly US$ 1 billion in China, whereas China has a cumulative investment of more than US$ 8 billion.[4] For last couple of years, India is experiencing a balance of trade vis-à-vis Vietnam, after years of massive trade surpluses. As to why this has happened, analysts point their fingers towards China, here too. It is believed that the period from 2018 to 2020 saw the heightening of the Sino-US trade war, which has forced China to scout for other destinations for diverting its supplies from the American market. There is apprehension that China is diverting its supplies to India through some ASEAN members to allow its products duty-free access. Therefore, much like Vietnam, an unusual 118 percent annual spurt in India's merchandise imports from Singapore to a record US$ 16.3 billion in 2019, raised an alarm among custom officials.[5] Similarly, India ran a trade deficit with Hong Kong for the first time in over two decades in 2019. Thus, this is an emerging and alarming trend that India must immediately look into.

For a detailed picture of the economic aspect of their relations during this period, **see** Tables 7 and 8 below.

Table 7: India's Trade Relations with Vietnam (April 2016–May 2020)

Values in US$ million

Year (April- March)	Export	Import	Total Trade	Balance of Trade
2016-17	6786.56	3320.56	10107.12	+3466
2017-18	7813.08	5018.55	12831.63	+2794.53
2018-19	6507.38	7192.33	13699.71	-684.95
2019-20	5059.88	7283.42	12343.3	-2223.54

Source: Prepared according to data available in Ministry of Commerce, Government of India, Annual Reports of Ministry of External Affairs, Government of India and General Statistics Office of Vietnam (Ministry of Planning and Investment, Government of Socialist Republic of Vietnam, Hanoi)

Table 8: India-Vietnam-China Total Trade (2016 onwards)

Values in US$ Million

Year (January-December)	Vietnam's Total Trade with India	Vietnam's Total Trade with China	Vietnam's Total Trade with World
2016	5432.7	71969.2	351559.2
2017	7710.9	93926.9	426430.6
2018	10690.8	106935.7	480879.3

Source: General Statistics Office of Vietnam, Hanoi (Government data of 2019 was not yet available)

As far as the political scenario between the three countries is concerned, in 2016, the 8th Round of the Annual Defence and Security Dialogue (ADSD) between India and China was held in New Delhi on November 8, 2016, and the 6th India-China Joint Training Exercise 'Hand- in-Hand 2016' was held in Pune from November 16-17, 2016. The main purpose behind these measures was to enhance the conviction and trust between both the armies and to acquaint them of each other's work procedures. Overall, in 2016, India's political ties with China remained smooth with general progress noted particularly in the economic sector. The Special Representatives Talks continued its search for a plausible solution on the border issue, besides regular high-level political visits, with President Pranab Mukherjee visiting China in May and Prime Minister Narendra Modi meeting Chinese President Xi Jinping on several occasions on the sidelines of multilateral events, such as the Shanghai Cooperation Organization (SCO) Summit in Tashkent in June, the G-20 Summit in Hangzhou in September and the BRICS Summit in Goa in October.

While analysing India's political ties with Vietnam this year, it must be noted that Prime Minister Modi paid an official visit to Vietnam from September 2-3 and the most significant achievement of this visit was the elevation of the Strategic Partnership between India and Vietnam to the level of Comprehensive Strategic Partnership. Twelve MoUs/Documents were signed during the visit, such as the Framework Agreement on Cooperation in the Exploration and Uses of Outer Spaces for Peaceful Purposes, Programme of Cooperation in

UN Peacekeeping Matters, MoU on Health Cooperation, MoU on Cooperation in IT, MoU on Cooperation in Cyber Security.[6] Moreover, PM Modi announced a new Line of Credit of US$ 500 million for strengthening their bilateral defence cooperation.[7] Further, he also announced a grant of US$ 5 million for the construction of an Army Software Park at the Telecommunications University in Nha Trang. For the first time, a Vietnamese ship participated in the International Fleet Review at Vishakhapatnam in February. Two Indian Naval Ships, INS Satpura and INS Kirch and one Indian Coast Guard Ship ICGS SAMRAT made port calls to Vietnam this year.[8] In fact, defence cooperation had become the cornerstone of their ties in the 'Act East' period, and Shri Manohar Parrikar, the then Defence Minister of India, lead a delegation of defence industry to Vietnam in June 2016. To follow it up, the then Defence Minister of Vietnam, General Ngo Xuan Lick paid a visit to India in December that year. Why this extra focus on defence cooperation? Can China possibly be the reason? Well, the perceived 'threat' from China in the psyche of Vietnamese people, did not seem to have found any remedy even in 2016. Skirmishes in the South China Sea continued unabated, and in fact aggravated, with reports of how China's plan of expanding the North Island and Tree Island in the Paracel Islands, along with constructions in the Fiery Cross Reef, was very much underway as per satellite images. It was also believed that China was operating a new lighthouse in the Subi Reef area. The US continued to remain vociferous of China's activities in the South China Sea and in May 2016, USS William P. Lawrence undertook freedom of navigation operations near the disputed Fiery Cross Reef, much to the chagrin of the PRC. In the same month, India deployed about four ships to the South China Sea and the North West Pacific Region for sometime before heading on to Philippines. Interestingly, in the same month, President Obama paid a visit to Vietnam and lifted the embargo on sales of lethal weapons to Vietnam completely, which was imposed since the Cold War days. This was a major breakthrough in Vietnam's growing ties with the US. Like India, the US supports freedom of navigation in the South China Sea and this lifting of the embargo was intended to provide Vietnam with an extra edge in any maritime territorial dispute with China.Therefore, the 'China factor' has been playing a major role in Vietnamese foreign policy and in its desire to beef up defence cooperation with its friends and allies, be it India, the US, Japan or Australia. The year 2016 also witnessed a tribunal ruling of the Permanent Court of Arbitration which rejected China's nine-dash line historical claims, in the month of July. However, China immediately rejected the ruling. Vietnam, India and the US welcomed the decision.

In the the first six to seven months of 2017, India's relations with China was relatively smooth without any major hiccup. Regular high-level visits continued with President Xi and PM Modi meeting along the sidelines of SCO in June, and at BRICS leaders' informal gathering at Hamburg in July. It is to be noted that at the meeting of the SCO on June 9 at Astana, India and Pakistan formally joined the SCO.This is an organization comprising China, Kazakhstan, Kyrgyztan, Russia, Tajikistan and Uzbekistan. PM Modi was gratified with the support that President Xi extended for India's entry into the group. However, this bonhomie received a sudden jolt when in the same month reports starting surfacing of a military stand-off between India and China in the strategically important Doklam area. This area is surrounded by the Chumbi Valley of Tibet, Ha Valley of Bhutan and has Sikkim on another side. Therefore, its proximity with the Siliguri corridor or the strategically vulnerable chicken-neck area which connects the Indian mainland with the North Eastern states makes the area sensitive to India's core interests. The Chinese intention to extend a road further south of Dokhlam, near the Bhutanese Army Camp in Jampheri Ridge was revealed when Chinese troops reached the area with equipment. This alarmed the Bhutanese authority as both Bhutan and India maintain that it is an integral part of the Bhutanese territory and reportedly Indian troops rushed to the area after Bhutan raised an alarm and called out for help. The Bhutanese government firmly retorted to China with an official statement that "the construction of the road inside Bhutanese territory is a direct violation of the agreements and the process of demarcating the boundary between our two countries."[9] The Chinese government accused the Indian government of trespassing into the Chinese territory and on the first week of August it released a statement which said, "India has no right to interfere in or impede the boundary talks between China and Bhutan."[10] The situation remained tense for about two months, despite some hasty parleys in the diplomatic circles, before a steady disengagement of the border personnel could be noticed on August 28.[11] Following this, the 10th round of the Working Mechanism for Consultation and Coordination on India-China Border Affairs (WMCC) was held at Beijing on November 16-17, that year, which stressed on maintaining peace and tranquility along the disputed border until a final resolution could be arrived at. In much contrast to India's political ties with China in 2017, her ties with Vietnam was all about celebrating the year of friendship to mark the 45th anniversary of establishment of their diplomatic ties and 10th anniversary of their Strategic Partnership. The Indian Cultural Centre was inaugurated at Hanoi in April 2017. With defence cooperation as the "significant pillar"[12]of their bilateral ties, New Delhi and Hanoi fast-tracked the procedures for implementation of the contract signed in September 2016, between M/s Larsen and Toubro Ltd and Vietnam Border Guards for procuring 12 offshore patrol vessels. This deal was particularly entered into keeping in mind Vietnam's perceived maritime threats from China in the disputed waters of South China Sea. As far as Vietnam's political ties with China in 2017 is concerned, the year started on a positive note with Secretary-General of the Communist Party of Vietnam (CPV) Nguyen Phu Trong visiting China in January. At the end of the four-day visit, a joint communiqué was arrived at which talked of upholding their mutual political trust and their commitment to strengthen the strategic cooperative partnership.[13] After the 12th National Congress of the Vietnam Communist Party and with President Trump's ascendancy to power, the growth of the US-Vietnam ties has hit a plateau. The gradual overshadowing of pro-Western ruling elite in Vietnam and President Trump's decision to withdraw from the Trans-Pacific Partnership (TPP) were very significant events of this year as far as future trends of Vietnam's foreign policy is concerned. These events have once again thrown at us important questions, like: first, will the Vietnamese leadership gradually lean towards China in the coming years? Secondly, if President Trump is re elected to power in late 2020, will the US-Vietnam relations cease to grow deeper than what was projected and hoped during the Obama period? Thirdly, if Vietnam inches closer towards China, will it be at the cost of its age-old friendship with India? Fourthly, if China continues its aggressive stance in the South China Sea, how far would Vietnam accept that? Questions are many, but answers few and sketchy.

Keeping aside the bitter Doklam incident, India and China started the next year on a positive note. The first informal summit between PM Modi and President Xi took place at Wuhan in April 2018. This was part of the newly crafted 'hometown diplomacy' in Sino-Indian ties. The Wuhan Consensus called for future direction of India-China relations to be built upon "mutual respect for each other's developmental aspirations and prudent management of differences with mutual sensitivity."[14] The spirit of the Wuhan Consensus influenced the follow-up meeting or the Special Representatives' Talks in November 2018 which focused on intensifying "their efforts to achieve a fair, reasonable and mutually acceptable solution to the India-China boundary question at an early date, and to ensure that the boundary question does not affect the overall development of the bilateral relationship."[15] Simultaneously, India continued her efforts to make her comprehensive strategic partnership with Vietnam reach a deeper level. The then Defence Minister Smt Nirmala Sitharaman laid the foundation stone for the Army Software Park in Nha Trang, during her visit to Vietnam from June 12–15, 2018. With defence termed as a 'significant pillar' of India's bilateral relations with Vietnam, New Delhi raised the ITEC slots it offers to Vietnamese personnel to 67.[16] Meanwhile, worrisome incidents from South China Sea were being reported, the most alarming of which was the news of China landing an H-6K bomber in the disputed Woody Island , thereby militarising and destabilising the region. The Woody Island is claimed by Vietnam and Taiwan. The bomber had the capacity to reach the entire Southeast Asia from the island.[17] Expectedly, such a move was highly criticised by the US Defence Secretary James Mattis, to which China's Lt Gen He Lei said, "Any irresponsible comments from other countries cannot be accepted."[18] With such incidents being frequently reported, Sino-Vietnamese ties remained on tenterhooks, and once again, possibilities of Vietnam not weaning away from the US orbit seemed strong by the end of the year.

The year 2019 witnessed the second informal meeting between PM Modi and President Xi at Chennai in October 2019. Both sides discussed ways to deepen their political ties and reiterated that "both sides should properly manage their differences and not allow them to become disputes."[19] With hydro-politics emerging to be another major area of concern and a potential point of discord, the 12th meeting of the India-China Expert Level Mechanism (ELM) on Trans-border Rivers took place at Ahmedabad in June 2019. During the meeting, both sides signed the 'Implementation plan on the provision of hydrological information of Yaluzangbu/Brahmaputra River in flood season'.[20] Another positive development that India could achieve vis-à-vis China this year was successfully persuading China to withdraw its veto in May 2019, which eventually paved the way for Masood Azhar to be listed as a global terrorist. China had long been vetoing such a move despite scathing criticisms and severe international pressure. This was a major diplomatic win for India. On the other hand, India's relations with Vietnam remained smooth and steady this year too and the highlight of it remained the launch of direct flights between New Delhi and Kolkata, Hanoi and Ho Chi Minh City. The lack of direct connectivity was a major lacuna and a long-standing demand of both the countries. On November 25, 2019, Vietnam released a *defence white paper*. Vietnam had published previous defence white papers in 1988, 2004 and 2009. It reiterated 'three no's'—no military alliances, no foreign bases, no siding with one country against another. About the South China Sea, this 2019 white paper is more vocal than its 2009 counterpart. It says, "New Developments in the East Sea, including unilateral actions, power-based coercion, violation of international law, militarisation, change in the status quo, and infringement upon Vietnam's sovereignty, sovereign rights, and jurisdiction as provided in international law have undermined the interests of nations concerned and threatened peace, stability, security, safety and freedom of navigation and overflight in the region."[21] Therefore, without naming China in the defence white paper, Vietnam has given a strong message to Beijing on the South China Sea issue. It does not seem that China is much concerned with the apprehensions and threat perceptions that India and Vietnam harbour towards China. The early developments in 2020 would prove that the Wuhan Consensus or the spirit of Chennai informal meeting is just an ephemeral narrative without any promise of enduring peace. When the world seemed to grapple with the Corona pandemic, China on the one hand, continued to heavily militarise the South China Sea and put India under pressure by instigating skirmishes in the strategically important Galwan Valley, which resulted in the death of several personnel on both sides, once again bringing down the Sino-Indian ties to a new low. New Delhi further believes that China's growing ties with Nepal has a major role to play behind Nepal to publish a new map in 2020 claiming Kalapani, Limpiyadhura and Lipulekh of Uttarakhand as their territories. India perhaps stuck in a quagmire of not-being-able-to-choose-neighbours-but-will-have-to-choose-friends-carefully, is being thrown into the US orbit much more than ever before, particularly due to the trust deficit that it has for China and some other neighbours. President Trump visited India in February 2020 and both sides reiterated their commitment to promote an open and free Indo-Pacific, including a comprehensive global strategic partnership. The US wants to see India as a major leveller in the Indian Ocean Region vis-à-vis China. India committed to procure the US military equipment worth US$ 3 billion. The US arms sales to India have grown from zero to about US$ 18 billion in the last 15 years.[22] Today, India is privy to such hi-tech armament from the US which is available only to its NATO allies. Therefore, it amply proves that the US attaches special importance to India, particularly to see

New Delhi grow as a great balancer against China in the region. As far as Vietnam is concerned, it is not one of the closest peers that the US has in the region. Thailand and Philippines have since long been US allies. However, today, the converging views between Vietnam, India and the US on the South China Sea issue have brought them closer to each other. The 'China factor' has indeed become an important consideration.

Notes

1. "India-Vietnam Relations," Embassy of India, Hanoi, Vietnam, https://www.indembassyhanoi.gov.in/page/india-vietnam-relations/ (accessed on July 20, 2020).
2. Ibid.
3. Chinese FDI in Vietnam: Growing Economic Ties, Despite Strains, *Vietnam Briefing*, 25 September 2017, https://www.vietnam-briefing.com/news/vietnam-and-china-growing-economic-ties-despite-strains.html/ (accessed on July 20, 2020).
4. 70 Years of Diplomatic Relations between China and India (1950-2020), *The Hindu*, March 31, 2020, https://www.thehindu.com/brandhub/70-years-of-diplomatic-relations-between-china-and-india-1950-2020/article31219737.ece (accessed on May 4, 2020).
5. Banikinkar Pattanayak, "China factor: India's trade with Vietnam swings from big surplus to large deficit," *Financial Express*, July 10, 2020, https://www.financialexpress.com/economy/china-factor-indias-trade-with-vietnam-swings-from-big-surplus-to-large-deficit/2019048 (accessed on July 15, 2020).
6. *Annual Report: 2016-2017*, Ministry of External Affairs, Government of India, New Delhi, 2017.
7. Ibid.
8. Ibid.
9. Josy Joseph, "What is the Doklam issue all about?," *The Hindu*, January 27, 2018.
10. Ibid.
11. Annual Report: 2017-2018, Ministry of External Affairs, Government of India, New Delhi, 2018.
12. Ibid.
13. Nguyen Minh Quang, "The Resurgence of China- Vietnam Ties," *The Diplomat*, January 25, 2017, https://thediplomat.com/2017/01/the-resurgence-of-china-vietnam-ties/ (accessed on May 6, 2020).
14. *Annual Report: 2018-2019*, Ministry of External Affairs, Government of India, New Delhi, 2019.
15. Ibid.
16. Ibid.
17. "South China Sea dispute: China lands bombers on island," *BBC News*, May19, 2018, https://www.bbc.com/news/world-asia-china-44180773, accessed on April 4, 2020.

18. South China Sea dispute: Beijing attacks 'irresponsible' US comments, BBC News, June 2, 2018, https://www.bbc.com/news/world-asia-44343368 (accessed on April 4, 2020).
19. *Annual Report: 2019-2020*, Ministry of External Affairs, Government of India, New Delhi, 2020.
20. Ibid.
21. Huong Le Thu, "Vietnam Draw Lines in the Sea," *Foreign Policy*, December 6, 2019, https://foreignpolicy.com/2019/12/06/vietnam-south-china-sea-united-states-draws-lines-in-the-sea/ (accessed on April 4, 2020).
22. Sameer Lalwani, "Trump's India trip didn't produce a trade deal. Here's what did result," The Washington Post, February 27, 2020, https://www.washingtonpost.com/politics/2020/02/27/trumps-india-trip-didnt-produce-trade-deal-heres-what-did-result/ (accessed on April 15, 2020).

SEVEN

Conclusion

Having analysed the various aspects of China Factor in India-Vietnam Relations, it is clear that, India's ties with Vietnam have only progressed towards betterment and higher achievements with each passing year since 1991. The main objective of the research endeavour was to analyse the nature of India's bilateral relations with Vietnam in the post-Cold War era, with the 'China factor' as its crucial determinant. Therefore, apart from discussing the issues where the bilateral relations have matured independent of the 'China factor' or any other external influences, particular focus has been given in the book on areas where the 'China factor' is especially influencing the foreign policies of India and Vietnam and motivating them to forge closer ties with each other. To set the things in context, *Chapter One* exclusively analyses the nature of India's bilateral friendship with Vietnam during the Cold War years as a prelude to the main focus of the thesis, that is the post-Cold War years. This chapter has discussed the developments during the fag end of the Second World War and post-Second World War phase, when the foundation stone of the bilateral relations of these two countries were laid down by Pandit Jawaharlal Nehru and Ho Chi Minh. It elaborates on how the Superpower Politics have influenced non-aligned India and Communist Vietnam to come closer to each other gradually, particularly during Mrs. Indira Gandhi's tenure as the Prime Minister of India, who was posthumously given the Golden Star Order Award, the highest civilian award in Vietnam, for her unforgettable contribution towards the cause of Vietnam and for elevating India-

Vietnam bilateral ties to a higher pedestal. Moreover, this chapter explores in detail, the incidents that brought these two countries closer and how the 'China factor' and the role played by the Soviet Union strengthened their ties t from the very beginning. The chapter reached the conclusion that the level of friendship and solidarity which India exhibited towards Vietnam during the Cold War years, was of the highest order and remains exemplary till date. At a time when ideology and ideological affiliations reigned supreme and divided the world into two halves, many groups, sub-groups and alliances, non-aligned India stood firmly behind Communist Vietnam. When in fact, Communist China refused to give any further economic assistance to Vietnam after the Sino-Soviet rift, India generously and to its best capacity helped Vietnam in its national reconstruction efforts, thereby proving that the ties of friendship that New Delhi forged with Hanoi and their people far surpassed any ideological considerations and thereby making ideology an irrelevant factor in Indo-Vietnam solidarity and friendship ties.

The *Second Chapter* of the book, which focused on explaining the economic relations between India and Vietnam and the 'China factor' since 1991, summarised after extensive analysis of India's trade figures and trade basket with Vietnam in these years, that India's trade ties with Vietnam is still far below its potentials and at the end of 2015, it was even less than 2 percent of India's total global trade volume. Therefore, it can be seen that despite excellent political and strategic relations between them, their economic relations have not been up to the satisfactory level. As probable reasons of this anomaly, certain points have been explained in the chapter. For instance, paucity in sufficient and cheap connectivity between them, similar trade basket hampering their export revenue, inadequate knowledge about each other's market potentials, higher taxes levied by India (as compared to China) on Vietnamese products, lack of business mindset on both sides, etc. However, Vietnam vis-à-vis China enjoys geographical proximity, similar political structures and very low taxes which have all facilitated Vietnam's excellent trade relations with China, so much so that despite all political tensions, China emerged as the largest trade partner of Vietnam till date.

In the *Third Chapter*, the various water-shed political events in global politics and in domestic politics of India and Vietnam of the post-Cold War era have been analysed, significant high level-political visits have been discussed, important agreements reached at by both the countries have been explained and China's reactions to various issues and factors of India-Vietnam collaboration have been studied thoroughly. This chapter discusses how both India and Vietnam are grappling to meet the challenges of China's aggressive outreach and expansionist attitude, fuelled by the 'China dream' under the leadership of President Xi Jinping. Furthermore, the chapter explores how both these countries are collaborating with other regional and extra-regional powers, for example, the US, Australia, Japan and France to counter Chinese 'not-so-benign' postures. On various issues, India also had to face the challenging posture adopted by China on the South China Sea issue, on the issue of its defence cooperation with Vietnam, on Arunachal Pradesh issue and border issue, on China's continuous economic and military assistance to Pakistan and building China-Pakistan economic corridor through disputed areas in Kashmir, on the issue of condemning Pakistan-based terrorists like Masood Azhar, who have regularly engaged in terrorist activities against India, on the issue of stapled visas and denying visa to Indian Lieutenant General and other multifarious controversial events that have occurred between 1991 and 2015. All these conflicting incidents have further influenced India to build very strong political ties with Vietnam, as a bulwark against Chinese political and strategic advances in the Southeast Asian region. Moreover, in this chapter, there is an analysis of gradual strengthening of India's 'Look East' Policy. It discusses in detail how India's gradual upward mobility in her ties with the ASEAN, whose spill-over effect improved her overall ties with Vietnam gradually. China's growing ties with the Southeast Asian region, with China being at a geographically advantageous position vis-à-vis the Southeast Asian region, as compared to India, has definitely propelled India to frame its Southeast Asia Policy more proactively. This chapter also analyses the rationale behind India and China watching each other's moves and projects involving the region and their apprehensions of each other's expanding clout in the region. In such a situation, Vietnam has emerged to be a prominent player in India's eastward proactive policy thrust, particularly because of the fact that Vietnam has been playing a creditable function in the security architecture of the region since it joined the ASEAN in 1995. Moreover, Vietnam shares with India the same fear of China's 'aggressive' advances as Hanoi itself has been embroiled in armed conflicts with Beijing twice in the late 20th century. Thus, Vietnam can play the role of a concrete bulwark against China's moves in Southeast Asia, which will certainly be to the advantage of India, who is keeping a close watch on China's 'One Belt One Road' Project in the region presently.

In the *Fourth Chapter*, detailed analysis has been made of the presence of 'China factor' in issues like South China Sea, Indian Ocean, hydro-politics, terrorism and such other factors which have cemented India's rise with Vietnam in the post-Cold War years. After analysing in detail each of these factors, this chapter concludes that indeed, strategic and political considerations are today playing a more important role than the economic factor. If the economic considerations were of supreme importance, such wide differences of opinion and raging conflicts in some cases would not have been exhibited such blatantly. It may also be concluded that both India and Vietnam are trying to keep their issues of conflict vis-à-vis China at one level, and at another level, both these countries are trying to improve their trade statistics with the mighty economic giant, China. So, on one hand, their good economic relations with China have not been able to ameliorate their bitter political and strategic ties with Beijing, and on another hand, they have so far been successful in keeping their political conflicts apart from their growing economic ties with China. Moreover, this chapter besides discussing the Indo-Vietnam bilateral issues where the 'China factor' is playing a major role, or the issues on which both India and Vietnam feel that they have been victimised by China's aggressive postures in the region, also discusses the multilateral issues like the Quadrilateral Security Dialogue Mechanism, the 'One Belt One Road' Project, US's 'Indo-Pacific' Strategy and China's reactions to each of these issues.

In the **Fifth Chapter**, India's cultural relations with Vietnam have been studied. Right at the outset, there is a discussion on the Cham Kingdom, which thrived in Central Vietnam and existed between the 2nd and the 15th century AD. There is a thorough discussion in the chapter on how Indian maritime traders went to Vietnam and settled there and established their kingdom in Central Vietnam most peacefully without any bloodshed. Cham artefacts, steles, handicrafts, temples, idols, apsara dances still form a core of Vietnamese society and have been preserved in the Da Nang museum. There is an analysis on how Buddhism has travelled from India to Vietnam and how it has always proved to be a linking philosophy between India and Vietnam. Also, presence of India's 'Soft Power' in Vietnam has been discussed along with the details of government initiatives adopted by both countries to foster better cultural cooperation between them. Furthermore, Chinese cultural influences in Vietnam owing to one thousand years of Chinese rule over Vietnam and presence of China's 'Soft Power' in Vietnam in the new millennium have been discussed exhaustively. Finally, it may be concluded that there is still ample scope for India to more proactively showcase her age-old cultural ties with Vietnam, one of the richest that India shared with any country, ever.

The *Sixth Chapter* discusses the recent developments and emerging trends in India-Vietnam-China relations during 2016–19 period, both in the economic sphere and at the political level and how both India and Vietnam continue to be wary of China.

Therefore, one can conclude that the irrelevance of 'ideology factor' in Indo-Vietnam ties became even more apparent in the post-Cold War years when after the dissolution of Soviet Union in 1991, Vietnam understood that the nature of global politics has changed its emphasis from the confrontation between Socialism and Capitalism to multi-polarity as the chief feature of international political structure. The then Politburo Member and the Prime Minister of Vietnam, Vo Van

Kiet was a pro-reform leader and exhorted his party members to accept the renovation in the post-Cold War years or risk the possibility of being removed from power. He was the Prime Minister of Vietnam for a major part of 1990s and was instrumental in motivating Vietnam to normalise ties with China on the one hand and the US on the other, join the ASEAN and display active participation in the affairs of region and also make efforts toward joining the World Trade Organization (WTO), as he realized that Vietnam should make good use of the then international economic environment and multi-polar political world structure, thereby ushering in economic renewal step by step, followed by political renewal. Therefore, it may be concluded that ideology as a factor was irrelevant in the Indo-Vietnam solidarity and friendship ties in the Cold War years, even more so in the post-Cold War years, primarily because the ideological considerations of a conflict-ridden world between Socialism and Capitalism has increasingly become irrelevant in Vietnam's internal politics, and successive Party Congresses have stressed on 'making friends' with as many countries as possible, besides emphasising on gradual assimilation with the global economy. Also, India's gesture of friendship and generous economic assistance in Vietnam's national reconstruction efforts has elevated their bilateral ties to such a high pedestal that well surpasses any ideological consideration.

Furthermore, through an in-depth analysis of various issues, it may be concluded that the 'China factor' has emerged to be a crucial consideration in the Indo-Vietnam bilateral bond in the post-Cold War years. The ASEAN as a regional organization has been playing a largely balancing role vis-à-vis China as some of its members are themselves involved in disputing claims in the South China Sea with China. However, the ASEAN has been successful to keep the pressure on China and on all other parties to enter into a Code of Conduct at an earliest possible date and adopt peaceful means to resolve the disputing claims. Besides this, the role of US in IndoVietnam bilateral ties has emerged to be very important in the post-Cold War years as both New Delhi and Hanoi are increasingly cooperating with the US on strategic and defence-related issues to ensure a check on China's belligerent moves particularly in the Indian Ocean and the South China Sea region. India has become a key player in US's 'Indo-Pacific' Security Strategy and Vietnam is also emerging to be a 'shadow-member', much to the chagrin of China. All these three countries—US, India and Vietnam have publicly voiced concern for freedom of navigation in international waters and the US has even carried out 'Freedom of Navigation' naval operations in the disputed South China Sea waters, which was fiercely protested by China. Moreover, India and the US have been holding regular Malabar naval exercises in the Indian Ocean since 1992, in which Japan became a permanent member in 2015. Therefore, China has been increasingly wary of India's and Vietnam's growing ties with the US, Japan, Australia (known as the Quad-Quadrilateral Security Dialogue Mechanism) and France, who share a common concern for China's aggressive postures, fuelled by the 'China dream' in the Asian Century, under Xi Jinping's strong and centralising leadership.

Most importantly, it must be remembered that India shares with China some outstanding issues of conflict, such as, the border issue, which even today is neither delimited nor demarcated and owing to such varying perception of the border, frequent flare-ups and infiltration only complicated the issue over the decades. India accuses China of wilful procrastination at arriving at the solution, with the primary motive to weigh down India's growth and keeping India occupied at multiple fronts. China's traditional belief in 'Tian Xia' (All Under Heaven) as belonging to 'Zhong Guo' (Middle Kingdom) or China has stopped them from accepting the McMahon Line as the demarcating border between India and China as it believes that this border is a Western construct and imposition. Thus, naturally, China still believes that Arunachal Pradesh belongs to China and issues stern statements when Indian Prime Ministers visit Arunachal Pradesh. Furthermore, China's 'all-weather friendship' with Pakistan and China's continuous and generous economic, military and infrastructural aid to Pakistan has further complicated Sino-Indian relations. China has officially maintained that Kashmir is a bilateral problem between India and

Pakistan, yet it has been planning and building the China-Pakistan economic corridor through the disputed region of Kashmir, which is the Pakistan-Occupied Kashmir (PoK), despite India's protests and warnings of "further political instability" by UN's regional development arm, named the Economic and Social Commission for Asia and the Pacific (ESCAP). Also, both India and Vietnam are facing a similar situation as lower riparian countries, bearing the brunt of China's dam-building activities as the upper riparian State in the Brahmaputra and the Mekong Rivers respectively. Therefore, hydro-politics has definitely emerged as a new bone of contention in the domain of Sino-Indian and Sino-Vietnam relations.

Summarily then, India's bilateral relations with Vietnam in the post-Cold War years have only gone from strength to strength. Truly, the kind of friendship that India has always shared with Vietnam is exceptional and unique. There are certain areas like cultural cooperation, tourism promotion, defence collaboration and economic exchanges, which all need further impetus and pro-activism on the part of Government of India, as performance in these areas is not at all commensurate with the excellent political and strategic relations that have evolved between India and Vietnam, and definitely concerted efforts have to be put in the their bilateral relations particularly on these areas in the coming years under India's 'Act East' Policy. The 'China factor' has emerged to be a crucial determinant in their bilateral ties in the post-Cold War years and both are trying to manage it in their own ways, by promoting their respective bilateral economic ties with China on the one hand and on the other hand, at the multilateral level uniting with other countries on the regional platforms like the ASEAN, ARF, ASEM, MGC, etc., to protest against 'Chinese excesses' in the South China Sea region and on other issues. So far, both India and Vietnam have been moderately successful in addressing the crucial and bitter outstanding issues in their ties with China, yet there is always a pestering discomfort in their political and strategic ties with China, which have proved to be a major impetus in strengthening their bilateral relations with each other in the post-Cold War years.

Therefore, after a detailed study of India's bilateral relations with Vietnam during the Cold War and post-Cold War era in the backdrop of 'China factor,' certain significant findings have been derived. **First**, India's solidarity with Vietnam during the Cold War period, especially during Prime Minister Indira Gandhi's leadership, remains exemplary till date. **Secondly**, in the economic realm, the trade figures and statistics most certainly reveal that New Delhi's trade volume with Hanoi is incommensurate with the former's excellent political and strategic ties with the latter. Conversely, China is way ahead of India in tapping its trade potentials with Vietnam. **Thirdly**, India's major political differences with China on some very crucial issues, have further influenced New Delhi to cultivate better political linkages with Vietnam and other countries of Southeast Asia and beyond. **Fourthly**, in the strategic sphere once again, India and Vietnam are increasingly coming together as a bulwark against China's 'excesses' to forge closer cooperation in issues and spheres like Defence, Science and Technology, Human Resources Development and Information Technology, Nuclear Collaboration, Border, Hydro-Politics, Anti-Terrorism drives, issues in Indian Ocean, etc., and in the post-Cold War period, it seems that the 'strategic factor' is playing a more crucial role than the 'economic factor'. Despite the fact that both India and Vietnam share an appreciable amount of trade intercourse with China, the outstanding strategic issues in their ties with China are acting as further impetus for Hanoi and New Delhi to strengthen their bilateral ties as a bulwark against China's actions which they construe to be 'aggressive' in nature and as genuine security threats. **Fifthly**, India has not yet been very successful in tapping the full potentials of her cultural ties with Vietnam and it has many opportunities to more proactively propagate the rich and deep cultural influences that she had on Vietnam since pre-historic times. **Sixthly**, Vietnam is the crucial springboard for India to look towards 'East' and beyond and keeping this bilateral relationship cordial and friendly will hugely determine the success of India's 'Look/Act East' Policy. **Finally**, although ideology always played a determining factor in relations between countries during the

Cold War period, but with reference to this research attempt, it may be concluded that the role of political 'ideology' is not at all a determining factor in Indo-Vietnam relations. Although during the Cold War period, their mutual friendship with the Socialist Soviet Union played a decisive role in forging closer ties between them, pitted against the imperialist West, India's generous help towards Vietnam's national reconstruction at a time when her own economy was in a tumultuous situation, elevated their bilateral ties to such a lofty pedestal that goes well beyond any ideological consideration, particularly at a time when the Communist China, ideologically closer to Vietnam than the non-aligned India, refused to give any further economic assistance towards economic reconstruction of Vietnam 1977 onwards. After the Cold War ended, the multilateral global structure and economic imperatives to rebuild their national economies totally overshadowed considerations of any ideological affiliations. Today, ironically, the Socialist Republic of Vietnam has many outstanding issues of conflict in relation to the Communist China and it is forging better ties with India and other countries like the USA, France, Australia and Japan to counter 'Chinese aggressive moves', particularly in the South China Sea region. It is true that similar political structures between China and Vietnam acts as a crucial tool to mitigate tensions and promote greater cooperation, yet, that has not yet been able to resolve the prickly issues in Sino-Vietnam relations. On the other side, in the post-Cold War years, India's relations with Vietnam have continued on the path of friendship that was followed in the Cold War period, and additionally, newer dimensions, issues and factors have further strengthened their age-old ties. Thus, how these two countries manage the 'China factor' in their bilateral friendship will to a large extent determine the destinies of South and Southeast Asian regions in the coming years.

Bibliography

Books

1. *85 Years of The Communist Party of Vietnam (1930–2015): A selection of documents from eleven Party Congresses*, The Gioi Publishers, Hanoi, 2015
2. Acharya, Amitav, *The Quest for Identity: International Relations of Southeast Asia*, Oxford University Press, Singapore, 2000
3. Amer, Ramses, *The ethnic Chinese in Vietnam and Sino-Vietnamese relations,* Forum, Kuala Lumpur, 1991.
4. Appadorai, A, and Rajan, M.S, India's Foreign Policy and Relations, South Asian Publishers Private Limited, New Delhi, 1985
5. Ayoob, Mohammed, India and Southeast Asia: Indian Perceptions and Policies, Routledge, London and New York, 1990
6. Ayres, A, and Raja Mohan, C (eds.), Power Realignments in Asia, Sage Publications, New Delhi, 2009
7. Bajpai, Kanti and Mattoo, Amitabh (eds.), The Peacock and Dragon: India- China Relations in the Twenty First Century, Har-Anand Publications, New Delhi, 2000.
8. Bajpai, Kanti, Jing, Huang, and Mahbubani, Kishore (eds.), *China- India Relations: Cooperation and Conflict*, Routledge, New York, 2016.
9. Baladas Ghoshal (ed.), India and Southeast Asia in the 1990s: New Perspectives, New Challenges, Konark Publishers Pvt. Ltd, New Delhi, 1996
10. Bandopadhyaya, Jayantanuja, The Making of India's Foreign Policy: Determinants, Institutions, Processes and Personalities, Allied Publisher Limited, New Delhi, 1970
11. Banerjee, Arun Kumar (ed.), Security Issues in South Asia: Domestic and External Sources of Threats to Security, Minerva Associates Pvt. Ltd, Calcutta, 1998
12. Bhatia, Rajiv, Sakhuja, Vijay and Ranjan, Vikash (eds.), *India- Vietnam: Agenda for Strengthening Partnership*, Shipra Publications, Delhi, 2013.
13. Biju, M.R (ed.), *New Horizons of Indian Foreign Policy*, Authors Press, New Delhi, 2007
14. Bose, Sugata, *A Hundred Horizons: The Indian Ocean in the Age of Global Empire*, Harvard University Press, USA, 2006.
15. Camilleri, Joseph, *Chinese Foreign Policy: The Maoist Era and Its Aftermath,* Martin Robertson and Co., Oxford, 1980.
16. Chakraborti, Tridib and Chakraborty, Mohor, *Expanding Horizon of India's Southeast Asia Policy: 'Look', 'Move' and 'Act' East*, KW Publishers Pvt. Ltd, New Delhi, 2018.
17. Chakraborti, Tridib, *India and Kampuchea: A Phase in their relations, 1978–81*, Minerva Associates Publications Pvt. Ltd, Calcutta, 1985.
18. Chakraborti, Tridib, Sen, Rabindra et al (eds.), *Power, Commerce and Influence: India's Look East Experience,* Lancers' Books, New Delhi, 2009.

19.. Chan, Yuk Wah, *Vietnamese- Chinese Relationships at the Borderlands: Trade, Tourism and Cultural Politics*, Routledge Contemporary Asia Series, Oxford and New York, 2013.

20. Chen, King C, *Vietnam and China, 1938-1954*, Princeton University Press, New Jersey, 1969.

21. Chopra, VD (ed.), India's Foreign Policy in the 21st Century, Kalpaz Publications, New Delhi, 2006

22. Chopra, VD (ed.), *Vietnam Today and Indo-Vietnam Relations*, Gyan Books Pvt. Ltd, New Delhi, 2001

23. Das, Suranjan and Muni, S.D. (eds.), *India and China: The Next Decades*, Rupa and Co., New Delhi, 2009.

24. Das, Suranjan, Chakraborti, Tridib and Bhattacharya, Subhadeep, *Indo-Vietnam Relations In The Emerging Global Order*, KW Publishers Pvt. Ltd, New Delhi, 2018.

25. De, Prabir (ed.), *ASEAN- India: Deepening Economic Partnership in Mekong Region*, Research and Information System for Developing Countries (RIS), New Delhi, 2014.

26. Deepak, B.R, *India China Relations in the first half of the Twentieth Century*, APH Publishers, New Delhi, 2001

27. Deepak, B.R, *India- China Relations*, A.P.H Publishing Corporation, New Delhi, 2001.

28. Dillon, Michael, *Contemporary China: An Introduction*, Routledge, London, 2009.

29. Dixit, J. N., *Indian Foreign Policy And Its Neighbours*, Gyan Publishing House, New Delhi, 2012.

30. Dutt, Sagarika and Bansal, Alok (eds.), South Asian Security: 21st Century Discourses, Routledge, London and New York, 2012

31. FitzGerald, C.P, *China and Southeast Asia Since 1945*, Vikas Publishing House Pvt. Ltd, Delhi, 1975.

32. Frankel, Francine R. and Harding, Harry (eds.), *The India- China Relationship: Rivalry and Engagement*, Oxford University Press, New Delhi, 2004.

33. Gandhi, P. Jagadish, India and China in the Asian Century: Global Economic Power Dynamics, Deep and Deep Publications Pvt. Ltd., New Delhi, 2007

34. Ganguly, Sumit, *India's Foreign Policy: Retrospect and Prospect*, Oxford University Press, New Delhi, 2010.

35. Garver, John .W, *Protracted Contest: Sino-Indian Rivalry in the Twentieth Century*, Oxford University Press, New Delhi, 2001.

36. Garver, John .W, *Protracted Contest: Sino-Indian Rivalry in the Twentieth Century*, Oxford University Press, New Delhi, 2001

37. Ghosh, Anjali, Chakraborti, Tridib, Majumdar, Anindyo J, and Chatterjee, Shibashis (eds.), *India's Foreign Policy*, Pearson, New Delhi, 2009.

38. Ghoshal, Baladas (ed.), ASEAN and South Asia: A Development Experience, Sterling Publishers Pvt. Ltd, New Delhi, 1998

39. Gilgoy, George J. and Bothm, Eric Hegin, *Chinese and Indian Strategic Behavior: Growing Power and Alarm*, Cambridge University Press, New Delhi, 2012.

40. Gordon, Sandy, India's Rise to Power in the Twentieth Century and Beyond, MacMillan Press Pvt. Ltd, Great Britain, 1995

41. Grare, Frederic and Mattoo, Amitabh (eds.), *Beyond the Rhetoric: The Economics of India's Look East Policy*, Manohar Publishers and Distributors, New Delhi, 2003.

42. Grare, Frederic and Mattoo, Amitabh (eds.), *India and ASEAN: The Politics of India's Look East Policy*, Manohar Publishers and Distributors, New Delhi, 2001.
43. Griffiths, Arlo, Lepoutre, Amandine, Southworth, William A. and Phan,Thanh, *The Inscriptions of Campa At The Museum of Cham Sculpture in Da Nang*, VNU- HCM Publishing House, Ho Chi Minh City, 2012.
44. Hall, D.G.E, *A History of South- East Asia*, Macmillan and Co., London, 1958.
45. Hiep, Le Hong and Tsvetov, Anton (eds.), *Vietnam's Foreign Policy under Doi Moi*, ISEAS, Singapore, 2018.
46. Hiep, Le Hong, *Living Next to the Giant: The Political Economy of Vietnam's Relations with China under Doi Moi*, Institute of Southeast Asian Studies- Yusof Ishak Institute, 2017
47. Jeshurun, Chandran (ed.), China, India, Japan and the Security of Southeast Asia, Institute of Southeast Asian Studies, Singapore, 1993
48. Jha, Ganganath and Shekhar, Vibhanshu (eds.), *Rising India in the Changing Asia-Pacific: Strategies and Challenges*, Pentagon Press, New Delhi, 2012.
49. Jha, Ganganath and Shekhar, Vibhanshu (eds.), *Rising India in the Changing Asia-Pacific: Strategies and Challenges*, Pentagon Press, New Delhi, 2012
50. Jha, N.Nand Singh, Sudhir (eds.), *Modi's Foreign Policy: Challenges and Opportunities*, Pentagon Press, New Delhi, 2016
51. Kapur, Harish, *India's Foreign Policy 1947-1992: Shadows and Substance*, Sage Publications, New Delhi, 1994
52. Kaul, T.N. (ed.), *India and Indochina: Perspectives of Cooperation*, Patriot Publishers, New Delhi, 1987.
53. Kondapalli, S (eds.), *Asian Security and China*, Institute for Defence Studies and Analyses, New Delhi, 2004
54. Kornberg, Judith F. and Faust, John R, *China in World Politics: Policies, Processes, Prospects*, Lynne Rienner Publishers Inc., Boulder, Colorado, 2007.
55. Majumdar, Ashis Kr., *Southeast Asia in Indian Foreign Policy: A Study of India's Relations with South East Asian Countries from 1962-82*, Naya Prokash, Calcutta, India, 1982.
56. Majumdar, R.C, *Champa: History and Culture of an Indian Colonial Kingdom in the Far East 2nd- 16th century A.D*, Gyan Publishing House, Delhi, 2008.
57. Majumdar, Ramesh C, *Ancient Indian Colonization in Southeast Asia*, Oriental Institute, Baroda, 1955.
58. Majumdar, Ramesh C, *India and Southeast Asia*, BR Publishing House, Delhi, 1979
59. Manivasakan, S. (ed.), *Security Dynamics of India's Future Relations with Southeast Asian Nations*, Centre for South and Southeast Asian Studies, University of Madras, 2012.
60. Martin, Edwin W., *Southeast Asia and China: The End of Containment*, Westview Press, Colorado, 1977.
61. Minh, Pham Quang, *Vietnam's foreign policy in the renovation period 1986-2010*, The Gioi Publishers, Hanoi, 2015.
62. Mohan, C. Raja, *Crossing the Rubicon- The Shaping of India's New Foreign Policy*, Viking, New Delhi, 2003.
63. Morris, Stephen J., Why Vietnam invaded Cambodia: Political Culture and the Causes of War, Stanford University Press, California, 1999
64. Nanda, Prakash, Rediscovering Asia: Evolution of India's Look East Policy, Lancer

Publishers and Distributors, New Delhi, 2003
65. Nathan, K.S (ed.), *India and ASEAN: The Growing Partnership for the 21st Century*, Institute of Diplomacy and Foreign Relations, Kuala Lumpur, 2000.
66. Nautiyal, Annapurna (ed.), Challenges to India's Foreign Policy in the New Era, Gyan Publishing House, New Delhi, 2006
67. Nautiyal, Annapurna and Mahapatra, Chintamani, *India- China Relations in the Contemporary Era Opportunities: Obstacles and Outlooks*, Kalpaz Publications, New Delhi, 2014
68. Panda, Rajaram (ed.), *India- Vietnam Relations: Retrospect and Prospect*, Northern Book Centre and Indian Council for Cultural Relations, New Delhi, 2016.
69. Pant, Harsh V. (ed.), *The Rise of China: Implications for India*, Cambridge University Press, India, 2012.
70. Papp, Daniel S., Vietnam: The View From Moscow, Peking, Washington, McFarland and Company, North Carolina, 1981
71. Paulino, Amelia U. Santos, and Wan Guanghua (eds.), The Rise of China and India: Impacts, Prospects and Implications, Palgrave, Macmillan, UK, 2010
72. Pokharna, Bhawna, *India-China Relations: Dimensions and Perspectives*, New Century Publications, New Delhi, 2009
73. Ram, Amar Nath (ed.), *Two Decades of India's Look East Policy: Partnership for Peace, Progress and Prosperity*, Manohar Publishers and Distributors, New Delhi, 2012.
74. Rao, P.V (ed.), *India and ASEAN: Partners at Summit*, KW Publishers Pvt. Ltd, New Delhi, 2008.
75. Ray, Santimoy and Chakraborti, Tridib (ed.), *Vietnam: A Changing Horizon*, Chatterjee Publisher, Calcutta, 1992.
76. Ray, Santimoy and Chakraborti, Tridib (eds.), *Vietnam: A Changing Horizon*, Chatterjee Publisher, Calcutta, 1992
77. Reddy, C. Ravindranatha, *India and Vietnam During Post- Cold War Era*, Centre For Southeast Asian and Pacific Studies, Sri Venkateswara University, Tirupati, 2012.
78. Reddy, C. Ravindranatha, *India and Vietnam: Era of Friendship and Cooperation, 1947-1991*, Emerald Publishers, Centre for Southeast Asian and Pacific Studies, Sri Venkateswara University, Tirupati, 2009.
79. Reddy, Gundre Jayachandra (ed.), *Dynamics of India and China Relations: Implications for New World Order*, UGC Centre For Southeast Asian and Pacific Studies, Sri Venkateswara University, Tirupati, 2016.
80. Reddy, Gundre Jayachandra (ed.), *India and China Relations: Historical, Cultural and Security Issues*, UGC Centre For Southeast Asian and Pacific Studies, Sri Venkateswara University, Tirupati, 2016.
81. Reddy, K. Raja (ed.), *India and ASEAN: Foreign Policy Dimensions for the 21st Century*, New Century Publications, New Delhi, 2005
82. Reddy, K. Raja, *India and ASEAN: Foreign Policy Dimensions For the 21st Century*, New Century Publications, New Delhi, 2005.
83. Reddy, K. Raja, Vietnam: Struggle for Unification, 1954-1975, Centre for Studies on Indo- China and South Pacific, Sri Venkateswara University, Tirupati, 1999.
84. Reddy, K.Raja (ed.), *Foreign Policy of India and Asia Pacific*, New Century Publications, New Delhi, 2012.
85. Reddy, Y. Yagama (ed.), *Emerging India in Asia-Pacific*, New Century Publications, New Delhi, 2007.

86. Reddy, Y. Yagama (ed.), *India- China Relations- Changing Profile in the 21st Century*, Gyan Publishing House, New Delhi, 2012.
87. Reddy, Y.Yagama (ed.), *Emerging India in Asia-Pacific*, New Century Publications, New Delhi, 2007.
88. Roberts, Priscilla, *Behind the Bamboo Curtain: China, Vietnam and the World beyond Asia*, Stanford University Press, United States, 2006
89. Roy, Arpita Basu and Bhattacharya, Subhadeep (eds.), *India and Southeast Asia: States, Borders and Culture*, Shipra Publications, New Delhi, 2015
90. Sakhuja, Vijay (ed.), *India- Vietnam Strategic Partnership: Exploring Vistas for Expanded Cooperation*, Pentagon Press and Indian Council of World Affairs, New Delhi, 2011.
91. Sardesai, D.R, *Indian Foreign Policy in Cambodia, Laos and Vietnam: 1947-1964*, University of California Press, USA, 1968.
92. Sawnhey, Pravin and Wahab, Ghazala, *Dragon on Our Doorstep: Managing China through Military Power*, Aleph Publishers, New Delhi, 2017
93. Sengupta, Arindam, *The Survivors: Kampuchea, 1984,* Patriot Publishers, 1984
94. Sharma, Geetesh, *Traces of Indian Culture in Vietnam*, Banyan Tree Books Pvt. Ltd, New Delhi, 2009.
95. Sharma, Geetesh, *Vietnam 1982-2017: Ruins To Incredible Progress*, Banyan Tree Books Pvt. Ltd, New Delhi, 2018.
96. Sharma, Geetesh, *Vietnam Liberation War: Role of Calcutta*, Bee Books, Kolkata, 2015.
97. Singh, Naunihal, China in the 21st Century, Mittal Publications, New Delhi, 2006
98. Sinha, Shakti and Trivedi, Sonu, *Emerging Horizons in India- Vietnam Relations*, Pentagon Press, Delhi, 2018
99. Sridharan, Kripa, *The ASEAN Region in India's Foreign Policy*, Dartmouth Publishing Co.Ltd., London, 1996.
100. Sucheta, Ghosh and Sen, Rabindra (eds.), Southeast Asia: Security in the Coming Millennium, Allied Publishers Ltd., Kolkata, 2000
101. Thakur, Ramesh and Thayer, Carlyle A. (eds.), *Soviet Relations with India and Vietnam 1945-1992*, Oxford University Press, New Delhi, 1993.
102. Thayer, Carlyle A. and Amer, Ramses, *Vietnamese Foreign Policy in Transition*, Institute of Southeast Asian Studies, Singapore, 1999.
103. Tripathi, D.P, and Deepak, B.R (eds.), *India- China Relations: Future Perspectives*, Vij Books India Pvt. Ltd, New Delhi, 2012
104. Vickery, Michael, *Cambodia: 1975-1982*, George Allen and Unwin, Sydney, 1984
105. Womack, Brantly, *China and Vietnam: The Politics of Asymmetry*, Cambridge University Press, 2006.
106. Yee, Herbert and Ian, Storey (eds.), The China Threat: Perceptions, Myths and Reality, Routledge, London, 2002
107. Yunling, Zhang *Rising China and the World Order*, World Scientific, Singapore, 2010.

Articles in Journals

1. Amador III, Julio S., Bobillo Ariane, and Penalber, Amirah, "Issues and Challenges in ASEAN- India Relations: Political- Security Aspects,"*India Quarterly*, June 2011
2. Amer, Ramses, "Sino- Vietnamese Normalization in the Light of the Crisis of the Late 1970s,"*Pacific Affairs*, Vol.67, No.3, Autumn 1994

3. Amer, Ramses, "The Territorial Disputes between China and Vietnam and Regional Stability," *Contemporary Southeast Asia*, Vol.19, No.1, June 1997
4. Amer, Ramses, "Vietnam and Its Neighbours: The Border Dispute Dimension," *Contemporary Southeast Asia*, Vol.17, No.3, December 1995
5. Amer, Ramses, "Vietnam in 2010," *Asian Survey*, Vol.51, No.1, January- February 2011
6. Amer, Ramses, "Vietnam's Proactive Foreign Relations," *Policy Brief*, No.167, Institute for Security and Development Policy (ISDP), December 2014
7. Amer, Ramses, and Jianwei, Li, "Creatively Managing China- Vietnam Relations In The South China Sea," *Policy Brief*, Institute for Security and Development Policy, No. 196, March 2017
8. Ba, Alice D, "China and ASEAN: Re- navigating Relations for a 21st Century," *Asian Survey*, Vol. XLIII, No.4, July-August 2003.
9. Bajpai, Arunoday, "The 'Rise of Asia' Thesis," *World Affairs*, Vol.16, No.2, April-June 2012
10. Balachandran, G., "India and NSG: Approaches to Indian Membership," *IDSA Issue Brief*, May 2013
11. Baladas Ghoshal, "The Rise of China: View From India," *Journal of Indian Ocean Studies*, Vol.18, No.2, August 2010
12. Banerjee, Paula, "Borders as Unsettled Markers in South Asia: A Case Study of the Sino- Indian Border," *International Studies*, Vol.35, No.2, 1998
13. Basu, A.R., "India's China Policy in Historical Perspective," *Contemporary Southeast Asia*, Vol.13, No.1, June 1991
14. Bhatia, Rajiv, "Indian Ocean: Challenges For India," *Journal of Indian Ocean Studies*, Vol.10, No.1, April 2011
15. Bhattacharya, Abanti, "Sixty Years of India- China Relations," *Strategic Analysis*, Vol.34, No.5, September 2010
16. Bhattacharya, Anushree, "China's Strategic Advancement in Southeast Asia: Trade, Diplomacy and Connectivity," *Maritime Affairs*, National Maritime Foundation, Routledge, Vol.6, No.1, Summer 2010
17. Brown, Frederick Z., "Rapprochement Between Vietnam and the US," *Contemporary Southeast Asia*, Vol.32, No.3, December 2010
18. Buszynski, Leszek and Sazlan, Iskandar, "Maritime Claims and Energy Cooperation in the South China Sea," *Contemporary Southeast Asia*, Vol.29, No.1, April 2007
19. Buszynski, Leszek, "ASEAN, the Declaration on Conduct, and the South China Sea, *Contemporary Southeast Asia*, Vol.25, No.3, December 2003
20. Chakraborti, Tridib and Bhattacharya, Subhadeep, "South China Sea Imbroglio: Problems, Outcome and India's Stand," *Policy Brief*, The University of Calcutta, Kolkata, No.5, December 2012
21. Chakraborti, Tridib, "China and Vietnam in the South China Sea Dispute: A Creeping 'Conflict- Peace- Trepidation' Syndrome," *China Report*, Vol.48, No.3, 2012
22. Chakraborti, Tridib, "India and the Indochina States in Emerging Global Politics: Challenges and Opportunities," *Policy Brief*, The University of Calcutta, Kolkata, No.4, December 2012
23. Chakraborti, Tridib, "India and Vietnam: Sprouting Strategic Partnership," *World Focus*, October 2011

24. Chakraborti, Tridib, "India's Look East Policy: Time for Stock- Taking," *World Focus*, November-December 2009, Vol.XXX
25. Chakraborti, Tridib, "India's Rendezvous with ASEAN in the New Global Order: Achievements and Pitfalls," *Politico*, Vol.2, No.2, 2014
26. Chakraborti, Tridib, "Indo-China States in the Canvas of India's Southeast Asia Policy," *World Focus*, Vol.27, No.4, April 2006
27. Chakraborty, Debashis and Kumar, Animesh, "ASEAN and China: New Dimensions in Economic Engagement," *China Report*, Vol.48, No.3, 2012
28. Chakravarty, Pinak Ranjan, "India's Foreign Policy in the Neighbourhood," *Indian Foreign Affairs Journal*, Vol.9, No.2, April– June 2014
29. Chang, Felix K., "China's Naval Rise and the South China Sea: An Operational Assessment," *Orbis*, Vol.56, No.1, Winter 2012
30. Chansoria, Monika, "Positioning Vietnam in India's 'Look East' Policy," *CLAWS Journal*, Winter 2011
31. Chaudhury, Rahul Roy, "Strategic Trends in the Indian Ocean," *Strategic Analysis*, September 1996
32. Cheng, Joseph Y.S., "Sino-Vietnamese Relations in the Early Twenty- first Century," *Asian Survey*, Vol.51, No.2, March–April 2011
33. Christensen, Thomas J., "Chinese Realpolitik," *Foreign Affairs*, Vol.75, No.5, September–October 1996
34. Cuong, Nguyen Anh, "The Principles of Vietnam's Communist Party In Its Relation with The US (1975-2013)," *Vietnam Social Sciences*, No.3 (161), 2014
35. Das, Krishnasri, "India's Growing Relations with South East Asia," *World Focus*, June 2012
36. Dinh, Do Duc, "Vietnam-US Relation: From Normalization To Comprehensive Partnership Then Alliance in the Future," *Vietnam Social Sciences*, No.3 (161), 2014
37. Fravel, M. Taylor, "China's Strategy in the South China Sea," *Contemporary Southeast Asia*, Vol.33, No.3, December 2011
38. Furtado, Xavier, "International Law and the Dispute over the Spratly Islands: Whither UNCLOS?," *Contemporary Southeast Asia*, Vol.21, No.3, December 1999
39. Ganguly, Sumit, "America and India at a Turning Point," *Current History*, March 2005
40. Ganguly, Sumit, and Pardesi, Manjeet S., "Can China and India Rise Peacefully," *Orbis*, Summer 2012
41. Garver, John W., "The Diplomacy of a Rising China in South Asia," *Orbis*, Summer 2012
42. Ghoshal, Baladas, "India's Engagement with ASEAN: Economic and Strategic Dimension," *Journal of Indian Ocean Studies*, Vol.20, No.3, December 2012
43. Ghoshal, Baladas, "The Rise of China: View From India," *Journal of Indian Ocean Studies*, Vol.18, No.2, August 2010
44. Goh, Evelyn, "Southeast Asian Perspectives on the China Challenge," *The Journal Of Strategic Studies*, Vol. 30, No.4-5, August- October 2007
45. Goldstein, Lyle, "Chinese Naval Strategy in the South China Sea: An Abundance of Noise and Smoke, but Little Fire," *Contemporary Southeast Asia*, Vol.33, No.3, December 2011
46. Goodman, Allan E., "The Political Consequences of Normalization of US- Vietnam Relations," *Contemporary Southeast Asia*, Vol.17, No.4, March 1996

47. Goud, R. Siddha, "China- Pakistan Economic Corridor- Game Changer in Indian Ocean Region," *Indian Ocean Digest*, Vol.35, No.1, Issue 55, January- June 2015
48. Grinter, Lawrence E., "China, the US, and Mainland Southeast Asia: Opportunism and the Limits of Power," *Contemporary Southeast Asia*, Vol.28, No.3, December 2006
49. Guihong, Zhang, "Sino- Indian Security Relations: Bilateral Issues, External Factors and Regional Implications," *South Asian Survey*, Vol.12, No.1, 2005
50. Gunnamani, Chongtham, "India and China: Reconfiguring Southeast Asia's Political Dynamics," *World Affairs*, Vol.14, No.4, October-December 2010
51. Han, Vo X., "Vietnam in 2008: A Dynamic Course Encountering Setbacks and Challenges," *Asian Survey*, Vol.49, No.1, January-February 2009
52. Herring, George C., "The Cold War and Vietnam," *Organization of American Historians Magazine of History*, Vol.18, No.5, October 2004
53. Hiep, Le Hong, "Performance-based Legitimacy: The Case of the Communist Party of Vietnam and Doi Moi," *Contemporary Southeast Asia*, Vol.34, No.2, 2012
54. Hiep, Le Hong, "Vietnam's Hedging Strategy against China since Normalization," *Contemporary Southeast Asia*, Vol.35, No.3, 2013
55. Hiep, Le Hong, "Vietnam's strategic trajectory: From internal development to external engagement," *Strategic Insights*, June 2012
56. Holmes, James R., "Inside, Outside: India's 'Exterior Lines' in the South China Sea," *Strategic Analysis*, Vol.36, No.3, May- June 2012
57. Hong, Zhao, "India and China: Rivals or Partners in Southeast Asia?," *Contemporary Southeast Asia*, Vol.29, No.1, April 2007
58. Hongyu, Wang, "Sino- Indian Relations: Present and Future," *Asian Survey*, Vol.35, No.6, June 1995
59. Hung, Nguyen Manh, "Vietnam in 1991: The Party's Choice," *Asian Survey*, Vol.40, No.1, January- February 2000
60. Hyer, Eric, "The South China Sea Disputes: Implications of China's Earlier Territorial Settlements," *Pacific Affairs*, Vol.68, No.1, Spring 1995
61. Jacob, Jabin T., "China in Southeast Asia: The Search for a Chinese Model of International Relations," *China Report*, Vol.48, No.3, 2012
62. Jha, Ganganath, "India's Vietnam Policy in Regional Perspective," *Strategic Analysis*, July 1996
63. Jha, Ganganath, "The Politics of Perestroika in Vietnam:1986-1990," *International Studies*, Vol.28, No.4, 1991
64. Jha, Pankaj K., "India-Vietnam Relations: Need for Enhanced Cooperation," *Strategic Analysis*, Vol.32, No.6, 2008
65. Kapoor, Deepak, "India's China Concern," *Strategic Analysis*, Vol.36, No.4, July- August 2012
66. Khurana, Gurpreet S., "Security of Sea Lines: India and Southeast Asia," *World Focus*, Vol.27, No.4, April 2006
67. Kim, Nguyen Van, "Vietnam-Japan Relationship: A View from the Sea Space," *Vietnam Social Sciences*, No.3 (161), 2014
68. Kim, Shee Poon, "The South China Sea in China's Strategic Thinking," *Contemporary Southeast Asia*, Vol.19, No.4, March 1998
69. Kondapalli, Srikanth, "Multilateral Accord, Bilateral Discord: India- China Relations in 2009-10," *World Focus*, September 2010
70. Kondapalli, Srikanth, "Premier Wen Jiabao's Visit To India: Setting Terms For

Engagement,"*Journal of Indian Ocean Studies*, Vol.18, No.2, August 2010
71. Kumar, Chanchal, "The Rise of India and China: Global Power Shift to Asia," *World Focus*, June 2012
72. Kumar, Pramod, "India and ASEAN Re- Linking for Eco- Political Gains," *World Focus*, June 2012
73. Kundu, Sampa, "India- Vietnam Bilateral Engagement,"*Journal of Indian Ocean Studies*, Vol.22, No.2, August 2014
74. Legro, Jeffrey W., "The Politics of the New Global Architecture,"*Strategic Analysis*, 2012
75. Liem, Nguyen Dinh, "China FDI in Vietnam after Twenty Years,"*Vietnam Social Sciences*, No.6 (170), 2015
76. Limaye, Satu P., "India's Relations with Southeast Asia Take a Wing,"*Southeast Asian Affairs*, 2003
77. Limaye, Satu P., "United States- ASEAN Relations on ASEAN's Fortieth Anniversary: A Glass Half Full,"*Contemporary Southeast Asia*, Vol.29, No.3, December 2007
78. Lou, Chunhao, "US- India- China Relations in the Indian Ocean: A Chinese Perspective,"*Strategic Analysis*, Vol.36, No.4, July- August 2012
79. Mahapatra, Chintamani, "India- US Strategic Dialogue: An Assessment,"*Strategic Analysis*, Vol.37, No.6, 2013
80. Maini, Tridivesh, "The 'New Silk Road': India's Pivotal Role,"*Strategic Analysis*, 2012
81. Marr, David G., "Sino- Vietnamese Relations,"*The Australian Journal of Chinese Affairs*, No.6, July 1981
82. Mehrotra, Lakhan, "India's Look East Policy: Its Origin and Development,"*Indian Foreign Affairs Journal*, Vol.7, No.1, January-March 2012
83. Min, Chang Pao, "Vietnam and China: New Opportunities and New Challenges,"*Contemporary Southeast Asia*, Vol.19, No.2, September 1997
84. Mishra, Binoda Kumar, "Cooperation and Discord in India- China Relationship: Key to the Future of South and South- East Asia,"*Indian Foreign Affairs Journal*, Vol.5, No.2, April-June 2010
85. Mohan, C. Raja, "India and the Balance of Power,"*Foreign Affairs*, Vol.85, No.4, July-August 2006
86. Muni, S.D and Mohan, C. Raja, "Emerging Asia: India's Options,"*International Studies*, Vol.41, No.3, 2004
87. Muni, S.D, and Mohan, C. Raja, "Emerging India: India's Options,"*International Studies*, Vol.41, No.3, 2004
88. Naidu, G.V.C, "India and Southeast Asia: An Activist Role for Indian Navy,"*Journal of Indian Ocean Studies*, Vol.11, No.2, August 2003.
89. Naidu, G.V.C, "India, ASEAN and the ARF,"*Strategic Analysis*, September 1996
90. Naidu, G.V.C, "Whither the Look East Policy: India and Southeast Asia,"*Strategic Analysis*, April-June 2004
91. Naidu, G.V.C., "India and ASEAN,"*Strategic Analysis*, April 1996
92. Nuri, Maqsudul Hasan, "China and South Asia in the 21st Century,"*Regional Studies*, Vol. XVII, No.4,
93. Odgaard, Liselotte, "Deterrence and Co- operation in the South China Sea,"*Contemporary Southeast Asia*, Vol.23, No.2, August 2001
94. Panda, Jagannath, "India- China Strategic Economic Diaogue: Progress and

Prognosis,"*Issue Brief*, Institute for Defence Studies and Analysis (IDSA), April 2014

95. Panda, Jagannath, "Maritime Silk Road and the India- China Conundrum,"*Indian Foreign Affairs Journal*, Vol.9, No.1, January-March 2014
96. Panda, Rajaram and Khan, Shamshad A, "China and South China Sea: Future Power Projections,"*Indian Foreign Affairs Journal*, Vol.5, No.3, July-September 2010
97. Pandit, Priyanka, "The Political Economy of China- ASEAN FTA,"*World Focus*, June 2012
98. Pant, Harsh V, "India's China Policy: Devoid of a Strategic Framework,"*South Asian Survey*, Vol.12, No.2, 2005
99. Pant, Harsh V., "China Shakes Up the Maritime Balance in the Indian Ocean,"*Strategic Analysis*, Vol.36, No.4, July-August 2012
100. Pant, Harsh V., "Great Power Politics in East Asia: The US and China in Competition,"*China Report*, Vol.48, No.3, 2012
101. Pao- min, Chang, "The Sino- Vietnamese Conflict and Its Implications for ASEAN,"*Pacific Affairs*, Vol.60, No.4, Winter 1987-88
102. Pedrozo, Raul, "Beijing's Coastal Real Estate, A History of Chinese Naval Aggression,"*Foreign Affairs*, November 2010
103. Pike, Douglas, "Vietnam in 1991: The Turning Point,"*Asian Survey*, Vol.32, No.1, January 1992
104. Pokharna, Bhawna, "Sub- Regional Co-operation in South and Southeast Asia: With Special Reference to BIMSTEC, MGCI and BCIM Regional Cooperation Forum,"*World Focus*, June 2012
105. Pradhan, Sanjay Kumar, "Spratly Dispute: Looking through Oil and Gas India's Energy Approaches,"*World Focus*, June 2012
106. Pringsheim, Klaus P, "China's Role in the Indo- Pakistani Conflict,"*The China Quarterly*, No.24, October-December 1965
107. Puri, Raman and Sahgal, Arun, "The South China Sea Dispute: Implications for India,"*Indian Foreign Affairs Journal*, Vol.6, No.4, October-December 2011
108. Rajagopalan, Rajeswari Pillai, and Biswas, Arka, "India's Membership to the Nuclear Suppliers Group,"*Issue Brief*, Observer Research Foundation, Issue No.141, May 2016
109. Ravikumar, Veena, "India-ASEAN Relations: From Milestones to Integration,"*World Focus*, June 2012
110. Rowan, Joshua P., "The US-Japan Security Alliance, ASEAN and the South China Sea Dispute,"*Asian Survey*, Vol.45, No.3, May-June 2005
111. Roy, Denny, "Southeast Asia and China: Balancing or Bandwagoning,"*Contemporary Southeast Asia*, Vol.27, No.2, August 2005
112. Roy, Mihir, "China's White Paper 2010 on National Defence: A Critique,"*Journal of Indian Ocean Studies*, Vol.19, No.1, April 2011
113. Schellhorn, Kai M., "Political and Economic Reforms in Vietnam,"*Contemporary Southeast Asia,* Vol.14, No.3, December 1992
114. Schultz II, Clifford J., and Ardrey IV, William J., "The Future Prospects of Sino-Vietnamese Relations: Are Trade and Commerce the Critical Factors for Sustainable Peace?,"*Contemporary Southeast Asia*, Vol.17, No.2, September 1995
115. Scott, David, "Conflict Irresolution in the South China Sea,"*Asian Survey*, Vol.52, No.6, November-December 2012

116. Severino, Rodolfo C, "ASEAN and the Growth of Regional Cooperation in Southeast Asia," *World Affairs*, Vol.3, No.3, July-September 1999
117. Severino, Rodolfo C., "ASEAN and the South China Sea," *Security Challenges*, Vol.6, No.2, Winter 2010
118. Shekhar, Vibhanshu, "ASEAN's Response to the Rise of China: Deploying a Hedging Strategy," *China Report*, Vol.48, No.3, 2012
119. Shekhar, Vibhanshu, "Introduction: Evolving Complexities of Southeast Asia-China Relations," *China Report*, Vol.48, No.3, August 2012
120. Shivakumar, M.S., "A New Era for Vietnam and US?," *Economic and Political Weekly*, Vol.40, No.31, July 30–August–2005
121. Simon, Sheldon W., "China and Southeast Asia: Suspicion and Hope," *The Journal of East Asian Affairs*, Vol.5, No.1, Winter/Spring 1991
122. Simon, Sheldon W., "China, Vietnam and ASEAN: The Politics of Polarization," *Asian Survey*, Vol.19, No.12, December 1979
123. Simon, Sheldon W., "Conflict and Diplomacy in the South China Sea: The View from Washington," *Asian Survey*, Vol.52, No.6, November 2012
124. Singh, Swaran, "Limitations of India- China Economic Engagement," *China Report*, Vol.45, No.4, 2009
125. Singh, Teshu, "China and the South China Sea: Recent Developments," *World Focus*, September 2012
126. Singh, Udai Bhanu, "India and the ASEAN Regional Forum," *Strategic Analysis*, July 1996
127. Singh, Udai Bhanu, "India and the ASEAN Regional Forum," *Strategic Analysis*, Vol.19, No.4, July 1996
128. Singh, Udai Bhanu, "Recent Trends in Sino- Vietnamese Relations," *Strategic Analysis*, May 1996
129. Smith Jr., Esmond D., "China's Aspirations in the Spratly Islands," *Contemporary Southeast Asia*, Vol.16, No.3, December 1994
130. Sundararaman, Shankari, "Politics and Security in Southeast Asia: Prospects for India- ASEAN Cooperation," *International Studies*, Vol.41, No.4, 2004
131. Surie, Nalin, "India- China Relations: Current State and Future Direction," *Foreign Affairs Journal*, Vol.7, No.1, January-March 2012
132. Thakur, Ramesh, "India's Vietnam Policy: 1946-1979," *Asian Survey*, Vol.19, No.10, October 1979
133. Thayer, Carlyle A., "ASEAN, China and the Code of Conduct in the South China Sea," *SAIS Review of International Affairs*, Vol.33, No.2, Summer-Fall 2013
134. Thayer, Carlyle A., "Force Modernization: The Case of Vietnam People's Army," *Contemporary Southeast Asia*, Vol.19, No.1, June 1997
135. Thayer, Carlyle A., "The Tyranny of Geography: Vietnamese Strategies to Constrain China in the South China Sea," *Contemporary Southeast Asia*, Vol.33, No.3, 2011
136. Thayer, Carlyle A., "Vietnam and ASEAN: A First Anniversary Assessment," *Southeast Asian Affairs*, 1997
137. Thayer, Carlyle A., "Vietnam and Rising China: The Structural Dynamics of Mature Asymmetry," *Southeast Asian Affairs*, 2010
138. Thayer, Carlyle A., "Vietnam in 2000: Toward the Ninth Party Congress," *Asian Survey*, Vol.41, No.1, January-February 2001
139. Thayer, Carlyle A., "Vietnam's Proactive International Integration: Case Studies in

Defence Cooperation,"*VNU Journal of Science*, Vol.32, No. IS, 2016

140. Thayer, Carlyle A., "Vietnamese Diplomacy, 1975-2015: From Member of the Socialist Camp to Proactive International Integration,"*Journal of Social Sciences and Humanities*, Vol.1 (3), 2015
141. Tuan, Hoang Anh, "ASEAN Dispute Management: Implications for Vietnam and an Expanded ASEAN,"*Contemporary Southeast Asia*, Vol.18, No.1, June 1996
142. Vatikiotis, Michael R.J, "Catching the Dragon's Tail: China and Southeast Asia in the 21st Century,"*Contemporary Southeast Asia*, Vol.25, No.1, April 2003
143. Vatikiotis, Michael, "Divided They Fall: ASEAN is losing its unity- and its clout,"*Far Eastern Economic Review*, December 1998
144. Vinh, Vo Xuan, "Realizing a Code of Conduct for Maintaining and Promoting Peace and Stability in South China Sea,"*World Focus*, June 2012
145. Vuving, Alexander L., "Strategy and Evolution of Vietnam's China Policy: A Changing Mixture of Pathways,"*Asian Survey*, Vol.46, No.6, November-December 2006
146. Vuving, Alexander L., "Vietnam: Arriving in the World- and at Crossroads,"*Southeast Asian Affairs*, 2008
147. Womack, Brantly, "China and Southeast Asia: Asymmetry, Leadership and Normalcy,"*Pacific Affairs*, Vol.76, No.4, Winter 2003-2004
148. Womack, Brantly, "China and Vietnam: Managing an Asymmetric Relationship in an Era of Economic Uncertainty,"*Asian Politics and Policy*, Vol.2, No.4, July 2010
149. Womack, Brantly, "China's Southeast Asia Policy: A Success Story for the Third Generation,"*Cross- Strait and International Affairs Quarterly*, Vol.1, No.1, 2004
150. Yahya, Faizal, "India and Southeast Asia: Revisited,"*Contemporary Southeast Asia*, Vol.25, No.1, April 2003
151. Yoshihara, Toshi and Holmes, James R., "Can China Defend a 'Core Interest' in the South China Sea?,"*The Washington Quarterly*, Spring 2011
152. Yuan, Jing-Dong, "China's Defence Modernization: Implications for Asia-Pacific Security,"*Contemporary Southeast Asia*, Vol.17, No.1, June 1995
153. Zha, Daojiong, "Security in the South China Sea,"*Alternatives: Global, Local, Political*, Vol. 26, No.1, January-March 2001

Articles/Documents from Internet

1. "East Asia Summit," Ministry of External Affairs, Government of India, mea.gov.in/aseanindia/about-eas.htm
2. "Vietnam taps potential of Indian tourism market,"Vietnam National Administration of Tourism, Ministry of Culture, Sports and Tourism, Hanoi, May 25, 2015, www.vietnamtourism.com/en/index.php/news/items/9402
3. Abuza, Zachary, Anh, Nguyen Nhat, "Vietnam's Military Modernization,"*The Diplomat*, October 28, 2016, https://thediplomat.com/2016/10/vietnams-military-modernization/
4. ASEAN- India Dialogue Relations," ASEAN Secretariat, Jakarta, http://www.aseansec.org/14802.htm
5. ASEAN Regional Forum," Ministry of External Affairs, Government of India. https://www.mea.gov.in/Portal/ForeignRelation/asean-regional-forum-august-2012.pdf
6. Chaturvedy, Rajeev Ranjan, "The 21st Century Maritime Silk Road,"*Observer*

Research Foundation Brief, February 10, 2017, https://www.orfonline.org/research/the-21st-century-maritime-silk-road/

7. Chauhan, Sadhavi, "Selling 'Brand India' in Vietnam," The Diplomat, November 25, 2014, https://thediplomat.com/2014/11/Selling-brand-india-in-vietnam/
8. Clinton, Hillary, "America's Pacific Century,"*Foreign Policy*, October 11, 2011, https://foreignpolicy.com/2011/10/11/americas-pacific-century/
9. Demombynes, Dinh, and Badiani- Magnusson, "Taking Stock: An Update on Vietnam's Recent Economic Developments," The World Bank, Hanoi, July 2014, p. 21, www.worldbank.org/content/dam/Worldbank/document/EAP/Vietnam/Taking_Stock_July2014_EN_final.pdf
10. Ghoshal, Baladas, "India's Look- East Policy and Vietnam,"*Mainstream Weekly*, Vol. XLVII, No.40, September 19, 2009, www.mainstreamweekly.net/article1639.html
11. Ghoshal, Baladas, "India's Look- East Policy and Vietnam,"*Mainstream Weekly*, Vol. XLVII, No.40, September 19, 2009, www.mainstreamweekly.net/article1639.html
12. Hiep, Le Hong, "The Belt and Road Initiative in Vietnam: Challenges and Prospects", Institute of Southeast Asian Studies, Singapore, March 29, 2018, p.3, https://www.iseas.edu.sg/images/pdf/ISEAS_Perspective_2018_18@50.pdf
13. Interview of Mr. Nguyen Minh Vu, Deputy Head of the APEC 2017 National Secretariat's Standing Committee, APEC 2017: Opportunities and Challenges for Vietnam, *VietNam Net*, December 15, 2016, english.vietnamnet.vn/fms/special-reports/171142/apec-2017—opportunities-and-challenges-for-vietnam.html
14. Kumar, Pranav "India- Vietnam Economic Relations: Opportunities and Challenges,"*Institute of Peace and Conflict Studies Special Report*, No.57, July 2008
15. Kuo, Mercy A, "The Origin of Indo- Pacific as Geopolitical Construct,"*The Diplomat*, January 25, 2018, https://thediplomat.com/2018/01/the-origin-of-indo-pacific-as-geopolitical-construct/
16. Lele, Ajay, "India-Vietnam Space Cooperation: Looking For New Frontiers,"*Society for the Study of Peace and Conflict*, 14 September 2011, www.sspconline.org/opinion/IndiaVietnamSpaceCooperationNewFrontiers_14092011
17. Malone, David M, "Soft Power in Indian Foreign Policy,"*Economic and Political Weekly*, Vol. XLVI, Issue No. 36, September 3, 2011, https://www.epw.in/journal/2011/36
18. Manish Chand, "India and Vietnam: Old Friends, New Vistas, Ministry of External Affairs, Government of India, August 24, 2014, https://www.mea.gov.in/in-focus-topic.htm?157
19. Marston, Hunter, "Why Tensions Are Rising Between Vietnam and China," Foreign Affairs, August 15, 2017, https://www.foreignaffairs.com/articles/asia/2017-08-15/why-tensions-are-rising-between-vietnam-and-china
20. Parameswaran, Prashanth, "Japan- Vietnam Defense Relations in the Indo- Pacific Spotlight,"*The Diplomat*, April 11, 2018https://thediplomat.com/2018/04/japan-vietnam-defense-relations-in-the-indo-pacific-spotlight
21. Ramachandran, Sudha, "Chinese and Indian Competition in Space Heats Up,"*China Brief*, Vol.17, Issue 13, October 20, 2017https://jamestown.org/program/chinese-indian-competition-space-heats/
22. Roche, Elizabeth, "India, Vietnam ink 5-year defence pact amid Chinese naval expansion,"*Livemint*, May 26, 2015, https://www.livemint.com/Politics/bUWnCvNDTwKT513o51TodP/India-Vietnam-ink-5year-defence-pact-amid-chinese-naval-ex.html

23. Scott, David, "India's Incremental Balancing in the South China Sea," *E-International Relations*, July 26, 2015, https://www.e-ir.info/2015/07/26/indias-incremental-balancing-in-the-south-china-sea
24. Thayer, Carl, "How India- Vietnam Strategic Ties Are Mutually Beneficial," The Diplomat, December 3, 2013, https://thediplomat.com/2013/12/how-india-vietnam-strategic-ties-are-mutually-beneficial/
25. Thayer, Carlyle A, "Vietnam: Relations with the US and China," Chenna Centre for China Studies, May 26, 2018, https://www.c3sindia.org/geopolitics-strategy/vietnam-relations-with-the-united-states-and-china-by-carlyle-a-thayer
26. Thayer, Carlyle A, Vietnamese Diplomacy, 1975-2015: From Member of the Socialist Camp to Proactive International Integration, Presentation to International Conference on Vietnam: 40 Years of Reunification, Development and Integration (1975-2015), April 25, 2015,https://auschamvn.org/wp-content/uploads/2015/04/Vietnamese-Diplomacy-1975-2015-by-Carl-Thayer_April-2015.pdf
27. Thayer, Carlyle A., "The Structure of Vietnam- China Relations: 1991-2008," Paper for the 3rd International Conference on Vietnamese Studies, Hanoi, Vietnam, December 4–7, 2008, https://www.scribd.com/document/16447513/Carlyle-Thayer-2008-Dec-The-Structures-of-Vietnam-China-Relations-1991-2008
28. The ASEAN Regional Forum: A Concept Paper". aseanregionalforum.asean.org/files/library/Terms of References and Concept Papers/Concept Paper of ARF. pdf
29. Tonnesson, Stein, "An International History of the Dispute in the South China Sea," EAI Working Paper No 71, March 16, 2001, www.cliostein.com/documents/2001/01repeai.pdf
30. Vietnam- China economic relations after 25 years," *VietnamNet*, November 6, 2015, https://english.vietnamnet.vn/fms/business/145683/Vietnam---china-economic-relations-after-25years.html
31. Vietnam To Join China's One Belt, One Road Project," *Executive Intelligence Review*, March 2, 2017. https://larouchepub.com/pr/2017/170302_vietnam_obor.html
32. Vy, Huynh Thuc, "Vietnam's Confucius Institute Distraction," *The Diplomat*, November 24, 2018, https://thediplomat.com/2013/11/vietnams-confucius-institute-distraction/
33. Womack, Brantly "Vietnam and China in an Era of Economic Uncertainty," *The Asia-Pacific Journal*, Vol. 36, No. 2, 2009, https://apjjf.org/site/view/3214
34. Xunhui, Yuan, Juan, Zhang and Tiezi, Shannon, "A Chinese Perspective on Obama's Asia Policy," *The Diplomat*, November 9, 2016, https://thediplomat.com/2016/11/a-chinese-perspective-on-obamas-asia-policy/

Official Documents

1. "61st Anniversary of the National Day, September 2, 1945-September 2, 2006," Publication of the Embassy of the Socialist Republic of Vietnam, New Delhi, 2006.
2. "Agreements/MoUs signed during the State Visit of Hon'ble President to Vietnam," Ministry of External Affairs, Government of India, www.mea.gov.in/bilateral-documents.htm?dtl/23996/AgreementsMoUs_signed_during_the_State_Visit_of_Honble_President_to_Vietnam_15_September_2014
3. "Chien Dan Towers," Vietnam National Administration of Tourism, www.vietnamtourism.com/en/index.phptourism/items/1628

4. "Full text of Obama speech in Parliament,"*India Today*, 8 November 2010, https://www.indiatoday.in/obama-visit/latest-updates/story/full-text-of-obama-speech-in-parliament-85230-2010-11-08
5. "India- Vietnam Relations," Ministry of External Affairs, Government of India, January 2013, http://www.mea.gov.in/Portal/ForeignRelation/Vietnam_Feb_2013.pdf
6. "Indian Maritime Doctrine," Ministry of Defence (Navy), Government of India, New Delhi, 2009, www.indiannavy.nic.in/sites/default/files/Indian-Maritime-Doctrine-2009-Updated-12Feb16.pdf
7. "Law on Enterprises," Vietnam National Assembly, Decision No. 13-199-QH10, August 31, 1999, http://www.vietnamlaws.com/freelaws/Lw60na29Nov05Enterprises[10April06].pdf;LawofInvestment
8. "My Son Sanctuary," UNESCO-World Heritage Convention, https://whc.unesco.org/en/list/949
9. "On the Occasion of the 40th Anniversary of Reunification Day of Vietnam, 125th Birth Anniversary of great leader- President Ho Chi Minh, 70th Anniversary of Vietnam's National Day," Publication of The Embassy of The Socialist Republic of Vietnam in India, New Delhi, Special Edition, 2015
10. "On the Occasion of the 68th Anniversary of Vietnam's National Day: 2nd September, 1945- 2nd September, 2013", Publication of the Embassy of the Socialist Republic of Vietnam in India, New Delhi, 2013
11. "On the Occasion of the National Day, September 2, 1945-September 2, 1998," Publication of the Embassy of the Socialist Republic of Vietnam in India, New Delhi, 1998
12. "President at Inauguration of India Study Centre in Ho Chi Minh National Academy of Politics," Centre for Indian Studies, Ho Chi Minh National Academy of Politics,April 7, 2015, cis.org.vn/artcle/7/president-at-inauguration-of-india-study-centre-in-ho-chi-minh-national-academy-of-politics.html
13. "Prime Minister Narendra Modi's Keynote address at Shangri La," Singapore, June 1, 2018, https://www.mea.gov.in/speeches-statements.htm?dtl/29943/Prime+Ministers+Keynote+Address+at+Shangri+La+Dialogue+June+01+2018
14. "Special Issue on the Occasion of the 55th Anniversary of the National Day, September 2, 1945-September 2, 2000," Publication of the Embassy of the Socialist Republic of Vietnam in India, New Delhi, 2000.
15. "US National Security Strategy of the United States of America," December 2017, https://www.whitehouse.gov/wp-content/uploads/2017/12/NSS-Final-12-18-2017-0905.pdf
16. "Vietnam National Defence," Ministry of National Defence, Socialist Republic of Vietnam, Hanoi, December 2009, https://www.files.ethz.ch/isn/155222/Vietnam2009.pdf
17. *Annual Report:1991*, Ministry of External Affairs, Government of India, New Delhi, 1991
18. *Annual Report:1992*, Ministry of External Affairs, Government of India, New Delhi, 1992
19. *Annual Report:1994-95*, Ministry of External Affairs, Government of India, New Delhi, 1995

20. *Annual Report:1996-97*, Ministry of External Affairs, Government of India, New Delhi, 1997
21. *Annual Report: 2001-02*, Ministry of External Affairs, Government of India, New Delhi, 2002
22. *Annual Report: 2003-04*, Ministry of External Affairs, Government of India, New Delhi, 2004
23. *Annual Report:2004-05*, Ministry of External Affairs, Government of India, New Delhi, 2005
24. *Annual Report:2005-06*, Ministry of External Affairs, Government of India, New Delhi, 2006
25. *Annual Report: 2006-07*, Ministry of External Affairs, Government of India, New Delhi, 2007
26. *Annual Report:2007-08*, Ministry of External Affairs, Government of India, New Delhi, 2008
27. *Annual Report:2009-10*, Ministry of External Affairs, Government of India, New Delhi, 2010
28. *Annual Report:2011-12*, Ministry of External Affairs, Government of India, New Delhi, 2012
29. *Annual Report:2012-13*, Ministry of External Affairs, Government of India, New Delhi, 2013
30. *Annual Report: 2013-14*, Ministry of External Affairs, Government of India, New Delhi, 2014
31. *Annual Report:2014-15*, Ministry of External Affairs, Government of India, New Delhi, 2015
32. *Chairman's Statement of the 3rd ASEAN- India Summit*, aic.ris.org.in/chairman's-statement-3rd-asean-india-summit-vientiane
33. Defence White Paper 2013," Department of Defence, Australia, www.defence.gov.au/whitepaper/2013/
34. Defense of Japan 2013," Japan Ministry of Defense, https://www.mod.go.jp/e/publ/w_paper/2013.html
35. Election Manifesto, Bharatiya Janta Party (BJP), 2014
36. Gandhi, Indira, *Aspects of our Foreign Policy*, Speeches and Writings, AICC, New Delhi, 1973
37. *I.K Gujral's speech*, "India's Role in World Affairs: Retrospective and Prospects," Nehru Centre, Bombay, 3 January 1997,http://www.indianembassy.org/policy/Foreign_Policy/global(gujral).htm
38. Joint Statement on the occasion of the State Visit of the General Secretary of the Communist Party of Vietnam to India," Ministry of External Affairs, Government of India, November 20, 2013, mea.gov.in/lok-sabha.htm?dtl/22510/Joint+Statement+on+the+occasion+of+the+State+Visit+of+the+General+Secretary+of+the+Communist+Party+of+Vietnam+to+India
39. Joint Statement on the occasion of the visit of the President of Vietnam, October 12, 2011, https://www.mea.gov.in/bilateral-documents.htm?dtl/5341/Joint_Statement_
40. Joint Statement on the State Visit of Prime Minister of the Socialist Republic of Vietnam (October 27–28, 2014), Ministry of External Affairs, Government of India, New Delhi, 28 October, 2014. See, https://www.mea.gov.in/bilateral-

documents.htm?dtl/24142/Joint+Statement+on+theState+Visit+of+Prime+Minister+of+the+Socialist+Republic+of+Vietnam+to+India+October+2728+2014

41. Nehru, Jawaharlal, "Note on Visit to China and Indo-China,"November 14, 1954. https://digitalarchive.wilsoncenter.org/document/121651.pdf?v=d7e143cb60346614a337c648500cf3a7
42. Official website of UN Commission on the Limits of the Continental Shelf (CLCS), http://www.un.org/Depts/los/clcs_new/clcs_home.htm
43. Patrick Ventrell, "South China Sea," Press Statement, U.S Department of State, August 3, 2012, www.state.gov/r/pa/prs/ps/2012/08/196022.htm
44. Project Mausam, Ministry of Culture, Government of India, https://indiaculture.nic.in/project-mausam
45. *Speech by External Affairs Minister Shri Yashwant Sinha*, Harvard University, September 29, 2003. For details see, https://www.mea.gov.in/Speeches-Statements.htm?dtl/4744
46. Speech of Donald J. Trump, Diplomatic Reception Room, White House, November 15, 2017, https://www.whitehouse.gov/briefings-statements/remarks-president-trump-trip-asia/
47. Speech of External Affairs Minister, Government of India at the 2nd Indian Ocean Conference, August 31, 2017, mea.gov.in/Speeches-Statements.htm?dtl/28907/Address+by+External+Affairs+Minister+at+the+2nd+Indian+Ocean+Conference+August+31+2017
48. Speech of Hillary Rodham Clinton, US Department of State, National Convention Center, Hanoi, July 23, 2010, https://2009-2017.state.gov/secretary/20092013.clinton/rm/2010/07/145095.htm
49. Speech of Prime Minister of Japan at the Indian Parliament, August 2007, https://www.mofa.go.jp/region/asia-paci/pm/0708/speech-2.html
50. Text of the Report "*The East Asian Miracle: Economic Growth and Public Policy*," The World Bank. documents.worldbank.org/curated/en/975081468244550798/Main-report
51. United Nations Convention on the Law of the Sea, 1982. See, https://www.un.org/Depts/los/convention_agreements/texts/unclos/unclos_e.pdf
52. *Vietnam Information Bulletin*, Embassy of Socialist Republic Of Vietnam, New Delhi, February 1999
53. *Vietnam Information Bulletin*, Embassy of Socialist Republic of Vietnam, New Delhi, October 1999
54. Vietnam: Consolidating National Defence, Safeguarding the Homeland," Vietnam Ministry of Defence, 1998
55. Vision and Actions on Jointly Building Silk Road Economic Belt and 21st Century Maritime Silk Road," National Development and Reform Commission, Ministry of Foreign Affairs and Ministry of Commerce of the People's Republic of China, March 28, 2015, en.ndrc.gov.cn/newsrelease/201503/t20150330_669367.html
56. Welcome address by Mr. P R Agarwala, former President, Bharat Chamber of Commerce on January 28, 2015, Kolkata
57. World Bank Report, July 2014, documents.worldbank.org/curated/en/641241468133544451/pdf./893100WPOP13240tock0July020140FINAL.pdf

Periodicals and Journals

1. Asian Survey
2. Area Studies
3. China Report
4. China Quarterly
5. Contemporary Southeast Asia
6. Cross-Strait and International Affairs Quarterly
7. Far Eastern Economic Review
8. Foreign Affairs Journal
9. Frontline
10. India Quarterly
11. Indian Foreign Affairs Journal
12. Indian Journal of Political Science
13. Indian Ocean Digest
14. Indo- Vietnam Chamber of Commerce and Industry Newsletters
15. Journal of Indian Ocean Studies
16. Orbis
17. Pacific Affairs
18. Publications of the Embassy of the Socialist Republic of Vietnam in India
19. Southeast Asian Affairs
20. Strategic Analysis
21. The Economic and Political Weekly
22. The Journal of East Asian Affairs
23. The Washington Quarterly
24. Vietnam Information Bulletin
25. Vietnam Social Sciences
26. Vietnam National University Journal of Science
27. World Affairs
28. World Focus
29. Indonesian Quarterly
30. Australia Quarterly

News Papers

1. The Economic Times
2. The Hindustan Times
3. The Hindu
4. The Times of India
5. The Telegraph
6. The Statesman
7. The Tribune
8. The Asian Age
9. The Patriot
10. Global Times
11. Peking Review

12. Beijing Review
13. Nhan Dan
14. The New York Times
15. The Washington Post
16. The Straits Times
17. The Bangkok Post
18. The Hanoi Times
19. The Saigon Times
20. The Vietnam News
21. The China Daily

Appendices

APPENDIX-I

Joint Declaration on Strategic Partnership between India and Vietnam (6 July, 2007)

The Joint Declaration on Establishing a Strategic Partnership between India and Vietnam seeks to diversify and deepen the relationship between India and Vietnam in rapidly changing environment. It will encompass bilateral relations in the political, economic, security, defence, cultural, science and technological dimensions and steer their cooperation in regional and multilateral fora in years to come. Some of the salient features of the Joint Declaration include the Establishment of a Strategic Dialogue, a Joint Working Group on Countering Terrorism, closer defence cooperation, India's commitment to assisting Vietnam through grants and concessional Lines of Credit, a joint commitment to working together to establish an Asian community and expansion of bilateral trade, enhancement of science and technology and cultural cooperation and closer cooperation in multilateral fora.

The Joint Declaration was signed by the two Prime Ministers.

[Source- Ministry of External Affairs, Government of India, New Delhi, 6 July 2007]

APPENDIX-II

Joint Statement on the occasion of the visit of the President of Vietnam (12 October, 2011)

1. At the invitation of H.E. Pratibha Devisingh Patil, President of the Republic of India, H.E. Truong Tan Sang, President of the Socialist Republic of Viet Nam and Madame Mai Thi Hanh paid a State visit to India on 11-13 October 2011.
2. The President was accorded an official ceremonial reception at Rashtrapati Bhawan in the capital New Delhi on 12th October 2011. The President laid a wreath at the memorial to Mahatma Gandhi at Rajghat. During the visit, President Truong Tan Sang called on the President of India Smt. Pratibha Devi Singh Patil who hosted a Banquet in his honour. He held talks with Prime Minister Dr. Manmohan Singh. Smt. Meira Kumar, Speaker of the Lok Sabha, Shri S.M. Krishna, External Affairs Minister, and Shri A.K. Antony, Minister of Defence and Smt. Sushma Swaraj, Leader of the Opposition called on the President.
3. President Truong Tan Sang visited Bangalore and met the Governor of the state of Karnataka. He also visited Mumbai where he met the Governor of the state of Maharashtra. President Sang met leaders of Indian business enterprises in New Delhi and Mumbai.
4. President Truong Tan Sang and Prime Minister Dr. Manmohan Singh also witnessed signing of Agreements and Memorandums of Understanding (MoUs) on bilateral cooperation.
5. President Smt. Pratibha Devisingh Patil and Prime Minister Dr. Manmohan Singh congratulated Viet Nam on the success of the 11th National Congress of the Communisty Party of Vietnam and the elections to the 13th National Assembly. President Truong Tan Sang highly valued the remarkable achievements made by the State, the Government and people of India in all fields in the course of national development which has increasingly enhanced the role and standing of India in the region and the world.
6. The leaders of the two countries exchanged views in an atmosphere of warmth,cordiality and mutul trust on all aspects of bilateral cooperation as well as on the regional and international issues of mutual interest. They welcomed the sustained development of the traditional friendship and

strategic partnership between India and Viet Nam. They recalled the glorious contributions of Prime Minsiter Jawaharlal Nehru and President Ho Chi Minh for the development of India-Viet Nam Friendship that had been preserved, nutured and further developed by generations of leaders and people of the two countries and had gone from strength to strength. Both countries agreed to celebrate 2012 as "the India - Viet Nam Friendship Year" to commemorate the 40th anniversary of the establishment of the full diplomatic relations (07/01/1972 - 07/01/2012) and the 5th anniversary of the establishment of the strategic partnership (06/07/2007 - 06/07/2012). The Indian side would also organize the "Year of India in Viet Nam" in 2012 with a series of cultural events including performing arts, film festivals, and other events in various cities across Viet Nam.

7. Both sides valued and agreed to further enhance high-level visits and meetings between the two countries. The leaders noted that there still remains considerable potential for cooperation and agreed to strongly enhance the comprehensive strategic partnership between the two countries, based on key pillars of politics, defense, security, economic, cultural and HRD cooperation. Both sides highly appreciated the results of the 14th Meeting of Joint Commission on Trade, Economic, Scientific and Technological Cooperation at the Foreign Minister level, the 5th Political Consultation and the 2nd Strategic Dialogue at the Deputy Foreign Minister level.
8. The leaders agreed to further deepen the strategic partnership, by adding more concrete programs and projects and broadening it to new areas for cooperation, taking into account the changing political and economic situation both at regional and international levels. Both sides agreed to continue strengthening cooperation in the areas of politics, economy,trade and investment, finance, science and technology, human resource development, culture, agriculture, fisheries, aquaculture etc., while striving to expand cooperation into other potential areas such as frontier areas of science and technology, justice, public health, information and communication, tourism, sports, press, and other areas of mutual interest. The two sides noted with satisfaction the establishment of the India-Viet Nam Business Forum, Advanced Resource Centre in Information and Communications Technologies (ARC-ICT) and the Institute for Indian and South-West Asian Studies under the Viet Nam Academy of Social

Sciences. Viet Nam welcomed the announcement of India to establish a Cultural Centre in Hanoi.

9. Both sides noted with satisfaction that the two-way trade had increased steadily in the recent years and the trade deficit of the Vietnamese side had declined. President Truong Tan Sang affirmed that Viet Nam would create favourable conditions for Indian enterprises to invest in the country. Both sides agreed to step up trade and investment linkages, inter-alia by encouraging cooperation between the private sectors. Both sides set a target of US$ 7 billion of bilateral trade by 2015. Both sides welcomed the entry into force of the India-ASEAN FTA in Goods and agreed to work for the early finalization of the India-ASEAN FTA in Services and Investments.
10. The two sides welcomed the strengthening of cooperation in the fields of defense and security. They expressed satisfaction at the outcome of the 6th Indo-Viet Nam Security Dialogue at the Deputy Defense Minister level and the establishment of a mechanism of biennial dialogue on security issues between the Ministry of Home Affairs of India and Ministry of Public Security of Viet Nam and agreed to work towards the early completion of the Indira Gandhi Hi-tech Forensic Laboratory in Ho Chi Minh City. The Vietnamese side welcomed the offer for training and capacity building of Vietnamese police forces.
11. Both sides welcomed the signing of the Extradition Treaty, Memorandum of Understanding on India-Viet Nam Frienship Year 2012, Agreement on Cooperation between Petrovietnam and ONGC Videsh Limited, Work Plan for the years 2011-2013 in the fields of agricultural and fishery research and education, Protocol of Cultural Activites in India-Vietnam Friendship Year 2012, and agreed to expedite negotiations for early signing of documents of cooperation in other fields as had been agreed in the 14th Meeting of the Joint Commission on Trade, Economic, Scientific and Technological Cooperation. The Vietnamese side welcomed the announcement by the Prime Minister of India to double the number of ITEC scholarships from 75 to 150 from the year 2012.
12. President Truong Tan Sang highly appreciated the support and assistance of the State, the Government and people of India rendered to Viet Nam in the past years, which was a vivid manifestation of the fine traditional relations of friendship and cooperation between the two countries. The Government of India agreed to extend new Lines of Credit to Viet Nam

on favorable terms and conditions for projects in infrastructure, oil and gas, power generation and transmission projects and in other areas as requested by the Vietnamese side; and agreed to consider earmaking a buyer's credit.

13. The leaders affirmed their desire and determination to work together for peace and stability in the region and the world, and agreed to further strengthen cooperation at regional and international fora, especially the ASEAN-India and Mekong-Ganga fora as well as in EAS, ASEM, ARF, WTO, UN and the Non-aligned Movement. The Vietnamese side reaffirmed its strong support for India's Look East Policy and the strengthening of ASEAN–India relationship. The Indian side congratulated Viet Nam for it's success in fulfilling its role as ASEAN Chair in 2010 and thanked Viet Nam for its support to India's candidature for permanent membership in an expanded United Nations Security Council and the G4 short draft resolution on reform of UNSC.
14. The two sides stressed the importance of maintaining peace, stability and of ensuring the safety, security and freedom of navigation in the high seas. The two sides agreed that disputes in the East Sea/South China Sea should be resolved by peaceful means, without resorting to the threat or use of force by the parties concerned, in accordance with universally recognized principles of international law, including the 1982 UN Convention on the Law of the Sea and the 2002 ASEAN-China Declaration on the Conduct of Parties in the South China Sea.
15. Both sides agreed to step up cooperation in the field of capacity building, technical assistance and information sharing between their respective relevant agencies for ensuring security of sea-lanes, including combating piracy, preventing pollution, conducting search and rescue, etc. on sea.
16. The two sides agreed to strengthen cooperation to effectively address the challenges posed by non-traditional security threats such as climate change, environmental degradation, natural disasters, energy security, HIV/AIDS and avian influenza.
17. Both sides also agreed to closely cooperate to promote dialogue and cooperation within the EAS with the aim of promoting peace, stability, development and prosperity in East Asia.
18. The two sides strongly condemned terrorism in all its forms and manifestations and resolved to increase cooperation in the common efforts of the international community in preventing this scourge in a

comprehensive manner. Both sides agreed to closely cooperate for an early finalization of a Comprehensive Convention on International Terrorism, for which India had presented a draft at the United Nations in 1996.

19. President Truong Tan Sang and Madame Mai Thi Hanh expressed their gratitude to the State and friendly people of India for the warm reception and hospitality accorded to the President and the Vietnamese delegation during their State visit to the Republic of India.

[Source- Ministry of External Affairs, Government of India, New Delhi, 12 October 2011]

APPENDIX-III

Agreements/MoUs signed during the State Visit of Hon'ble President to Vietnam (15 September, 2014)

Sl. No.	Agreement/MoU	Signatories		Brief description of the Agreement/MoU
		India	Vietnam	
1.	Agreement between the Government of the Republic of India and the Government of the Socialist Republic of Vietnam on Cooperation and Mutual Assistance in Customs Matters	Mrs. J.M. Shanti Sundharam, Chairperson, Central Board of Excise and Customs	Mr. Truong Chi Trung, Deputy Minister of Finance	The Agreement aims to strengthen, promote and develop cooperation and mutual assistance on matters pertaining to customs between India and Vietnam. The two countries shall assist each other for the prevention, investigation and combating customs offences for the proper application of customs laws and for facilitating legitimate trade. The two countries shall also cooperate and exchange information in their enforcement against the illicit trafficking of narcotic drugs, psychotropic substances, precursor chemicals and other prohibited goods.

Sl. No.	Agreement/MoU	Signatories		Brief description of the Agreement/MoU
2.	MoU on $ 100 million Line of Credit for Defence Procurement	Ms. Geeta Poojary, General Manager, Exim Bank of India	Mr. Truong Chi Trung, Deputy Minister of Finance	The MoU provides concessional line of credit for procurement of defence equipment from India. Details of equipment to be procured by Vietnam are under finalization. The LoC opens new opportunities in our defence cooperation.
3.	MoU between the Ministry of Agriculture of the Republic of India and the Ministry of Agriculture and Rural Development of the Socialist Republic of Vietnam in the field of Animal Health	Mrs. Preeti Saran, Ambassador of India to Vietnam	Mr. Le Quoc Doanh, Deputy Minister, Ministry of Agriculture and Rural Development	The MoU establishes cooperation between India and Vietnam in the field of Animal Health including protecting territory of each other from introduction of animal diseases and infection caused by the trade of animals, products of animal origin and materials of animal reproduction. India and Vietnam shall also share special information on meat processing, meat products and slaughter houses/abattoirs. They shall cooperate in the training and upgrading of human resources in the field of animal health through exchange of delegations, workshops, expert visits, training and share information on veterinary research.

Sl. No.	Agreement/MoU	Signatories		Brief description of the Agreement/MoU
4.	MoU between National Fisheries Development Board, Hyderabad, Department of Animal Husbandry, Dairying and Fisheries, Ministry of Agriculture of the Republic of India and Directorate of Fisheries, Ministry of Agriculture and Rural Development, Government of the Socialist Republic of Vietnam on Cooperation in the Field of Setting up of Pangasius Breeding and Farming in India	Mrs. Preeti Saran, Ambassador of India to Vietnam	>Mr. Le Quoc Doanh, Deputy Minister, Ministry of Agriculture and Rural Development	This MoU between India and Vietnam is aimed at cooperation in transfer of technology and setting up of Pangasius (catfish) breeding and farming in India and allied activities between the two countries through joint activities, programmes, exchange of scientific material, information and personnel. The joint activities shall be environmentally sound and sustainable. Annual Work Plan will be drawn and a Joint Technical Committee shall be formed to provide guidance, review progress and facilitate cooperation.

Sl. No.	Agreement/MoU	Signatories		Brief description of the Agreement/MoU
5.	MoU between the Ministry of Skill Development, Entrepreneurship, Youth Affairs and Sports of the Republic of India and the Central Committee of the Ho Chi Minh Communist Youth Union of the Socialist Republic of Vietnam on Cooperation in Youth Affairs	Mrs. Preeti Saran, Ambassador of India to Vietnam	Mr. Nguyen Dac Vinh, First Secretary of the Central Committee, Ho Chi Minh Communist Youth Union	The MoU provides the framework for programmes of cooperation between India and Vietnam in the field of youth development and excellence by encouraging and promoting an exchange of programmes, experience, skills, techniques, information and knowledge. The youth programmes shall include participation of young politicians, young entrepreneurs, young doctors, young journalists etc. It shall also involve participation of young people from both countries in youth festivals, seminars and conferences on youth related issues.

Sl. No.	Agreement/MoU	Signatories		Brief description of the Agreement/MoU
6.	Letter of Intent between ONGC Videsh Limited, India and Vietnam Oil and Gas Group (PetroVietnam)	Mr. N.K. Verma, Managing Director, ONGC Videsh Ltd.	Mr. Do Van Hau, President and CEO, PetroVietnam	ONGC Videsh Limited (OVL) and PetroVietnam signed an MoU on 20 November, 2013 in the presence of Prime Minister of India and General Secretary of the Communist Party of Vietnam with an objective to enhance mutual cooperation in hydrocarbon sector. PetroVietnam offered new blocks to OVL for oil and gas exploration and production. OVL is keen to expand its presence in Vietnam and is evaluating the blocks on offer. This Letter of Intent will further consolidate cooperation between India and Vietnam in energy sector and pave way for future collaboration between the two countries in this area.

Sl. No.	Agreement/MoU	Signatories		Brief description of the Agreement/MoU
7.	MoU between Jet Airways (India) and Vietnam Airlines Company Limited	Mr. Naresh Goyal, Chairman, Jet Airways (India)	Dr. Pham Ngoc Minh, President and CEO, Vietnam Airlines Company Limited	Jet Airways and Vietnam Airlines have entered into this MoU for enhancing their presence in each other's markets. The scope of the MoU involves code sharing on services of each other. From 5 November 2014, Jet Airways intends to extend its Mumbai-Bangkok flight to Ho Chi Minh City, Vietnam. This service will also enable passengers travelling from Delhi to Bangkok, to connect on the extension flight beyond Bangkok to Ho Chi Minh City.

[Source- Ministry of External Affairs, Government of India, New Delhi, 15 September 2014]

APPENDIX-IV

DECLARATION ON THE CONDUCT OF PARTIES IN THE SOUTH CHINA SEA (4 November, 2002)

The Governments of the Member States of ASEAN and the Government of the People's Republic of China,

REAFFIRMING their determination to consolidate and develop the friendship and cooperation existing between their people and governments with the view to promoting a 21st century-oriented partnership of good neighbourliness and mutual trust;

COGNIZANT of the need to promote a peaceful, friendly and harmonious environment in the South China Sea between ASEAN and China for the enhancement of peace, stability, economic growth and prosperity in the region;

COMMITTED to enhancing the principles and objectives of the 1997 Joint Statement of the Meeting of the Heads of State/Government of the Member States of ASEAN and President of the People's Republic of China;

DESIRING to enhance favourable conditions for a peaceful and durable solution of differences and disputes among countries concerned;

HEREBY DECLARE the following:

1. The Parties reaffirm their commitment to the purposes and principles of the Charter of the United Nations, the 1982 UN Convention on the Law of the Sea, the Treaty of Amity and Cooperation in Southeast Asia, the Five Principles of Peaceful Coexistence, and other universally recognized principles of international law which shall serve as the basic norms governing state-to-state relations;
2. The Parties are committed to exploring ways for building trust and confidence in accordance with the above-mentioned principles and on the basis of equality and mutual respect;
3. The Parties reaffirm their respect for and commitment to the freedom of navigation in and overflight above the South China Sea as provided for by the universally recognized principles of international law, including the 1982 UN Convention on the Law of the Sea;
4. The Parties concerned undertake to resolve their territorial and jurisdictional disputes by peaceful means, without resorting to the threat or use of force, through friendly consultations and negotiations by sovereign

states directly concerned, in accordance with universally recognized principles of international law, including the 1982 UN Convention on the Law of the Sea;

5. The Parties undertake to exercise self-restraint in the conduct of activities that would complicate or escalate disputes and affect peace and stability including, among others, refraining from action of inhabiting on the presently uninhabited islands, reefs, shoals, cays, and other features and to handle their differences in a constructive manner.

Pending the peaceful settlement of territorial and jurisdictional disputes, the Parties concerned undertake to intensify efforts to seek ways, in the spirit of cooperation and understanding, to build trust and confidence between and among them, including:

   a. holding dialogues and exchange of views as appropriate between their defense and military officials;
   b. ensuring just and humane treatment of all persons who are either in danger or in distress;
   c. notifying, on a voluntary basis, other Parties concerned of any impending joint/combined military exercise; and
   d. exchanging, on a voluntary basis, relevant information.

6. Pending a comprehensive and durable settlement of the disputes, the Parties concerned may explore or undertake cooperative activities. These may include the following:
   a. marine environmental protection;
   b. marine scientific research;
   c. safety of navigation and communication at sea;
   d. search and rescue operation; and
   e. combating transnational crime, including but not limited to trafficking in illicit drugs, piracy and armed robbery at sea, and illegal traffic in arms.

The modalities, scope and locations, in respect of bilateral and multilateral cooperation should be agreed upon by the Parties concerned prior to their actual implementation.

7. The Parties concerned stand ready to continue their consultations and dialogues concerning relevant issues, through modalities to be agreed by them, including regular consultations on the observance of

this Declaration, for the purpose of promoting good neighbourliness and transparency, establishing harmony, mutual understanding and cooperation, and facilitating peaceful resolution of disputes among them;

8. The Parties undertake to respect the provisions of this Declaration and take actions consistent therewith;
9. The Parties encourage other countries to respect the principles contained in this Declaration;
10. The Parties concerned reaffirm that the adoption of a code of conduct in the South China Sea would further promote peace and stability in the region and agree to work, on the basis of consensus, towards the eventual attainment of this objective.

Done on the Fourth Day of November in the Year Two Thousand and Two in Phnom Penh, the Kingdom of Cambodia.

[Source-Official Website of ASEAN, 4 November 2002]